Bodily Self-Sacrifice in Indian Buddhist Literature

Bodily Self-Sacrifice in Indian Buddhist Literature

Reiko Ohnuma

MOTILAL BANARSIDASS PUBLISHERS
PRIVATE LIMITED • DELHI

First Indian Edition : Delhi, ***2009***
Earlier published by Columbia University Press *unaer the title*
'Head, Eyes, Flesh and Blood : *Giving Away the Body*
in Indian Buddhist Literature'

ISBN: 978-81-208-3360-9

MOTILAL BANARSIDASS
41 U.A. Bungalow Road, Jawahar Nagar, Delhi 110 007
8 Mahalaxmi Chamber, 22 Bhulabhai Desai Road, Mumbai 400 026
203 Royapettah High Road, Mylapore, Chennai 600 004
236, 9th Main III Block, Jayanagar, Bangalore 560 011
Sanas Plaza, 1302 Baji Rao Road, Pune 411 002
8 Camac Street, Kolkata 700 017
Ashok Rajpath, Patna 800 004
Chowk, Varanasi 221 001

Printed in India

By Jainendra Prakash Jain at Shri Jainendra Press,
A-45 Naraina, Phase-I, New Delhi 110 028
and Published by Narendra Prakash Jain for
Motilal Banarsidass Publishers Private Limited,
Bungalow Road, Delhi 110 007

For Toshi and Shoroku Ohnuma

All good things began with you

CONTENTS

ILLUSTRATIONS

TABLES

CONVENTIONS USED IN THIS BOOK

1. Throughout this book, I refer repeatedly to many different gift-of-the-body *jātakas* (which collectively make up the corpus from which I draw my conclusions). Since it is cumbersome to cite all of the available editions, translations, and discussions of each *jātaka* every time it is mentioned, and since it is confusing (for the reader) to cite such information only the first time each *jātaka* is mentioned, I have collected all of this information together in the Appendix (where I hope it will be easier to locate) and left it out of the endnotes completely. The endnotes are thus reserved for direct citations and relevant discussions only. However, when citing a text or story that is not a part of my corpus (and therefore not covered in the Appendix), I try to give somewhat fuller information in the endnotes.

2. Passages translated by me from the original sources are cited according to the edition used (ed.); passages borrowed from other people's translations are cited according to the translation used (trans.). For passages translated by me, I have provided the original text in the endnotes in the case of shorter passages, but not in the case of longer passages.

3. Many of the stories I discuss exist in both Pāli and Sanskrit versions. In order to avoid the confusion caused by variant names, I consistently

use the Sanskrit form throughout (e.g., King Śibi rather than King Sivi), regardless of whether I am talking about a Pāli or a Sanskrit source. The same goes for technical terms (e.g., *anātman* rather than *anatta*). The only exceptions are a few instances in which it made more sense to me (for various reasons) to use the Pāli form rather than the Sanskrit (e.g., *Vessantara Jātaka* rather than *Viśvaṃtara Jātaka*). In such cases, I clearly indicate that the language is Pāli.

ACKNOWLEDGMENTS

Many people and institutions have helped me in the completion of this book (as well as the Ph.D. dissertation on which it is based), and it is a pleasure to be able to acknowledge them. First and foremost, I would like to thank the members of my dissertation committee at the University of Michigan: my advisor Luis Gómez, for his unflagging help and support (along with many mysterious and enigmatic kernels of wisdom); Don Lopez, for his enduring friendship and expert guidance over the last fifteen years; Bob Sharf, whose scholarship I deeply admire; and Madhav Deshpande, for much help with the Sanskrit.

For funding that made the completion of the dissertation possible, I would like to thank the Rackham Graduate School of the University of Michigan (for a Rackham Pre-Doctoral Fellowship and a Rackham Thesis/Dissertation Grant) and the Woodrow Wilson National Fellowship Foundation (for a Charlotte Newcombe Doctoral Dissertation Fellowship).

During the many years that have elapsed since completion of the original dissertation, I have had three institutional homes, all of whom I thank for providing me and my family with equally warm and hospitable environments: the Department of Asian Studies at the University of Texas, the

Department of Religious Studies at the University of Alabama, and the Department of Religion at Dartmouth College—with a special thanks to Susan Ackerman, Amy Hollywood (now of Harvard), and Ehud Benor, for help with various aspects of this book. I would also like to thank Dartmouth College for a Junior Faculty Fellowship during 2002–2003 that made the significant revision of the dissertation possible.

Other scholars to whom I am grateful for helping me over the years and showing an interest in my work include Tom Trautmann, Griff Foulk, Charles Hallisey, Phyllis Granoff, Jonathan Silk, Liz Wilson, Richard Cohen, Jake Dalton, Dan Boucher, and Gregory Schopen. I also thank four anonymous reviewers (for both Columbia and another press) who made many valuable comments about my original manuscript—some incorporated and others ignored—and one very *un*anonymous reviewer, John Strong, whose extensive comments were particularly helpful. Wendy Lochner at Columbia University Press has made my first experience in publishing a very pleasant one. Finally, I thank two scholars who stand at the very beginning and very end of the process: At the end was Michael Hahn, who found many unforgivable errors of translation in a piece I had published and then most graciously agreed to review the bulk of the translations that appear in this book, thus saving me from many embarrassing mistakes. And at the beginning of the process was Padmanabh Jaini, my inspiring undergraduate teacher at U.C. Berkeley. Though I sat at the back of his classroom and never said a word, I now take this opportunity to thank him publicly for his wonderful courses on Buddhism and Hinduism that first set the direction for my future. I only hope I have begun to live up to the startling comment he made at the end of my final paper: "Graduate work in Buddhist Studies appears to be a natural direction for your future!"

On the nonacademic side of my life, I thank my older sister, Keiko, for leading an interesting, tropical life, and my wonderful in-laws, the Pults, for unbelievably good food over many years' time. Closer to home are my husband, Richard, and my beautiful kids, Attie and Astro—none of whom were any help at all in the completion of this book—as well as Ike and Dusty (who weren't much help either, since they spend most of their time bumping into each other). Still, I feel lucky and blessed every single day to have surrounded myself with such a gorgeous and motley array of creatures. Nothing would mean anything without them. Finally, words cannot express the debt of gratitude I owe to my parents, Toshi and

Shoroku Ohnuma, who have helped me, supported me, and loved me for my entire life. I have often been a difficult, petulant, and ungrateful daughter. I hope that I can begin to repay them in some small way for everything they have done for me by dedicating this work wholly—and whole-heartedly—to them.

Head, Eyes, Flesh, and Blood

INTRODUCTION

In 399 C.E. a Chinese Buddhist monk by the name of Faxian set out from his home in Chang'an to undertake a fourteen-year pilgrimage to the Buddhist holy land of India. After following a path westward across the length of China, he eventually worked his way south via the Karakorum trail and entered the northwestern portion of the Indian subcontinent, in the regions of Uḍḍiyāna and Gandhāra (in what is currently northern Pakistan).

At the time of Faxian's visit, Buddhism in this region (under the Later Kuṣāṇas and Śakas) was flourishing, and in addition to the many large monasteries and thriving monastic communities Faxian encountered, there were a number of impressive Buddhist holy sites associated with the biography of the Buddha. But since the original homeland of the historical Buddha lay far away in the central Gangetic plain, this region of northwest India could not lay claim to the more standard and well known episodes of the Buddha's life. Instead, the holy sites of northwest India were of two major types: Some commemorated the events that took place during a purely apocryphal and supernatural nighttime journey the Buddha is said to have taken to the region in the company of the *yakṣa* Vajrapāṇi, during which he tamed and converted many nonhuman beings by means of his magical powers.[1] (Thus Faxian visited the famous cave in which the Buddha, after taming the *nāga*-king Gopāla, had left an imprint of his shadow as a continuing reminder of his presence.) Most of the northwestern sites, however, were associated with the Buddha's *previous* lifetimes (before his birth as Siddhārtha Gautama) and commemorated the various heroic deeds he had performed while still a bodhisattva. Since northwest India could not be clearly associated with the Buddha's last life, it made sense to localize and acclimatize Buddhism within the region by identifying various northwestern sites as the locales of some of his previous lives, as recorded in the Buddhist *jātakas.*[2]

If we follow Faxian along his journey (by means of the detailed account he left behind),[3] it is striking to observe that virtually all of these sites connected to the Buddha's previous lives commemorate deeds of *bodily self-sacrifice.* Though the bodhisattva of the *jātakas* performs different virtuous deeds, it is the act of bodily sacrifice, above all, that seems to have excited the imagination of those who erected the holy sites of the northwest. In a place called Suvastu, for example, Faxian came across a large *stūpa* "adorned . . . with gold and silver ornaments" and marking the spot where the Buddha, in his previous life as King Śibi, had "cut off a piece of his own flesh" and used it to ransom a dove from the clutches of a hungry hawk.[4] Five days later, in Gandhāra, Faxian encountered another large *stūpa,* similarly adorned with gold and silver, where the same King Śibi "gave away his eyes as alms to others."[5] Seven days later, while visiting a *stūpa* in Takṣaśilā, Faxian informs us that the name Takṣaśilā means "decapitation" and refers to the Buddha's birth as King Candraprabha, who "gave away his head as alms at this place; hence the name."[6] And from there, several days' journey to the east, Faxian and his companions visited yet another *stūpa,* which marked the place where the bodhisattva, born as Prince Mahāsattva, "gave his body to feed a starving tigress."[7] These acts of bodily sacrifice seem to have inspired abundant worship and devotion, for Faxian further informs us that the people of the region referred to these sites as the "Four Great Stupas," where "kings, ministers, and people of different countries vied with one another in making offerings" and "the practices of scattering flowers and lighting lamps at the stupa never ceased."[8] A virtual cult of the bodhisattva's bodily sacrifice appears to have been active throughout the region.

Approximately two hundred years later, in the seventh century C.E., another Chinese Buddhist monk by the name of Xuanzang also made the holy pilgrimage to India, visiting many of the same sites as his predecessor Faxian and writing an even more detailed account of his travels.[9] By this time the situation in northwest India had changed considerably, however. Buddhism had suffered greatly under the ravages of the Ephthalites, or White Huns, and in many of the places where Faxian had described beautiful monasteries and thriving monastic communities, Xuanzang found only neglected and crumbling buildings inhabited by dwindling numbers of monks.

Nevertheless, while traveling through the northwest, Xuanzang once again paid his respects at the same four *stūpas,* his account of them offering us several additional details. The *stūpa* commemorating King Śibi's sacrifice of his eyes, for example, is described by Xuanzang as having "wood carvings and stone sculptures [that] are quite different from work done by human artisans."[10] Xuanzang dates this *stūpa* to the era of King Aśoka, and further informs us that the bodhisattva gave his eyes away at this spot not just once, but in a thousand consecutive lifetimes. The same repetitive quality also characterizes King Candraprabha's gift of his head, for Xuanzang tells us that this king, too, made such a gift "a thousand times in past lives."[11] The potency of this repetitive self-decapitation was such that its effects were still apparent in the time of Xuanzang. "On fast days," he tells us, "[the *stūpa*] sometimes emits a light amid divine flowers and heavenly music," and its powers had recently cured a devout woman suffering from leprosy.[12] Supernatural occurrences also characterized the fourth *stūpa,* commemorating Prince Mahāsattva's gift of his body to the hungry tigress. Xuanzang tells us that because the prince had "pricked himself with a dry bamboo splinter so as to feed the tigress with his blood . . . the soil and plants of this place are dark reddish in color, as if they have been stained by the blood," and "when people come to this spot, they feel nervous and uneasy, as if they had prickles hurting their backs."[13]

Unlike Faxian, Xuanzang does not single out these sites as the "Four Great Stupas." In fact, his account of his travels through the northwest suggests that many additional sites associated with the bodhisattva's bodily sacrifice also existed in this region.[14] Thus, the Mahāvana ("Great Forest") monastery marked the spot where the bodhisattva, as King Sarvadatta, had offered his own head to a wandering supplicant.[15] In the Sanirāja valley stood a monastery called Sarpauṣadhi ("Serpent Medicine") with an eighty-foot high *stūpa* whose story Xuanzang relates as follows:

> This was the place where a famine occurred with a pestilence when the Tathāgata was [the deity] Indra in a former life. Medical treatment failed to cure the people, who died one after another on the road. With a mind of pity, Indra wished to save them, and so he transformed himself into a huge python lying dead in the valley, and an announcement echoed in the air. Those who heard about it were glad to rush to the spot to cut off pieces of flesh, which were at once replaced, to satisfy their hunger and cure their disease.[16]

Strangely enough, nearby was yet another *stūpa* where a very similar deed had occurred: during a great famine, the bodhisattva (born once again as the deity Indra) "changed himself into a large *sūma* (water) serpent, and all those who ate its flesh were cured."[17] And finally, the appropriately-named Rohitaka (Red) *Stūpa* marked the spot where the bodhisattva, as King Maitrībala, "drew blood from his body to feed five yakṣas."[18]

Head, eyes, flesh, and blood—the land of northwest India itself was a virtual map of the bodhisattva's gruesome gifts. Over and over again, throughout his long career—whether as king, prince, ascetic, elephant, hare, serpent, or god—the bodhisattva quite literally gave of himself, repeatedly jumping off cliffs or into fires, drowning himself in the ocean, slashing his throat, cutting the flesh from his thighs, ripping out his tusks, gouging out his eyes, or letting mosquitoes drink from his blood. He offered his body as food, as drink, as medicine to cure all ills, as a raft to hang onto in pursuit of the other shore, as ransom for the life of another—or for no good reason at all, but merely because someone had asked. And always with the same motivation—to benefit other beings out of selflessness and compassion, to fulfill the "perfection of generosity" (*dāna-pāramitā*), and ultimately, to win the highest estate of Buddhahood.

Visual depictions of such gifts are scattered throughout the archaeological remains of ancient India and beyond. In a sculptural frieze from Gandhāra, the bodhisattva, born as a noble elephant, kneels down and allows a cruel hunter to saw off his magnificent tusks for the sake of an evil queen who desires them.[19] The same legend is depicted at Ajaṇṭā Cave 17 (see figure 1), except that in this case the elephant himself performs the difficult task, wrapping his enormous trunk around one of his tusks and enduring excruciating pain as he wrenches it out, while the hunter kneels beside him in awe.[20] In another Gandhāran frieze now kept at the British

FIGURE 1 The elephant Ṣaḍdanta removes his own tusk on behalf of a hunter. Wall painting, Cave 17 at Ajaṇṭā, ca. late 5th century C.E. Courtesy of Benoy K. Behl.

Museum (see figure 4 in chapter 3), we see King Śibi having a chunk of flesh removed from his thigh and placed on a scale in order to match the exact weight of the dove whose life is being ransomed, while in a painting from Ajaṇṭā Cave 1 we see him heaving his entire body up onto the scale itself, since—through a bit of divine magic—the weight of the dove cannot be matched no matter how much flesh is cut (see figure 2).[21]

For textual references to the bodhisattva's bodily gifts, we need not rely solely on the accounts of Chinese travelers, but can turn to the vast literature of Indian Buddhism itself. In some texts these gifts are merely alluded to in a general way. The *Mahāprajñāpāramitā Śāstra*, for example, says of the Buddha: "When he was still only a bodhisattva, he offered to his enemies who came to kill him his body, his flesh, his head, his eyes, his marrow, and his brain."[22] In other texts, they are enumerated more specifically. The *Lalitavistara*, *Rāṣṭrapālaparipṛcchā Sūtra*, and *Jātakastava* of Jñānayaśas, for example, contain long lists of the Buddha's previous births in which multiple instances of bodily sacrifice are briefly summarized and praised.[23] (The bodhisattva of the *Jātakastava* is especially busy; in just twenty verses, he throws himself off two cliffs, drowns himself in the ocean, jumps into a raging fire, and gives away his head, tusks, eyes,

FIGURE 2 King Śibi, unable to cut enough of his flesh to equal the weight of the dove, steps onto the scale itself. Wall painting, Cave 1 at Ajaṇṭā, ca. late 5th century C.E. Courtesy of Benoy K. Behl.

and flesh on three different occasions.) Such descriptions, though brief, do make us privy to certain new and lush details. From the *Jātakastava,* for example, we learn that King Maitrībala's flesh was "cut out in slices with a sword," and after being cut, was "still warm . . . with blood flowing from the apertures of the cloven veins."[24]

In many Mahāyāna *sūtras,* on the other hand, the bodhisattva's gifts are treated as examples to be imitated, and all bodhisattvas are encouraged to give their bodies away, either literally or figuratively. "I have renounced and abandoned my body to all living beings," the *Nārāyaṇaparipṛcchā Sūtra* advises the bodhisattva to think, "not to mention external things. If any being needs anything for any reason whatsoever, I will give it, as long as it seems right. I will give my hands to whoever asks for my hands, my feet to whoever asks for my feet, my eyes to whoever asks for my eyes. I will abandon flesh, blood, bone marrow, major and minor limbs—not to mention external things . . ."[25] The *Vajradhvaja Sūtra* likewise advises the bodhisattva to renounce his own body, reasoning with himself: "If I should give to this supplicant the intestines, the liver, the heart, or the lungs from my body, or if I should not give them—either way, my body is not permanent; at the end of my life, it is destined for the cremation ground."[26] Such passages remove the act of bodily self-sacrifice from the specific context of Śākyamuni Buddha's biography and begin to place it within the more generic context of the bodhisattva path and vocation.

The bodhisattva's gift of his body appears in many different guises, then, throughout the traditions of Indian Buddhism. Nevertheless, it is first and foremost in the Buddhist literary genres known in Sanskrit as *jātaka* and *avadāna* that such gifts and deeds truly come alive. In these two prominent Indian Buddhist narrative forms, the human stories behind such gifts are told, the heroes are brought to life, and the consequences of their gifts on themselves and those around them are narrated in painstaking detail. It is only through the reading of such fully elaborated stories that we stop thinking of bodily sacrifice as merely "something bodhisattvas do"—routinely, repetitively, as a matter of course—and are instead momentarily drawn into a world in which a *real creature inflicts horrible pain and mutilation upon his own self.* It is only within the context of the story, in other words, that we lose sight of the generic "bodhisattva path"—a cosmological pattern that replays itself in much the same way over and over again throughout time—and instead become embroiled within a smaller and more detailed world concerned with this-or-that king, this-or-that rabbit, and the integrity of this-or-that physical body. Through the skill of the storyteller and the flow of the narrative, the bodhisattva's deeds become visceral experiences for the reader. No matter how many stories one reads in which the bodhisattva agrees to give his body away, one still holds one's breath every time the momentous decision is made. One still feels a shudder run up the spine whenever the bodhisattva cuts open his flesh, and the text dwells almost lovingly on the pain and agony endured. It is only the story that engages us to such an extent that we become as children again, listening to the same tale over and over but experiencing delight upon every retelling.

Thus, in the various Pāli and Sanskrit versions of the *jātaka* involving King Śibi's gift of his eyes, we hear not merely of the gift itself, but of the dramatic events leading to it. King Śibi is described as a generous and compassionate king—one who has six alms-halls established throughout his capital city and distributes six hundred thousand pieces of gold to beggars and supplicants every day, "showering forth a great rain of gifts, like a cloud in the Golden Age."[27] Surely, he is the very model of the generous king! But still—it is not enough; he is unhappy and discontented; something is not right, "so addicted was he to giving."[28] We see him sitting on his throne, chin in hand, mulling over his gifts, wondering why they no longer satisfy him. What is it that he truly wishes to give?

"I've got it!," he exclaims, suddenly seating himself bolt upright.

> Today, when I go to the alms-hall, if any supplicant asks not for an external object, but names something internal, I will give it. If anyone names the flesh of my heart, I will strike my chest with a spear, and as if I were uprooting a lotus with its stalk from a clear pool of water, I will tear out my heart, oozing with drops of blood, and give it to him. If anyone names the flesh of my body, I will strip the flesh off my body as if I were engraving with an engraving tool and give it to him. If anyone names my blood, I will give him my blood, placing it in his mouth or filling up the bowl he holds forth. . . . If anyone names my eyes, I will tear out my eyes, as if I were removing the pith from a palm tree, and give them to him. . . . There is not a single human gift that has not been given by me. Even if someone should ask for my eye, without trembling I will give it.[29]

Sure enough, later that day, a blind old brahmin comes and asks the king for an eye, and King Śibi agrees to give him not one, but both of his eyes. This terrible decision throws his kingdom into chaos; officials and ministers protest, people are torn with grief, and ladies cry and lament. But King Śibi cannot be swayed. He calls his court physician and orders him to remove an eye. The physician reluctantly applies a powdered medication, and the eye rolls around in its socket. He applies another powder, and the eye begins to come out. He applies a third powder, and the eye comes out of the socket and dangles at the end of a tendon. The pain is extreme, blood flows, the ladies cry and lament. "My friend, be quick," says the king. So the physician picks up a knife, severs the tendon, and hands the king his eye, whereupon the king gives his eye to the brahmin, who places it in his own eye-socket. The same procedure is repeated for the second eye, as well. King Śibi is now blind, but the brahmin can see, and King Śibi is at last satisfied. "The eye of omniscient knowledge," he says, "is dearer to me than this eye by a hundred-fold, by a thousand-fold! This is the reason for [my action]."[30]

The story does not end there. Later on we will find out that the blind man was really the god Śakra in disguise, who was merely testing the bodhisattva's virtue. We will also see King Śibi's eyes magically restored to health and hear him preach a sermon on generosity to his subjects. But already we have begun to enter the king's world. What a strange man he is—but we feel that we know him somewhat; we have entered into his world and listened to him think, all by means of the story. He is no longer just the generic bodhisattva; now he is the proud and magnanimous king and the fallible human being—depressed when his unnatural addiction to generosity cannot be satisfied, stubbornly determined when his subjects oppose him, nearly suicidal (though never regretful) upon becoming blind. The story has given him flesh, and bone, and life.

One way in which we might begin to appreciate the possibilities brought about by the story-form is to compare two different versions of the same story, in this case both composed by the same author, the great Buddhist poet Kṣemendra, who included many such stories in his eleventh-century C.E. Sanskrit collection of versified *jātakas,* the *Bodhisattvāvadānakalpalatā* (hereafter *Avadānakalpalatā*). This is the well-known story of the hungry tigress, which differs in its details from one version to the next, but always involves the bodhisattva's sacrifice of his life in order to feed a hungry tigress who is about to devour her own cubs (see figure 3). In *Avadānakalpalatā* 95, Kṣemendra relates this story in the briefest of terms. One day, two criminals who have been sentenced to death are pardoned through the intervention of the Buddha, who then explains to his disciples:

> These two were saved by me in a previous birth, as well, when their mother was a hideous tigress. At that time, I was a king's son named Karuṇarekha. I was a bodhisattva and a compassionate friend of all beings. A tigress was once emaciated by hunger and ready to eat her two young cubs. I gave her my own body and thus prevented her from doing so. And now, these same two [cubs] have become thieves through their remaining karma, and have [again] been rescued by me. Their mother was none other than that tigress.[31]

This version of the story is brief and uninteresting, providing all of the essential "facts" but otherwise failing to exploit any of the possibilities of the storytelling form. In *Avadānakalpalatā* 51, on the other hand, Kṣemendra is much more loquacious, telling what is basically the same story again (aside from minor details), but this time in a manner that brings out all of the richness made possible by the characteristics of narrative literature.

One day, so the story goes, the Buddha suddenly smiles. When the deity Śakra asks him why, the Buddha replies that his smile is a result of him remembering some of the deeds from his previous lives that occurred on precisely this spot of ground. He then goes on to relate (speaking

FIGURE 3 Story of the starving tigress, as depicted on an eighteenth-century Tibetan *thangka* now kept in the St. Louis Art Museum (detail). On the lower left, the Buddha relates the story of his previous life as a brahmin ascetic. On the lower right, the brahmin ascetic and his disciple cross a bridge. In the center, they discover and preach to the starving tigress. On the upper left, the bodhisattva is devoured by the tigress while his disciple searches for him. Courtesy of the Saint Louis Art Museum, William K. Bixby Trust for Asian Art.

in the third-person rather than the first-person) a series of four of his previous lives, the fourth of which involves the hungry tigress. In order to give one a sufficient taste of this literature, I now quote the episode in full:

[Once upon a time, there was a brahmin's son] named Satyavrata who was highly esteemed by the people. He was learned in all the sciences, his heart was devoted to compassion, he was fond of tranquility, and his mind was opposed to marriage.

> A noble birth, the acquisition of virtues,
> a mind adorned with discrimination,
> and love and compassion for all beings—
> These are the marks of those whose karma is good!

Taking delight in his indifference to worldly desires, he went to a hermitage when he was still just a young man. He undertook a vow to serve two great sages and lived comfortably at the hermitage.

Then, in time, when he had attained the pure eye of wisdom, he saw a tigress who was about to give birth. He reflected: "She is afflicted by hunger and will give birth in seven days. Then an intense longing will arise [in her] to eat her own young." Thinking thus about her suffering, he informed the two sages and made a wish, out of compassion, to prevent it.

Then, after seven days had passed, the tigress—exhausted by the weight of the fetuses, and tormented by her long abstinence from food—brought forth her young in pain. Satyavrata saw that the smell of her own blood had produced an intense longing within her, and full of compassion, he thought: "Because of the pain of hunger, this miserable [creature] is prepared to eat her own cub! Alas! Out of regard for one's own welfare, one forgets even the love of offspring! Everyone is tormented by their own suffering, but cool to the torments of others. Rarely is a person born who is especially pained by the pain of others. I will give away my body to rescue this tigress and her young! I cannot endure their copious suffering when their lives are at stake. [And besides:]

> Those who abandon their bodies in order to save the lives of others,
> treating [their bodies] as if they were [mere] blades of grass—
> they have an enduring body of fame,
> brought about by the arising of abundant merit!
> [For] this [mortal body] is intent upon death.

It is a speck of life, like a drop of water,
trembling on the surface of a lotus leaf
shaken by the advancing wind.

Having thus reflected, that treasure-store of compassion fell down in front of the tigress, and with a bamboo stick, made a wound on his neck that oozed with blood.

For the minds of those who are magnanimous—
which are sweet with compassion
and intent upon protecting the unfortunate—
cannot at all endure the torments of others!

Then the tigress, stimulated by a desire for his blood, fell down upon his broad chest as he lay immobile, tearing into it with the glistening tips of her claws, which seemed to smile with joy, as if they were engraving into his chest the wonder of his noble conduct in this world.

Without moving at all, his body, full of courage, endured with compassion the burden of the terrible and cruel injuries brought about by the attack of the tigress—just as love endures faults, forbearance endures wickedness, wisdom endures a multitude of anxieties, firm resolution endures miserable and unbearable calamity, and ascetic radiance endures affliction. His body was covered with bristling hairs, and as his unblemished chest was torn apart by the sport of the tigress' rows of claws, it looked for a moment as if it were full of shooting rays of light whose purity was as bright as the moon. As he joyfully gazed at the tigress, intoxicated by eating his flesh and drinking his blood, his innate life-force—bewildered at the prospect of a long journey abroad—held its ground for a moment, clinging on in his throat.

[At last, the tigress] was satiated by moving back and forth as if she were circumambulating him, holding her face down continuously as if from bashfulness, and intent upon taking his hand [like a bride]. Thus did she cause excitement to his heart—even though he was hostile to marriage!

Those who are good-hearted have hearts
that are purified by benevolence,
imperturbable, noble by nature,
rivers of kindness and merit,
[enjoying] fame among [all] worlds.
Their very nature is to benefit others,

> and although they are completely in control of themselves,
> they are also ornamented by compassion for the miserable.
>
> Then, as he was being torn apart by the tips of the tigress' claws, the earth-lady, who is girdled by the playful tides of her four oceans, noticed his unequalled courage and suddenly trembled for a long time, as if with dread at the moment when his life would be destroyed.
>
> [The Buddha concluded]: "I myself was that man Satyavrata, who delighted in compassion. Remembering here and now my own [former] deeds, I gave rise to a smile."
>
> Having heard the Conqueror speak of his past conduct, Śakra's mind was amazed and his face stood motionless.[32]

Here, we have the same basic theme as before—the bodhisattva's gift of his body to a hungry tigress—yet the characters and their actions have now been vividly brought to life. We see the tigress, her belly heavy with the weight of her cubs, bringing them forth in great pain, giving rise to an insatiable hunger brought about by the smell of her own uterine blood, and finally ripping into the bodhisattva's flesh with utter abandon, satiating her hunger until she is drunk with blood and joy. And we see the bodhisattva himself—a calm, dispassionate, and wise renunciant, but at the very same time, a true bodhisattva, so full of compassion for the miserable beast and so excited by the opportunity to help her that she actually appears to him like a bashful bride, circumambulating the wedding-fire and "causing excitement to his heart, even though he was hostile to marriage." The use of such erotic imagery within the context of a body being ripped to shreds underscores for us just how *odd* this bodhisattva's values really are. Other paradoxes are also evident: The bodhisattva's neck is violently torn open and oozes with blood, yet at just the same time he is described as being "sweet with compassion"—as if the oozing blood itself were transformed, through his great compassion, into sweet, delicious nectar. The act of self-sacrifice is gory and bloody, with repeated images of claws ripping flesh—but it is also a fantastic spectacle, full of "shooting rays of light" and making the earth herself tremble like a fainthearted woman. Standard Buddhist doctrinal themes are also brought to life: the impermanent and unsatisfying human body becomes a drop of water clinging hopelessly onto a shaking leaf, while the attachment-to-self afflicting all unenlightened beings becomes a desperate mother ready to devour her own young.

On the other hand, even though they are duly mentioned, virtually no attention at all is paid in this version to the two sages with whom the bodhisattva lives—but they will similarly be brought to life in yet further versions of the same tale. In one version,[33] in which the bodhisattva is a prince rather than an ascetic, these two sages are replaced by the two older brothers of the bodhisattva, who, in spite of being royal princes themselves, are also men full of fear: even before entering the forest where they will encounter the hungry tigress, one brother says that he is afraid of being destroyed by a wild animal, while the other brother says that he is afraid of being separated from their parents—exactly the fate that their younger brother will later willingly and gladly undergo (whereupon we watch these two brothers utterly fall apart as a result of their enormous grief). In another version,[34] they are not only fearful but foolishly boastful—two sages who assure the bodhisattva that *they* will provide the hungry tigress with food, only to use their magical powers to fly away in fright once they realize how vicious the tigress really is. We also discover that one of these sages was a previous birth of the future Buddha Maitreya, and it was his failure to act in the same exalted manner as Śākyamuni that made him lose the cosmic race toward perfect Buddhahood. The highest and most exalted beings within the Buddhist universe are thus intimately connected to a single, long-ago human episode involving three ascetics wandering around in a lonely forest.

Same story, different versions—and a myriad of ways in which the awesome, cosmic pattern of the bodhisattva's repetitive bodily self-sacrifice is individualized, brought to life, and placed within a universe that *matters to us.* It *is* an awesome deed, to be sure, but perhaps it becomes something we can actually imagine when it is related to us in a simple, first-person voice and involves one's life as a lowly rabbit—such as we find in *Cariyāpiṭaka* 1.10 from the Khuddaka Nikāya of the Pāli Canon. Here the Buddha explains:

> When I was a hare living in the woods, feeding on grass, leaves, vegetables, and fruit, and abstaining from injuring others, a monkey, a jackal, an otter cub, and I lived in the same neighborhood and were seen [together] morning and evening. I instructed them as to virtuous and sinful deeds, saying, "Shun the sinful and stick to the virtuous!"
>
> Seeing the full moon on an Observance Day, I told them: "Today is an Observance Day. Prepare gifts to give to one who is worthy of gifts. After giving gifts to one who is worthy of gifts, observe the Observance Day."

"Very well," they said to me, and after preparing gifts in accordance with their ability and their means, they searched for one worthy of gifts.

Seated [there], I thought about a worthy, suitable gift: "If I should find someone worthy of gifts, what will be *my* gift? I have no sesame seeds, beans, rice, or clarified butter [to offer]. I live on grass, and it is impossible to give [someone] grass. If someone worthy of gifts comes to me for food, I will give him my own self! He will not leave [with an] empty [stomach]!"

Understanding my intention, [the god] Śakra came to my dwelling disguised as a Brahmin in order to test my generosity. When I saw him, I was delighted, and I spoke these words:

"It is indeed wonderful that you have come to me for the sake of food. Today I will give you an excellent gift that has never been given before! [But] you are endowed with moral virtue, and it is not suitable for you to injure others. [So] come, gather various types of wood, and light a fire. I will cook my own self, and you will eat [my] cooked [body]!"

"Very well," he replied, and with a delighted mind, he gathered various types of wood and fashioned a great pyre out of a womb of burning embers. He lit the fire there in such a way that it would quickly grow great.

Shaking my dusty limbs, I approached to one side. When the great pile of wood was blazing and roaring, I jumped up and fell into the middle of the flames.

Just as cool water relieves the anxiety and fever of whoever enters into it, and gives them satisfaction and joy, so did the blazing fire, when I entered it, relieve all of my anxiety, as if it were cool water.

My outer skin, my inner skin, my flesh, my muscles, my bones, and the sinews of my heart—I gave my whole entire body to the Brahmin.[35]

What a delightfully silly image—four little animals gathered together in the woods, listening intently to a sermon preached by a bunny rabbit, followed by the bunny rabbit himself, full of shame due to his poor food-gathering abilities, diving headlong into a blazing fire in order to feed a solitary Brahmin wanderer. And yet the Brahmin wanderer is really the great deity Śakra in disguise, the bunny rabbit is the bodhisattva himself, the blazing fire that ought to consume him magically becomes like cool, fresh water, and, as the *Cariyāpiṭaka* itself later informs us, this single deed constituted the bodhisattva's "fulfillment of the perfection [of giving]" and thus directly contributed to Śākyamuni's Buddhahood.[36]

In *Avadānakalpalatā* 104, by contrast, Kṣemendra turns the rabbit into a significantly more austere figure, and a much more sophisticated preacher. In this version, the rabbit lives in the forest with an ascetic, but when the forest is suddenly afflicted by drought, the ascetic becomes determined to leave it and go to a village where there will be more food. The rabbit dissuades him, however, by speaking eloquently and poetically about the dangers of ordinary, worldly life within a village. "O Holy Man, rich in austerities," he says,

> Is it really proper for a wise man like you
> to abandon an ascetic grove?
> The grounds of a village are teeming with people
> who are immersed in all kinds of distress
> as a result of being separated [from whatever they are attached to].
> They are breeding grounds for the trouble caused
> by the demon known as "delusions of the household life."
> The household is crowded with servants;
> it is rattled by the chain called "wife";
> it is made intolerable by the fetter called "son";
> it firmly strangles one with the snare called "relatives."
> It is made terrible by its crowds of wicked people;
> it is a great darkness that envelops one in stupidity.
> What wise man, having abandoned the household,
> would ever touch it again?
> The sorrow that results from being separated from what one loves
> is a constant source of bewilderment.
> Food that is salty with material wealth
> only makes one's thirst grow greater.
> People whose minds are made stupid
> by their habitual, wicked desire for sensual pleasures
> dwell in the house called "field of mental afflictions"
> and see their welfare come to ruin.
> [But] in a deserted forest,
> those who are satisfied by sublime tranquility
> do not have minds shaking with intoxication
> by the passionate liquor of sensual enjoyments;
> or eyes full of tears welling up
> from the smoke of separation from loved ones;
> or burning pain brought about
> by the heat of anger and fighting.
> When men have an aversion to tranquility,

they continually long for the village
because of the distress caused by the forest,
or they fondly remember the forest
because of the distress caused by the village.
Please don't look longingly upon the village,
for the village is unfavorable to discipline!
And how much more does contact with the village
bind those who are attached to sensual pleasures!
You'll be able to get fruit right here, sooner or later.
And for now, you can survive on my own clean flesh.[37]

Same basic scenario, but no longer is he an insignificant bunny rabbit worrying about how to gather food; now he is a most talented Buddhist preacher (superior even to the human ascetic) whose sermon skillfully gives voice to the enduring Buddhist themes of the pitfalls of worldly life and the benefits of renunciation. Bold images such as the "rattling chain called 'wife'" and the "intolerable fetter called 'son'" also remind us that this particular preacher is the future Buddha himself, and the simple plotline involving a rabbit jumping into a fire here recedes somewhat into the background.

In yet other cases, however, such sermons might be kept to a minimum, while the plotline itself becomes significantly more complicated and capable of conveying complex ideas by means of its very intricacy. Consider, for example, the twenty-sixth story in the (Tibetan) *Sūtra of the Wise and the Fool,* a story with a complicated pedigree[38] but clearly related to several Sanskrit parallels. While this story resembles the other stories I have discussed, its depiction of the act of bodily sacrifice is clearly more complicated than we find in the cases of King Śibi, the tigress, or the hare. Once again, in order to provide a sufficient taste of this literature, I will translate this delightful story in full:

Thus did I hear at one time. The Blessed One was [once] dwelling at Veṇuvana, at Kalandakanivāpa, in Rājagaha. At that time, the Venerable Ānanda got up from his seat, arranged his robes, put his knees on the ground with his palms joined, and requested the Blessed One thus:

"I ask you to explain this. Why is it that as soon as the Blessed One [first] turned the wheel of the dharma in the world, the five monks headed by Kauṇḍinya were the very first to taste the nectar of the dharma?"

The Blessed One said to Ānanda: "Previously, these five monks were the first to eat my flesh and be satiated. Therefore, in this life as well, they were the first to taste the flavor of the dharma and be liberated."

Ānanda requested of the Blessed One: "Please tell us what these five monks previously did." The Blessed One spoke to Ānanda, [and he told him a story of the past].

• • •

Formerly, in the past, a long time ago, immeasurable, innumerable, inconceivable eons ago, here in Jambudvīpa, there was a king named Śudolagarne who ruled over the 84,000 or so minor kings of Jambudvīpa. At one time, a soothsayer predicted that no rain would come to the country for a period of twelve years. Hearing this news, the king was greatly afflicted by suffering, thinking about how much food there was and for how many years it would feed so many people if such a great famine arose. He gathered all the minor kings and ministers together and consulted with them, calculating how much grain was in the storehouse and how many people were present. But when they calculated [how much grain] must be given directly to each person [in order to last] for twelve years, [they saw that the grain they had] would not last for twelve years, and they announced this in a bell-ringing proclamation.

Then, later on, a great famine arose and many people died. The king thought about what he could do to save many people's lives. [One day, the king], the queen, and the royal retinue went walking in the park and stopped somewhere to rest. After the queen and all of the numerous people [in the retinue] had fallen asleep, [the king] got up from his couch, bowed down in the four directions, and made a solemn vow, as follows:

"In this country, a famine has arisen, and all the food is gone. May I abandon my body through hunger, and after I have died, may I be reborn as a giant fish! May everyone feed on my flesh and be satiated!"

Having made this solemn vow, he climbed up into a tree. He threw his body from the tree into an abyss. After dying there, he was miraculously transformed into a giant fish, five hundred *yojanas* [long], [swimming] in a great river.

At that time, there were five woodcutters in the country who came to the riverbank to gather wood. The giant fish saw them and said to them in a human voice:

"If you are hungry, then cut off my flesh and eat as much as you want! Even after you are full, take home with you as much as you can carry! You will be the first to eat my flesh and be satiated; therefore, later on, as well, when I have attained complete enlightenment, you will be the first to taste the food of the dharma!

[Go and] tell the people of the country that anyone who is hungry should take as much of my flesh as they wish."

So the five men cut up his flesh and ate it, and told the people of the country [to do likewise]. The word spread from one to another until everyone in Jambudvīpa gathered to cut up his flesh and eat it. When one side of his ribs was completely exhausted, [the fish], on his own accord, turned over [and offered] the other side. Similarly, when the top half of him was not yet completely exhausted, he offered the bottom half. With the fish turning over and over in this way, from his belly to his back, everyone cut his flesh and ate it for a period of twelve years. [During this time], everyone gave rise to thoughts of compassion, and thus, everyone who ate his flesh, even after dying, was reborn as a god in heaven.

• • •

"Ānanda," [the Buddha concluded,] "the king who became a fish at that time and on that occasion is now me. The five woodcutters who were the first to cut and eat my flesh are [now] the five monks headed by Kauṇḍinya. The many beings who later ate my flesh are [now] 80,000 *devas* and my liberated disciples. At that time, I gave [my body] to those five men first and saved their lives, and therefore, in the present time, as well, I taught the dharma first to them, and by means of the limbs of my dharma-Body, I extinguished the fire of the three poisons."

Ānanda and the great assembly were delighted and rejoiced at the Blessed One's words.[39]

In this case, we have *two* separate instances of bodily self-sacrifice, along with a miraculous transformation. The king first sacrifices his life in order to transform himself into a gigantic fish, and the fish then sacrifices its life by allowing all beings to feed on his flesh. This seems to change the nature of the self-sacrifice itself. In fact, if we consider all of the stories I have discussed thus far, it is possible to place this instance of self-sacrifice on the far end of a continuum of bodily destruction and/or transformation: in the story of the tigress, an ascetic's body is wholly ripped to shreds and lost for good; in the story of the hare, the outside world itself (in the form of the fire) refuses to destroy the hare's body at all; in the story of King Śibi, the eyes are pulled out but later magically restored in a better and more powerful form than before; and now finally, in the story of King Śudolagarne, the act of self-sacrifice actually *transforms* the ineffectual human body into a gigantic creature whose flesh heals thousands of other beings. The image of the dispassionate bodhisattva who is willing to throw away his worthless body on behalf of other beings gradually gives way to another, quite different image: that of a boastful bodhisattva who is determined to physically force the transformation of his body into something monstrous and almost grotesquely effective. Clearly, the act of bodily self-sacrifice is more complicated than it first seems.

There is a further complexity in this story, as well, in the intriguing identifications made between past and present characters: the five woodcutters who were the very first to feed on the fish's flesh were subsequently reborn as the Buddha's first five disciples (headed by Kauṇḍinya), who were "the very first to taste the nectar of the dharma." There are no lengthy sermons or extended doctrinal reflections, yet from these identifications (and similar identifications made in other stories), it is possible to discern, as I have done elsewhere,[40] an underlying message about the nature of Buddhahood and the path that leads to it: the bodhisattva gives away his physical body and enacts a physical salvation of beings, the story suggests, whereas the Buddha gives away a *spiritual* body—the body of dharma—and enacts a *spiritual* salvation of beings. An intriguing parallel—but also hierarchy—is thus drawn between the bodhisattva's gift of his physical body in the past and the Buddha's gift of his dharma-body in the present, between life-saving food and soul-saving nectar, between physical satiety and spiritual satisfaction.

Complex plotlines, intriguing identifications, beautiful imagery, and so many different elaborations of the same basic theme. Perhaps we can now understand why the theme of the bodhisattva's gift of his body proved to be such a compelling one in the literary traditions of Indian Buddhism.[41] In the Pāli Canon preserved by the Theravāda school (whose roots extend back to perhaps the third century B.C.E. but whose final codification and commentarial appendages were not completed until the fifth century C.E.), there are several such stories (for example, those of King Śibi, the hare, and the elephant) contained in the *Jātaka* collection of verses (the tenth book of the Khuddaka Nikāya), together with its prose commentary, the *Jātakaṭṭhakathā* (hereafter "Pāli *Jātaka* collection"). Two of these stories (those of King Śibi and the hare) are also related more briefly in the *Cariyāpiṭaka* (the fifteenth book of the Khuddaka Nikāya), where they are celebrated as paradigmatic instances of the bodhisattva's *dāna-pāramitā*, or "perfection of generosity."

Nevertheless, although the theme of the bodhisattva's bodily sacrifice would become quite popular in the later Theravāda tradition of Southeast Asia (there are many such stories, for example, in the 15th–16th century *Paññāsa Jātaka*),[42] in the earlier tradition represented by the Pāli Canon, it does not seem to have attained much prominence—overshadowed, perhaps, by the complete dominance within this tradition of the *Vessantara Jātaka,* which is another story involving extreme generosity (in this case, the gift of one's wife and children).[43] In the Sanskrit tradition, on the other hand, stories involving the bodhisattva's bodily self-sacrifice seem to have become something of a minor obsession, the same stories appearing over and over again in story-collections of diverse provenance. This would include, for example, relatively earlier collections such as the *Avadānaśataka,* the *Mahāvastu,* the *Divyāvadāna,*[44] Kumāralāta's *Kalpanāmaṇḍitikā* (now extant only in Chinese),[45] and the *Jātakamālā* of Āryaśūra, as well as later collections such as the *Jātakamālās* of Haribhaṭṭa and Gopadatta,[46] Kṣemendra's *Avadānakalpalatā,* and the (much later) *Mahajjātakamālā*[47]—texts which range in date from perhaps the first century C.E. to relatively recent times, come from both Mainstream and Mahāyāna origins,[48] and vary in style all the way from simple Buddhist Hybrid Sanskrit prose attributed to no individual author to elegant, literary Sanskrit composed at the courts of kings by named and celebrated poets.

In some cases, gift-of-the-body stories appear in unexpected places—such as the version of the tigress-story contained in the eighteenth chapter of the Mahāyāna *Suvarṇabhāsottama Sūtra* (which is otherwise a typical Mahāyāna *sūtra*)—while in other cases, the theme is developed at great length and merits its own, independent text, such as we find in the *Maṇicūḍāvadāna,* a long rendition of the story of King Maṇicūḍa, and in the *Lokānandanāṭaka* of Candragomin, a dramatic play in five acts (again dealing with King Maṇicūḍa) that is now extant only in Tibetan. Finally, some story collections preserved in languages such as Chinese and Tibetan and having a very uncertain relationship to any presumed Indic originals might also be included within this general grouping, since the stories themselves clearly draw on Indic tradition and often run parallel to stories existing in Sanskrit or Pāli. Two such collections I will refer to throughout this book are the Chinese *Liudu ji jing* (*Sūtra on the Collection of Six Perfections,* T. 152), which is supposed to have been translated by Kang Senghui between 222 and 280 C.E. but which has no extant Indic original,[49] and the Tibetan *mDzangs bLun* (commonly known as the *Sūtra of the Wise and the Fool*), which is a collection of stories that were supposedly heard orally in some Indic language by eight Chinese monks living in Khotan, transcribed by them in Chinese in 445 C.E., and subsequently translated into Tibetan, Mongolian, and Oirat versions.[50]

How can texts of such diverse provenance, existing in different social, historical, cultural, and literary contexts, be brought together merely by sharing the single theme of the bodhisattva's bodily self-sacrifice? Does it, indeed, make any sense to view them as a single grouping? In this book, I will be advancing precisely this argument. Despite each story's individual flavor (some of which I have tried to convey through the excerpts given above), the premise of the book as a whole is that the gift-of-the-body theme itself has its own internal logic and significance, and was conveyed through a set of conventions that seem to have remained remarkably consistent over wide areas of space and time, and in spite of significant linguistic and stylistic diversity. In fact, as I will argue, gift-of-the-body stories might best be seen as constituting a discrete subgenre of Indian Buddhist narrative literature—a subgenre that is worthy of a close and careful reading that gives due weight to the literary forms of the stories and takes them seriously as crafted pieces of literature.

One of the earliest scholars to address the gift-of-the-body theme in any detail was Har Dayal, who collected, summarized, and discussed a series of gift-of-the-body stories in his classic work *The Bodhisattva Doctrine in Buddhist Sanskrit Literature.*[51] But despite the usefulness of his discussion, I cannot share his opinion of the value of such stories or the manner in which they should be read. "The idea of giving away one's limbs has given rise to some curious stories," he states, "which are intended to be highly instructive and inspiring, but which are simply silly and puerile."[52] A few pages later, he continues:

> The heroes and heroines of these stories give away wealth, limbs, life, wives and children in a spirit of exaggerated and fantastic philanthropy. The lack of a sense of proportion and harmony is the fatal flaw of the Indian temperament as exhibited in literature and religion. The Indian thinkers and writers often push a good idea to such extremes that it becomes grotesque and ridiculous. But we can read these quaint parables with pleasure and interest, if we appreciate their spirit without thinking too critically of the details.[53]

"Thinking critically of the details" is precisely what I aim to do herein. Instead of abstracting the "spirit" of the gift-of-the-body theme from the context of the stories in which it is developed, I aim here to treat the theme *as it is developed within the* jātakas *and* avadānas *themselves.* I am interested not merely in the meaning and significance of the gift-of-the-body theme, but also in how this theme reveals and unfolds itself within the world of

Indian Buddhist storytelling. We know that bodhisattvas tend to give away their bodies, but how does this actually occur? What kind of beings are they, why do they do such things, how do the people around them react to their deeds, does it hurt—and what happens next? It is the *stories* and not the theme alone that captivate my attention, and this book is a first attempt to problematize and analyze the reactions that I—and perhaps other audiences—have experienced as a reader of these tales.

The book is based on a highly idiosyncratic (and by no means complete) corpus of Indian Buddhist gift-of-the-body stories preserved in Pāli and Sanskrit (with a few Tibetan and Chinese translations for support) and classified as either *jātakas* or *avadānas.* The stories in question date anywhere from perhaps the third century B.C.E. to the late second millennium C.E. and are drawn from the narrative literature of both the Mainstream and Mahāyāna traditions. They include several of the most famous and well-known gift-of-the-body tales—such as those of King Śibi, the elephant, and the tigress—and many less prominent tales as well. A full description of the corpus is given in the Appendix.

My discussion can be divided naturally into two halves. In chapter 1, which is methodological and introductory in nature, I lay out my argument in favor of approaching gift-of-the-body stories from a genre-based perspective and through a largely ahistorical approach. I then situate my corpus of gift-of-the-body stories within the larger context provided by the *jātaka* and *avadāna* genres, arguing that gift-of-the-body stories should be treated as a distinct subgenre within this larger context, proposing a definition of the gift-of-the-body subgenre, and distinguishing it from several other, closely related subgenres. This chapter thus sets the literary and conceptual background for chapters 2 and 3.

In chapter 2 I begin my analysis of the tales by looking closely at the genre's conventions of plot: What are some of the major plotlines employed within gift-of-the-body stories? How does each plotline "work," how do different plotlines relate to each other, and how do variations in the plotline serve to bring different emphases to the fore? This analysis is continued in chapter 3, where I turn from conventions of plot to conventions of rhetoric: What kind of rhetorical and ideological logic underlies the gift-of-the-body genre? What do these stories wish to argue, and how do they go about doing so? How do they use the narrative form to acknowledge, confront, and grapple with various alternative ideologies that are directly opposed to their own, most cherished ideals? These two chapters together provide the reader with a close analysis of the genre and make a conscious attempt to complicate our perception of these seemingly "simple" stories and instead demonstrate to the reader their complexity, nuance, and ideological power.

After examining my corpus in terms of genre, in the second half of the book, I move away from a strictly genre-based approach (though without losing sight of the literary forms of the stories) to examine more closely some of the major religious issues that come to the fore within gift-of-the-body tales. Chapters 4 and 5 focus on the "gift" portion of the gift-of-the-body theme. The bodhisattva's bodily self-sacrifice is usually explicitly conceived of as a type of "gift" (*dāna*)—indeed, as a most extraordinary type of gift and a fulfillment of the bodhisattva's "perfection of generosity" (*dāna-pāramitā*). These two chapters thus attempt to situate the gift-of-the-body theme within the larger context of Buddhist ethical discourse on gifts, gift-giving, and the virtue of generosity: What kind of gift is the bodhisattva's gift of his body, and how does it bring together several different Buddhist ideals of generosity? Since *dāna* constitutes a profoundly important concept in Indian Buddhist thought whose many contours are just beginning to be untangled, in chapter 4 I first set the context for this discussion by proposing two different conceptual schema by means of which the many notions of *dāna* put forth in Indian Buddhist literature might be classified. In chapter 5 I then turn to the gift-of-the-body theme itself and attempt to situate it within this larger discourse, arguing that the theme is multivocal and flexible in nature and relates to the larger discourse in a variety of different ways (and again paying ample attention to the types of narrative strategies that allow for this degree of flexibility).

Chapter 6, in contrast, focuses on the "body" portion of the gift-of-the-body theme. The bodhisattva's gift is not just any gift, but specifically a gift of his *body.* Thus this chapter discusses several prominent Buddhist lines of thinking about the body—both the ordinary human body and the very special body of the bodhisattva—and demonstrates how they are invoked within gift-of-the-body stories, once again arguing for the genre's multivocality and flexibility as brought about through the narrative form. Chapters 5 and 6 together thus begin to move away from an intensive focus upon the stories themselves to demonstrate how the stories relate to wider spheres of Buddhist intellectual discourse.

Finally, chapter 7 briefly points toward several further contexts of interpretation that might be brought to bear on the gift-of-the-body theme—including kingship and its legitimation, the category of sacrifice, the category of the ritual offering, and the Buddhist discourse on death—while the Conclusions offer a summarizing discussion of the major points made throughout the book.

In speaking of the hundreds of versions of the Rāmāyaṇa epic that have crisscrossed their way across ancient and modern India, A. K. Ramanujan once observed that the Rāmāyaṇa is not just a series of "texts" or "stories" or "versions," but instead a set of cultural resources—or what he termed a "pool of signifiers" that each individual version dips into to bring out a "unique crystallization."[54] Each "version" has its own unique internal logic and necessity, but relies for its ability to convey meaning on the overall "pool" from which it draws. I find this to be a most felicitous image for thinking about Buddhist gift-of-the-body stories. It is my hope that within these pages I have thrown some light on both the art and artistry of individual "crystallizations" and the basic "pool of signifiers" from which all such stories draw.

1

THE GIFT-OF-THE-BODY GENRE

In the twenty-second chapter of the *Divyāvadāna* we find a long and elaborate rendition of the story of King Candraprabha, who gave away his head to an evil and greedy brahmin. The story opens with a description of King Candraprabha's magnanimous generosity and the beneficial effects it has on his kingdom. King Candraprabha is described as "a giver of everything, a renouncer of everything, one who gave without attachment and engaged in great generosity."[1] He gives away so many material gifts that everyone in Jambudvīpa's 68,000 cities becomes exceedingly wealthy. No one goes around on foot anymore; instead, they ride around on the backs of richly caparisoned elephants or in golden chariots drawn by horses. So weighed down are they by the jewelry, parasols, crowns, and ornaments given to them by the king that everyone in Jambudvīpa begins to look exactly like the royal king himself. They live in pleasure and luxury, and instead of working for a living, they listen to musical performances, surround themselves with beautiful women, and "amuse themselves with the amusements of kings."[2]

The turning point in the story comes with the introduction of an evil brahmin named Raudrākṣa, who lives on Gandhamādana Mountain. For as soon as he hears of King Candraprabha's great reputation as an "all-giving" (*sarvaṃdada*) king, he muses to himself:

> What if I were to go and ask for his head? If he were really "all-giving," then he would give me his head! But it is difficult, impossible, and out of the question that he would renounce the most excellent, beloved, cherished, dear, and charming part of his body—his head, that is! This is impossible![3]

When I first translated this story many years ago, I did not find anything particularly humorous in Raudrākṣa's musings. Instead, I wondered right along with him whether King Candraprabha could really be convinced to offer up his own head. It was only after reading many more gift-of-the-body stories that I began to find Raudrākṣa's words incredulous, ridiculous, and maybe even funny. For by the conventions of the gift-of-the-body genre, of course, there is no question as to whether the bodhisattva will agree to give away his head. Every dull-witted reader knows that he will—that it is *impossible* that he should *not*—and thus, for Raudrākṣa to state repeatedly that such a thing is "difficult, impossible, and out of the question" turns him into a caricature of the foolish, evil brahmin, and makes his statement appear humorous. The humor is not intrinsic to the statement itself, but derives from one's understanding of the conventions of the gift-of-the-body genre. Once I understood this, my education as a reader had begun.

Here is another example of the play of generic conventions. In the sixth chapter of Āryaśūra's *Jātakamālā,* we find an interesting version of the famous story of the Buddha's previous birth as a hare, roughly the same story as the one I previously quoted from the *Cariyāpiṭaka.* Once again, this hare lives in the forest with an otter, a jackal, and a monkey, and once again, he delivers a sermon to them on the necessity of offering food and hospitality to wandering travelers, but then immediately begins to fret about his own ability to do so. Just when the hare is about to despair, however, he hits upon a momentous idea: he will offer to any wandering travelers who happen by the flesh from his own body. This sincere intention to sacrifice his own body in order to feed a guest causes the earth and mountains to shake with delight, which alerts the celestial beings above. The god Śakra, eager to test the hare's virtue, disguises himself as a brahmin wanderer who is hungry and lost in the woods. When he calls out for help, the otter comes and offers him seven fish, the jackal offers him a dead lizard and a bowl of sour milk, and the monkey offers him some mangoes. The hare then bravely steps forward and offers to the brahmin his own body. A heap of flaming coals suddenly materializes, and the hare throws himself into the fire—thus sacrificing his very life to provide the brahmin wanderer with a nice meal of rabbit. Impressed and filled with astonishment, Śakra abandons his brahmin-disguise, praises the hare's deed at length, and then places the image of the hare in the moon as a permanent reminder of this magnificent gift.

For the uninitiated reader, there is nothing especially odd here—nothing that would immediately stand out and garner one's attention. It is only for one who has read many of these tales and is familiar with the conventions of the genre that the plot of this particular tale marks it as an especially extreme example. For, as we will see in chapter 2, gift-of-the-body stories fall into two main types. In some stories, the request for the gift might be described as "real." That is, an ordinary living being who finds himself in dire straits of some kind makes a sincere request for the bodhisattva's body, or is obviously in need of the bodhisattva's body. The bodhisattva gives away his body, and generally dies in the process. This death is entirely appropriate—for the theme of extreme and uncompromising generosity on behalf of suffering living beings finds its greatest fulfillment only when the bodhisattva actually loses his life and is therefore seen to have sacrificed everything for the sake of generosity and compassion. (Having the bodhisattva survive the gift or somehow get his body back would obviously dilute the ethical message.)

In other stories, however, the request for the gift is not "real," but might rather be described as a "ruse"—for the recipient who demands the gift is not truly a suffering being in need, but rather the god Śakra in disguise, who is merely testing the bodhisattva's generosity. The request for the gift is *not real*—it is a *ruse*—and thus the bodhisattva in these stories *does not die.* Instead, the normal outcome of such stories is that once the bodhisattva passes Śakra's test by demonstrating his willingness to give, Śakra reveals his true identity, praises the bodhisattva, and then encourages him to perform an "Act of Truth" that restores his injured body to perfect health. The story has a "happy ending"—and this, again, is entirely appropriate. For it is never Śakra's intention to make the bodhisattva *die;* it is only his intention to *test* him, and once he passes this test, it is perfectly appropriate that he should get his body back. This correspondence between the identity of the recipient and the ultimate fate of the bodhisattva appears to be a solid generic convention. That is, although such conventions never constitute ironclad rules, we can state with some assurance that most gift-of-the-body episodes in which the recipient is Śakra-in-disguise end with the bodhisattva restoring his body by performing an Act of Truth, while most gift-of-the-body episodes in which the recipient is someone other than Śakra end with the bodhisattva losing his life.

Once we are schooled in these generic conventions, Āryaśūra's rendition of the hare-story suddenly jumps out at us and strikes us as significant. For the story begins with the typical setup involving Śakra's desire to test the bodhisattva's generosity—yet it ends with a fiery death for the hare. Something has gone wrong here. *He wasn't supposed to die, it was only a test.* Generic conventions have been violated, generic expectations thwarted—and it is here that interpretation takes place. We might speculate, for example, that Āryaśūra is particularly concerned to emphasize the theme of extreme self-sacrifice, and thus violates certain generic conventions in his retelling of the hare-story in order to achieve this end. *Even when the gift was only a ruse,* he seems to be saying, *the bodhisattva still gave up his life.* The competent reader will, on some level, recognize the divergence of Āryaśūra's version not only from the Pāli versions on which it is likely based[4]—in which the hare survives the gift rather than dying—but more important, its divergence from *all* gift-of-the-body stories in which the recipient is Śakra-in-disguise. It is the violation of the larger generic convention that signals to the reader the possible significance of this particular tale. Ideally, such a reader has heard or read many different stories in which Śakra tests the bodhisattva—and has seen the bodhisattva pass and survive this test in good health over and over again. Thus, when the hare unexpectedly *dies,* this death calls attention to itself; it brings home to one the reality of extreme self-sacrifice with new and unanticipated force. This forcefulness derives from the story's relationship to the larger generic tradition rather than from the story itself.

In support of this interpretation, I might point out that Peter Khoroche has claimed that the *Jātakamālā* does indeed show a much greater concern with emphasizing the bodhisattva ideal of self-sacrifice than does the Pāli *Jātaka* collection. He notes, for example, that three of the four tales in the *Jātakamālā* that are not shared in common with the Pāli *Jātaka* collection involve the gift-of-the-body theme.[5] Thus one could argue that Āryaśūra, when deciding which tales from the earlier tradition to include within his collection, showed disproportionate favor toward the theme of extreme self-sacrifice. The collection as a whole thus confirms what we can already gather from just a single story—once we approach it in terms of its *genre.*

The Concept of Genre

"Genre," in my usage, does not refer to a prescriptive body of rules, theoretical model, or universal archetype. Instead, I adhere to a broadly historical conception of genre, as advanced by many literary critics.[6] In the understanding of such critics, the term "genre" should be restricted to those historically situated sets of institutionalized conventions that have presumably governed the writing and reading of literature at a particular place and time. Thus any genre, by this definition, should be characterized by both historical/cultural specificity, in terms of being restricted in time and space, and discursive specificity, or its own distinctive complex of generic conventions. A genre becomes recognizable to its readers as an entire complex of generic conventions—formal, substantive, structural, functional, etc.—that appear to characterize a body of related texts. Each genre can be described as an abstract body of such conventions, which constitutes its "generic repertoire." Genres can be named and defined by the culture in question (*jātaka, avadāna,* etc.), but it is also possible for scholars to make historically and critically persuasive arguments for genres that are not explicitly named by the culture in which they operate—which is the project I will undertake here.

Despite modern declarations of the increasing irrelevance or even "death" of genre, genre is, in fact, intrinsic to the everyday processes of writing, reading, and interpreting.[7] Writing cannot take place in a vacuum; a writer always writes within the context of the repertoire of genres characteristic of his or her culture. Even those works that seem to violate generic codes beyond recognition derive at least some of their meaning against the framework provided by the very codes violated and contribute (if they become influential) to the future make-up of the codes. Readers, too, can interpret a text only by placing it within the context of a particular genre or genres. Thus literary critics (especially reader-response critics) often speak of the way in which the opening section of a text establishes a "generic contract" between the text and the competent reader, providing the reader with a set of "generic expectations" against which to interpret the text. These expectations are often violated or broken, but they provide the framework within which interpretation takes place, and they make the violations meaningful. Far from limiting the creativity of either author or reader, generic conventions (and other elements of literary competence brought to bear on the text) provide the very means by which literature can be made to bear meaning. Thus, if we think of genre not in terms of ironclad rules and prescriptions that stifle creativity, or rigid, taxonomic classes into which every work of literature must fit, but rather in the looser terms of an "invitation to form"[8] for the writer and a "horizon of expectations"[9] for the reader, then it seems that genre is very much alive.

The phrase "horizon of expectations" is also useful for indicating the status of the generic conventions one describes within one's analysis. Rather than seeing these conventions as collectively constituting some kind of "underlying structure" or "essence" that is intrinsic to the genre in question—as Vladimir Propp does, for example, in *Morphology of the Folktale*[10]—I favor an approach which theoretically shifts such "structures" from the text to the expectations of the competent reader.[11] That is, whatever conventions one uncovers through the reading of multiple texts should not be seen as properties *intrinsic* to those texts, but rather, as the norms, expectations, and interpretive operations on the part of the reader that are required to account for the effects of signification the texts are seen to have. Thus, in my own discussion of the gift-of-the-body genre, whatever conventions I discern and describe should be seen merely as abstractions that attempt to render explicit the body of literary and generic expectations any qualified and competent Indian Buddhist reader might have brought to bear on a story of this type, based on his or her previous experiences with literary tradition. From this perspective, deviations from the expected conventions found in any particular story do not "disqualify" the story as a gift-of-the-body story, but rather, highlight possible points at which the reader might derive meaning from the violation of his or her "generic expectations" (as we saw with Āryaśūra's version of the story of the hare). Alternatively, if we wish to imagine genre from the perspective of the writer rather than the reader, then these same conventions might be seen as a hypothetical reconstruction of the basic set of discursive possibilities such a writer had available to him in composing or reworking a story of this type—whether or not he ultimately chose to fulfill them.

The concept of genre, as I have defined it, always includes a historical dimension.[12] Because literature is historically situated and constantly subject to transformation and change, genres that are given "once-and-for-all" definitions and conceived as ideal, immutable, Platonic forms tend to lack any explanatory power when applied to actual texts. Therefore, one's analysis of a genre should always specify a historical frame of reference. Moreover, depending on the width of this frame, there will generally be a trade-off between the range of texts accounted for and the level of explanatory detail: a very wide historical frame will include a greater range of texts at the expense of explanatory detail, while a very narrow historical frame will be rich in explanatory detail but have the power to explain a smaller number of texts. I do not necessarily agree with Alastair Fowler, however, when he states categorically that "correspondingly little can be said" within a frame of wider limits, or that such discussion always "tends toward the vacuous."[13] True, one can probably say considerably less of general import about "the novel" than one could about "the nineteenth-century British novel"—but what one does say might be equally interesting and persuasive and serve just as well to bring out the value and literariness of those texts understood to be "novels." Ultimately, the success or failure of this trade-off depends on the critic's overall purpose and should be evaluated in those terms.

Methodologically, then, I conceive of genre in a manner that steers a middle way between two theoretical extremes. On the one hand, I am broadly committed to historicity and would reject any generic interpretation—however rhetorically convincing—that would be impossible for historical authors and readers to recognize. On the other hand, however, I also recognize that history itself is a matter of interpretation—not the objective ground for such interpretation—and in that sense, all generic "description" is ultimately interpretive and pragmatic in nature. Genres are always grounded in the critic's explanatory purpose, defined by the critic herself in order to achieve certain ends, and constitutively powerful of the texts being examined. As Adena Rosmarin states in *The Power of Genre,* genre is "the critic's heuristic tool"—a "pragmatic thought-experiment" that is "justified wholly insofar as it helps us make better or more convincing critical arguments."[14]

These theoretical issues are especially pertinent to the project I undertake here because the historical frame of reference I invoke throughout this book is a very wide one indeed. In fact, the category of "Indian Buddhism" is perhaps the only historical frame that brings my corpus of stories together (and in some cases even this frame is stretched to its very limit). Thus, although I am ostensibly aiming to reconstruct the generic expectations of a "qualified and competent Indian Buddhist reader," it is worthwhile asking who, exactly, this phantom figure might be. After all, a Pāli story from the Pāli *Jātaka* collection written in a simple style and perhaps deriving from early oral tradition (though not redacted in its final form until fifth-century C.E. Sri Lanka) is something very different from a Sanskrit story from Āryaśūra's fourth-century C.E. *Jātakamālā,* which is written in an elegant, courtly style and directed at connoisseurs of fine poetry—and both of those are quite different, again, from a much later Tibetan story translated from a Chinese collection originally based upon oral tales heard in some Indic language by Chinese monks in Khotan.[15] What kind of "qualified and competent Indian Buddhist reader" could we possibly posit as the audience for all three of these tales? Where would such a person come from, what gender or social class would he (or she) belong to, when would he (or she) have lived, and under what local circumstances would he (or she) have encountered such a genre?

Perhaps the best way to answer such questions is to admit that while this kind of local specificity—even in the case of premodern Indian Buddhism—*is* sometimes possible,[16] and while it has garnered increasing attention in the field of Buddhist Studies, it is simply *not* the project I am interested in pursuing here. Since I am interested in a set of stories that spans the entire length and breadth of the Indian Buddhist tradition (and involving many texts whose provenance and reception are full of uncertainty), and since I nevertheless wish to hold onto the conception of genre in terms of the generic competence and expectations of the reader, I suppose that my "qualified and competent Indian Buddhist reader" is something of a phantom figure. Not only is he (or she) fully literate—for in my conception of a "reader," I have completely ignored the oral/aural dimension of these texts and their possible adaptation to performative, storytelling contexts—but he or she also stands at the very end of the tradition, looking back, and is familiar with texts in several different languages and styles of writing.

In a sense this reader is not any single historical person who might have potentially existed, but instead a personification of *Indian Buddhist literary tradition*—and even perhaps a personification of the not-necessarily-chronological intertextuality so characteristic of this material. For the texts within my corpus are not just isolated texts—they are texts that are often aware of one another, refer to one another, quote from one another, draw from the same shared context of reference and allusion, and borrow and adapt the same stories and conventions over and over again—in some cases, seeming to "speak" to each other in a way that would be historically impossible. It is this—admittedly diffuse and historically vague—Indian Buddhist discursive space that I am after when I conceive of my "competent reader." It is the overall "pool of signifiers" that most persuasively (I hope) accounts for the "unique crystallization" embodied by each individual tale. This competent reader, moreover, is—unavoidably—a projection of my own reading practices, but one that is available for the scrutiny of other qualified readers.

Ultimately, then, in spite of its reliance upon a broadly historical conception of genre, the project that I undertake here is clearly *not* well-rooted in a particular historical context, and although I recognize that this methodology leaves me open to the risk of considerable criticism, I am convinced that this is a risk worth taking. Otherwise, one would have to hold the position that nothing at all can ever be said about a general "Indian Buddhist discursive world" that shows definite continuity over time and space (not only in terms of plotlines, characters, and religious conceptions, but even in terms of individual clichés and phraseology, and between Pāli, Sanskrit, and Tibetan/Chinese translations), simply because "Indian Buddhism" is too long and too broad for one's statement to be historically responsible—and I am unconvinced that this is the case. I would loosely compare the scope of my methodology, perhaps, to John Strong's description of his work as "the exegetical exploration of a world of meaning,"[17] in which "particular texts or particular issues [from widely varying historical contexts] are taken as focal points for presenting and discussing the problematics of a given tradition,"[18] or to Steven Collins' exploration of a wide-ranging "Pali imaginaire," which he specifies as consisting of "any and every Pali text from the premodern period, but only those of which there is a western edition."[19] And finally, I would also defend the basic claim that careful reading and a sympathetic imagination can make up, to some extent, for a lack of historical precision. As Hallisey and Hansen have stated:

> As yet we know very little about what individual Buddhists did in particular historical circumstances, and it is unlikely that we will ever recover all that we would like to know. There will be very few instances where we will have an independent historical witness to the impact that the retelling of a story may have had on a particular individual. [But] [a]ttention to the worklike aspects of the texts may help us to educate our imaginations, such that we do feel that we have a reasonable idea about what subsequent Buddhists . . . might have learned from a story—if only because our own horizon of values and expectations is altered by our attempt to think through the possibilities of a text.[20]

I follow them here in believing in the value of such imaginative enterprises.

Jātakas, Avadānas, *and Gift-of-the-Body Tales*

The vast majority of gift-of-the-body stories that constitute my corpus do not refer to themselves explicitly as "gift-of-the-body stories." Though the bodhisattva's gift of his body is referred to in Sanskrit with several different terms—such as *ātma-parityāga* ("self-sacrifice"), *śarīra-parityāga* ("renunciation of the body"), *adhyātma-dāna* ("internal gift"), and *kāya-dāna* or *deha-dāna* ("gift of the body")—none of these terms is regularly used, either alone or in combination with other terms, to indicate a specific literary genre.[21] The gift-of-the-body genre I am proposing constitutes my own hypothetical construction and is not a genre that was specifically named by the culture in question. I have underscored this point throughout by consistently making use of the hyphenated English adjective "gift-of-the-body" (as in "gift-of-the-body theme," "gift-of-the-body story," and "gift-of-the-body genre") rather than any Sanskrit equivalent.

Instead of referring to themselves as "gift-of-the-body stories," most of the stories within my corpus identify themselves more generally as *jātakas* or *avadānas*. Three different versions of the hare story,[22] for example, call themselves the *Sasa Jātaka* (Pāli), the *Śaśa Jātaka* (Sanskrit), and the *Śaśāvadāna* (Sanskrit)—meaning either "the *jātaka* of the hare" or "the *avadāna* of the hare." The Buddhist narrative genres of *jātaka* and *avadāna* thus constitute the larger generic context within which gift-of-the-body tales might be seen as a distinct *subgenre*—a "subgenre" being defined by Fowler as a class with the same basic generic repertoire as its corresponding genre, but additional specification of content.[23] This raises the obvious question, however, of how gift-of-the-body stories can constitute a subgenre of two different genres at once. Are gift-of-the-body stories *jātakas?* Are they *avadānas?* Or does it depend on the particular story?

A brief discussion of the *jātaka* and *avadāna* genres will help to clarify these issues. Both in terms of etymology[24] and consistent usage, the meaning of the term *jātaka* in Indian Buddhism is quite clear: a *jātaka,* in brief, is a story in which one of the characters—usually the hero—is identified as a previous birth of the historical Buddha, generally appearing in the form of a man, a deity, or one of the higher animals (but only rarely as a female of any kind).[25] Such stories exist within all kinds of Buddhist texts, both canonical and noncanonical—including *sūtra, vinaya, abhidharma, śāstras,* and commentaries, as well as individual *jātaka* texts and *jātaka* collections. The *jātaka* as a genre appears to be very old, for in the ancient system enumerating nine "limbs" (*aṅga*) of the Buddha's teaching mentioned throughout the Pāli Nikāyas, *jātaka* constituted the seventh "limb."[26] Since this is an ancient classification that predates the texts in which it now appears, *jātaka* as an *aṅga* refers not to specific extant texts, but rather to a particular genre of composition and category of *buddhavacana.* The great age of the *jātaka* genre is also suggested by the fact that depictions of *jātaka* stories appear in Indian Buddhist art at Bhārhut and Sāñcī as early as the second century B.C.E.

The existence of the *jātaka* genre is based on the notion that the Buddha, during the "first watch" of the night of his enlightenment, attained the recollection of his previous lives.[27] Throughout his career he often had occasion to relate one of these former lives to his audience in order to illustrate a point, drive home a moral lesson, or shed light on some situation. It is these stories that constitute the *jātakas.* Because samsara is beginningless, of course, the Buddha—like all beings—has a potentially infinite number of these previous lives. The *jātakas,* however, do not stretch back into the infinite past. In Indian Buddhist tradition, the lives related in the *jātakas* are understood to be restricted to those that took place during the Buddha's bodhisattva career. In several important texts, such as the *Jātakanidāna* and the *Buddhavaṃsa* (both in Pāli), the story is told that four "innumerable eons" and one hundred thousand (regular) eons ago, when the Buddha was a young brahmin ascetic named Sumedha, he encountered the former Buddha Dīpaṃkara, became full of faith, made a religious vow in Dīpaṃkara's presence to become a Buddha himself in the far distant future, and received from Dīpaṃkara a firm and detailed prediction of his future success.[28] This was the moment that inaugurated the Buddha's bodhisattva career, and it is only the lives that occurred *after* this crucial point that are worthy of being related in the *jātakas. Jātakas* are about the Buddha's previous lives *as a bodhisattva on the bodhisattva path* rather than as an ordinary being.[29]

The general function of the *jātakas,* then, is to illustrate how the bodhisattva, in life after life, cultivated various virtues on the bodhisattva path that ultimately contributed to his attainment of Buddhahood. Accordingly, most *jātakas* portray the bodhisattva as an exemplary figure, highlighting such features as his wisdom, compassion, and ascetic detachment. Many *jātakas,* in fact, are explicitly intended to illustrate the bodhisattva's cultivation of one of the six or ten "perfections" (*pāramitā*) needed for the attainment of Buddhahood. In the *Aviṣahya Jātaka,* for example, the bodhisattva is a wealthy merchant who continues to give alms to supplicants even after he is reduced to absolute poverty, thus cultivating the "perfection of generosity" (*dāna-pāramitā*); in the *Brāhmaṇa Jātaka* he is a boy who refuses to steal even when his brahmin teacher urges him to do so, thus cultivating the "perfection of morality" (*śīla-pāramitā*); and in the *Kṣāntivādin Jātaka* he is an ascetic who calmly tolerates the mutilation inflicted on him by an angry king, thus cultivating the "perfection of forbearance" (*kṣānti-pāramitā*).[30]

Some *jātaka* collections are even arranged on this basis: the *Jātakamālā* of Āryaśūra arranges the bulk of its thirty-four *jātakas* (including the three mentioned above) in accordance with the first three of the Sarvāstivādin list of six perfections, while the *Cariyāpiṭaka* of the Pāli Canon arranges its thirty-five versified *jātakas* in accordance with the Theravādin list of ten perfections. In spite of the didactic nature of these and many other *jātakas,* however, it is also the case that any preexisting tale could be transformed into a *jātaka* simply by turning one of its characters into a previous birth of the Buddha. The *jātaka* genre was thus used to assimilate an enormous variety of traditional Indian folklore into the Buddhist fold—including some tales whose moral lessons were not specifically Buddhist, or that had no discernible moral lesson at all. This is especially true of the massive Pāli *Jātaka* collection, much of whose contents are likely non-Buddhist in origin, including many traditional animal fables, folktales, and fairy tales.

In terms of narrative structure, many *jātakas* possess or imply a threefold structure consisting of a "story of the present" (in Pāli, *paccuppannavatthu*), explaining on what occasion the Buddha told this tale; a "story of the past" (*atītavatthu*), which is the past-life story itself; and the final "identifications" (*samodhāna*), in which the perspective shifts back to the present, and the Buddha identifies characters in the "story of the past" as the previous births of those in the "story of the present" and other well-known Buddhist figures of his time (always including himself). These identifications are often predictable, for the relationships the Buddha has with other people during his last life often mirror the relationships he had with them during his numerous previous lives. (Thus, the bodhisattva's mother is usually identified as a previous birth of the Buddha's mother Queen Māya, the bodhisattva's father is usually a previous birth of King Śuddhodhana, and any "villain" in the story is usually a previous birth of the Buddha's cousin and nemesis Devadatta.)

The "story of the present" and the "identifications" both pertain to the "present" time, and together serve as an outer framework that encompasses and contextualizes the "story of the past," or *jātaka* proper. In many cases, however, this outer framework is largely ignored, and only the "story of the past" appears—although at least some indication that one of the characters is a previous birth of the Buddha is required in order to indicate that the story is a *jātaka.* Often this is accomplished simply by referring to one of the characters as "the bodhisattva."

In contrast to the relatively easy task of describing what constitutes a *jātaka,* far greater problems are presented by our second relevant genre, the *avadāna.* Etymologically, the term *avadāna* has been given at least two different derivations,[31] and there is no consensus on what the term originally meant. It seems fairly clear, in fact, that both the etymology and the original meaning of the term *avadāna* must have been lost at an early date, and the Buddhist tradition itself did not clearly understand the precise meaning of the term. Given these uncertainties, many scholars have eschewed the quest for etymology or original meaning and have been content to conclude that the term *avadāna* within Buddhist literature has the broad meaning of "legend," "narrative," or "tale."[32] In some cases, however, scholars have also come up with more descriptive definitions, based on the characteristics of those works labeled as *avadānas.* A perusal of descriptive definitions put forth by scholars and ranging in date from 1844 to 2000[33] leads one to the conclusion that although they differ in emphasis, they are generally in accord with one another, and seem to revolve around three major aspects: (1) *Avadānas* are stories that illustrate the workings of karma and rebirth, demonstrating how past actions have resulted in present circumstances, and how present actions will result in future circumstances. (2) Often the types of actions depicted take place in a Buddhist devotional context; thus positive actions are generally good deeds done toward Buddha, Dharma, Saṃgha, or some other religious object, while negative actions are the opposite. (3) The heroes of *avadānas* are generally Buddhist disciples or layfollowers.

Taken together, these three elements do provide an adequate descriptive definition of the *avadāna* genre—one that is in general concord with important *avadāna* collections, such as the *Avadānaśataka, Divyāvadāna, Karmaśataka,* (Pāli) *Apadāna,* and a later collection of texts known as the *Avadānamālās.* It is also possible in many cases to distinguish (as some scholars have done) between several distinct types of *avadānas: avadānas* of the past (relating the previous lives of the heroes), *avadānas* of the present (relating deeds and their consequences within a single lifetime), *avadānas* of the future, or *vyākaraṇas* ("prophecies," relating present deeds and the Buddha's prediction of their future consequences), and mixed *avadānas,* which combine several different types.[34] Further complicating the matter, however, is that many "*avadānas* of the past" deal with previous lives of the Buddha; these are referred to as *bodhisattvāvadānas* and are technically equivalent to *jātakas*. Thus, *jātakas* can be seen as a subset of *avadānas*, and any *jātaka*, in theory, could be called an *avadāna* (while only some *avadānas* could be called *jātakas*).

Just as the existence of the *jātaka* genre is based on what happened during the "first watch" of the night of the Buddha's enlightenment, so the existence of the *avadāna* genre is based on what happened during the "second watch."[35] During this watch the Buddha gained the "divine eye," which allowed him to see, with perfect clarity, the intricate workings of karma and rebirth and the "passing away and reappearance" of all beings. Thus, in addition to perceiving his own previous lives, he could also perceive the previous (and future) lives of other beings. Throughout the remainder of his career, he often had occasion to relate the previous or future lives of his disciples and layfollowers—focusing especially on karmic deeds and their consequences—and it is these stories that constitute the *avadānas*.

Like the *jātaka*, the *avadāna* appears to be a very old genre, for in addition to the ancient system of nine *aṅgas*, or "limbs," of the Buddha's teaching mentioned earlier, there is also a list of twelve *aṅgas* that retains the original nine but adds three additional categories, including *avadāna* as the eleventh.[36] Once again, since this twelvefold system predates the texts in which it now appears, *avadāna* as an *aṅga* refers not to specific extant texts, but rather to a genre of composition or category of *buddhavacana*. It is even possible, moreover, that there existed a class of monks who specialized in composing and passing down the texts belonging to this genre, since two verses in the *Kalpadrumāvadānamālā* refer specifically to "avadānists" and to "experts in the *avadānas*."[37]

From the preceding discussion, the answers to the questions I posed above become obvious: although the gift-of-the-body stories within our corpus are variously labeled either *jātaka* or *avadāna*, we are justified in seeing them strictly as *jātakas* because all of them involve previous births of the Buddha, which is the technical definition of the *jātaka*. Thus the title *jātaka* versus the title *avadāna* has little significance within this corpus, since *avadāna*, in this case, really stands for *bodhisattvāvadāna*, a term synonymous with *jātaka*. Gift-of-the-body stories are clearly *jātakas*.

In the following section, however, I would like to approach and answer this question from a slightly different perspective by considering not merely the technical definitions of the terms *jātaka* and *avadāna,* but also the religious meaning or significance of each genre and the relationship obtaining between them. For *jātakas* and *avadānas* do not exist in isolation; instead, they are both part of an Indian Buddhist generic system marked by particular relations between different genres. I will argue that gift-of-the-body stories are *jātakas* not merely because they involve previous births of the Buddha, but also because they embody what might be called the "ethos of the *jātaka*" rather than the "ethos of the *avadāna.*" I will argue, in fact, that gift-of-the-body stories are a kind of "super-*jātaka*"—and that part of the significance of the "super-*jātaka*" derives from its stark contrast to the *avadāna.*

*Perfections, Devotions, and Super-*Jātakas

Several scholars have pointed to a fundamental difference between the religious perspectives of the *jātaka* and the *avadāna.* Weeraratne states that *jātakas* involve the long moral career of the bodhisattva and his gradual acquisition of virtues and perfections over an extremely long period of time. They never suggest that one can achieve complete Buddhahood merely through worshiping other Buddhas. "But in the *avadānas,*" he states, "we detect a subtle change of emphasis. . . . Though these *avadānas* are termed stories about karma . . . the karma referred to . . . is not the karma . . . described in the *jātaka* stories, but action with a certain amount of devotion . . . towards the Buddha."[38] Speyer makes a similar observation that is worth quoting at length (despite his use of the word "trivial" to characterize the *avadānas*):

> The *avadāna* class comprises a great many of invented stories of a trivial kind, which are never or seldom met with among the *jātakas* proper. To perform an *avadāna,* that is to say: a glorious deed, common people may suffice with something less than the world-famed heroic performances of the Bodhisattvas of old, who offered their body as food to a famished tigress, their eyes, their flesh and blood, their head . . . who gave away wife and children to a begging brahman, etc. Gifts to the Saṅgha; glorification of the Master or his disciples by presenting them with incense, flowers, silver, gold, jewels; the adorning, repairing, honouring of *stūpas* and *caityas* . . . in short any deed or performance beneficial to the Church and its Clergy may constitute actions entitled to that name and worth celebrating in *avadāna*-tales.[39]

And finally, John Strong, in a somewhat similar manner, contrasts "*jātaka*-acts" with "*avadāna*-acts"—noting that *jātaka*-acts are "acts of compassion" while *avadāna*-acts are "acts of devotion."[40] Taking all three observations together, we might say that *jātakas* illustrate the bodhisattva's arduous cultivation of certain moral perfections, whereas *avadānas* take place in a Buddhist devotional context and involve the performance of devotional acts by disciples and layfollowers. In short, we might say that *jātakas* are about "perfections" whereas *avadānas* are about "devotions."

Taking *jātakas* and *avadānas* as a whole, of course, this is not strictly true. It is more of a general tendency—yet general enough so that it constitutes a generic expectation whose violation causes confusion about whether something is "really" a *jātaka* or an *avadāna*. Take, for example, the stories that appear in the second *varga* (division) of the *Avadānaśataka* or the various narratives contained in the *Buddhavaṃsa*.[41] These relate the previous lives of the Buddha and therefore meet the technical definition of the *jātaka*. But rather than dealing with the bodhisattva's cultivation of the *perfections*, they instead deal with the bodhisattva's *devotions* toward previous Buddhas. For this is the second major activity a bodhisattva engages in: when there is no Buddha in the world, the bodhisattva cultivates the six or ten moral perfections needed for Buddhahood (as described in the *jātakas*), but when there *is* a Buddha in the world, the bodhisattva encounters this Buddha and engages in acts of worship and devotion. Thus the Buddha himself, as a bodhisattva, encountered every one of the twenty-four Buddhas that arose in the world beginning with the time of his original bodhisattva-vow (as the ascetic Sumedha) and ending with his own final attainment of Buddhahood—and it is these devotional encounters that fill the pages of the *Buddhavaṃsa* and the *Avadānaśataka*'s second *varga*. Because these narratives focus on this second type of action—"devotions" rather than "perfections"—they are more akin in spirit to *avadānas* than to *jātakas*. Consequently, there is confusion among scholars about whether they are really *jātakas*, and most surveys of *jātaka* literature and descriptions of the *Buddhavaṃsa* and *Avadānaśataka* do not refer to them as *jātakas*. In the case of the *Avadānaśataka*, in fact, the term *jātaka* is usually reserved for the stories that appear in the fourth (rather than second) *varga* of the text, which do deal with the bodhisattva's cultivation of the moral perfections. Thus, even though the second and fourth *vargas* of the text both focus on the Buddha's previous lives, only the latter is consistently seen as containing *jātakas*.

This distinction between the second and fourth *vargas* of the *Avadānaśataka* is not merely a product of scholarly confusion, moreover, for the Buddhist tradition itself appears to make the very same distinction. From approximately 400 to 1000 C.E., most of the stories of the *Avadānaśataka* were systematically reworked, elaborated, and rekeyed in the tone of the Mahāyāna in a later series of four texts known as the *Avadānamālās* (or "Garlands of Avadānas"). It is striking to observe, as Strong has pointed out in his discussion of this issue, that the author-compilers who produced these later texts on the basis of the *Avadānaśataka* consistently included the stories of the second *varga* but ignored those from the fourth.[42] This suggests that the author-compilers themselves drew a distinction between *avadānas* as stories about "devotions" and *jātakas* as stories about "perfections." The stories in the second *varga* fit the implicit definition of the *avadāna* and were thus included in the *Avadānamālās*, even though they involved previous births of the Buddha and were therefore technically *jātakas*, while the stories in the fourth *varga*, though called *avadānas*, were recognized by them to be *jātakas* and thus left out of the *Avadānamālās*.

In terms of their ethos or religious significance, then, we might say that *jātakas* are about "perfections," while *avadānas* are about "devotions." The former deal with *moral* acts, while the latter deal with *ritual* acts. The split between morality and ritual, of course, is by no means a definitive one. Buddhist texts make it clear that moral acts (such as saving somebody else's life) very often involve ritualistic elements (such as vows), while ritual acts (such as offering flowers to a *stūpa*) are both driven by and help to cultivate moral attitudes (such as faith). In fact, the frequently voiced notion that Buddhism replaces ritual with ethics or ethicizes ritualistic notions has been shown to be vastly oversimplified; the moral and the ritual always implicate each other and can never be wholly separated.[43] Nevertheless, there *is* a difference of emphasis between the predominantly-moral and the predominantly-ritual, and it is this contrast, I contend, that constitutes one of the major differences between the *jātaka* and *avadāna* genres.

This contrast can be further clarified, perhaps, if we consider the two genres in terms of the *absence* or *presence* of Buddhism in the world to function as a "field of merit" (*puṇya-kṣetra*). In the *avadānas* Buddhism is present in the world as a powerful "field of merit." The heroes of the *avadānas* thus engage in devotional acts that ritually draw upon the power of this field to produce religious merit—or they fail to take advantage of this field, which produces religious demerit. In the *jātakas*, by contrast, the world is devoid of Buddhism as a field of merit whose power can be ritually tapped. The heroes of the *jātakas* thus engage in moral (rather than devotional) acts to produce religious merit. Moreover, because they do not have access to such a powerful field of merit, the moral acts they perform must often be more extreme in nature than the ritual acts performed by the heroes of the *avadānas,* who do have access to such a field. Thus, generosity in the *avadānas* might involve the offering of alms to a Buddhist monk, whereas generosity in the *jātakas* might involve chopping off one's own head. Ascetic detachment in the *avadānas* might involve depriving oneself of material goods by offering them to the Saṃgha, whereas ascetic detachment in the *jātakas* might involve renouncing one's family and glorious kingship to endure a difficult life in the wilderness.

In part, no doubt, this difference between the *jātaka* and the *avadāna* derives from the fact that the hero of the former is the bodhisattva himself, whereas the hero of the latter is generally an ordinary person. (Naturally, we would expect the bodhisattva to engage in more heroic feats than an ordinary disciple or layfollower.) Quite apart from this, however, I contend that part of the logic of the distinction between *jātakas* and *avadānas* is to highlight the difference between the *pre-Buddha* and *post-Buddha* ages. Without a Buddha in the world, King Śibi had to gouge out his eyes and give them to a stranger in order to adhere to the imperative of *dāna,* whereas a layperson living in the age of Śākyamuni can offer alms to a monk and perhaps gain just as much. Why? Because the latter gift constitutes an act of *dāna* to the Saṃgha—a potent field of merit that was unavailable to King Śibi. Thus, moral deeds in a Buddha-less age ("perfections") are both compared to and contrasted with ritual transactions in an age of Buddhadharma ("devotions"). By means of the *jātakas,* the bodhisattva is lauded and exalted for the magnificent lengths he went to during his previous lives—but by means of the *avadānas,* ordinary Buddhists receive the message that such magnificent lengths are now *unnecessary,* thanks to the presence of Buddhism in the world as a powerful field of merit. The life of the Buddha can be replaced by the ritual of the Buddhist. For "perfections" and "devotions" are, on some level, equivalent: the sort of ritual logic at work here means that every offering made, every act of devotion performed, no matter how small, is multiplied by the great field of merit in which it is bestowed—the resulting product calling to mind the magnificent past deeds of the Buddha himself (such as King Śibi's gift of his eyes). Thus it is neither the *jātakas* alone nor the *avadānas* alone but only the two genres taken together that illuminate for the reader the ritual magic worked by Buddhism—a magic that allows pre-Buddha "perfections" to be replaced by post-Buddha "devotions."[46]

jātakas and *avadānas,* then, are not distinguished from each other solely by the technical matter of whether they focus upon the Buddha or someone other than the Buddha. Instead, each of the two genres conveys certain characteristic religious values and assumptions, and the two genres work together to encompass an entire set of contrastive relations (as well as parallels and connections) between the past and the present, the Buddha-less age and the age of Buddhadharma, moral deeds and ritual transactions, Buddhas and ordinary beings. Within the discursive space occupied by these two genres, some tales embody the ethos of the *jātaka,* some tales embody the ethos of the *avadāna,* some tales consciously attempt to forge connections between the two,[45] and some tales have little relevance to either side of this distinction—but in that case, I contend, the generic label of *jātaka* or *avadāna* strikes us almost as adventitious or irrelevant to the story's interpretation.

Gift-of-the-body stories are *jātakas* in this second and more significant sense as well. That is, not only do they involve previous births of the Buddha, but they do so in a manner consistent with the ethos of the *jātaka*—by focusing on "perfections" within a Buddha-less age rather than "devotions" within an age of Buddhadharma. In fact, if we imagine a kind of continuum in which stories can be judged as either more or less "*jātaka*-like," then gift-of-the-body stories, I maintain, are "super-*jātakas,*" or some of the most "*jātaka*-like" *jātakas* of all. Within the *jātaka* genre as a whole, there is an implicit hierarchy of tales, and gift-of-the-body stories inhabit the highest rungs of this hierarchy. In order to demonstrate this, let me draw a few distinctions between different varieties of *jātakas* and their corresponding degrees of "*jātaka*-ness" or adherence to the ethos of the *jātaka:*

1. The first major distinction I would draw is between those *jātakas* that illustrate one of the six or ten perfections (*pāramitā*) and those *jātakas* that do not, with the former having more "*jātaka*-ness." This is not a question of relative numbers, since a very large number of the latter type of *jātaka* also exist. Many of the stories in the Pāli *Jātaka* collection, for example, are simple animal fables teaching cleverness, shrewdness, or worldly wisdom (*nīti*), rather than illustrating one of the perfections. And yet one cannot help but notice a persistent tendency in the scholarship to *exclude* such tales from the *jātaka*-category. Thus Speyer, in the above quote, speaks of "*jātakas* proper," and there are similar references throughout the scholarly literature to "real *jātakas,*" "unequivocal *jātakas,*" "true *jātakas,*" "classical *jātakas,*" "distinctly Buddhist *jātakas,*" and so forth.[46] Presumably, such

real, true, unequivocal *jātakas* are those that illustrate, in some way, the bodhisattva's cultivation of the perfections.

The same underlying assumption about what constitutes a "true" *jātaka* is also evident within the Buddhist tradition itself. Despite the heterogeneous contents of the Pāli *Jātaka* collection, for example, the Theravādin tradition has always given a special status to the last ten *jātakas* in the collection because they are understood to be the preeminent examples of each of the ten perfections. Likewise, if we look at the history of the *jātaka* genre as a whole, there is a clear tendency over time for later authors to selectively choose and rework earlier traditions. Within these patterns of choice, many such authors (for example, Āryaśūra and Haribhaṭṭa) clearly favor those tales that illustrate the bodhisattva's cultivation of the perfections and generally ignore the simple animal fables, fairy tales, and folktales found so frequently in the Pāli *Jātaka* collection. The fact that some later collections (such as the *Jātakamālā*) are even arranged on the basis of the perfections further underscores this obvious hierarchy.

2. Among those *jātakas* that illustrate one of the six or ten perfections, *dāna-pāramitā,* or the "perfection of generosity," seems to be a highly favored choice. This is clear not only from a subjective reading of many *jātakas* but also in the layout of those *jātaka*-collections that are arranged on the basis of the perfections. The final ten *jātakas* of the Pāli *Jātaka* collection mentioned above (which deal with the ten perfections) save the last and longest story of all (that of Prince Vessantara) for the "perfection of generosity"—clearly giving it the most exalted status among the ten perfections.

In other cases, this favoritism toward *dāna* is a matter of relative numbers. The *Cariyāpiṭaka* of the Pāli Canon consists of thirty-five versified *jātakas* (told in the first-person by the Buddha himself) arranged according to the Theravādin list of ten perfections. Among these, there are ten stories each for "generosity" (*dāna*) and "moral virtue" (*sīla*), followed by five for "renunciation" (*nekkhamma*), one for "resolution" (*adhiṭṭhāna*), six for 'truth" (*sacca*), two for "benevolence" (*mettā*), and one for "equanimity" (*upekkhā*)—with one of the concluding verses of the work implying that the remaining three perfections have been achieved as well. Āryaśūra's *Jātakamālā* is arranged in a similar way, with the first ten stories illustrating "generosity," the second ten "moral virtue," and the third ten "forbearance"; the pattern breaks down with the last four stories of the collection, however, which do not illustrate "energy" (the fourth Sarvāstivādin perfection), and the fifth and sixth perfections ("meditation" and "wisdom") are not represented at all. In both texts, then, *dāna* is clearly one of the favored perfections. Many early scholars could not understand this: Barua and Morris felt that the *Cariyāpiṭaka* must be incomplete because it was "missing" three perfections; Horner felt that even if the "lost" sections were found, one still could not account for the overrepresentation of "generosity" and "moral virtue"; and Rhys Davids surmised that the text must originally have consisted of a hundred tales—ten for each perfection—basing himself on a similar claim concerning the *Jātakamālā* recorded by the Tibetan historian Tāranātha.[47] However, recent scholarship has insisted that both works are complete as they stand,[48] and indeed it is not so difficult to imagine that *dāna* and *śīla* were simply held in higher esteem and thought to warrant greater attention, as the most "*jātaka*-like" virtues of all.

3. Finally, within the favored category of *jātakas* illustrating *dāna-pāramitā,* the gift-of-the-body theme was one of the favored means of so doing. Out of the great wealth of *jātakas* involving generosity that must have been available to their authors, the *Cariyāpiṭaka* uses two gift-of-the-body stories (out of ten) to illustrate *dāna-pāramitā,* while the *Jātakamālā* uses four; similarly, in a list found in the *Jātakanidāna,* two out of eleven *jātakas* illustrating *dāna-pāramitā* are also gift-of-the-body stories.[49] Similarly, gift-of-the-body stories are frequently invoked within exegetical discussions of *dāna-pāramitā.* In fact, the gift of the body is consistently described not as an ordinary act of *dāna* but as the paradigmatic example or fullest embodiment of *dāna-pāramitā.*

Thus, gift-of-the-body stories are not only *jātakas* in a strictly technical sense. In addition, they are *jātakas* in the further senses of illustrating the cultivation of moral perfections in a Buddha-less world, focusing in particular upon the highly favored "perfection of generosity," and illustrating this perfection in an extreme and especially paradigmatic way. Gift-of-the-body tales are very special *jātakas*—"super-*jātakas*" that occupy the highest rungs in an implicit *jātaka*-hierarchy. Moreover, if the ethos of the *jātaka* contrasts with the ethos of the *avadāna,* then it is the "super-*jātaka*" that provides the greatest contrast of all. Part of the significance of the "super-*jātaka,*" I contend, comes from its extreme "non-*avadāna*-ness." In the bodhisattva's gift of his body, we have perhaps *the* paradigmatic example of the *heroic and inimitable moral exploit performed by a worthy and superior being in a difficult, Buddha-less age of the past*—and standing in stark opposition to the commonplace ritual and devotional transactions performed by ordinary Buddhists in the narrative present.

This contrast, in fact, sometimes seems to be invoked within the Buddhist tradition itself. One of the most interesting examples comes from Faxian's experience of the festival of the Buddha's tooth relic, as it was celebrated in Sri Lanka during the fifth century C.E. For ten days prior to the festival, Faxian reports, the king took care to whip up the devotional fervor of the public by having a man dressed in royal robes parade around the city on a huge elephant, reminding people (in the following words) of everything the Buddha had done on their behalf:

> The Bodhisattva practiced for the incalculably long time of three *asamkhyeya* (immeasurable) *kalpas*, never sparing his own life. He gave up his kingdom, his wife, and his child. He even tore out his eyes to give them to others. He cut his own flesh to ransom a dove, gave his head as alms, offered his body to feed a famished tigress, and did not begrudge his marrow and brain. Having suffered these pains, he achieved Buddhahood at last for the sake of all living beings.[50]

It was explicitly in remembrance of *these* particular deeds that people were then encouraged to "level the streets, decorate the roads, and prepare all kinds of flowers, incense, and other offerings"—or in other words, engage in typical, *avadāna*-like deeds. The fervor of their devotion, in other words, was to be fueled by the obvious and enormous *chasm* existing between what the bodhisattva did for them—expressed most effectively in the gifts of his body—and what they were able to do in return, out of gratitude and devotion. Implicit in this man's message is the very contrast I have been discussing—the contrast between the "ethos of the *jātaka*" and the "ethos of the *avadāna*"—as well as the status of the gift of the body as perhaps the most preeminent expression of the former.[51]

Understanding the position inhabited by gift-of-the-body tales within the larger generic context provided by *jātakas* and *avadānas*, I believe, is helpful in interpreting the rhetorical strategies employed by individual gift-of-the-body stories. One of the recurring themes throughout the remainder of this book will be my contention that gift-of-the-body stories are "super-*jātakas*" that embody the ethos of the *jātaka* in a particularly paradigmatic way and derive part of their meaning from the contrast they pose with the ethos of the *avadāna*. This contrast, however, is neither simple nor straightforward; indeed, I will demonstrate that gift-of-the-body stories often make playful and creative use of this contrast by highlighting it, exaggerating it, undermining it, denying it, or manipulating it in some other manner. On the one hand, the bodhisattva's gift of his body is a paradigmatic example of the *jātaka*-type moral deed; on the other hand, the *avadāna*-type ritual deed is never far away. In different circumstances, and through a variety of rhetorical strategies, the line between the two may be hardened, blurred, moved around, or dissolved altogether. It is only by means of an approach that considers this larger generic context that such strategies can be brought to the fore.

The Gift-of-the-Body Subgenre: A Definition

Now that I have demonstrated that gift-of-the-body stories are *jātakas* and made the further argument that they belong to an elite group of "super-*jātakas*," it is time for me to provide a stipulative definition of the gift-of-the-body subgenre by considering more specifically the subject matter of the stories I assign to this category. For if we follow Fowler[52] in thinking of genre in terms of "family resemblance"—that is, as a group of texts that have certain similarities or family resemblances to each other—then we still have to determine the *size* of the family we wish to treat. Genres, as families, can be small, medium, or large, and the size of the family one treats will determine the limits and parameters of the discussion, as well as the status of particular stories as either "belonging" to the genre in question or having more or less "relatedness" to it.

In this case, stories involving the basic theme of bodily sacrifice can be classified into several different categories. Many Indian Buddhist stories involve animal or human characters who in some way sacrifice either the entire body or a part of the body, but I am focusing in this book only on a specific type of these stories. The definition of this type can proceed through a process of elimination by identifying several closely related subgenres that fall outside the scope of my analysis:

1. Some stories feature the theme of altruistic self-sacrifice of one's life for someone else, but do not explicitly conceive of this act as a gift of the *body*. For example, in the *Nigrodhamiga Jātaka* of the Pāli *Jātaka* collection,[53] there are two herds of deer who alternately take turns sending one of their members (drawn by lot) to the palace kitchen of the king of Benaras to be cooked for the king's royal meals. On one occasion, when the lot falls to a pregnant doe, the leader of one of the herds decides to sacrifice himself for the king's meal in order to spare her and her unborn fawn. In this case,

the deer-king (who is a previous birth of the Buddha) is said to "give his life" (*jīvitaṃ datvā*)[54] to the doe, but the gift is not explicitly a gift of the *body;* instead, it is a generalized act of self-sacrifice. Though these stories share much in common with the stories I am focusing on, they lack our stories' characteristic emphasis on and conceptions of the body, which are dealt with in chapter 6.

2. On the other hand, some stories involve the loss of a body part and its religious ramifications, but do not explicitly conceive of this loss as a *gift.* Two examples involving the eyes are the *Kunālāvadāna* (from the *Divyāvadāna*), in which King Aśoka's son Kunāla has his eyes gouged out at the command of his evil stepmother, and the *Subhā Jīvakambavanikā* (from the Pāli *Therīgāthā*), in which the nun Subhā pulls out her own eye in order to stop a man who is sexually threatening her.[55] Though very similar in some respects to the story of King Śibi's gift of his eyes, these stories—and others of their kind—lack the primacy given to *dāna* characteristic of the stories I am focusing on, which is the subject of chapters 4 and 5.[56] Likewise, in *jātakas* featuring the bodhisattva, the act of bodily self-sacrifice is sometimes treated as an illustration of *kṣānti-pāramitā* (the perfection of forbearance) rather than *dāna-pāramitā* (the perfection of generosity). The most prominent example, of course, is the famous story of Kṣāntivādin (mentioned earlier), in which an ascetic calmly tolerates the mutilation inflicted upon him by an angry king, thereby fulfilling the perfection of forbearance.[57] Again, since the bodily mutilation here constitutes a passive act of "forbearance" rather than an active deed of "generosity," such stories lie outside the scope of my discussion.

3. A third type of story I am not dealing with here includes those stories in which a character gives away his body in exchange for a religious teaching (often referred to as *subhāṣita,* "well-spoken words," or *subhāṣita-gāthā,* "a well-spoken verse").[58] In the *Surūpa Jātaka* of the *Mahāvastu,* for example, a deer-king named Surūpa offers his body to a hunter in exchange for a single verse of teaching.[59] Many such stories exist, and in some cases are strikingly similar in character and plot structure to the gift-of-the-body stories within my corpus: in *Avadānakalpalatā* 91, for example, King Śibi purchases a verse of religious teaching by feeding his own flesh and blood to a demon—who is really the god Śakra in disguise—and later restores his body by performing an Act of Truth. Despite the obvious similarities, however, there is a crucial difference: whereas gift-of-the-body stories emphasize one-sided *generosity,* these stories deal explicitly with the

notion of *exchange.* Because the act of bodily sacrifice in such stories is always performed *in exchange for* receiving a religious teaching, it is very far removed from the bodhisattva's *dāna-pāramitā.*

4. A fourth type I exclude from my discussion involves those stories in which a character uses his body to make a religious offering. Examples are chapter 23 of the *Lotus Sūtra,* in which a bodhisattva burns his arm as an offering to a Buddha,[60] and the many stories in which a bodhisattva copies the dharma using his skin as parchment, his bones as a pen, and his blood or marrow as ink.[61] Such stories deal with ritual "offerings" rather than "gifts," and generally take place within a Buddhist devotional context rather than in the Buddha-less past. They thereby construe the act of bodily sacrifice more in accordance with the ethos of the *avadāna* than the ethos of the *jātaka,* which distinguishes them significantly from the stories I focus on here.

5. A final category of stories excluded from my discussion is those in which the gift of the body is given by someone other than the Buddha in a previous birth. In several different Buddhist texts recently analyzed by Hubert Durt, there are stories about women who give away the flesh from their thighs in order to feed Buddhist monks who need meat because they are ill.[62] Although these stories involve both the gift-aspect and the body-aspect of the gift-of-the-body theme, they do not feature the bodhisattva as the hero. Such stories lack the basic features of the *jātaka* so characteristic of gift-of-the-body stories (such as taking place in a Buddha-less age) and clearly follow a different narrative pattern.[63]

• • •

From the above exclusions, it is clear that stories belonging to the gift-of-the-body subgenre (as I define it) are characterized by three necessary elements—*gift, body,* and *bodhisattva.* They must feature the bodhisattva as the hero; they must conceive of the act of bodily sacrifice as a gift; and they must emphasize the physical body as the item being given away. In order to highlight these three elements simultaneously, I will consistently refer to these stories henceforth as "gift-of-the-body *jātakas.*" Although, as mentioned before, this genre is my own hypothetical construction and is not a genre that was named by the culture in question, I believe there is evidence that such a category was recognized to some extent by the tradition itself. Exegetical discussions of *dāna* or *dāna-pāramitā* and narrative collections illustrating the six *pāramitās,* for example, often invoke this same group of gift-of-the-body *jātakas* over and over again, while stories of the other types (nos. 1–5 above) are not generally invoked within the same contexts.

Nevertheless, I clearly recognize that the distinctions I have drawn above are somewhat artificial and sometimes hard to defend. It is often difficult, for example, to determine whether the bodhisattva is really giving up his "body" or his "life," and whether or not his action is primarily an expression of "generosity." I have used the concept of the "gift-of-the-body *jātaka*" pragmatically to limit my material, but I believe that ultimately all such story-types as I have described above must be seen as one large and interwoven thematic group, with the various types playing off each other in interesting ways. Many such interconnections can be adduced, and I therefore attempt in my discussion to refer briefly to other types wherever applicable.

Since even the narrow definition of the gift-of-the-body genre I draw above includes a very large amount of material, I have selected a limited number of stories that constitute the corpus from which I draw my conclusions. The corpus is drawn mostly from Sanskrit and Pāli sources easily available in published editions (including, for example, the Pāli *Jātaka* collection, *Cariyāpiṭaka, Jātakamālā, Avadānakalpalatā, Divyāvadāna, Avadānaśataka, Mahāvastu, Avadānasārasamuccaya, Mahajjātakamālā,* and *Maṇicūḍāvadāna*). Since my access to the Tibetan Buddhist canon is limited—and my facility with classical Tibetan mediocre at best—I have made use of only two Tibetan texts: the *mDzangs blun zhes bya ba'i mdo* (commonly called the *Sūtra of the Wise and the Fool*), which contains several interesting gift-of-the-body *jātakas,* and the *Lokānandanāṭaka* (a dramatized version of the story of King Maṇicūḍa), a Sanskrit drama by Candragomin that now exists only in Tibetan. Finally, I have also taken into consideration several Chinese texts presumably based upon Indic originals and read in French translation. Though I have tried to include within the corpus some of the most prominent gift-of-the-body stories (such as those of King Śibi, the tigress, and the hare), my selection is otherwise idiosyncratic, covering a very broad period and including both Mainstream and Mahāyāna examples. A full description of the corpus can be found in the Appendix.

II

CONVENTIONS OF PLOT

In chapter 1 I argued that gift-of-the-body *jātakas* can be usefully treated as a discrete subgenre of "super-*jātakas*" within the larger generic context provided by *jātakas* and *avadānas* as a whole—even though the stories I place in this category are widely divergent in terms of language, style, dating, and historical context. The purpose of this and the following chapter, therefore, will be to demonstrate in a more concrete manner that gift-of-the-body *jātakas* constitute a separate and identifiable grouping of texts marked by consistent features and conventions that make it meaningful to speak of them as a subgenre. Gift-of-the-body *jātakas,* in other words, share more than merely the central theme of a gift of the body. In plotline, characters, structure, imagery, and even the use of stereotypical phraseology, all gift-of-the-body *jātakas* share a certain "family resemblance" that immediately recalls the category to mind.

The first and largest aspect of this "family resemblance" is that of *plot.* The bodhisattva's gift of his body is always a climactic moment, but it is not a moment that exists in isolation; instead it is integrated into a narrative plotline that allows the gift to develop gradually and then traces its various consequences. This is perhaps the most profound distinction between the gift-of-the-body theme when taken in isolation and the same theme when treated in the *jātakas.* Instead of the mere *fact* of the bodhisattva's self-sacrifice—experienced as something isolated and already complete—the *jātakas* integrate this self-sacrifice into a particular narrative sequence and allow it to unfold in a processual and emergent manner. The readers of these stories watch the gift *come into being and occur over time,* and they also experience the outcome of the gift and how it affects the surrounding world. This unfolding of the gift, however, is never arbitrary or idiosyncratic in nature, but instead follows certain conventional patterns. These patterns, which are limited in number, constitute the conventional plotlines of the gift-of-the-body genre.

Although there are several possible ways one might classify individual gift-of-the-body *jātakas* into different categories based on plotline, I have found that the most useful criterion of classification—the one which has the greatest effect on plotline as a whole—is the identity of the recipient. As already alluded to in the previous chapter, stories in which the recipient is an *ordinary being* (who makes a "real" request for the bodhisattva's body) are quite different in character and development from stories in which the recipient is the deity *Śakra in disguise* (whose request for the bodhisattva's body is nothing more than an elaborate "ruse"). Based primarily on this distinction, I will enumerate two "major" conventional plotlines characteristic of the gift-of-the-body genre (as well as one plotline I designate as "minor"). I will also advance the argument that, quite apart from the question of how each plotline may have developed historically, the resulting effect is significant: variations in plot are much more than simply superficial differences in narrative sequence, for each conventional plotline consistently conveys particular messages and emphasizes particular themes.

When the Recipient Is an Ordinary Being

Our first major category consists of those gift-of-the-body *jātakas* in which the recipient of the gift is an ordinary being, rather than the deity Śakra in disguise. Though such stories are obviously quite diverse in nature and content, it is my contention that when taken as a group, they function in a similar manner and consistently emphasize the same themes. These themes include the extraordinary heroism of the bodhisattva, the extreme purity of his generosity and compassion, his exaltation above all other living beings, and the sense of amazement and awe surrounding his act of self-sacrifice. These stories, in other words, make use of ordinary, lowly beings as the recipients of the bodhisattva's self-sacrifice in order to emphasize the chasm that exists between him and everyone else and turn him into an object worthy of the highest devotion and adoration. Returning once again to the idea of the "super-*jātaka*" and its portrayal of truly heroic and utterly *in*imitable deeds, these stories are perhaps the "super-est" *jātakas* of them all.

We can recognize this more clearly when we consider the fact that the ordinary beings who serve as the recipients of the bodhisattva's gift are never just generic "ordinary beings"; instead, they are thoroughly conventional in nature. They can be roughly divided into two groups—those who are *pitiful* and those who are *evil.* The *pitiful* recipients (for example, hungry animals, thirsty insects, or destitute wanderers) are usually in dire straits and do not make any direct demand for the bodhisattva's body. The bodhisattva simply encounters their pitiful situation—very often a situation of hunger, thirst, illness, or the threat of imminent death—and decides, on his own initiative, to give up his body in order to save their lives. I call these recipients "pitiful" not only because of the dire situation in which they find themselves, but also because the lack of any explicit request for the bodhisattva's body distinguishes them from those recipients who are "evil." Pitiful recipients, in other words, are innocent of any conscious desire for the bodhisattva's self-sacrifice; though they might ask the bodhisattva for help, they would never dream of asking him to cut off his head, gouge out his eyes, or sacrifice his life on their behalf. Instead, they are wholly pitiful creatures—starving to death, dying of thirst, lost in the wilderness and about to collapse, stricken by horrible illnesses, drowning in the ocean, or consigned to a low animal birth driven solely by the unconscious instinct for survival. They present themselves, in all their misery, before the bodhisattva's eyes, and he—on his own initiative—decides to give his body away.

One classic example involving a "pitiful" recipient is the story of the starving tigress, which exists in several different Sanskrit versions. Here the bodhisattva is either a prince or a brahmin ascetic who encounters a tigress in the wilderness. The tigress has just given birth to several cubs and is so overcome by hunger and fatigue that she is on the verge of devouring her own offspring. In order to save the lives of both the tigress and her cubs, the bodhisattva throws himself off a cliff or slits his own throat and allows the tigress to devour him. In other stories, as well, the bodhisattva is devoured by insects and mosquitoes, dogs and jackals, or birds of prey such as vultures. Such animals are presented as objects of pity rather than blame, for in being consigned to an animal rebirth, they are incapable of making a conscious moral decision to kill or hurt the bodhisattva.[1] Instead, they are merely wild animals, afflicted by suffering and driven wholly by the animal instincts of hunger and self-preservation. This is underscored by the fact that it is always the purely physical needs of hunger and thirst that drive such animals to take advantage of the bodhisattva's body, and their inner thoughts and conscious intentions are never depicted.

In other cases, however, it is morally conscious human beings rather than instinct-driven animals who serve as such "pitiful" recipients, with several different strategies being utilized to preserve their "pitiful" status. In some cases the human recipients who find themselves in such dire situations throw themselves at the bodhisattva's feet and beg for his help, but only in the most generalized manner and without any explicit reference to his giving up his body. In *Avadānaśataka* 31, for example, when the subjects of King Padmaka's kingdom are dying from a terrible epidemic, they cry out to the king in despair, "Save us, Great King, from this disease! Give us life!"[2]—yet they never imagine that he will throw himself off the roof of his palace in order to transform himself into a particular type of fish whose flesh will cure their disease. As soon as this happens, of course, they do take full advantage of the situation—"carrying baskets and gripping weapons in their hands" and ruthlessly "cutting up the flesh of the fish while he was still alive"[3]—yet their innocence is preserved by the fact that they never *intended* for him to help them in this way.

It is also pertinent to note that when they do devour the fish so ravenously, they do so in the midst of an epidemic—while in a similar story from the *Sūtra of the Wise and the Fool,* the situation is one of great famine.[4] Epidemic and famine are both conditions that strip one of moral agency; one of the common themes we find in these stories (and elsewhere in Buddhist literature) is the idea that extreme hunger, thirst, and illness reduce morally conscious human beings to an animal-like status in which they lose their moral agency and act purely through the instinct for survival.[5] Desperate physical circumstances, we might say, temporarily consign these human beings to an animal rebirth, thus ensuring their status as objects of pity.

In other stories, however, human moral agency is preserved, even in the most calamitous of circumstances, and the author must go to yet further lengths to protect his characters' innocence. One strategy is to have the same human recipients who initially beg the bodhisattva for help become shocked, repulsed, and horrified when they discover what he intends to do. Thus, in *Jātakamālā* 30, the bodhisattva is a magnificent elephant who encounters a group of seven hundred men who are wandering through the desert, suffering from hunger and thirst. These men beg the elephant for help, calling him "relief incarnate," a "refuge," and a "friend for we who are friendless," and explicitly asking him to "please save us in whatever way you know how!"[6] Realizing that they will never make it across the desert without food and water, the elephant tells them where they can find an elephant carcass, whose flesh will serve as food and whose entrails will serve as water bags. Racing ahead to the predetermined spot, the elephant throws himself off a mountain in order to provide the carcass that will save the men's lives. In this case, even though the men beg for the elephant's help, they certainly have no intention that he should kill himself, and once they come across the elephant carcass and realize it is the same elephant as before, they are shocked and horrified:

> Who could possibly eat the flesh of one whose love for us was greater than that of the most affectionate friends and relatives, who was kind enough to help us in such a way, who was eager to undertake our welfare even at the cost of his own life, and who has acted in such an exceedingly noble manner? Instead, it would be more appropriate for us to repay our debt to him by worshipping and cremating his body![7]

It is only through some argument amongst the men and a consideration of what the elephant would have wanted them to do that they are ultimately persuaded to make use of his physical body, as he intended. Thus their innocence of any explicit demand for the bodhisattva's body is preserved, and they remain wholly "pitiful" characters.

A comparison of several different versions of a single story can further demonstrate how the blamelessness of human recipients is preserved, even as they are given greater and greater moral agency. In one story, the bodhisattva is the leader of a band of merchants who are drowning in the ocean after their ship has been demolished. Remembering that the ocean cannot stand to have a dead body in it for even a single night, the bodhisattva instructs his companions to hang on to his body and then slits his own throat, whereupon the ocean casts his corpse onto shore, thus saving the others' lives.

In the version of this story that appears in the *Mahāvastu*,[8] we hear nothing from the bodhisattva's companions. They do not beg him for help, they don't seem to have any knowledge of his intention to kill himself beforehand, and once he does kill himself, we hear nothing of their reaction to his deed. Instead they are mute characters who serve only as the objects of the bodhisattva's compassion and might just as well be depicted as animals. In contrast, *Avadānasārasamuccaya* 2,[9] which is a later version of the same story, dramatically expands the role of these companions and turns them into morally conscious beings. Now, as they are drowning, they throw themselves at the bodhisattva's feet and beg him for help at great length:

> We have abandoned all effort, fixing all our aims and hopes upon you. Whatever needs to be done here, do it quickly! Our lives are in danger! As you look on, these hopeless men are drowning in the ocean right before your very eyes. Any delay would be improper, so use your strength and act now! . . . Rescue these people who are wandering aimlessly in the face of adversity. . . . Deliver us from danger, like a father showing compassion for his sons, for we are in the very belly of death. . . . Display your manly strength, O Kinsman of the World! . . . Please rescue us![10]

Yet despite the urgency and intensity of this request, once these companions hear that the bodhisattva intends to kill himself, they are shocked and horrified. Their minds are "utterly blown away," their hearts "tremble with fear," they are "overcome with sadness and despair," and they consider his intention to be "inconceivable, unendurable, and exceedingly awesome."[11] They start crying uncontrollably and beg him to reconsider:

> All of us will willingly go to our deaths right here in this great ocean, but we cannot do this ignoble deed! An excellent friend like you is difficult to find; if we saw you destroyed, what use would we have for worldly life or riches? So refrain from this reckless deed, O Resolute-Minded One![12]

In a third version of this story, found in *Sambhadrāvadānamālā* 4, even this protest is not enough, for the helmsman of the ship then steps forward and argues against the bodhisattva's self-sacrifice for an additional fourteen verses, employing a number of fairly complicated moral arguments.[13] It is only after all of this shock, horror, and moral protest have been registered that the bodhisattva (through another lengthy speech) finally convinces his reluctant companions to accept his intention to kill himself and make use of his physical body.

"Pitiful" recipients, then, can be mute and instinct-driven animals, desperate human beings temporarily reduced to an animal-like condition, innocent people who make only the most generalized request for help, or wholly conscious—even morally sophisticated—human beings who are fully aware of what the bodhisattva intends to do. But in all cases, their moral innocence in bringing about the bodhisattva's death is always preserved. They do not ask the bodhisattva to give up his body, and they have no intention that he should do so. In this sense, they constitute objects of pity rather than blame or censure.

In contrast, I classify *evil* recipients (for example, evil brahmins, evil kings, or evil women) as those who make a direct, explicit, and conscious demand for the bodhisattva to give up his body. "Evil," of course, is a relative term, with some recipients being far more "evil" than others, but with all of them being presented in a highly negative manner. The most evil recipients of all are those who have no discernible reason for demanding the bodhisattva's body, other than outright cruelty. The story of King Candraprabha alluded to earlier[14] never gives us any explicit reason *why* the brahmin Raudrākṣa must have King Candraprabha's head, other than intimating that the brahmin is a cruel and malicious person. Slightly less evil, perhaps, are those who demand the bodhisattva's body for purely selfish purposes—such as the queen who demands an elephant's tusks to get revenge upon him for some perceived slight, or the brahmin who asks for King Sarvaṃdada's head because another king has offered a reward. Finally, the least evil of the "evil" recipients are those who demand the bodhisattva's body for a seemingly legitimate reason. These recipients have a legitimate need for the gift that makes them overlap somewhat with those who are "pitiful," yet I classify them as "evil" because of the explicit demand they make for the bodhisattva's body—a demand perceived by those around them (and presented by the story itself) as being excessive, cruel, and repugnant.

In the story of King Maṇicūḍa (as found in the *Maṇicūḍāvadāna*), for example, the bodhisattva is a generous king named Maṇicūḍa who has a magical crest-jewel embedded in his head, while the recipient of the gift is a neighboring king named Duṣprasaha who demands the crest-jewel so he can use its curative powers to end an epidemic within his own kingdom. Despite this seemingly legitimate need for the crest-jewel, the story goes out of its way to depict Duṣprasaha in as negative a manner as possible. The name Duṣprasaha itself means "difficult to endure," and the character lives up to this name from the moment he is introduced. Long before the epidemic afflicts his kingdom, Duṣprasaha is said to be greedy for an excellent elephant belonging to Maṇicūḍa. He repeatedly hankers after the elephant and then becomes angry and jealous when the elephant is given to someone else. He gathers his army together and proceeds to wage war against Maṇicūḍa's kingdom—an act Maṇicūḍa himself attributes to the "wickedness of the afflictions."[15]

It is only after this thoroughly unpleasant character has been established that we see Duṣprasaha demand Maṇicūḍa's crest-jewel in order to cure the epidemic afflicting his kingdom. In the *Lokānandanāṭaka* (a dramatized version of the Maṇicūḍa story preserved only in Tibetan), even this request is suspect, for Maṇicūḍa's prime minister calls it a "trick" and a "means of deception" intended to kill Maṇicūḍa, rather than a benevolent attempt by Duṣprasaha to save his own subjects' lives.[16] This negative portrayal is further reinforced at the end of the *Maṇicūḍāvadāna,* when Duṣprasaha is identified as a previous birth of Devadatta. Whether or not there is a legitimate use for the bodhisattva's body, then, *any* recipient who would even *think* of asking the bodhisattva to intentionally injure or kill himself tends to be presented by the story in a negative and highly unflattering manner. In this sense, such recipients are "evil" rather than "pitiful."

The ordinary beings who receive the bodhisattva's gift of his body are thus thoroughly conventional in nature. In some cases they are "pitiful" and in other cases they are "evil"—but they are never just generic "ordinary beings." Why should this be the case? Perhaps the most important reason is that those who are "pitiful" and those who are "evil" both clearly fall into the category of those who are "unworthy" of receiving gifts. As I will explain at greater length in chapters 4 and 5, gift-of-the-body *jātakas* must be seen within the context of a larger Buddhist discourse on giving (*dāna*) and, in particular, in relation to the doctrine of the "worthy recipient" (*supātra*). The doctrine of the worthy recipient was pan-Indic in nature. Buddhism, Hinduism, and Jainism all hold that religious gifts should generally be directed *upward* toward religiously worthy and superior recipients (such as monks, brahmins, Buddhas, and Jinas) because these gifts are productive of the greatest amount of merit (*puṇya*). Indeed, the merit accruing from a gift is dependent on the spiritual worth of the recipient: the more worthy the recipient is—or the better "field of merit" he or she constitutes—the more merit the donor will accrue. Any ordinary giver will thus aim to direct his or her gifts toward the worthiest recipients of all, in order to acquire the greatest merit. Correspondingly, it follows that gifts which flow in the opposite direction—that is, *downward* toward *unworthy* recipients—are productive of very little merit, since they are planted within a poor-quality "field." In the Buddhist discourse on giving, the gift given to an unworthy recipient is thus an *unproductive* gift—and as such it becomes the site of pure, unmitigated generosity. Although ordinary people are sometimes exhorted to make such gifts, it is characteristic of Buddhist literature in general that the gift given to an unworthy recipient is usually attributed only to highly exceptional beings (such as bodhisattvas and Buddhas) and is often used as a marker for pure generosity and altruism.

As those who are "unworthy" of receiving gifts, then, "pitiful" and "evil" recipients fulfill a very specific function within gift-of-the-body stories: they mark the bodhisattva as an *extraordinary* giver, not an ordinary giver, and serve to highlight the extreme and uncompromising nature of his generosity. So extreme is his generosity that he gives away his body even to lowly and pathetic creatures such as insects, and so uncompromising is his generosity that he gives away his body even to evil people who have no legitimate use for it—and in both cases he does so not for the sake of merit, but purely out of generosity and compassion. Pitiful and evil recipients thereby represent extreme test-cases of *dāna-pāramitā* (the "perfection of generosity"), a theme I explore in more detail in chapter 5. By the use of such lowly recipients, the bodhisattva's status is elevated and he becomes a highly exalted giver, capable of giving in a manner that no ordinary giver could ever hope to emulate. Stories featuring ordinary beings as the recipients of the gift thus promote a highly idealized portrait of the bodhisattva's generosity.

The same point can be made again if we consider "pitiful" and "evil" recipients from the point of view of the audience's response. For the audience, the two types of recipients represent quite different situations and merit quite different reactions. When the recipients are *pitiful* in nature—with their miserable situations often being described in excruciating detail—it is clear that the audience should be moved by their plight and respond with a feeling of pity ("pity," or *kṛpā,* being one of the standard *rasas,* or appropriate aesthetic responses, outlined in the classical Sanskrit theory of aesthetics). In contrast, when the recipients are *evil* in nature, the audience's reaction is likely very different and probably involves feelings of anger or indignation rather than sympathy or pity. In case an audience doesn't know how to respond, there are certain subsidiary characters—especially lower deities and other supernatural beings—who seem to serve as the audience's guide by demonstrating for them the "correct" response to the gift. These "correct" responses are fairly consistent in nature: sympathetic and compassionate if the recipients are pitiful, angry and indignant if the recipients are evil.[17] Thus, for the gods and other subsidiary characters in the narrative—and by extension, for the audience, as well—pitiful and evil recipients merit very different responses.

From the perspective of the bodhisattva, however, such is not the case—and once again, the extraordinary nature of the bodhisattva and his essential difference from all other beings is thus highlighted. For the bodhisattva in these stories makes no distinction whatsoever between "pitiful" and "evil" recipients. "Evil" recipients, for him, are as equally the objects of pity as those who are more conventionally "pitiful." This is because the bodhisattva understands that just as "pitiful" recipients suffer from hunger, thirst, illness, and other life-threatening conditions, so "evil" recipients are equally tormented by the mental afflictions of anger, hatred, and delusion—afflictions, moreover, that will surely condemn them to hell, where they will suffer physical torments even worse than those now suffered by the "pitiful."

This compassion the bodhisattva feels for even the most evil of recipients is made explicit in story after story. The bodhisattva is often described as intentionally "generating thoughts of benevolence and compassion" toward evil recipients,[18] and sometimes patiently explains to those around him why such recipients merit pity rather than blame. In the *Maṇicūḍāvadāna,* for example, when the evil King Duṣprasaha demands the crest-jewel embedded in King Maṇicūḍa's head, Maṇicūḍa tells his ministers they ought to feel sympathy for him, for it is only because the poor king is "intoxicated with the pride of royal power" and "deluded by lust for this life" that he "intends to do something unprofitable both in this world and the world to come, thus assuring his own ruin!"[19] His ministers are amazed at this reaction and wonder how Maṇicūḍa can be so compassionate "even to a killer whose weapon is poised to strike."[20] Similarly, in *Kalpanāmaṇḍitikā* 69, the bodhisattva, as an elephant, explains to his female companion why it is foolish for her to react with anger toward the cruel hunter who has come to remove his tusks:

> If a man whose heart had been invaded by demons
> in his madness insulted his doctor,
> the doctor would only think of subduing the demons,
> he would not blame the poor patient!
> Afflictions and bonds are like these demons.
> Only when one is enveloped by the bonds of ignorance

> does one give rise to anger and hatred.
> . . . So why become vexed against this man?[21]

By comparing the hunter's cruelty to a physical disease suffered by a wholly innocent patient, the bodhisattva equalizes those who are "pitiful" and those who are "evil" in a way that ordinary people would find difficult. The bodhisattva's ability to look beyond worldly ideas about who deserves "pity" and who deserves "blame" and to see all beings as equally pitiful and in need of compassion within the larger context of a world governed by suffering and rebirth distinguishes him sharply from other people and once again highlights his extraordinary nature.[22]

The same effect is heightened even further in those cases in which the bodhisattva actually *exalts* the evil recipient *above* the pitiful recipient, speaking of him not merely as an object of pity and compassion, but, in fact, as one who deserves great *praise, gratitude,* and *esteem.* The idea that it is precisely one's worst enemy that gives one the greatest opportunity to cultivate the wholesome attitudes of benevolence, forbearance, and compassion—and that this enemy therefore deserves gratitude and esteem rather than blame or censure—is common to many Buddhist texts dealing with meditative techniques.[23] In gift-of-the-body *jātakas* involving evil recipients, we sometimes see the same idea put into play within a narrative situation. Thus, when an enemy king viciously attacks King Sarvaṃdada's kingdom, his reaction is one of *gratitude* rather than anger. He exalts the enemy king as an "auspicious friend" who is "truly teaching" him in the ways of patient forbearance, and wishes only the best for this cruel invader: "From now on, let even evil conduct be of benefit to him, his friends, and his relations for hundreds of years!"[24] Once again, it is the contrast between the bodhisattva's reaction and that of the other characters that is often highlighted: in the *Maṇicūḍāvadāna,* even a wise sage refers to the five brahmins who have come to remove the crest-jewel from Maṇicūḍa's head as "killers with violent minds and cruel hearts, sinners who pay no heed to the other world and are ungrateful and merciless"—only to hear Maṇicūḍa himself refer to the very same brahmins as "wish-fulfilling jewels, vessels of good fortune, desire-granting cows, like gurus, like gods."[25] In a Tibetan version of the same story, in fact, these cruel brahmins are even *better* than wish-fulfilling jewels, "for a wish-fulfilling jewel grants material wealth alone, while a supplicant brings about all virtues."[26] In fact, from the bodhisattva's exalted point of view, the situation is the very *reverse* of what the ignorant presume it to be. Thus King Maṇicūḍa says of the evil king Duṣprasaha who has sent the brahmins to remove his crest-jewel: "This man here is the donor, and it is I who am the supplicant! O Friend, why have you turned it all around?"[27] Since the audience likely identifies with the sentiments of the other characters rather than those of Maṇicūḍa, the extraordinary nature of the bodhisattva and the chasm between his values and ours are once again highlighted and brought to the fore.

"Pitiful" and "evil" recipients thus fulfill a variety of different functions, yet in every case the same themes are reinforced—the extraordinary heroism of the bodhisattva, the extreme purity of his generosity and compassion, his exaltation above all other beings, and the sense of amazement and awe surrounding his act of self-sacrifice. Perhaps we can now understand why the most common and appropriate outcome for such stories is to have the bodhisattva *die* as a result of making his gift. The extreme and uncompromising generosity that constitutes the main emphasis of such stories can find its greatest consummation only in the bodhisattva's tragic death. Our sense of the extraordinary character of the bodhisattva and our amazement at his self-sacrifice on behalf of the lowliest of creatures can be sustained only if the bodhisattva actually dies; for him to survive the gift or experience giving's rewards would run counter to all of the effects initiated by featuring pitiful and evil recipients in the first place. Although the bodhisattva is sometimes reborn in heaven or receives some other comparable "reward" for his gift, more emphasis is laid in these stories on his tragic loss of life and the grief and sadness of those he leaves behind. Extreme generosity is the predominant theme, and amazement mixed with grief, the predominant emotional tone.

If "sainthood," as one volume has put it, is always a complicated mixture of *otherness* and *imitability*,[28] then stories in which the recipient is an ordinary being come down clearly on the side of the bodhisattva's "otherness." He sacrifices his body on behalf of the lowliest of beings, he does so purely out of disinterested generosity and without any ulterior motives, and in the vast majority of cases he suffers death as a result—a tragic death that is usually lamented at great length by other beings. He is *other* to us, and his deed invites a response of *worship* and *devotion* rather than direct *imitation*—for the ordinary reader cannot hope to imitate such an extraordinary deed. Moreover, though I previously argued that all gift-of-the-body *jātakas* constitute "super-*jātakas*" whose significance, in part, derives from their contrast with the ethos of the *avadāna,* I now contend that this is especially and particularly true of those stories featuring ordinary beings as their recipients. The *inimitable heroic exploit performed by an extraordinary being in a difficult, Buddha-less age of the past* that defines the ethos of the *jātaka* finds perhaps its most perfect manifestation in the spectacle of the bodhisattva's tragic loss of life on behalf of those who are pitiful and evil.

When the Recipient Is Śakra-in-Disguise

Quite different in nature from the above are stories falling into our second major category, in which the recipient of the gift is really the deity Śakra in disguise rather than an ordinary being. Once again, these stories follow a thoroughly conventional plotline—but one that brings quite different emphases to the fore from those characteristic of the first category. Let me first summarize the conventional plotline adhered to by such stories, and then turn to a discussion of how its concerns and messages differ fundamentally from those of the stories addressed previously.

The pattern of Śakra's involvement in these stories is fairly consistent and includes the following elements. First, Śakra is introduced into the story by being aroused or alerted in some way as to the existence of the bodhisattva and the extremity of his generosity. Usually this occurs because the bodhisattva forms a generalized aspiration to give away his body (before any specific opportunity to do so has arisen). Śakra is alerted because the power of this aspiration causes his marble throne to become hot (a common Indic convention in speaking of virtuous human beings),[29] or because it causes the trembling of earth and mountains, whereupon Śakra discerns the reason for such omens,[30] or because Śakra simply "understands" or "realizes" the bodhisattva's intention[31]—as one text puts it, because he has "knowledge and vision of what goes on in the lower regions."[32]

In any case, once Śakra is alerted to the bodhisattva's intentions, he then decides to *test* the bodhisattva's generosity by asking him for his body. In order to carry out this test, Śakra dons some sort of disguise; he never approaches the bodhisattva in his own form. Śakra's disguises again fall into the general categories of the *pitiful* recipient or the *evil* recipient—but whether the recipient is pitiful or evil matters little, since the audience always knows that he is Śakra-in-disguise. Using this disguise, Śakra goes to the bodhisattva and requests a part of his body (or makes a generalized plea for help that he knows will result in a gift of the body), and the bodhisattva, with no hesitation, agrees to give his body away and generally begins the process of doing so.

Rather than allowing the bodhisattva to die, however, these stories generally interrupt the gift at some point and make it clear to the audience that the bodhisattva has successfully passed Śakra's "test" and does not need to lose his life. Although it is difficult to determine the exact moment when the test has been "passed," it seems to be marked by several narrative elements in combination. In many cases, for example, the gift-giving is interrupted when Śakra suddenly reveals his true identity to the bodhisattva, sometimes explaining that he was merely testing him. At some point also, Śakra usually expresses a wish (generally to himself) to help the bodhisattva restore his injured body to perfect health.[33] He then does so in almost all cases by encouraging the bodhisattva to perform an Act of Truth.

The "Act of Truth" (*satya-kriyā*), a common motif in Indic narrative literature, is a ritualistic act in which a person enunciates some truthful statement and then ritually draws upon the power of this truth to make some desired consequence occur.[34] It generally takes the form of: "If X is true, then by the power of this truth, let Y occur." The natures of both truth and consequence vary widely from one story to another and can range from the trivial to the very profound. In gift-of-the-body *jātakas,* however, they are again quite conventional in nature: the truth invoked by the bodhisattva always concerns the purity and sincerity of his frame of mind when he gave his body away, while the desired consequence is always a request to see this same body restored. The truth may be stated either negatively (for example, his mind experienced no regret, displeasure, hostility, or other negative emotions while giving his body away) or positively (for example, his mind experienced only unconditional love for all supplicants, joy and pleasure in giving the gift, etc.). As a "negative" example, we might take Maṇicūḍa's first Act of Truth in the *Maṇicūḍāvadāna:*

> When I gave away my own flesh today, through the force of compassion and intent upon enlightenment, my mind did not give rise to any regret, and was free of both stinginess and distress. O Thousand-Eyed One, by this truth, and by the power of my merit, let this body of mine become just as it was before, fully handsome![35]

As a "positive" example, we might take King Śibi's two Acts of Truth after giving away his eyes, as stated in the *Jātakamālā:*

> Since the voices of supplicants freely asking for favors, both then and now, are as dear to me as if they were blessings, let one of my eyes arise! . . . Moreover, since I gladly gave both of my eyes to he who asked for only one, and did so with single-minded joy and pleasure, let my second eye also arise![36]

While the first Act of Truth deals with the absence of certain mental qualities and the second one deals with the presence of certain (other) mental qualities, both statements attest to the bodhisattva's absolute sincerity in giving the gift. It is the power of this sincerity that then allows the bodhisattva's injured body to be restored to perfect health. Naturally, the Act of Truth is always effective, and once the bodhisattva's body has been restored, we know for certain—in fact, we have physical evidence—that the bodhisattva has passed the test successfully and convinced Śakra that he constitutes a true bodhisattva.

One final indication that the test has been successfully passed occurs when Śakra makes some kind of effusive, positive response to the bodhisattva—for example, he praises the gift, he confirms the bodhisattva's generosity and pure intentions, or he predicts the bodhisattva's imminent Buddhahood:

> His resolution is firm and sincere; he will not be long in becoming a Buddha![37]

> Wonderful, wonderful, O Lord of the Earth! Your mind is firmly resolved, your vow is unshakable, and your great compassion seeks out beings because you are fearless in the midst of those conditions which cause terror. Because of your determination, it won't be long before you awaken to unsurpassed, perfect, full enlightenment![38]

> Look, honorable gods who live in heaven! Rejoice at this Great Being's truly extraordinary and remarkable deed! Look how he has fearlessly given up his body today out of love for his guest![39]

Thus, a number of narrative elements in combination—Śakra's revelation of his true identity, his wish to restore the bodhisattva's body, his role in encouraging the Act of Truth, the bodhisattva's survival and restoration of his body, and Śakra's positive reaction to the gift—all conspire to signal to the audience that the test is over, and the bodhisattva has passed. Rather than culminating in a tragic loss of life, such stories conclude with a "happy ending"—with Śakra fully satisfied and the bodhisattva in robust health.

Clearly such stories are quite different in nature from the stories I discussed previously. I would characterize this difference in two major ways: On the one hand, the theme of generosity itself is deemphasized, to some extent, so that other concerns can come to the fore—first and foremost, a concern with clarifying the relationship between the Buddha and the gods. On the other hand, while generosity does remain a predominant theme, such stories present us with quite a different model of generosity than the extreme and uncompromising generosity characteristic of the stories discussed earlier. I will deal with each of these topics in turn.

BUDDHA, GODS, AND COSMOS

Whereas effective illustration of the "perfection of generosity" appears to be the very *raison d'être* of the stories discussed earlier, stories involving Śakra as the recipient of the gift seem to deemphasize generosity, to some extent, so that other concerns can come to the fore. This deemphasizing of generosity will become apparent if we pause to consider some of the implications of the basic test-by-Śakra motif. When Śakra decides to "test" the bodhisattva, the terms used consistently for the notion of "testing" all derive from the desiderative of the verbal root *man* (or occasionally *jñā*), meaning "to want to know," "to investigate," or "to test."[40] The very consistent use of these forms is important, for they clearly mark Śakra's request for the bodhisattva's body as a *test* or a *trial* that the bodhisattva must successfully "pass," rather than a sincere appeal for his body. This already indicates to the audience that quite apart from the specific virtue of "generosity," Śakra's testing of the bodhisattva (and the bodhisattva's successful passing of this test) itself becomes a predominant theme. The question of the narrative is not merely "Is he generous?" or "Will he give the gift?" but also "Will he pass the test?" Though generosity is the specific quality being tested here, generosity is deemphasized to the extent that other qualities appropriate to bodhisattvas might just as well be tested in its place—and in other stories this is indeed the case.

In fact, the theme of Śakra's testing of the bodhisattva appears in many different stories and does not need to be tied to the virtue of generosity at all. In *Jātakamālā* 19, for example, the bodhisattva is an ascetic who lives in the forest with his seven siblings.[41] Alerted to his great virtue, Śakra takes his meals away every day and waits to see if he will accuse his siblings of having done so. This seems to constitute a general test of morality or virtue and is clearly not a test of generosity. Similar tests by

Śakra concerning other virtues occur throughout the bodhisattva's career. From this perspective, we might see Śakra's testing of the bodhisattva as a theme in itself, with "generosity" as the incidental quality being tested in these particular stories.

The deemphasizing of generosity per se and the highlighting of Śakra's testing of the bodhisattva also have important implications for the outcome of the plot. The initial setup of the story already indicates to the audience that the story ought to end with the bodhisattva *surviving* the gift rather than dying—for if the bodhisattva *dies* when the gift was nothing more than a test, the story will seem like a cruel joke rather than a noble illustration of generosity (unless, of course, the author is intentionally subverting these generic expectations, as I argued earlier in the case of Āryaśūra's version of the story of the hare). Thus the emphasis on the bodhisattva's "tragic loss of life on behalf of suffering beings" so characteristic of the earlier set of stories here recedes into the background: we do not wish to see the bodhisattva lose his life out of compassion for others; instead, we wish to see him *best the god* and *pass the test.* The bodhisattva must succeed, the deity Śakra must be sufficiently humbled, and the story must have a positive outcome. Compassion, self-sacrifice, and generosity are all present, but the manner in which they manifest themselves is now governed by the larger theme of a *contest between god and bodhisattva.* The gift alone is insufficient, precisely because it is the exigencies of the *test* that control the narrative, rather than the theme of generosity alone. Thus, whereas stories in which the recipient is an ordinary being often place the bodhisattva's gift of his body toward the *end* of the narrative—as climax and culmination of the entire plot—stories involving Śakra as the recipient generally locate the gift at a much earlier point in the narrative, subordinating it to the larger concerns of the test-by-Śakra motif.

One of these concerns, as I have already suggested, is the theme of an *agonistic contest between god and bodhisattva.* Indeed, quite apart from the promotion of generosity, I believe that these stories can be placed within a larger Buddhist discourse concerned with illuminating the careful balance of power between the Buddha and traditional deities such as Śakra. In order to explore this theme, let us begin by considering Śakra's position relative to the bodhisattva and the complex motives that drive him to initiate the test.

In some cases, it seems that Śakra tests the bodhisattva purely out of a sense of personal curiosity. In *Jātakamālā* 6, for example, Śakra is "filled with astonishment and curiosity" when he learns of the bodhisattva's desire to give away his body and "wishes to find out more about the nature of this Great Being."[42] Likewise, in *Mahajjātakamālā* 44, he thinks to himself: "This king is obsessed with giving! What is he thinking? I must go and see whether or not this intention of his is sincere!"[43] Although these sentiments of personal curiosity do provide a sufficient rationale for the undertaking of the test, they do little to illuminate Śakra's status as king of the *devas* and his relationship to the aspiring bodhisattva.

More interesting to consider are those statements that begin to place Śakra's motives within a wider cosmological perspective. In some cases Śakra seems to be working for the welfare of the cosmos as a whole when he tests the bodhisattva, allowing the bodhisattva to fulfill the perfection of generosity by giving away his body and thereby move one step closer to perfect Buddhahood on behalf of the entire world. In *Kalpanāmaṇḍitikā* 64,[44] for example, Śakra is overcome with sorrow when an heretical teacher denies the existence of anyone in the universe who is capable of achieving perfect, full enlightenment. He searches the universe for such a being and, with the help of Viśvakarman, locates the generous King Śibi and decides to put him to the test. Once King Śibi has passed the test by giving away his flesh, both Śakra and Viśvakarman are full of joy. They offer their respect and homage to the bodhisattva and express a wish for the future that all beings might take refuge in the Buddha and attain the goal of perfect enlightenment.

From a cosmological perspective, the specific quality of "generosity" is almost irrelevant here. Instead, the primary concern of the test-by-Śakra motif in this case seems to be to demonstrate the proper place of the *devas* within a Buddhist universe and their relationship to the bodhisattva: The *devas,* such a story suggests, are committed Buddhists. They are benevolent in nature and work for the welfare of the world by aiding the bodhisattva in his progress toward Buddhahood—and despite the fact that they are *devas* (while the bodhisattva is just a human being or even an animal), they submit to his greater spiritual authority. Historically, we might interpret such a story as part of the larger attempt Buddhist authors undertook to integrate Buddhism into the wider Indic religious context and make an argument for the Buddha's superiority over traditional deities such as Śakra.

Śakra's benevolent role in aiding the bodhisattva's progress is by no means devoid of some ambivalence, however. Perhaps most interesting of all are those occasions on which Śakra is depicted as becoming *anxious, worried,* or *fearful* when he learns of the existence of the bodhisattva and the perfection of his virtue and generosity. The reason for Śakra's worry has to do with the status of Śakrahood itself and how it is achieved. In the Buddhist understanding, Śakra is not a unique and immortal being; instead, the position of "Śakrahood" is a particularly high station of rebirth achieved through virtuous, merit-making deeds and inhabitable by any human being who exhibits sufficient virtue. (This is why Śakra's marble throne begins to heat up every time a human being is excessively virtuous.)

Moreover, among the virtuous deeds that result in rebirth as Śakra, generosity seems to occupy a prominent place. In the *Sakkasaṃyutta* of the *Saṃyutta Nikāya,* for example, we are told that Śakra was previously a human being who undertook seven vows "by the undertaking of which he attained the position of Śakrahood," and the fifth of these vows was to be "freely generous, open-handed, devoted to liberality, ready to give, delighted in giving and sharing."[45] In the section of this text devoted to Śakra's epithets, moreover, we are told that Śakra is called Purindada because in the past "he gave gifts in one city after another (*pure pure*)," he is called Śakra (Pāli Sakka) because "he gave gifts respectfully (*sakkaccham*)," and he is called Vāsava because he once "gave a dwelling-place (*āvasatham*)";[46] while in the commentary to the *Dīgha Nikāya,* Buddhaghosa tells us explicitly that "one attains the state of Śakrahood in this world by giving gifts."[47]

Śakra's anxiety and worry over the generous bodhisattva are thus well justified, for if the bodhisattva continues to engage in abundant generosity, he will be well on his way to usurping Śakra's position. (In fact, according to a passage in the *Aṅguttara Nikāya,* the bodhisattva did indeed occupy the position of Śakrahood a total of thirty-six times throughout his career.)[48] In some of our stories, Śakra's fear of being displaced by the bodhisattva becomes quite explicit. When the bodhisattva is born as a very generous woman named Rūpāvatī, for example, one version of her story has Śakra think to himself, "I fear that the woman Rūpāvatī might thus cause Śakra to fall from his palace!"—while in another version he wonders: "Does Rūpāvatī wish to expel me from the City of the Immortals and herself assume sovereignty over the gods?"[49] Similarly, a Chinese version of the story of King Śibi's gift of his flesh (to ransom a dove) begins with a group of *devas* and other supernatural beings discussing the fact that Śakra is replaceable, whereupon Śakra becomes "fearful" that the virtuous King Śibi might replace him.[50] Later on in the story, Śakra sheepishly apologizes to King Śibi, saying: "In my stupidity, I thought, O Great King, that you wanted to take my place from me, and that's why I harassed you."[51]

In many Hindu stories making use of this motif—that is, a deity's position being threatened by a virtuous human being—an ascetic's extreme power and virtue cause Śakra's (or in Hinduism, Indra's) marble throne to heat up, and Śakra becomes worried lest the ascetic should displace him. His response at this point often involves sending down a celestial nymph to seduce the ascetic and diminish his ascetic power, thus circumventing the threat to himself. In Indian Buddhist literature too we have at least one example of a similar nature in the *Alambusā Jātaka* of the Pāli *Jātaka* collection, in which Śakra, fearful of losing his position, sends the heavenly nymph Alambusā down to earth to seduce the powerful ascetic Isisiṅga, who then loses his powers for three long years as he immerses himself in sexual distraction.[52] In the perpetual struggle between god and man, a god must encourage an overly virtuous man's downfall, lest the man become so virtuous that he displace the god himself. But why, then, in our stories, would Śakra decide to test the bodhisattva's virtue by asking him for his body? If his position is already threatened by the generous bodhisattva, why would he give him the opportunity to engage in an even more magnificent display of generosity?

One of the consistent features of the role played by the higher *devas* within gift-of-the-body *jātakas* is that they seem to have a longer and wider perspective on the bodhisattva's gift of his body than do those of more lowly status. While animals, human beings, and lower deities often lament the terrible consequences of the gift, the higher *devas* generally express celebration and joy because they understand the larger significance of the gift within the context of the bodhisattva's career (perhaps by virtue of their incredibly long lives and their witnessing of numerous bodhisattva-careers). Śakra, too, falls into this pattern. Śakra clearly understands that the gift of the body is not merely another gift that will move the bodhisattva ever closer to usurping Śakra's throne, but is instead the kind of deed that will propel the bodhisattva on toward full Buddhahood and thus out of the karmic race for Śakrahood altogether. In functional terms, encouraging the bodhisattva to give away his body is no different from sending down a celestial nymph: while the latter protects Śakra's position by kicking the virtuous human back down the karmic ladder, the former protects Śakra's position by propelling the virtuous human on toward full Buddhahood and thus out of the karmic hierarchy altogether. Thus Śakra tests the bodhisattva not merely out of personal curiosity or for the welfare of the world—though both elements are no doubt present—but also as a way of defending his own position in the universe.

This defensiveness and self-interest on the part of Śakra are never quite made explicit within our stories, but are implicit in several elements of the plot, taken together—his stated fear that the bodhisattva might displace him, his decision to test the bodhisattva by asking him for his body, his pleasure and satisfaction when the bodhisattva demonstrates a willingness to give his body away, and his frequent predictions of the bodhisattva's future Buddhahood. Moreover, as I discuss in more detail in the next chapter, Śakra often goads the bodhisattva into making a specific statement of the motives underlying his gift—and in many cases this statement includes an *explicit denial of any desire for the status of Śakrahood.* The gift of the body in these stories is thus not merely an opportunity to illustrate the bodhisattva's perfection of generosity; it is also an *agonistic contest between god and bodhisattva* in which the god protects his own position in the universe, while the man propels himself toward the ultimate position of Buddhahood.

The relationship between Śakra and the bodhisattva in these stories is complicated and constantly shifting. While Śakra is king of the gods and the bodhisattva is just an ordinary human being (or even animal), Śakra clearly understands that the bodhisattva is on a course that will ultimately make him far superior not only to other human beings but to any god as well. In testing the bodhisattva and asking him for his body, Śakra protects his own position at the top of the karmic hierarchy and removes the bodhisattva as a threat, yet at the same time he acknowledges the bodhisattva's ultimate superiority and provides him with the opportunity to propel himself toward Buddhahood. Likewise, the bodhisattva is superior to Śakra and rejects the kind of goal represented by Śakra's position, yet he also depends upon Śakra's godly powers and intervention to make his leap out of the karmic hierarchy. Śakra and the bodhisattva dance a complicated dance of interdependence that ultimately illuminates the relationship between the Buddha and the *devas.* Gift-of-the-body *jātakas* involving Śakra as the recipient thus place the gift of the body within a larger cosmological perspective balancing humans, gods, and Buddhas.[53]

The role that Śakra, as a higher *deva,* plays within these previous lives of the Buddha continues on, of course, into his final life as Prince Siddhārtha. Though Prince Siddhārtha is the one who renounces the world, engages in many years of religious striving, defeats Māra underneath the bodhi tree, attains enlightenment, becomes a Buddha, and initiates the spread of the dharma, he is aided at every step of the way by the intervention of the *devas.* In Buddha-biographies such as the *Jātakanidāna,* for example, when Prince Siddhārtha is living a hedonistic life of luxury within his palace compound and has no exposure to suffering, it is the gods who engineer the Four Sights that will cause him to renounce the world. When he decides to leave the world even though his father has locked him up within the palace compound, it is the gods who cause the palace guards to fall asleep, open the palace gates, and even hold up the hooves of his horse so that his departure will go unnoticed. And when he finally attains enlightenment but then hesitates to teach to others, it is the gods who intervene and beg him to teach, thus assuring the spread of the dharma. Throughout the entire biography, we see the same complicated interdependence and shifting hierarchies that we see in gift-of-the-body *jātakas* involving Śakra: the Buddha is superior to the gods, yet he depends upon the gods in order to become a Buddha; the gods are more powerful than Prince Siddhārtha, yet they use their divine powers to help the lowly human reach a status superior to any godhood. Gift-of-the-body *jātakas* in which Śakra is the recipient thus fall into a larger category of stories concerned with illuminating this complex relationship—quite apart from their illustration of generosity.

IMITABLE GIVING

The particular virtue of generosity, of course, does remain a predominant theme. Yet even if we bracket the test-by-Śakra motif and consider these stories purely from the perspective of the theme of generosity, it is clear that they differ significantly in their illustration of generosity from stories of the earlier type. We can see this difference most clearly, perhaps, when we consider the physical restoration of the bodhisattva's body and the contradictory nature of the Act of Truth that brings it about. The Act of Truth within these stories strikes us as inherently contradictory, for on the one hand the bodhisattva asserts his perfect willingness to give his body away, his joy in doing so, and his absolute lack of any regret, while on the other the obvious purpose of the Act of Truth is to *get his body back.* In chapter 5, I will address this contradiction in more detail; for now, I simply observe that the extreme and uncompromising generosity so characteristic of the stories discussed earlier is here significantly deflated by the fact that, in these stories, the bodhisattva *gets his body back.* We know from the Act of Truth that the bodhisattva's generosity *is* perfect and sincere, yet the illustration of this generosity cannot help but be affected by the spectacle of the bodhisattva's body being restored to perfect health. Instead of watching the bodhisattva suffer a tragic loss of life as a result of giving the gift, here we watch him give the gift—only to see this gift restored back to him in the end, often in a *better* and more powerful form than before. The emphasis on perfect and one-sided generosity is thus significantly weakened.

This weakness in the illustration of generosity, however, is balanced by a corresponding strength: the survival of the bodhisattva and the restoration of his body allow these stories to emphasize the *rewards* of the gift much more so than those stories in which the bodhisattva dies. Consequently, although the bodhisattva's gift itself remains extreme and inimitable in nature, it often serves implicitly as a model for more ordinary types of giving (such as the offering of alms to monks) and the karmic rewards they bestow. The ordinary Buddhist giver could not hope to imitate the bodhisattva's bodily sacrifice—and in that sense the bodhisattva is exalted—but perhaps he or she *can* identify with the bodhisattva's enjoyment of giving's rewards and thus be encouraged to engage in generosity of his or her own. This identification with the bodhisattva is reinforced on an emotional level as well: the survival of the bodhisattva and the restoration of his body give to these tales a much more joyful and celebratory tone than those in which the bodhisattva dies—one that offers the reader a vicarious satisfaction and further motivates his or her own generosity. Thus, in contrast to the highly idealized and extreme generosity characteristic of the stories discussed earlier, stories involving Śakra as the recipient of the gift present the virtue of generosity in a more palatable and accessible form, one that appeals to the ordinary giver.

We might say, in other words, that in the balance between the saint's "imitability" and "otherness," these gifts remain wholly "other" to the ordinary giver—yet they begin to make a nod toward "imitability." In these stories the bodhisattva's generosity is not merely the object of awe-inspired worship and devotion, but also an appropriate object of *imitation:* the ordinary reader, too, can give gifts generously and experience giving's many rewards. On the level of genre, moreover, it also follows that although these stories remain "super-*jātakas*" that perfectly embody the ethos of the *jātaka,* they do so in a manner that at least begins to form a bridge to the ethos of the *avadāna.* In contrast to the stories discussed earlier, stories featuring Śakra as the recipient begin to draw connections between the bodhisattva's "perfections" and the ordinary Buddhist's "devotions"—between heroic bodily gifts and ordinary ritual offerings. These ideas will be treated at greater length in chapters 4 and 5, when I turn to a discussion

TABLE 1
Differences Between the Two Major Plotlines of the Gift-of-the-Body Genre

RECIPIENT OF THE GIFT	Ordinary being (pitiful or evil)	Śakra-in-disguise
MOST COMMON OUTCOME OF THE PLOT	Bodhisattva dies	Bodhisattva survives and restores his body through an Act of Truth
TYPE OF GIVING	Extraordinary giving	Ordinary giving
QUALITY EMPHASIZED	Bodhisattva's "otherness"	Bodhisattva's "imitability"
APPROPRIATE RESPONSE	Worship and devotion	Direct imitation
JĀTAKA VS. *AVADĀNA* ETHOS	"Super-*jātaka*"	"*Avadāna*-like" *jātaka*

of the Buddhist discourse on *dāna.* For now, I refer the reader to table 1, which summarizes the major distinctions I have enumerated between these two major plotlines.

When the Gift Is Interrupted

So far I have enumerated the two major plotlines that are most characteristic of the gift-of-the-body genre. In the first plotline, the recipient of the gift is an ordinary being, and the bodhisattva dies as a result of giving the gift; in the second plotline, the recipient of the gift is the god Śakra in disguise, and the bodhisattva survives the gift and restores his body through an Act of Truth. In addition, I would also define a third and less common plotline. This plotline, which might make use of either an ordinary being or the god Śakra as the recipient of the gift, is defined by the single fact that the *gift is not initiated once the bodhisattva's willingness to give has been established.* Here the bodhisattva's mere willingness to give performs the same function as the actual gift itself, and the bodhisattva therefore neither needs to lose his life nor restore his body through an Act of Truth. These stories have a somewhat different flavor than the others, since there is none of the usual emphasis on the mutilation of the body or the pain undergone by the bodhisattva so characteristic of the types described above. Nevertheless, some of the themes we have already seen are also present here.

In some cases, the gift is not initiated because whoever was demanding the gift or in need of the gift is so moved by the bodhisattva's mere willingness to give that he puts a stop to the gift before it is even begun. The bodhisattva's ability to cause this profound change of heart in the recipient through the sheer magnitude of his virtue once again highlights the extreme and uncompromising nature of the bodhisattva's generosity, as well as the awe-inspiring power and charisma he exerts over others. Thus in *Avadānaśataka* 34 Śakra disguises himself as a brahmin and makes a request for King Śibi's eyes in order to test his generosity. In contrast to other versions of the story, however, as soon as King Śibi demonstrates his complete willingness to give—saying, "Take whatever you want, Great Brahmin! There is no obstacle here on my part!"[54]—Śakra puts a stop to the test before the gift is even begun. In this case, it appears that the bodhisattva's mere verbalization of his willingness to give is so powerful that Śakra becomes convinced of his generosity, and the physical gift itself then becomes unnecessary. The bodhisattva's resolve, in and of itself, has the power to circumvent the test.

This power to bring about such a profound change of heart in the recipient is especially strong, of course, in the case of those recipients I have classified as "evil." In the traditional story of King Sarvaṃdada, for example, the bodhisattva is a virtuous and generous king named Sarvaṃdada ("All-Giving") who first loses his kingdom to an immoral, enemy king and then offers his own head to a wandering supplicant to bring to the enemy king for a reward. This gift of Sarvaṃdada's head is never completed, however, because the enemy king is so moved and profoundly shaken by Sarvaṃdada's generous intentions that he immediately gives up his immoral ways and is converted wholly to the side of virtue. Various versions of the Sarvaṃdada story take pains to convey the profound nature of the enemy king's conversion. In *Avadānasārasamuccaya* 3, for example, when the enemy king first learns of Sarvaṃdada's intention to offer up his own head, he "trembles with fear," his mind is "overwhelmed by terror," and he wonders who this magnificent being might be.[55] By the time he has come face to face with Sarvaṃdada himself, his moral conversion is complete. "O King," he says to Sarvaṃdada,

> if one who is capable of gratifying his subjects deserves to be called a 'king,' then you alone are a king, O Treasure-House of Excellent Virtues! . . . Go rule over your own city, just as you did before. We are intent on submitting to the authority of someone like you. And please forgive us our deviation from proper conduct—for one who has no eyes stumbles even when the ground is even.[56]

He "renounces the poison known as anger,"[57] bows his head down at Sarvaṃdada's feet, and retreats to his own kingdom, where he becomes a virtuous ruler thereafter. In *Kalpanāmaṇḍitikā* 71, the situation is similar, with the enemy king confessing his "remorse" and chastising himself as "an idiot and a fool, a conceited man deprived of intelligence."[58] In all such cases, the bodhisattva's mere *intention to give* affects the world around him in powerful ways and has almost-magical consequences upon others. Thus, even though the gift itself never occurs, the spectacle of the gift is replaced, in a sense, by the spectacle of the powerful moral effects the bodhisattva's generosity wields upon others.

In other cases, it is not the recipient of the gift who experiences such a profound conversion, but the very universe itself. The gift is not completed, in other words, because of some kind of magical or miraculous response on the part of the cosmos. Thus in several different versions of the hare story the hare offers his body to a brahmin supplicant (sometimes Śakra, sometimes not) by throwing himself into a fire, but the fire refuses to burn him. In Pāli *Jātaka* 316, the fire is "unable to heat even as much as the pores of the bodhisattva's skin";[59] in *Cariyāpiṭaka* 1.10 the fire becomes like "cool water relieving a fever";[60] and in a Chinese version of the story the fire itself is extinguished as soon as it touches the bodhisattva's body.[61] Likewise, in a Chinese story involving a mother swan who intends to feed her own flesh to her young during a drought, the cosmos itself responds to this magnanimous intention by immediately showering down rain and food, thus obviating the need for such a gift.[62] In these cases, the physical universe itself seems to respond in powerful ways to the bodhisattva's intention. The spectacle of the gift is here replaced by the spectacle of the universe's response; the universe confirms the bodhisattva's generosity, and the gift does not need to be completed. These physical responses on the part of the universe are ultimately equivalent to the moral changes of heart discussed earlier: the universe, in a sense, becomes a moral character who is so moved by the bodhisattva's intention that it puts a stop to the gift before it is made.

Such dramatic interruptions of the gift, whether moral or cosmological in nature, once again serve to underscore the enormous power of the bodhisattva's resolve, his essential difference from other beings, and his status as an object of awe and devotion. In this sense, we might compare such stories to those of the first plotline I dealt with above, since both plotlines engage in an extreme idealization of the bodhisattva. At the same time, however, these stories also share something in common with the second plotline I dealt with above, in terms of presenting a more palatable, accessible, and imitable model of generosity than one that results in the giver's death. For just as stories following the second plotline suggest that you can give away a gift and later get it back (as long as your intentions are pure), so stories following this third plotline seem to suggest that perhaps you don't really have to give away the gift at all (as long as your intentions are pure). Stories in which the gift is interrupted thus seem to combine the extreme idealization of the bodhisattva characteristic of the first plotline with the palatable and appealing model of generosity characteristic of the second.

What, then, is the basic purpose of the noncompletion of the gift? If we observe the simple fact that in all such stories the bodhisattva's mere *willingness to give* functions like the gift itself, and the need for an actual gift is thus obviated, then perhaps the underlying purpose of such a plotline is to draw a strict equivalence between the *intention or volition to give* and the actual act of giving itself. Not only would this help to ensure that aspiring bodhisattvas all over India were not throwing themselves off mountains or jumping into fires, but it also accords doctrinally with many Buddhist definitions of *dāna.* The *Mahāprajñāpāramitā Śāstra,* for example, defines *dāna* as a "wholesome volition associated with the mind," and then adds that "certain people say that from this wholesome volition comes a bodily or vocal act which is also called *dāna.*"[63] In a similar manner, the *Bodhicaryāvatāra* says that the bodhisattva's *dāna-pāramitā* "is called such because of the intention to give everything one has to all people, along with the fruit of the gift," and then adds, "Therefore, the perfection is nothing other than this intention."[64] Such definitions give primary emphasis to the *intention behind the gift,* and seem to include the actual act of giving as a secondary element. This is in consonance, of course, with Buddhism's much-vaunted "ethic of intention" and the

Buddha's famous definition of action in the *Aṅguttara Nikāya:* "O Monks, I say that action is volition. Having made a volition, one acts by means of body, speech, or mind."[65]

Variations

In the above discussion I have enumerated the two "major" plotlines and one "minor" plotline most characteristic of the gift-of-the-body genre, as well as elucidating the basic themes each plotline highlights. Thus I hope to have shown that stories featuring ordinary beings as the recipients of the gift promote a highly idealized and extreme generosity that invites a response of worship and devotion; stories featuring Śakra as the recipient of the gift temper this ideal and make it more accessible and "imitable" by leaving space for the rewards of giving (as well as addressing other concerns); and stories in which the gift is not completed draw a strict equivalence between the intention or volition to give and the actual gift itself.

Despite the usefulness of these categories, however, gift-of-the-body *jātakas* demonstrate an endless variety in creative detail, character, imagery, and plot. The schema I have presented above cannot be treated too mechanistically because there will always be individual stories that fail to conform; indeed, there are probably almost as many exceptions as there are stories that adhere to the expected patterns. My purpose in laying out such a typology is not to designate certain plotlines as the only "acceptable" alternatives, but rather to construct a basic interpretive framework for the genre—one that is solidly based on the stories themselves, but also one that helps us make sense of even those stories that fail to conform. I would describe these plotlines as being *interpretive* in function rather than *classificatory:* in other words, rather than using them as boxes in which to classify individual stories, I perceive them only as a well-grounded conceptual framework against which to interpret stories that may or may not necessarily conform. In order to demonstrate this largely heuristic function, I will conclude this chapter by looking at three such instances of "failure to conform." This enumeration is by no means exhaustive, but is only intended to provide a range of representative examples and to demonstrate the types of questions and answers that become possible by constructing such a framework in the first place.

AN UNSTABLE CONVENTION: THE BODHISATTVA'S RESTORATION OF HIS OWN BODY

I will begin with the case of an unstable convention—that is, a convention that is characteristic of one of the plotlines I enumerated above, but that seems to be inherently unstable and is therefore frequently violated. As we have seen, in those gift-of-the-body *jātakas* involving the test-by-Śakra motif, it is generally the case that Śakra puts a stop to the test at some point and encourages the bodhisattva to perform an Act of Truth, which alone is responsible for restoring his body back to health. Narratively speaking, this makes sense: if the purpose of the story is to test the bodhisattva's generosity, then the Act of Truth constitutes the "proof" we need that this test has been successfully passed. For by means of the Act of Truth, we know for certain that the bodhisattva's generosity is genuine; after all, if his claim to be perfectly generous were *not* true, then the Act of Truth would fail and his body would *not* be restored—but since his body *is* restored, we know for sure that this claim must be true. Restoring the bodhisattva's body in some other manner would clearly not have the same proof-giving effect. This is emphasized for us, in fact, in a discussion from the *Milindapañha,* for when King Milinda (the interlocutor in this text) wonders how King Śibi's eyes could be restored after being so completely destroyed, the wise monk Nāgasena answers him by emphasizing the power of the Act of Truth alone: "Through the power of the truth *and without any other cause,* Great King, did that divine eye arise. Truth itself was the cause, in this case, for the arising of the divine eye."[66]

In spite of this narrative logic, however, the exclusive role of the Act of Truth in restoring the bodhisattva's body appears to be an inherently unstable convention. In many stories, in fact, Śakra's crucial role in encouraging the Act of Truth seems to result in some ambiguity about whether *Śakra* might be partially responsible as well. Thus, in company with the Act of Truth, Śakra sometimes tells the bodhisattva to "choose a boon" (which suggests that he himself is granting the restoration); or the restored body part is said to have been "given by Śakra"; or the Act of Truth is paired with Śakra's administration of supernatural medicines (which obscures the true cause of the restoration).[67] Finally, there are some stories in which the Act of Truth is dispensed with completely, and it is Śakra himself (or sometimes another divine being) who restores the bodhisattva's body directly.[68] In other words, although the genre as a whole ostensibly wishes to show that the bodhisattva's sincerity alone has the power to heal and restore his own body, individual stories consistently falter in this assertion and imply that Śakra is partially or wholly responsible as well.

Why is this particular convention so unstable, resulting in frequent deviations from the plotline one would normally expect? I noted before that all stories involving the basic motif of bodily self-sacrifice should ultimately be seen as one large and interweaving thematic group, and that gift-of-the-body *jātakas* most likely have close connections to stories of other types. In this case, in trying to explain why there is a consistent tendency to give Śakra part or all of the responsibility for restoring the bodhisattva's body, I would perhaps point to Phyllis Granoff's discussion of a large body of Indic stories (Hindu, Buddhist, and Jain) sharing a common complex of ideas.[69] The stories that conform to this pattern have nothing to do with the virtue of generosity. Instead, all of them depict a hero embarking on some kind of quest and having an agonistic encounter with a god-in-disguise, in which the hero must show himself to be willing to risk his life. He is ritually humbled, or wounded, or "killed" (sometimes symbolically, sometimes literally), and then restored to health and given a new and purified body *by the deity himself.* In an episode from the *Mahābhārata,* for example, Arjuna goes on a quest to obtain some magical weapons and the mantras that control them. His journey takes him into the forest, where he encounters the god Śiva, disguised as a hunter. Śiva and Arjuna fight; Arjuna loses the fight and is severely wounded. Śiva then reveals his true identity and touches Arjuna's body, whereupon "all that was impure in Arjuna's body was at once destroyed."[70] It is only then that Arjuna is able to obtain the weapons and mantras he needs. Granoff interprets such stories as being similar in structure to "rites of passage" (as described by Arnold van Gennep and Victor Turner),[71] in which the hero is stripped of his personal identity through an agonistic encounter with a deity-in-disguise, and then purified, renewed, and transformed at the hands of the deity himself.

Keeping this larger group of stories in mind, then, perhaps we could speculate that gift-of-the-body stories in which Śakra is the recipient either play upon or derive from this traditional complex of ideas, but recast it in terms of Śakra's testing of the bodhisattva's generosity. Many of the themes seem quite similar—the hero on a quest (this time, for Buddhahood), the god in disguise, the agonistic quality of the encounter, the hero's willingness to risk his life, and his ultimate renewal and restoration to health. One could speculate, however, that because our stories adapt this complex of ideas to illustrate the Buddhist virtue of *dāna,* they must shift responsibility for the restoration of the body from the god to the bodhisattva's own sincerity in giving the gift; however, as we have seen, they sometimes fail to do so completely. On a grander scale, one might even try to make the argument that a traditional Indic narrative or ritual pattern has here been "Buddhicized" and/or "ethicized"—but the transformation, in some cases, remains incomplete.

Determining whether this particular argument is valid, of course, would require much more substantial evidence. The methodological point I am making, however, is hopefully clear: Once we have an "expected" generic framework against which to interpret our stories, minor deviations from the expected plotline are flagged, the inherent instability of certain generic conventions becomes visible, and it then becomes possible to speculate about the instability itself. The questions we ask and the answers we give take shape only against the initial framework with which we begin.

Distorting the Plotline: Multiple Episodes of Bodily Giving

Another example of the failure to conform to an expected plotline occurs in those stories that depict multiple episodes of bodily giving. Some authors were not content to depict the bodhisattva making a single gift of his body, but instead composed stories in which multiple gifts of the body occur, and the bodhisattva seems to engage in an orgy of extreme generosity. Rather than watching a single gift come into being and unfold in the expected manner, such stories present us with a quick succession of gifts that stretch and distort the characteristic plotlines—though not beyond recognition.

Thus in *Avadānaśataka* 34 the familiar character of King Śibi performs three such gifts in quick succession. First, he cuts open his body and allows mosquitoes to feast on his blood. Before this episode can reach any kind of resolution, however, the story proceeds onward to a second gruesome episode, in which the deity Śakra, disguised as a vulture, receives permission to pluck out King Śibi's eyes. Rather than revealing his true identity and encouraging King Śibi to perform an Act of Truth, however, Śakra then quickly dons yet another disguise, appearing as a brahmin supplicant who requests these same eyes, whereupon King Śibi freely agrees to give them. It is only when we get to this third and final episode that one of our "expected" outcomes occurs—in this case, what I have designated as the "minor plotline," in which the gift is interrupted once the bodhisattva's willingness to give has been established. Three episodes of bodily giving are thus related within four short pages of text, with two of these episodes lacking any characteristic outcome and the resolution of the story being delayed until the last and final gift. In stark contrast to a story such as *Mahajjātakamālā* 44, which takes eighteen (much longer) pages to relate a single gift of King Śibi, the reader here is clobbered with a quick succession of bodily gifts—narratively *immersed* in the relentless flow of the bodhisattva's bodily sacrifices, which only comes to a conclusion (and an expected resolution) with the third and final gift. The conventions of the gift-of-the-body genre are here being stretched and manipulated in order to achieve a certain effect, and the resulting experience for the reader is quite different.

If we were to imagine this process being taken to its logical conclusion, we might envision something like a gift-of-the-body "story" that has lost all narrative structure and become nothing more than a relentless listing of bodily gifts. It is interesting to note that as the Mahāyāna discourse on the bodhisattva's generosity becomes more and more hyperbolic and extravagant in nature, we do indeed find gift-of-the-body stories in the Mahāyāna *sūtras* that tend in this direction. With their multiple episodes of bodily sacrifice and their lack of characteristic plot outcomes, these stories contain many of the traditional elements we might expect to find in a gift-of-the-body story—such as generous donors, evil or pitiful recipients, gifts of the body, and Acts of Truth—but their discourse seems fundamentally different. They are less "narrative" in nature, less intelligible as self-contained "stories" with definite plotlines, and more embedded within the surrounding *sūtra* text.

In the fifth chapter of the (Mahāyāna) *Karuṇāpuṇḍarīka Sūtra,* for example, there is a story involving the Buddha's previous birth as a *cakravartin* king named Ambara. But rather than focusing on a single gift of Ambara's body, this text inundates the reader with a veritable deluge of bodily gifts: in quick succession, Ambara gives away to various recipients his feet, eyes, ears, genitals, flesh, blood, and hands. His ministers dump his mutilated body into a charnel ground, where the remainder is devoured by flies, mosquitoes, dogs, jackals, and vultures. He (or whatever is left of him) then performs an Act of Truth that begins in a thoroughly conventional manner but ends in such a way that the orgy of giving can continue:

> If, when I gave up my whole body, with its major and minor limbs, and thereby gave up all of my royal sovereignty, I did not feel regret for even a moment, nor did I give rise to anger, then may my wish be fulfilled: May this body of mine

> become a mountain of flesh! May whatever beings have flesh for food and blood for drink come eat my flesh and drink my blood. And, by the power of my vow, may my body grow enough to accommodate as many beings as may eat my flesh and drink my blood, until it is a hundred thousand *yojanas* in height and five thousand *yojanas* in width![72]

Once this occurs and he becomes a flesh-mountain, he continues to feed beings his flesh for a full one thousand years. He is then reborn as a *nāga*-king who discovers and gives away "hundreds of thousands of millions of billions of treasure-stores full of treasures," during "seven hundred thousand millions of billions of seven-year intervals," and in universes "equal in number to grains of sand in the Ganges River."[73] Thus the story doesn't so much come to a definitive conclusion as get lost in a cloud of Mahāyāna hyperbole and seamlessly merge back into the surrounding *sūtra* discourse.

The experience and effects of such a narrative are quite different, of course, from those of the traditional gift-of-the-body *jātaka.* Instead of allowing the reader to focus on a single gift and experience its unfolding in a processual and emergent manner (as well as contemplate its possible consequences on the surrounding world), this text hits the reader over the head with an incessant wave of multiple bodily sacrifices described briefly and in quick succession, so that the language of the narrative as a whole becomes almost numinous in nature. Nevertheless, individual elements of the traditional plotlines are still recognizable, along with the manner in which they have been reinterpreted.

Understanding the conventions of the gift-of-the-body genre might thus help us to understand the nature of Mahāyāna discourse and the types of adaptations Mahāyāna authors made to traditional Buddhist genres in order to fulfill new ends. In fact, the manipulation of the gift-of-the-body genre in this instance might even be aligned with other such manipulations characteristic of Mahāyāna discourse. The audience who listens to a Mahāyāna *sūtra,* for example, is often described in a much more elaborate and fantastical manner than the audience who listens to a Mainstream *sūtra*—sometimes consisting of billions of bodhisattvas and celestial beings spread out in multiple universes, rather than the standard 1,250 monks gathered at Jetavana. The growth of the audience to such unimaginable and inconceivable proportions is somewhat similar to the extension of the gift-of-the-body theme from a single gift to an incessant wave of bodily sacrifices that become difficult to keep track of or visualize. Taking both manipulations together, it then becomes possible to say something about Mahāyāna discourse more generally—about its tendency toward excess and hyperbole, perhaps, or its numinous use of language and imagery. Such discussions become convincing, however, only when they are built upon a solid understanding of the conventions of earlier genres.

The Individual Story: An Analysis of Jātakamālā *8*

While the previous two discussions have focused on "anomalies" that are common to more than one gift-of-the-body story, I turn now to the case of an individual story that fails to conform to the expected plotlines—most likely for purely individual reasons. Every story is unique, of course, and has its own internal logic and necessity—but once again I hope to demonstrate that the conceptual framework I have constructed can serve as a background against which this logic becomes illuminated.

Jātakamālā 8 relates the story of the virtuous King Maitrībala, who slices up his own body on behalf of five cruel and murderous *yakṣas* who have begged him for food but are unsatisfied with anything less than human flesh and blood. Because these *yakṣas* constitute "evil recipients," we might expect King Maitrībala to die as a result of making this gift. These expectations are subverted, however, when the god Śakra suddenly appears on the scene and praises his great generosity. However, rather than encouraging him to perform an Act of Truth to restore his body—as we might then expect—Śakra restores his body directly by applying natural and supernatural medicines. Looked at purely in terms of plotline, then, this story appears to be make use of elements common to several different types: the *yakṣas,* as "evil" recipients, are characteristic of the first plotline I discussed; Śakra's sudden appearance on the scene, his formal praise of the bodhisattva, and the bodhisattva's survival and restoration of his body are common to the second plotline I discussed; while the fact that it is *Śakra* who restores the bodhisattva's body (rather than the bodhisattva's own Act of Truth) is characteristic of the "unstable convention" I have described. Rather than merely classifying each element of the story, however, it is also possible to use our conventional plotlines as a framework against which the logic of this individual story might be elucidated.

The first thing to note is that a reading of the story as a whole makes it clear that one of the major themes of this particular story is the illustration of "good kingship" and the fundamental connection Buddhism posits between the virtue of the king and the prosperity and flourishing of his kingdom. This theme is highlighted throughout the entire story. At the beginning of the story, when the *yakṣas* are first introduced, we see them going around King Maitrībala's kingdom, trying to sap the people of their vital forces so they can devour their bodies for food. When they are unsuccessful at weakening even a single person, however, they ask a simple cowherd in the forest why the people of this kingdom are so invulnerable to horrible, man-eating demons, whereupon the cowherd tells them that the kingdom is protected by a "powerful good-luck charm"—the virtuous King Maitrībala himself.[74] As the cowherd explains, the virtue of the king is like a physical force-shield that ensures the prosperity of the kingdom and the robust health of its citizens:

> The power of our great king derives from his own noble character. . . . His power is nothing other than his benevolence—and his army, with its colorful flags, is merely a matter of traditional custom. He has never experienced anger, and he is incapable of speaking harshly. He rules the earth in a proper manner, and the dharma he follows is one of good governance, not deceitful statecraft. . . . Our Lord is endowed with hundreds of virtues such as these, and this is why no misfortune could ever afflict the people who live in his realm.[75]

It is this information that makes the *yakṣas* decide that they should simply ask King Maitrībala for his own flesh and blood—hoping, in one fell swoop, to both satiate their immediate hunger and destroy the protective "good-luck charm" that prevents them from getting more food.

With this initial opening, it becomes clear that one of the purposes of this particular story will be to illustrate what "good kingship" is (from the Buddhist perspective) and to demonstrate its beneficial consequences. The gift-of-the-body theme is clearly subordinated to this end, for once the *yakṣas* have requested the king's flesh and blood, the lengthy arguments that occur between Maitrībala and his ministers are really arguments about the nature of "good kingship." While Maitrībala's ministers repeatedly advance the basic *dharmaśāstric* argument that the king has a duty to serve the entire kingdom and should therefore not sacrifice his life merely for the sake of a few hungry demons, the story has Maitrībala put forth a more typically Buddhist view: the king is a moral exemplar, and the virtue of the entire kingdom is dependent, first and foremost, upon the virtue of the king himself. "Being your leader in matters of dharma and the law," he tells his ministers, "if I myself were to take the wrong course [of action], what would be the condition of my subjects, who would follow my path of conduct? Therefore, it is in consideration of my subjects themselves [that I am giving away my body]."[76] Thus, in sharp contrast to the Hindu political discourse on *nīti* and *arthaśāstra,* with its paramount concern with political expediency, this story wishes to argue that a king who gives his body to a few cannibalistic demons out of perfect generosity is indeed the *best king of all*—and not merely for himself and his own progress as a bodhisattva, but for the worldly prosperity of his kingdom as well.[77] In this Buddhist view of ideal kingship, the moral virtue of the king is paramount and serves as the very fountainhead of the kingdom's prosperity.

In this situation, it is, of course, impossible to have King Maitrībala *die* as a result of making his gift, for if he were to die his kingdom would be left leaderless and all the worst fears of his ministers proven correct. In order to demonstrate that the bodhisattva's compassion and self-sacrifice on behalf of the lowliest of creatures is *also* the best possible policy for the worldly welfare of his kingdom, King Maitrībala must survive and prosper, and the story must have a positive resolution. Thus it is no surprise that the story ends with the deity Śakra quite suddenly appearing on the scene, praising the king's excellent conduct, and using various supernatural medicines that instantly heal his wounds and restore his body to its former condition. It is only in this way that Maitrībala's virtuous deeds can be justified as an appropriate manifestation of good kingship. Thus, in spite of the presence of the *yakṣas* as "evil recipients," it is essential for the bodhisattva to survive this gift and prosper, rather than suffer a tragic death.

On the other hand, if one asks why the story didn't simply make *Śakra* the recipient of the gift—which might more easily have ensured the king's survival—this, too, it seems to me, can be explained by the emphasis on good kingship. It is the good king's ability to show compassion for *everyone* (including the unworthiest of beings) and still be an effective leader that is at stake here, not merely his ability to pass some deity's test. In order to demonstrate that generosity toward the lowly really can be reconciled with effective political leadership, the request for the king's body must be *real* and not just a deity's ruse. The recipients of the gift must therefore be ordinary, lowly beings—the more evil, the better—and not simply a curious deity undertaking an elaborate deception. For if the entire gift were nothing more than Śakra's trick, the viability of compassionate Buddhist kingship would not truly be tested.

Depicting the *yakṣas* as "evil" recipients is useful to the story in another way as well. Throughout the Buddhist discourse on good kingship, a consistent emphasis is placed on the manner in which the king's virtue leads inexorably to the virtue of those around him. In the present case this theme is reinforced by having the *yakṣas* be "evil" recipients, for the story is then able to depict the dramatic moral conversion they undergo upon receiving the king's flesh. In fact, when faced with the king's willingness to give up his very life, these formerly murderous *yakṣas* become "completely serene and full of wonder"; they beg for the king's forgiveness and ask him to give them a command, whereupon he orders them to "avoid, as if they were poison, injury to others, greed for their wives or possessions, vile speech, and the sin of drunkenness."[78] The story thus demonstrates that not only did the king's extreme generosity *not* result in his death and loss to the kingdom, but in fact it even protected the kingdom forever after from the further incursions of these murderous *yakṣas.* The power of the king's virtue to spread to those around him and thus ensure the prosperity of his kingdom is dependent upon the *yakṣas* being "evil recipients."

Finally, if one asks why the story depicts *Śakra* magically restoring the king's body rather than having the king himself perform an Act of Truth, I would argue that this again makes sense within the context of the "good kingship" theme. Since this particular story is really more concerned with justifying the ideal of compassionate Buddhist kingship than it is with underscoring the bodhisattva's "perfect generosity," there is less of a need, perhaps, to focus so explicitly (as the Act of Truth does) on the purity of the king's generosity. The Act of Truth can thus be sacrificed in favor of an element that here makes better narrative sense: Śakra, the king of the *devas,* suddenly appears on the scene, praises King Maitrībala's conduct, and magically restores his body. The ideal of compassionate Buddhist kingship embodied by the human king Maitrībala is thus dramatically confirmed and validated by the king of the gods himself.

Every element of the story, then, makes a positive contribution to the story's paramount concern with illustrating the viability of compassionate Buddhist kingship. In analyzing this story against the background of our "conventional plotlines," however, I do not wish to convey the impression of an author who consciously lays these plotlines out before him and then selectively chooses elements in order to achieve a certain effect. Instead, my argument throughout this chapter is simply this: looking closely at a body of related texts that strike one as belonging to a single genre and then uncovering that which a reader experiences as the standard conventions of this genre allows us to construct a coherent world of meaning against which the details of an individual story suddenly become significant—and gives us a language in which to ask meaningful questions about a narrative and offer persuasive arguments as to why it has been constructed in a particular way. It is a way of diving—from a distant time and place—into the "pool of signifiers" historical writers and readers perhaps swam in with little conscious effort.

III

CONVENTIONS OF RHETORIC

As we saw in the previous chapter, gift-of-the-body *jātakas* show significant variations in plotline, with each conventional plotline emphasizing different themes and allowing different concerns to be brought to the fore. Nevertheless, the unity of the genre is ensured by the fact that all such tales share in common the central theme of the bodhisattva's gift of his body and the rhetoric surrounding this gift. Whether or not the gift is completed, whether or not the bodhisattva dies in the process, and regardless of who the recipient is, certain aspects of the *rhetoric* or argumentation remain the same: the bodhisattva wishes to give away his body, other characters oppose this wish, arguments for and against the gift are provided, a resolution is reached, and in every case, the point is ultimately made that the bodhisattva's intention was good, true, and right all along, while those who opposed his intention were wrong. Throughout the story, there is a dialectical push-and-pull between the bodhisattva and those who oppose him—between the drive to complete the gift and the drive to stop it—that always resolves itself by demonstrating the rightness of the bodhisattva's intention (even in those cases in which the gift is not ultimately made). A distinction might be drawn here between *plot* and *rhetoric:* stories showing significant variations in plot nevertheless share in common the same basic rhetoric.

This chapter seeks to elucidate the conventions of rhetoric characteristic of the gift-of-the-body genre. It proceeds in the following manner. I first offer a brief, holistic interpretation of the genre's basic rhetoric—that is, an argument about what the genre wishes to persuade us of and how it goes about doing so. Using this discussion as a framework, I then go back and look in more detail at how this "power to persuade" proceeds throughout the course of the story, focusing especially on particular types of characters and the roles they play within this rhetoric.

Conflict and Resolution

The rhetoric of the gift-of-the-body genre is organized, I contend, around *conflict* and *resolution*—that is, the positing of a fundamental conflict and some attempt at its eventual resolution. In order to understand both the nature of this conflict and the possibilities of its resolution, it is first necessary to consider what the character of the bodhisattva stands for—and what happens when this character is immersed within a narrative setting.

As I will demonstrate in more detail in chapter 5, the bodhisattva's gift of his body is frequently described in Indian Buddhist literature as the most extreme manifestation possible of the virtue of *dāna* (generosity) and the paradigmatic example or fullest embodiment of *dāna-pāramitā* (the "perfection of generosity"). The bodhisattva who engages in a gift of the body thus constitutes a human (or anthropomorphic) embodiment of the abstract Buddhist ideal of *dāna* or *dāna-pāramitā.* Accordingly, he does not strike one as a fully-rounded or "realistic" character; instead, he is a highly idealized stereotype of virtue with whom the reader has difficulty identifying, and his major purpose is to embody the ideal of *dāna* in a wholly uncompromising way. Indeed, the statements made about the bodhisattva by the narrative voice of the text, the way in which the bodhisattva speaks and acts throughout the story, and other conventions surrounding the bodhisattva are generally in close agreement with the abstract ideal of *dāna* discussed within exegetical and philosophical literature.

The *difference* between the bodhisattva and the abstract ideal, however, is that while the abstract ideal may exist in isolation, the bodhisattva must embody this ideal as a human or animal character acting within a semi-realistic narrative setting, where he is surrounded by other characters who react to his thoughts and deeds, as well as a physical universe potentially affected by the various consequences of his actions. This, it seems to me, is precisely the point: the basic rhetorical purpose of gift-of-the-body stories, I contend, is to provide a concrete manifestation of an abstract Buddhist ideal, locating this ideal within a dramatic character and allowing it to unfold within a recognizable human context replete with personal and social consequences. In contrast to many philosophical and technical discussions of *dāna,* then, these depictions often lay particular emphasis upon both the bodhisattva's difficulties in executing the ideal and the community's ambivalence toward it. The opposition and conflict surrounding the ideal must be depicted and worked out.

The primary conflict depicted within gift-of-the-body stories consists of the obvious and inevitable clash that occurs between the abstract imperative of *dāna* and the value systems of everyday life—between the universalistic demands of "perfect generosity" and the particularistic claims of family, community, and kingdom. The *dāna* of the bodhisattva, one must remember, is not just ordinary, everday *dāna,* but rather *dāna-pāramitā,* the "perfection" of generosity, or (using the traditional etymology of *pāramitā*) *dāna* that has "gone to the other shore," been taken to its utmost limit, followed through to its logical conclusion—in other words, *dāna* as an absolute and transcendent value that brooks no concession or compromise. While this absolute imperative of *dāna* dictates that the bodhisattva should give to any recipient whatever gift that recipient requests, this gift is consistently portrayed as conflicting with the bodhisattva's social and familial obligations. Gift-of-the-body stories do not shy away from this conflict; instead, they confront it directly.

Certain types of characters (whom I refer to as *opposers*) traditionally play the role of exposing such conflict and vigorously opposing the bodhisattva's intention to give, employing a variety of non-Buddhist (often Hindu dharmaśāstric) and general Indic cultural viewpoints that openly conflict with the Buddhist ideal of *dāna* in its more extreme forms. While the logic of such stories always assumes from the very beginning that such characters will never succeed in persuading the bodhisattva to refrain, they are often given ample opportunity to voice their concerns and make their arguments. The concerns and doubts they express about the gift constitute a multitude of competing voices and show that the ideal of *dāna* promoted by gift-of-the-body stories was by no means presumed to be self-evident. In fact, it is a basic feature of the genre that because the bodhisattva is such a static embodiment of virtue, it is his *opposers* with whom the reader is most likely to identify, and the utter reasonableness of *their* arguments that are perhaps most likely to persuade.

Ultimately, however, this conflict between the transcendent Buddhist values embodied by the bodhisattva and the everyday, pragmatic concerns embodied by those who oppose him must reach some sort of resolution in favor of the bodhisattva's point of view. Thus no matter how much resistance and opposition to the gift might be depicted, the bodhisattva is always allowed to answer his opposers, in many cases putting forth detailed counterarguments in favor of the gift and persuading them of the correctness of his conduct. Ethical argument alone is not enough, however—particularly when it pertains to transcendent values whose correctness and justifiability are far less obvious than the more immediate objections raised by the opposers[1]—and it is here that we see one of the strengths of the narrative form, for in some cases the story itself must attempt to persuade where ethical arguments fail to do so.

Thus no matter how much pain and tragedy is involved in making the gift, the bodhisattva's conduct is always ultimately vindicated by the outcome of the story: Sometimes, the bodhisattva's mere willingness to give melts the heart of the recipient, so that the gift does not have to be made, and the recipient is no longer a danger. Sometimes, the gift is made and the bodhisattva dies, but he is often reborn in heaven and leaves behind something of significant worth (such as relics or *caityas*)—and his opposers too usually gain an understanding of the larger significance of the gift in terms of its contribution to perfect Buddhahood. In those stories involving Śakra, Śakra either reveals his identity and puts a stop to the test before the gift is made, or he reveals his identity after the gift is made and then helps the bodhisattva restore his body by performing an Act of Truth. And in all cases, the bodhisattva's sincere show of generosity sets a moral example and induces others to do good. The outcome of the story, no matter how tragic, is never one of chaos, misfortune, or misery. By employing such stock "happy endings," gift-of-the-body stories suggest that the seeming conflict between *dāna* and other obligations is only illusory and results from a limited perspective. Appeal is made to a kind of overarching Buddhist cosmic and moral order that encompasses and overrides all narrower and more limited realms of interest, such that adherence to even the most extreme Buddhist ideals ultimately results in the greatest benefit for everyone.[2]

The degree and tidiness of this resolution vary, however, from one story to another, and once again we can point to some general differences between our three most typical plotlines. Stories featuring ordinary beings as the recipients of the gift and resulting in the bodhisattva's tragic loss of life on behalf of those who are pitiful or evil tend to offer the least satisfactory resolution. Because of the bodhisattva's tragic death and the grief and sadness of those he leaves behind, the absolute conflict between transcendent and pragmatic values initially posed by the gift is often allowed to hang numinously in the air, despite perfunctory and pro forma statements of its resolution. This, I contend, is fully intentional. It is in keeping, once again, with the status of these stories as the paradigmatic example of the "super-*jātaka,*" and the way in which the super-*jātaka* highlights the extraordinary nature of the bodhisattva, invites a response of awe, worship, and devotion, and makes little attempt to relate the heroic deeds of the bodhisattva to the everyday actions of ordinary Buddhists.

In contrast, stories in which Śakra is the recipient of the gift and the bodhisattva restores his body by performing an Act of Truth offer a greater degree of resolution—not merely because the bodhisattva *survives* the gift, but also because the very notion of *giving the gift and then getting it back* provides the reader with a concrete image of the conflict's resolution: the bodhisattva wants to give his body away, his opposers want him to keep his body, and the point is ultimately made that if he gives it away with utter sincerity, he will get to keep it as well. The universalistic demands of perfect generosity and the particularistic demands of family, community, and kingdom are thereby brought together through the give-and-get-back movement of the gift. The character of Śakra also plays a crucial role in the development of this resolution. Śakra, I believe, constitutes a kind of mediator between the Buddhist values of the bodhisattva and the everyday, worldly values of his opposers. As king of the gods, Śakra stands at the apex of the everyday world. Śakra's test of the bodhisattva thus constitutes a direct contest between worldly values and the Buddhist ideal. When the bodhisattva passes this test and Śakra must acknowledge his superiority, the Buddhist ideal is fully justified even from the worldly perspective most fully embodied by Śakra. Moreover, as I will demonstrate further below, the character of Śakra fulfills a number of "discursive functions" throughout the narrative that help to develop this resolution in a gradual manner and allow the reader to experience it dialectically. Again, all of this is in keeping with the status of these stories as "super-*jātakas*" that nevertheless begin to form a bridge to the ethos of the *avadāna*—compromising the "perfection" of generosity just enough to make the bodhisattva's heroic deeds of self-sacrifice in the past relatable to the ordinary Buddhist's actions and motivations in the present.

Finally, stories in which the gift is interrupted by either dramatic moral conversions on the part of the recipients or cosmic reactions on the part of the universe seem to go so far in resolving the conflict that they perhaps abort it rather than truly resolving it. On the one hand, the conflict between the bodhisattva and his opposers does reach some sort of resolution; on the other hand, because the gift itself is not depicted and the need to make the gift simply evaporates, this "resolution" seems to occur all too easily, and the mental "work" of resolution on the part of the reader is somehow absent. As a result, stories that follow this pattern strike the modern reader at least as the most didactic and unrealistic in nature. However, because these stories are presumably arguing that the *intention to give* is equivalent to the gift itself, perhaps it makes sense that the gift's supposed conflict with more pragmatic and worldly concerns would not require such elaborate resolution. Developing this resolution through the narrative can thus be sacrificed in favor of other ends.

The gift-of-the-body genre as a whole thus posits a fundamental conflict between the transcendent Buddhist ideal of *dāna-pāramitā* and the more pragmatic value systems of everyday life, with each of the three conventional plotlines resolving this conflict in different ways. In placing the three plotlines along a continuum running from "least" to "greatest" resolution of the conflict, however, I want to emphasize that the terms "least" and "greatest" suggest nothing whatsoever about the relative "success" or "failure" of a particular story. A story offering the "greatest" resolution is not necessarily the most "successful" story—nor does one offering the "least" resolution represent any kind of "failure." Instead, the intentional manipulation of conflict and resolution on the level of each individual story allows for the achievement of different effects, messages, and reading experiences across the genre as a whole—a way of gradually working out and thinking through the difficulties of the conflict and the possibilities (or impossibilities) of its resolution. Thus all gift-of-the-body stories are concerned with positing the conflict and then resolving it, but they make very different choices about how starkly to depict the initial conflict and how tidily to portray its resolution. Some stories are highly idealistic and propagandistic in nature, going out of their way to convince their readers of the ease and tidiness of Buddhist ideology's accommodation with the everyday world—while other stories are far more ambivalent. Moral ambiguity, multivalence, irony, and subversion are all present, and rather than reducing all texts of the genre to a simple (and simplistic) judgment—i.e., "These are nice, happy, didactic stories that promote the virtue of *dāna*"—any serious attention to Buddhist narrative must recognize this complexity and diversity. I follow Steven Collins here in invoking the "offensiveness" of Buddhist ideology—indeed, of all transcendentalist ideologies—or the manner in which such ideologies *affront* and *offend against* the ordinary concerns of everyday human life and community.[3] Buddhist authors were fully aware of this "offensiveness," and they grappled with it in sophisticated and creative ways.

Despite the complex and open-ended nature of this process, however, I also follow Collins in pointing to the importance of the concept of nirvana—or in our case, the concept of full and perfect Buddhahood—in acting as a *syntactical marker of closure* within the world of Buddhist narrative, particularly within the world imagined by the *jātakas*.[4] In other words, the *jātaka* genre, by its very definition (and whether or not this is made explicit), presupposes as its final teleological end point the bodhisattva's achievement of perfect Buddhahood. This end point, or "marker of closure," is always in the background and serves in some sense as an ultimate justification for whatever happens within the *jātaka* itself (should more mundane forms of justification fail to satisfy). In fact, I believe that it is precisely because of the implicit presence of this end point—Buddhahood as a presupposed Ultimate Good—that the gift-of-the-body genre becomes free to acknowledge (in some cases, to emphasize) the intractable difficulties posed by "perfect generosity": *Is perfect generosity really everything it's cracked up to be?* The image of a highly beloved figure taking a knife to his own flesh amidst the cries and protestations of those around him poses this question in the starkest possible manner, and the understood teleological end point of perfect Buddhahood allows for enormous creativity and freedom in suggesting a possible answer.

By the same token, however, if the ambivalence toward perfect *dāna* such stories sometimes display is ultimately made possible by the understood end point and *summum bonum* of perfect Buddhahood, then the reverse is perhaps equally true: the value of perfect Buddhahood itself depends upon the messiness in which it is sometimes immersed. Ultimate goals and universal ethical ideals are nothing more than cold and lifeless abstractions unless they are imaginatively placed within a world that *matters to us;* they are meaningless unless they are forced to grapple with the particular—and it is narrative that does this most effectively. This dependence of the universal upon the particular has been nicely stated by Alasdair MacIntyre in the following terms:

> The fact that the self has to find its moral identity in and through its membership in communities such as those of the family, the neighborhood, the city, and the tribe does not entail that the self has to accept the moral *limitations* of the particularity of those forms of community. Without those moral particularities to begin from there would never be anywhere to begin; but it is in moving forward from such particularity that the search for the good, for the universal, consists.[5]

This point was recognized by the Buddhist authors of gift-of-the-body tales, and its implications were explored within the world most amenable to such exploration—the imaginative world of the story.

In what follows, I hope to flesh out the interpretation I have offered above through a closer consideration of the conventional characters of gift-of-the-body stories and the roles they play within this rhetoric.

The Bodhisattva and His Motive

One way to bolster the claim that the bodhisattva within gift-of-the-body stories represents a perfect anthropomorphic embodiment of the abstract Buddhist ideal of *dāna* is by looking at the conventions used to depict him and the manner in which these conventions tend to be in close agreement with systematic and philosophical discussions of *dāna* found, for example, in exegetical (rather than narrative) texts. Although there are several different conventions that might be used for this purpose, I will here focus on only one—the statements made by the bodhisattva concerning his motive in giving the gift: what is the motive behind the gift, and what does the bodhisattva hope to accomplish by means of the gift?

Statements made by the bodhisattva in answer to these questions vary widely from story to story; in some stories, he barely mentions his motives at all, whereas in other stories (particularly from later texts), he may go on for several pages. Such statements form a large and heterogenous group and differ widely from one story to the next. However, there is also a smaller group of statements that are formalistic (and often ritualistic) in nature, conventional across a range of stories, and immediately recognizable as a group, employing the same phrases and ideas over and over again. These statements constitute one of the conventions associated with the bodhisattva and indicating his ideal nature as a perfect embodiment of *dāna*. They may be loosely divided into four different patterns of increasing complexity, which can be represented formulaically as follows:

1. *Simple Vows* (often explicitly referred to as *praṇidhāna* or *praṇidhi*): "By means of this gift, let A-B-C occur."
2. *Statements of Motive (stated positively, negatively, or both):* "I give this gift only for the sake of A-B-C" (*positive*); "I do not give this gift for the sake of X-Y-Z" (*negative*); "I do not give this gift for the sake of X-Y-Z, but only for the sake of A-B-C" (*positive and negative*).
3. *Vows including Statements of Motive:* "I do not give this gift for the sake of X-Y-Z, but only for the sake of A-B-C, and by means of this gift, let A-B-C occur."
4. *Vows including Statements of Motive and formulated as Acts of Truth* (sometimes explicitly referred to as *satyakriyā, satyādhiṣṭhāna,* or some equivalent expression): "I do not give this gift for the sake of X-Y-Z, but only for the sake of A-B-C, and if this is true, then by means of this gift, let A-B-C occur."[6]

While these patterns, as I have stated them, are somewhat artificial, and not all such statements will match up perfectly with one of these categories, nevertheless there is a significant group of immediately recognizable, formalistic statements that conform in a general way to these four basic patterns. Individual statements may be more or less elaborate, more or less complete, yet they all share a certain "family resemblance" that recalls them mutually to mind. Let us look at a few examples of different types:

(*Simple Vow*) By the gift of my head, may I quickly attain enlightenment![7]

(*Simple Vow*) [By means of this gift,] may I become a Buddha in this blind world, without leader and without guide. May I ferry across those who have not crossed, may I liberate those who are not liberated, may I console those who are despondent, and may I bring to complete nirvana those who have not attained complete nirvana![8]

(*Statement of Motive [negative]*) I do not give this [gift] for the sake of glory, nor do I desire sons or wealth or kingdoms.[9]

(*Statement of Motive [negative and positive]*) [By means of this gift,] there is nothing I wish to obtain in this world. Rather, having benefited all beings, I strive to obtain unsurpassed, perfect, full enlightenment.[10]

(*Statement of Motive [negative and positive]*) If I sacrifice my body, it is not in order to win riches, nor for sensual pleasure, nor for the love of my wife, children, or relations. What I covet is enlightenment, so that I can procure the welfare of all beings.[11]

(*Statement of Motive [negative and positive]*) The merit that I obtain from giving my head to you is not for the sake of [acquiring rebirth as] a Māra, a Brahmā, a Śakra, or a Cakravartin, nor because I desire the pleasures and enjoyments of the three worlds. Rather, I do this [only] because I wish to attain unsurpassed, perfect, full enlightenment, and to rescue all beings and establish them in nirvana.[12]

(*Vow including a Statement of Motive [negative and positive]*) O Kauśika, by means of this gift of my own body, I do not wish to become a Śakra, a Māra, a Brahmā, or a World-Protector, nor for rebirth in heaven, nor for the kingship of a Cakravartin, nor for any other human kingship. Rather, by means of this [gift], may I attain unsurpassed, perfect, full enlightenment! May I ferry across those who have not crossed, may I liberate those who are not liberated, may I console those who are despondent, and may I bring to complete nirvana those who have not attained complete nirvana! This is what I want.[13]

(*Vow including a Statement of Motive [negative and positive]*) This is not an attempt to win for myself a happy destiny, or the royal majesty of a universal king, or heaven with its singularly excellent joys, or even the bliss of liberation. But by whatever merit I may gain from wanting to rescue these people immersed in the wilderness, may I become the savior of the world, which is immersed in the wilderness of samsara![14]

(*Vow including a Statement of Motive [negative and positive] and formulated as an Act of Truth*) I am making a gift—an extraordinary gift, a gift exceeding all other gifts, a sacrifice of my own throat! But I make this sacrifice not for the sake of kingship, not for the sake of wealth, not to become Śakra, not to acquire the territories of kings and Cakravartins, and how much less for anything else! Rather, when I have awakened to unsurpassed, perfect, full enlightenment, may I tame those who are untamed, ferry across those who have not crossed, liberate those who are not liberated, comfort those who are despondent, and bring to complete nirvana those who have not attained complete nirvana. By these true words of truth, may my sacrifice bear fruit![15]

(*Vow including a Statement of Motive [negative and positive] and formulated as an Act of Truth*) I go to this trouble not out of ambition, nor out of a desire for fame, heaven, or kingship, nor even [to attain] perfect bliss for myself. On the contrary, I do this only in order to benefit others. As this is true, may I forever have the power to remove the world's suffering and simultaneously give it happiness and prosperity, just as the sun has the power to remove darkness and give off light.[16]

Examining these four patterns, it is clear that all such statements are concerned with the *denial of unacceptable motives for the gift* (X-Y-Z) and the *affirmation of acceptable motives for the gift* (A-B-C). The constant and repetitive invocation of the same items for A-B-C and X-Y-Z is what gives to these statements their conventional quality. What, then, are these "acceptable" and "unacceptable" motives, and what do they tell us about the bodhisattva?

The *unacceptable motives* denied by the bodhisattva are stereotypical in nature and include three basic types of inappropriate desire: the desire for a high karmic station (such as kingship, Cakravartinhood, devahood, Śakrahood, Mārahood, or Brahmāhood), the desire for the rewards of such high stations (such as kingdoms, wealth, glory, sensual pleasures, sons, or family), and the desire for individual tranquility, final emancipation, or final bliss. "Unacceptable motives" for the gift thus include all worldly and heavenly goals, all karmic goals, and even individual nirvanic goals that do not include a consideration of the welfare of others. The *acceptable motives* affirmed by the bodhisattva are overwhelmingly limited to two: the desire for omniscience or enlightenment or Buddhahood, and the desire to help beings, rescue beings, work for the welfare of the world, and so forth. Particularly clever in this regard is the bodhisattva's statement in *Jātakamālā* 1 that he gives the gift only *parārthasiddheḥ*—a phrase which, as Speyer has pointed out, can be interpreted as *either* "in order to benefit others" *or* "to attain the highest goal [of Buddhahood]," thus suggesting both "acceptable motives" within the same phrase.[17]

These "acceptable" and "unacceptable" motives invoked by the bodhisattva have not been chosen at random; in fact, they accord very closely with those hierarchical classifications of different types of *dāna* based on the motive behind the gift found throughout Mainstream and Mahāyāna *sūtra* and *śāstra* literature. A passage found in both the *Dīgha* and *Aṅguttara Nikāyas,*[18] for example, speaks of eight types of givers who give gifts with the hope of being reborn within specific high karmic stations—as a rich *kṣatriya,* brahmin, or householder, or as one of seven different types of deities. Although the passage promises such rewards to the virtuous giver (but not the nonvirtuous giver), it also assumes that any such desire to attain a high karmic station constitutes the motives of an "ordinary" giver, and for each case, it states (somewhat dismissively): "This intention of his, being directed at an inferior level and not cultivated to a higher level, will [only] result in rebirth within that realm."[19] In our stories, as we have seen, it is precisely the desire for such self-interested and limited karmic rewards that is invoked by the bodhisattva, but that must be denied, since the bodhisattva is an embodiment of ideal *dāna,* not an ordinary giver.

In general, classifications of *dāna* based on the motive behind the gift tend to subordinate all worldly and rebirth-oriented goals to the higher soteriological goal of attaining nirvana, or at least cultivating the mental states that lead to it. Very common throughout the Pāli Canon and other Buddhist texts are passages listing eight different types of gift, in which the eighth gift is contrasted to and made superior to the previous seven. In a passage from the *Abhidharmakośabhāṣya,* for example, the eight gifts are listed as: (1) the gift one gives because the recipient is nearby; (2) the gift one gives out of fear that the object will be destroyed anyway; (3) the gift one gives because the recipient had previously given to them; (4) the gift one gives with the hope that the recipient will return something greater; (5) the gift one gives because one's fathers and grandfathers gave; (6) the gift one gives with the hope of reaching heaven; (7) the gift one gives for the sake of one's reputation; and (8) the gift one gives "to ornament one's mind, to prepare one's mind, to [acquire] the equipment of yoga, and to obtain the highest goal [of nirvana]."[20] Of these, the first seven gifts are motivated by worldly and heavenly rewards, while the eighth gift is motivated by the aspiration for nirvana; correspondingly, the eighth gift is described as being "foremost" (*agra*).

Slight variations on this list also appear in two different passages from the *Aṅguttara Nikāya,* where (in both cases), the eighth gift is again given "to ornament and prepare one's mind [for nirvana]."[21] Also common is a distinction between those gifts that are "impure" (*aviśuddha*) and those that are "pure" (*viśuddha*), in which the latter is sometimes defined in terms of the goal of nirvana. Thus the *Mahāprajñāpāramitā Śāstra* in one passage defines the "pure" gift as "a gift made in view of the Path [to nirvana] . . . [and] not searching for happiness either in this world or the world beyond."[22] Thus the goals of mental and religious cultivation and individual liberation are consistently placed above all lesser worldly and heavenly goals.

But for the bodhisattva who aspires to Buddhahood, of course, even this does not suffice, and our stories thus consider even the goal of individual liberation to be an "unacceptable" motive that is often explicitly denied. In fact, the *only* "acceptable" motives for the bodhisattva's gift of his body are those motives that should incite *all* the actions of the bodhisattva (not merely giving)—that is, the desire to obtain Buddhahood and the desire to liberate and succor all beings. In some doctrinal texts this gift is placed alongside the gift aiming at nirvana as another variety of "foremost" gift appropriate specifically to the bodhisattva. In the *Abhidharmakośabhāṣya*'s discussion, for example, it is said that in addition to the gift given with the goal of attaining nirvana, "the gift that a bodhisattva gives for the welfare of all beings is [also] the foremost gift"[23]—as the sub-commentary by Yaśomitra further explains, "because it is given for the sake of perfect Buddhahood and for the sake of all beings."[24] In many Mahāyāna texts, on the other hand, this gift is exalted far above the gift aiming at nirvana. Thus, the *Mahāprajñāpāramitā Śāstra,* in spite of its praise of the "pure" gift aiming at nirvana, later distinguishes the gift of a *śrāvaka* from that of a Buddha or bodhisattva in the following terms:

> When one gives out of fear of old age, sickness, and death, this is the gift of a Śrāvaka. When one gives in order to acquire the state of a Buddha, in order to convert beings, and without fear of old age, sickness, and death, this is the gift of a Buddha or bodhisattva.[25]

Similarly, the *Bodhisattvabhūmi* defines the "pure gift" of the bodhisattva as a gift that is "indifferent to reward" in the form of either "material or bodily good fortune," but is made by the bodhisattva "seeing supreme Buddhahood [alone] as a blessing."[26]

The statements made by the bodhisattva concerning the motive underlying his gift are thus not random in nature, but intentionally chosen to be in close accord with the highest ideal of *dāna* expressed within exegetical and philosophical texts. These formalistic statements of motive are only one of the many conventions associated with the bodhisattva. Here I have merely used this convention as an example of the way in which the bodhisattva in these stories can be seen as constituting a perfect manifestation of *dāna*—or, as one story puts it, "the very embodiment of *dāna-pāramitā*."[27] As I argued above, however, this ideal cannot exist in isolation, but must be immersed within a real-world setting of opposition and conflict. Let me turn now to explore the conventional forms such opposition normally takes.

Opposition to the Gift

Just as certainly as the bodhisattva is willing and eager to give his body away, so also there are always one or more characters who *oppose* the bodhisattva's gift of his body and give active voice to this opposition throughout the course of the story. These characters, whom I will call *opposers,* are again conventional in nature and type, falling into four recognizable and consistent categories across a wide range of different tales: (1) *officials and ministers,* when the bodhisattva is a king (such as the army commander, the brahmin *purohita,* the king's vassals, or other types of officials and ministers); (2) *women* close to the bodhisattva (such as mothers, wives, and lovers); (3) *commoners* beholden to the bodhisattva (such as the king's subjects or a man's friends and companions); and (4) *minor deities,* usually those who preside over the location where the gift is taking place (such as the deity of a hermitage, a city-gate, a tree, or a pleasure-park).

I will argue below that each group of "opposers" represents some kind of limited social, familial, political, or religious realm of interest against which the absolute and transcendent value of *dāna* must be shown to take priority.[28] To foreshadow my argument a bit: The category of *officials and ministers* represents the realm of worldly political interests (the interests embodied in the concept of *nīti* or *realpolitik*), as well as traditional Hindu dharmaśāstric arguments concerning the conduct appropriate to each class of individuals in each stage of life (*varṅāśramadharma*), including the conduct proper to a king (*rājadharma*)—or, in broader terms, the interests of social and political order more generally. The category of *women* represents the realm of familial and affective interests, or the interests of specific and particularistic love and duty (especially those pertaining to wife and children). The category of *commoners* seems to represent the interests of traditional Indian extensions of the male head-of-household, such as servants, employees, and beggars, and the householder's paternalistic responsibility to such groups. Finally, the category of *minor deities* represents the limited religious interests of popular, local religious tradition over and against the universalistic religious interests of Buddhism.

Each of these realms of interest, embodied in the appropriate characters, puts forth its own variety of opposition to the gift. When the bodhisattva succeeds in overcoming each type of opposition and winning over all those who had opposed him, the Buddhist ideal of *dāna* in its most extreme form is seen to take precedence over all more limited realms of interest—indeed to *include* all more limited realms of interest—and the triumph of the Buddhist values embodied in the bodhisattva is thus assured (though again the degree and nature of this "triumph" are quite variable). It is through this opposition and its eventual resolution that the rhetoric of the genre manifests itself.

To support my association of each group of "opposers" with a particular limited realm of interest, in the following sections I examine more closely the specific arguments made against the gift by each of these four groups.

OFFICIALS AND MINISTERS: COMPETING NOTIONS OF KINGSHIP

In those stories in which the bodhisattva is a king, it is generally the king's officials and ministers who argue against the gift most vociferously. Moreover, out of all the characters I have labeled as "opposers," officials and ministers offer the most sustained and developed opposition, using a wide range of arguments and often opposing the gift from several points of view at once. Because they constitute the opposers par excellence, I will deal with these characters at some length and treat the other three categories more briefly.

The most immediate opposition to the gift offered by officials and ministers is the attempt to *substitute* material gifts for the gift of the body. "A supplicant should be given material goods," King Śibi's ministers urge him in *Mahajjātakamālā* 44,

> such as precious metals, jewels, and money; various types of ornaments, clothing, and so forth; furnishings, houses, etc.; elephants, horses, chariots, and vehicles . . . delectables such as food and drink . . . rice, corn, and other edibles; wonder-drugs and elixirs; kingdoms and so forth—all those things that are fit to be given, you should give. . . . Why should one give what is not to be given? One should give only that which is supposed to be given![29]

"What use does a poor man have for an eye?"—they further reason in *Jātakamālā* 2—"It will [only] see the prosperity of others! Therefore, Lord, give him money instead. Don't do anything rash!"[30]

Such substitutions are also urged on the recipient. In *Divyāvadāna* 22, for example, King Candraprabha's chief minister tries to prevent an evil brahmin from asking for the king's head by enticing him with a large pile of jeweled heads instead: "Great Brahmin, you take these many jeweled heads, and I will give you such abundant gold and silver that it will be the livelihood of your sons and grandsons. What do you want with the Lord's head, full of marrow, mucus, and fat?"[31] The stark contrast drawn in such passages between the attractive material riches that could be given to the recipient and the dismembered body parts the king proposes to give underscores the utter reasonableness of the ministers' urgings and the inconceivability of the king's intentions—particularly in a premodern South Asian context in which the description of material riches would no doubt be quite appealing to the majority of ordinary listeners, and in which strong cultural notions of bodily impurity would make the gift of the body (full of "marrow, mucus, and fat") rather *un*appealing. The conflict between the bodhisattva and his opposers is thus posed in a particularly stark manner, with the reader's own sentiments likely to be firmly on the side of the opposers.

What might simply appear, on the surface, to be a simple argument over what kind of object it is more reasonable to give, however, also contains an underlying discourse contrasting two competing notions of kingship and the dharma proper to a king (*rājadharma*). By urging the king to substitute material gifts for the gift of the body, officials and ministers uphold the king's proclivity for generosity, yet also try to force him to express this generosity through the means proper and appropriate to an Indian king—the traditional means of material gifting. In the dharmaśāstric literature dealing with kingship, generosity is one of the foremost virtues incumbent upon the Indian king, but this generosity is traditionally understood in the limited sense of material support of the people through the giving of material gifts.[32] By desiring to give away his *body* the bodhisattva-king clearly takes this ideal of royal generosity to an extreme that openly conflicts with his duties as a king—for how can a king who is blind, mutilated, or dead possibly continue to be a good king? The ministers' attempt to substitute material gifts for the gift of the body thus constitutes an attempt to keep the king bound within the limits of traditional Indic kingship, as well as to avoid whatever political chaos and instability might ensue from the death of the king. By rejecting such attempts at substitution, the bodhisattva-king rejects both the dharmaśāstric notion that moral conduct is relative to and dependent upon one's particular social position, and the arthaśāstric notion that a king's moral conduct must be limited to whatever is politically expedient—and in their place he embodies an idealistic Buddhist notion of kingship in which the best king is also one who adheres rigorously and without concession to the highest of Buddhist virtues (as we saw previously in the story of King Maitrībala). Or, to put it another way: the ministers promote a *sva-dharma*—literally, "one's own dharma," or the dharma that pertains to a particular social position (in this case, that of "king")—whereas the bodhisattva promotes a *sāmānya-dharma,* that is, a "universal" dharma that transcends any particular social position. The story itself, by means of the "happy endings" discussed earlier, resolves this conflict by arguing that the two are, in fact, wholly compatible: the *sāmānya-dharma* adhered to by the good bodhisattva is also the best *sva-dharma* for any good king.

The argument I have advanced here might be usefully compared to Steven Collins' discussion of kingly violence in *Nirvana and Other Buddhist Felicities.*[33] Collins maintains that one of the fundamental conflicts facing the authors of Pāli Buddhist texts in dealing with the theme of kingship was the issue of violence: How can the violence inherent in the institutions of kingship and political power be reconciled with the transcendent ideal of perfect nonviolence espoused by Buddhist monastic ideology? Collins maintains that Pāli texts, rather than positing any single answer to this question, offer a range of possible answers by means of a plethora of stories about kings.

In order to impose some order upon this range, he puts forth two contrasting notions of dharma (or "what is right") in relation to the kingly use of violence (particularly in the form of punishment). "Mode 1 dharma" is "an ethics of reciprocity, in which the assessment of violence is context-dependent and negotiable. Buddhist advice to kings in Mode 1 tells them not to pass judgment in haste or anger, but appropriately, such that the punishment fits the crime"[34]—in other words, some violence is necessary, and as long as it is administered fairly, it falls within the confines of dharma. "Mode 2 dharma," on the other hand, is "an ethic of absolute values, in which the assessment of violence is context-independent and non-negotiable, and punishment, as a species of violence, is itself a crime. The only advice possible for kings in Mode 2 might seem to be 'Don't be one!', 'Renounce the world!', 'Leave everything to the law of karma!'"[35]—in other words, violence is never acceptable, not even for a king. Using these two concepts to analyze and discuss an array of Pāli stories about kings, Collins demonstrates that some stories promote the negotiable Mode 1 dharma and suggest that a king who engages in appropriate and just punishment is a perfectly good king; some stories promote the non-negotiable Mode 2 dharma in such a way that kingship becomes impossible (the only good king being one who renounces the kingship altogether); and some stories imagine a world in which kingship *is* compatible with Mode 2 dharma by putting forth the "utopian paradox of the nonviolent king" ruling over a "Perfect Moral Commonwealth."[36] In other words, perfect nonviolence and the maintenance of social order become compatible because—in the utopian scenario envisioned by such texts—the king's virtue spreads to those around him, everyone behaves morally, and the law courts and prisons stand empty.

Though Collins' discussion deals with the theme of violence rather than the theme of generosity, on a larger level the conflict is much the same. In gift-of-the-body stories, we might say, the officials and ministers, promoting Mode 1 dharma, advocate a "context-dependent and negotiable" generosity, such that a king should give certain types of gifts to certain types of recipients in certain types of appropriate situations; while the bodhisattva, promoting Mode 2 dharma, advocates a "context-independent and non-negotiable" generosity, such that one should give whatever object is asked for to anyone who requests it.[37] The stories as a whole, rather than offering a full range of possible relationships between these two modes, generally come down in favor of Mode 2 and its compatibility with kingship within the context of a utopian vision of the "Perfect Moral Commonwealth." Thus, the king *can* give away his body and still be a good king with a prosperous and flourishing kingdom because of the very power of his virtue—which spreads to those around him, converts evil recipients so that they are no longer any danger, influences his own subjects to behave as perfect moral citizens, results (in many cases) in the restoration of his own injured body, and often causes nature itself to be bounteous and shower the kingdom with ever-replenishing wealth.[38] Thus, contrary to the ministers' expectations, the king's duty to uphold the transcendent ideal of *dāna* does not conflict in any way with his duty to be a good king.

Much the same fundamental conflict is found in a second major type of opposition to the gift offered by officials and ministers, which is to cite the disastrous consequences of the king's gift for various groups of people

In this case, it is not a question of *what type of gift* a king should give, but rather, *to whom he owes his allegiance:* Do some people deserve his loyalty and protection over others? In the *Maṇicūḍāvadāna,* for example, King Maṇicūḍa's brahmin *purohita* points out that if the king gives away his body, the wretched, blind, and miserable will be deprived of all protection, beggars and mendicants will be deprived of all support, the king's subjects will be sorrowful and despondent, and the queen and women of the harem will all die of grief.[39] Of course these are precisely the parties to whom the king owes a particular allegiance, and any reasonable reader will feel that they deserve more consideration than, say, a cannibalistic demon or an evil brahmin from a faraway land. The conflict once again can be reduced to competing notions of kingship; as King Maitrībala's ministers remark in *Jātakamālā* 8,

> O Lord . . . you bear the burden of kingship solely for the benefit of your people, [but] your determination to give away your flesh runs contrary to your own intentions! So let it go! . . . What kind of dharma is this by which the Lord would make the whole world fall into misfortune for the sake of these five [*yakṣas*] alone?[40]

As we saw already in chapter 2, however, King Maitrībala answers his ministers by citing his role as a moral exemplar as the very foundation of his kingly dharma—and the ending of the story ultimately bears him out. Effective political leadership and particularistic duty toward one's own subjects are thus shown to be reconcilable with universal compassion for all.

In some cases, in fact, a particular emphasis is placed once again on the inexorable and relentless *spread* of the king's virtue to others—which eventually makes meaningless any distinction between "one's own" subjects and everybody else. In *Mahajjātakamālā* 45, for example, King Sarvaṃdada's willingness to make a gift of his own head has a positive moral influence not only on the subjects of his own kingdom, but on *all other kings* as well: "Then, all of those kings, desirous of the happiness which comes from being renown for righteousness, gave gifts and worked for the world's welfare as much as they were able. . . . Thus, by the power of the bodhisattva's merit, everywhere on earth, a faultless and virtuous effort was set in motion on all sides."[41] Again in *Mahajātakamālā* 44 it is not merely the people of King Śibi's own kingdom who are affected by his version of kingly dharma, but rather, "through the truth, power, and strength of that dharma, there was happiness everywhere, in all kingdoms."[42] In the face of such radiant power, particularistic duties toward one's own subjects are easily subsumed within the bodhisattva's universal compassion for all.

In addition to attempting to substitute material gifts for the gift of the body and citing the king's responsibility toward particular groups of people, officials and ministers employ a wide variety of further arguments—for example, they invoke the glory of kingship and express amazement at the idea that anyone would do something to jeopardize such a high station; they cite commonsense, logical arguments against the gift (such as the impossibility of attaching one person's eye to another); and they warn the king that the recipient is a fraud whose only intention is to bring the king to ruin. But the general gist of such argumentation should by now be clear. In all of these cases, officials and ministers represent the worldly and pragmatic realm of politics, the interests of maintaining social order and political dominance, and traditional dharmaśāstric interests in enforcing *varṇāśramadharma*—all of which, by the end of the story, must somehow be reconciled with the absolute imperative of *dāna.*

This is similar to the role such characters play in many other types of Buddhist stories as well—a prominent example being stories of royal figures who wish to renounce the world and retire to the life of the forest, including the story of Siddhārtha Gautama himself. In a famous passage from the *Buddhacarita,* for example, King Śuddhodana's chief minister and brahmin *purohita* are sent to the forest to persuade the young Prince Siddhārtha to return to the kingdom after he has renounced the world.[43] Their arguments against Siddhārtha's renunciation are very similar to those we encounter in gift-of-the-body stories: first, they offer the dharmaśāstric argument that one should renounce the world only at the proper stage of one's life; second, they appeal to Siddhārtha's compassion for his family; third, they argue that renunciation is for the weak and timid (thus invoking the martial ethic of the *kṣatriya*); and fourth, they employ the argument of the *Bhagavad Gītā* that salvation is attainable through the disinterested fulfillment of one's traditional duties. Siddhārtha, of course, successfully counters each of these arguments and refuses to return back home.

This dialogue between radical bodhisattva-kings and their more traditional ministers continues throughout the Buddhist story tradition. Buddhist stories about bodhisattva-kings are not merely stories promoting the Buddhist ideals of *dāna,* nonviolence, and renunciation, but also stories that actively engage a much wider Indic and Hindu discourse on such matters as kingship, caste, good governance, and the ideal social and political order. Within this plethora of stories, we find a wide range of possible solutions offered to the conflict between Buddhist ideology and the realities of social and political life. In any particular story the two might be depicted as being completely compatible, completely incompatible, coexisting in a state of tension, or placed in a hierarchical relationship in which one is subordinate to the other. It is through the sheer diversity of narrative possibilities that the relationship between the two is negotiated.

OFFICIALS AND MINISTERS: A CASE STUDY

To further illuminate the opposition to the gift put forth by officials and ministers, I turn now to a specific case study. In this case study, a later text tells the same basic story as an earlier text but significantly expands the argumentation that occurs between the king and his ministers. Opposition to the gift is considerably heightened in the later text, with the ministers becoming more confrontational and adversarial characters and arguing against the gift more intensively than they do in the earlier version. Thus, even though the two texts tell the same basic story, the later text shows a greater willingness to use these conventional characters to confront and challenge the bodhisattva and suggest the possible problems inherent in his "perfect generosity." I include this case study not only to further illuminate the opposition to the gift offered by officials and ministers, but also to provide the reader with a specific example of generic variation—or how a later version of a story can extend and manipulate the rhetorical discourse of an earlier version while still remaining within the basic constraints of the genre.

Jātakamālā 2 (hereafter *JM* 2) and *Mahajjātakamālā* 44 (hereafter *MJM* 44) both tell the story of King Śibi's gift of his eyes to a brahmin supplicant (the god Śakra in disguise) and their eventual restoration by means of an Act of Truth. Moreover, the two texts are closely related, with the later text, *MJM* 44, being significantly based upon the earlier, *JM* 2. Out of the 220 verses that comprise *MJM* 44, thirty verses are borrowed directly from *JM* 2, 105 more verses are directly parallel to the corresponding material in *JM* 2 (in many cases being simple versifications or elaborations of the prose portions of *JM* 2), and only eighty-five verses (approximately thirty-eight percent of the total) represent content that is substantially new. Nevertheless, by identifying these eighty-five "new" verses and considering the kinds of adaptations they make, we can see that the author of *MJM* 44 had some very specific concerns in mind in his reworking of *JM* 2—in particular, a concern with heightening the opposition to the gift put forth by officials

TABLE 2
The Structure of *Mahajjātakamālā* 44 and Its Relationship to *Jātakamālā* 2

VERSES	CONTENT	
1–4:	Dialogue between Aśoka and Upagupta	external frame added
5–10:	Bodhisattva intentionally takes birth in the world as King Śibi to rescue all beings and make them "devoted to dharma"	internal frame added
11–94:	*Parallels with* Jātakamālā *2 (except for 8 verses, 6 of which involve dharma)*	
95–122:	The ministers oppose the gift as "bad dharma"	new arguments added
123–46:	King Śibi argues for the gift as "good dharma"	new arguments added
147–209:	*Parallels with* Jātakamālā *2 (except for 4 verses)*	
210–213	King Śibi's dharma spreads throughout the earth and he is reborn in heaven	internal frame added
214–220	Dialogue between Aśoka and Upagupta	external frame added

and ministers (as well as the countering of this opposition on the part of the bodhisattva), and a concern with resolving the conflict between them in a more explicit manner. (The relationship between the two stories is outlined in Table 2 as an aid to the following discussion.)

In the earlier version of the story found in *JM* 2, when King Śibi agrees to give both of his eyes to the brahmin supplicant, his officials and ministers put forth many standard varieties of opposition to the gift: They urge him to offer material gifts instead, they remind him of his duty to his own subjects, they wonder why anybody would be willing to give up the hard-won status of kingship, and they wonder how one person's eyes can possibly be attached to another. The bodhisattva, in refuting them, essentially ignores all of these pragmatic arguments and seems to speak purely from his transcendent status as a perfect bodhisattva who is concerned solely with fulfilling the imperative of *dāna,* regardless of whatever effect this might have on his kingdom. Two opposing sets of values are thus set in conflict with one another, and it is only the outcome of the story that resolves this conflict for us—for once King Śibi has survived the gift and prospered, we understand implicitly that his transcendent dharma as a bodhisattva overrides and encompasses the more worldly dharma espoused by his officials and ministers. This resolution remains implicit, however, being conveyed through the narrative action itself rather than being given any direct expression.

In *MJM* 44, on the other hand, it is clear that the author wishes to recast this entire exchange so that the underlying question becomes explicit: What is it that constitutes "dharma," and which variety of "dharma" is most beneficial, not only for the bodhisattva's own progress, but for the worldly welfare of his kingdom as well? In fact, it is striking to observe that a very long passage of the text running from verses 11 to 94 essentially repeats the entire argument between King Śibi and his ministers, as found in *JM* 2, with only eight new verses containing substantially different content—yet out of these eight new verses, six of them deal explicitly with the concept of dharma. Thus, in verses 54–56, the brahmin supplicant now frames his request for King Śibi's eyes specifically in terms of dharma:

> O Great King, I have come to you with the hope that you will give me an eye. By fulfilling this hope of mine, *you will increase your fame for dharma.* By respectfully giving to all supplicants whatever material goods they want . . . you have only begun to shine. Now fulfill my desire by giving me one of your eyes, and in this way, you will conquer all other givers and *attain fame for your excellent dharma*![44]

Likewise, in verse 83 King Śibi warns his ministers that they should not interfere with the gift of his eyes, "*for when it comes to dharma,* servants share in the efforts of their master"—only to have his ministers reply in verse 86: "O Lord . . . we servants are only conducting ourselves *in devotion to dharma.*"[45] Finally, in verse 90 the chief minister tries to prevent the gift of King Śibi's eyes by urging the king: "If one wants happiness and success *in the excellent dharma,* one should thoroughly and quickly investigate the effectiveness of his actions, and only then should one act."[46] Clearly the king and his ministers both believe that they are pursuing "dharma," even though they are proposing completely different courses of action. Through the strategic addition of these six new verses to what is otherwise a straightforward replay of the material found in *JM* 2, the author of *MJM* 44 succeeds in reframing the entire discussion as an argument over competing notions of dharma.

This subtle reframing of the argument then serves as an underpinning for *MJM* 44's single largest innovation on the earlier version. In a long passage spanning fifty-two "new" verses, the king and his ministers continue to debate the gift, offering wholly new arguments not found in the earlier text. From verses 95 to 122 the ministers argue against the gift, and from verses 123 to 146 the king counters by arguing in favor of the gift. The author of *MJM* 44 uses these extra passages to heighten both the ministers' opposition and the bodhisattva's resolve, as well as to frame the entire conflict in terms of competing notions of dharma. In verses 96–99, for example, one of the ministers, speaking for the others, states their position in the starkest possible terms—and makes clear what the ministers stand for and what the bodhisattva is so opposed to—by drawing an explicit equation between *nīti* and *dharma,* between the "art of politics" and "what is right":

O Master and Great King, for the sake of your own welfare, you should listen to what I have to say. You are practicing a brand of politics (*nīti-dharma*) that is not beneficial to the world! Neglecting your people through this foolish brand of politics (*anīti*), how will you attain dharma? And without dharma, there is suffering, and the one who suffers is tormented. . . . [Therefore,] respecting that which is honored as the art of politics (*nīti*), if one wishes to rescue people, one should place the practice of the art of politics (*nīti-dharma*) above everything else, and then give the gifts that are desired.[47]

By twice using the compound *nīti-dharma,* the ministers suggest that *nīti* itself is a kind of dharma—but by also stating explicitly that *without nīti, there is no dharma,* they make the further suggestion that, at least when it comes to King Śibi, *nīti* is *dharma.* King Śibi, however, states his rebuttal just as clearly: the universal dharma he adheres to as a bodhisattva overrides but also encompasses any royal dharma incumbent upon him as a king:

Dharma is the only thing that death can never conquer. Therefore, dharma is a great hero and should be perfected for the welfare of the world. Dharma can conquer everything, everywhere, at all times, while not even a multitude of sins can conquer dharma. . . . Therefore, those good people who seek virtue should abandon everything else and always zealously perfect dharma alone, for the welfare of the world.

And among all dharmas, the dharma of the Buddhas (*saugataṃ dharmam*) is the best, for it renders all sin throughout the triple world completely harmless. It is through the power of the dharma that all Sugatas of the past benefited the world, attained enlightenment, and were liberated. It is through the power of the dharma that all of those who are Conquerors right now, having attained complete enlightenment, stand ready to bring about the welfare of the triple world. And it is through the power of the dharma, again, that all those who will be [Buddhas in the future] will conquer all of Māra's troops and effect the welfare of the world.

And I, too, wish in every way to follow the dharma, attain complete enlightenment, conquer Māra and his troops, and do good on behalf of the world. This is why I wish to give to this old brahmin even the eye attached to my own body. . . . Because I yearn for the welfare brought about by the good dharma right here within samsara, I am indifferent even to my own life and quite capable of giving up my eye. Therefore, you should not hinder my gift. For when it comes to the practice of the dharma, servants should only be of assistance. Realizing this, you should sympathetically rejoice in my gift, for by the power of this dharma, you, too, will attain enlightenment.[48]

On the one hand, King Śibi's invocation of the innumerable Buddhas of the past, present, and future, their attainment of perfect enlightenment, and their conquering of Māra calls forth all of the authority and grandeur of the transcendent Buddhist dharma manifested by his gift—a cosmic dharma which is the "best among all dharmas" that might exist. But on the other hand, he further makes it clear that this dharma also leads to happiness and welfare "right here within samsara" and is thereby equivalent to his dharma as a worldly king.

The priority of King Śibi's universal dharma over the *nīti-dharma* advocated by his ministers must be reinforced, of course, by the story as a whole, and it is interesting to note the manner in which the remaining "new" verses added by the author of *MJM* 44 function to do exactly that. In his narration of the story, the author of *MJM* 44 adds two new frames that are absent from the earlier version. The first new "framing" of the basic story occurs in verses 5–10 at the beginning of the tale and verses 210–213 at the end. In verses 5–10, we learn that the bodhisattva's birth as King Śibi was neither random nor accidental, but took place for a very specific reason: the bodhisattva was "a wise king of the gods in heaven" who looked down upon the earth one day, saw that "all beings everywhere on earth were behaving wickedly," became "determined to rescue them" and "to make mortal humans devoted to dharma," and thus "took birth in the royal family of the Śibis."[49] The bodhisattva's birth as King Śibi is now made fully intentional—and his intent is not merely to be a good king to the Śibi people, but to rescue all beings and make them "devoted to dharma." The universalizing effect these verses have on the basic story is subsequently reinforced at the end of the story, in verses 210–213, where we learn that the moral example the king sets by giving away his eyes spreads inexorably to all kingdoms throughout the world, and the king himself is subsequently reborn up in heaven, where he "continued to work for the welfare and benefit of the world with a mind directed toward full enlightenment."[50] The addition of this frame demonstrates for the reader the larger significance of the dharma adhered to by King Śibi and its complete compatibility with his ministers' more immediate (and local) concerns.

The second new "framing" of the basic story added by the author of *MJM* 44 occurs in verses 1–4 at the beginning of the story and verses 214–220 at the end. This is an external frame story in which the tale of King Śibi is set within the context of a dialogue between the great Buddhist king Aśoka and the famous arhat Upagupta. In verses 1–4, King Aśoka asks Upagupta to tell him the story of a "well-done deed" performed by the Buddha in a previous birth, and Upagupta agrees to do so.[51] After relating the entire story of King Śibi, the text returns to this external frame-story in verses 214–220, where Upagupta concludes by telling King Aśoka that it was by means of giving away his eyes that the bodhisattva "engaged in the practice of dharma," and that King Aśoka himself must "tell the people about the Teacher's practice of excellent dharma, place them on the paths leading to enlightenment, and rule over them," whereupon Aśoka and his retinue rejoice.[52]

By means of this external frame, the story of King Śibi is now located within a very specific context: it is a story told to a *king,* and it is narrated by a *Buddhist monk.* We could say that the monk, as representative of Buddhist transcendentalist ideology, is thus placed in a position of authority and instruction over the king, as representative of the realm of worldly, political power—yet the message of the monk's story is that the two realms are wholly compatible. In fact, in the end Upagupta addresses King Aśoka himself as a bona fide bodhisattva, for his final words to the king are: "Through the power of this meritorious work, may you always have good fortune! And having gradually fulfilled the requisites for enlightenment, may you finally attain it!"[53] The compatibility of kingship and bodhisattvahood suggested by the story of King Śibi is thus reinforced by the addition of this external frame.[54] Through this and other strategically placed additions, the author of *MJM* 44 succeeds in both heightening and sharpening the ministers' opposition to King Śibi's gift and demonstrating the correctness of the bodhisattva's reply.

OTHER OPPOSERS: WOMEN, COMMONERS, AND MINOR DEITIES

The three remaining groups of opposers and the limited realms of interest they embody can be treated more briefly, since many themes similar to those we have seen above also come into play here.

Women close to the bodhisattva (such as mothers, wives, and lovers) tend to respond to the gift with abundant emotion—frequently crying, wailing, fainting, and lamenting—which is suitable, I contend, to their role as representatives of affective, familial, and sexual interests, or the interests of specific and particularistic love. Again we see a close correspondence between stories involving renunciation and stories involving self-sacrifice: just as angry wives constitute the major obstacle to their husbands' renunciation of the world and ordination as Buddhist monks in so many Buddhist tales,[55] here also women oppose the bodhisattva's self-sacrifice because of the way in which it breaks up the family, leaves the woman abandoned and grieving, and otherwise conflicts with the male bodhisattva's traditional obligations toward wife and children. The opposition expressed by women thus pits the particularistic claims of familial love and affection against the universal compassion for all beings characteristic of the bodhisattva.

A good example of such arguments is the long, passionate speech delivered by Queen Padmāvatī in the *Maṇicūḍāvadāna,* when King Maṇicūḍa is on the verge of death, having cut up his body to feed a hungry *rākṣasa:*

> Alas, alas, Lord, alas, you who are supremely virtuous and greatly compassionate, Hero in Generosity, Protector of the World! Where have you gone, abandoning me without a protector, extremely depressed and wandering in the wilderness? Alas, Lord, please turn back! . . . Oh Lord, I am blameless, yet you have abandoned me. Alas, Illustrious One, I am ruined, miserable, and depressed. . . . O Sinless One, you even promised Bhavabhuti, my father, that you would never abandon his daughter. Did you make such a promise in vain? . . . So please turn back! . . . Or, if you have decided that you absolutely must go, O Brave One, then take me along as well—your queen and slave, who is devoted to your feet. Having entered the fire out of love for you, I will die together with you.[56]

Female characters are frequently used in this way in traditional Indian literature: we might cite, for example, the pitiful lamentations of Siddhārtha's wife and the women of his harem after he renounces the world in the *Buddhacarita,*[57] Queen Maddi's long and sorrowful lament for her missing children in the *Vessantara Jātaka,*[58] and, as a Hindu example, Draupadī's somewhat angry rebuke of her husbands for failing to protect her in the *Mahābhārata.*[59] By virtue of their lower social and political status, I would argue, women come to be representative of the personal and familial bonds of love. They thus constitute effective agents for presenting emotionally compelling arguments with which the reader can easily identify, and which seem to make a mockery of the coldly abstract ideal embodied by the male hero. In Victor Turner's terms, they possess the "powers of the weak" that allow them to stand in temporary moral judgment of the superior bodhisattva.[60] Thus, while the male hero is valiantly pursuing some abstract and universalistic ideal, it is the women in his life who tend to remind us who gets hurt in the process. It is interesting to note, as well, that while the bodhisattva generally expends enormous energy in refuting the objections of his officials and ministers, his most common response to the women in his life is one of utter silence. Queen Padmāvatī, for example, gets no reply to her impassioned speech because the story—perhaps all too conveniently—has Maṇicūḍa faint from his injuries just before it begins and wake up only once it has concluded.[61] (Perhaps he's a typical husband after all!) Nevertheless, the conclusion of the story, in one way or another and to varying degrees, always vindicates the bodhisattva's conduct: the best bodhisattva also makes the best husband.

Our third category of "opposers," that of *commoners* beholden to the bodhisattva (such as the king's subjects or a man's friends and companions), is much less frequently encountered than the first two. In fact, commoners do not frequently speak for themselves, but as we have seen, their interests are often taken up by officials and ministers. In any case, in arguments against the gift from the point of view of commoners beholden to the bodhisattva, their affection for the bodhisattva, the grief they will feel if he abandons them, their dependence on him, and his paternalistic responsibility toward them are emphasized. Within such arguments commoners are frequently depicted as children losing a parent, or inferiors losing a paternalistic superior. Therefore, I believe that the category of commoners represents the interests of traditional Indian extensions of the male head-of-household, such as servants, employees, and beggars, as well as the subjects of the king (a sort of "super" head-of-household, as it were). Inasmuch as such groups constitute extensions of the householder's self, for the householder to give himself away (by giving away his body) constitutes an abrogation of his responsibilities toward them. Once again, however, the outcome of such stories fully justifies the bodhisattva, for whether or not he survives the gift, his conduct is always depicted as having a positive moral effect on the commoners beholden to him. As King Śibi puts it: "When it comes to dharma, servants share in the efforts of their master."

Finally, *minor deities,* the fourth category of "opposers," generally react to the gift in childish, emotional, and sometimes violent ways. They do not offer specific, logical arguments against the gift, but simply lash out at the recipient. In the *Maṇicūḍāvadāna* the deity of the hermitage where King Maṇicūḍa is about to give away the jewel embedded in his head yells at the brahmin recipients: "Alas, alas, you sinful brahmins! How can you cause the death of this royal sage, who is most compassionate, devoted to all beings, blameless and harmless?"[62] Likewise, in *Divyāvadāna* 22 the deity of a city-gate tries to prevent a brahmin recipient from entering the city to ask for King Candraprabha's head, saying: "Do not enter, you evil and vicious brahmin!"[63]—while in the *Sūtra of the Wise and the Fool* 22, it is a tree-deity who becomes incensed, going so far as to strike the brahmin recipient across the face, causing him to fall to the ground.

As far as I can tell, such reactions on the part of minor deities occur primarily in those stories in which the bodhisattva is a king. When seen from this perspective, such reactions are, in a sense, entirely appropriate to the protective functions of such deities, for as the guardians and benefactors of the territory, they have a duty to protect the king who rules over it. In all such cases, however, there seems to be an attempt to make such deities seem not merely protective, but also irrational and short-sighted, especially in contrast to the bodhisattva himself. I believe that such deities represent the realm of local, popular religious interests, and that the translocal and cosmological authority of Buddhism over such interests is demonstrated by the fact that the bodhisattva always sternly rebukes the deity and is successful in making him[64] "fall silent."

By means of this rebuke, the bodhisattva-king thus proclaims his territory to be a realm in which the Buddhist dharma holds priority over popular folk religion (even in the absence of "Buddhism" itself!). The *way* in which the bodhisattva rebukes such deities is also significant. Rather than employing ethical argument (as in the case of officials and ministers) or simply remaining silent (as in the case of females), the bodhisattva tends to rebuke minor deities through a very specific type of appeal: usually, the local deity's opposition to the gift is shown to be short-sighted through an appeal to Buddhist cosmology and sacred geography. That is, by placing events in an ages-long, cosmic and mythological perspective, the bodhisattva succeeds in demonstrating the deity's purely local concerns to be trivial, and the deity falls silent and allows the gift to be made.

In the *Maṇicūḍāvadāna* episode mentioned above, for example, whereas the deity of the hermitage is concerned with *this particular king* giving away *this particular crest-jewel,* King Maṇicūḍa rebukes him by placing the gift within a much larger context—the bodhisattva's long journey to perfect enlightenment and the similar deeds performed by him at the very same spot during thousands of previous lives:

> Enough, enough, deity! Do not obstruct my supplicant! Do not hinder my enlightenment! And why is that? In the past, deity, a supplicant approached me, asking for my body. He was hindered by some deities. By hindering him, they hindered my enlightenment and produced a lot of demerit for themselves. If they had not hindered my supplicant, I would have very soon attained unsurpassed, perfect, full enlightenment. Moreover, deity, at this very spot of earth, I have sacrificed my body a thousand times, and no one has ever hindered me before. Therefore, I say to you: Do not hinder my supplicant! Do not cast my unsurpassed, perfect, full enlightenment into the far distance![65]

By means of this rebuke, the deity's objections to the gift are now dramatically reconfigured within a wholly new frame: his misguided attempt to protect the local territory might, in fact, be delaying the appearance of a Buddha in the world—and not a single one of his one thousand predecessors has ever made such a fatal mistake before.

In *Sūtra of the Wise and the Fool* 22, a similar statement is made, but the aura of cosmic inevitability surrounding the gift becomes even stronger, for King Candraprabha explains to the tree-deity:

> In the past, I have given my head away at this tree nine-hundred-and-ninety-nine times. Now, with this head, I will complete one thousand gifts and fulfill the perfection of giving! So please do not hinder my aspiration for the highest enlightenment![66]

And finally, in *Divyāvadāna* 22, King Candraprabha's rebuke of the deity expands to include a well-known Buddhist mythological figure as well:

> Do not hinder the supplicant who wants my head! For it was here in this very [pleasure-park], deity, that I once sacrificed myself to a tigress and thus outdistanced

Maitreya, who had set out [for Buddhahood] forty eons before. Maitreya Bodhisattva was outdistanced by a single gift of my head![67]

Now the local deity learns that not only is he delaying the appearance of a fully enlightened Buddha in the world, but he may in fact be interfering in two bodhisattvas' cosmic race toward Buddhahood—ruining Śākyamuni's "lead," as it were.

Within the bodhisattva's rebuke, then, the imperative to make the gift is not merely a moral imperative but becomes a matter of cosmological inevitability. The full authority and grandeur of the Buddhist universe is solemnly invoked, and the deity's purely local religious concerns are revealed to be trivial and insignificant. In terms of history, we might see such passages as reflecting, on the narrative level, the complicated process by which Buddhism, as an elite and translocal ideology expressed through formal languages such as Sanskrit and Pāli, coexisted with popular, local religious traditions.[68] In terms of literature, on the other hand, such passages once again take us back to a consideration of genre—for the shift in perspective between a "local" frame and a "cosmological" frame employed so effectively by such passages is possible precisely because of the double time-perspective inherent to the *jātaka:* within the bodhisattva's rebuke, we are suddenly reminded of what we have known all along—that this particular human king will one day become the exalted Buddha himself.

CAN THE BODHISATTVA BE ALL THINGS TO ALL BEINGS?

As we have seen, the four standard groups of opposers I have identified above are used to represent various limited realms of interest against which the Buddhist ideal of *dāna* must be shown to take priority—such as worldly political interests (*nīti*), Hindu dharmaśāstric interests in maintaining *varṇāśramadharma,* familial and affective interests, the interests of traditional Indian extensions of the male head-of-household, and the interests of popular, local religious tradition. Each of these realms of interest is defined in terms of social structure; in other words, the representatives of each realm of interest have legitimate claims upon the bodhisattva (as king, husband, etc.) because of the social-structural position they themselves inhabit (as official, minister, wife, etc.)—position-bound claims that have been specified and authorized in a long tradition of Indian śāstric literature.

FIGURE 4 King Śibi, with the help of his attendants, has his flesh cut and weighed on a scale in order to ransom the life of a dove (lower left); the deity Śakra is the crowned figure second from right. Sculptural frieze from Gandhāra, ca. 2nd century C.E. © Copyright The Trustees of the British Museum.

In some passages, however, we encounter a form of opposition that is far more general and philosophical in nature and perhaps more difficult to answer: How can universal compassion be shown toward beings with very particularistic desires? What if one generic being's demands upon the bodhisattva conflict with those of another generic being? In this case, it is not a question of specific groups of people who have legitimate claims upon the bodhisattva's allegiance that have been vouchsafed by Indic tradition, but rather, the more basic question: *Can the bodhisattva really be all things to all beings?*

In *Avadānakalpalatā* 55, a frightened dove takes refuge with King Śibi (here called King Sarvaṃdada), who resolves to safeguard the dove's life. A hunter, however, soon appears on the scene and argues that the dove ought to be released to him. After all, he observes, hunting for such prey is his "birth-given occupation," the dove constitutes food that is "natural" to him, and if he cannot hunt for such doves, his whole family will soon die.[69] This seems reasonable enough, but since King Śibi is determined to safeguard the dove's life, what can he possibly do? Since both the hunter and the dove must be assumed to be subjects of Śibi's kingdom, this is not a situation pitting insider against outsider, but a more fundamental conflict between one creature and another. The hunter himself poses this conflict in the starkest possible terms: "You should not show hatred to me out of affection for the dove. . . . As he is, so am I. What difference is there between us to you? Good people who are impartial toward all beings should not show compassion to one alone."[70]

This conflict is further heightened by the phrases used to describe the king throughout the story: he is favorably compared to a "wish-fulfilling jewel that grants whatever one can think of" and a "tree of plenty that produces exactly what one wants," and described as one who "listens to the needs of all the world, as if with innumerable bodies"—yet here he is, a single mortal body stuck between the competing claims of a hunter and a dove.[71] In *Kalpanāmaṇḍitikā* 64—in which the dove is being sought by a hawk rather than a hunter—King Śibi states that the dove must be protected because "when I made the vow to attain enlightenment, I accorded my protection to all beings"—only to have the hawk turn his own words against him: "If your words are true," he points out, "then quickly give me the dove. For if you cause me to die of hunger, you will no longer be showing compassion." Even King Śibi is momentarily undone by this reasoning, for he says to himself: "I find myself in an extremely difficult situation."[72]

In keeping with the "utopian" nature of the gift-of-the-body genre, of course, even this intractable situation is easily resolved (in both versions of the story) by means of the gift of the body: the king gives his own flesh away, and the needs of both the dove and the hunter/hawk are satisfied (see figure 4). Nevertheless, the question has been raised, and it hangs in the air: What if more doves, hunters, and hawks continued to make the very same requests? What would the bodhisattva do then? Can the bodhisattva really be all things to all beings?

In the first three acts of the *Lokānandanāṭaka,* a dramatized version of the Maṇicūḍa story authored by Candragomin in the fifth century C.E. but now extant only in a Tibetan translation, this question is posed in a particularly bold and daring manner. This first half of the play—which takes place during King Maṇicūḍa's youth—deals not with the two gifts of the body for which Maṇicūḍa is famous (the gift of his flesh to a *rākṣasa* and the gift of his crest-jewel to an enemy king), but rather with the issue of marriage. The maiden Padmāvatī is deeply in love with Prince Maṇicūḍa, and everyone wishes to see them married, including both of their parents. Maṇicūḍa, however, has no interest in marriage; he sees marriage as an "incurable sickness"[73] and wishes only to renounce the world so that he can work on becoming a Buddha.

After several different characters have tried and failed to persuade him to go along with his family's wishes, the heavenly fairy Ratnāvalī, understanding that Maṇicūḍa is a bodhisattva intent upon universal compassion, hits upon the perfect plan. Toward the end of act 2 she approaches Maṇicūḍa and throws herself at his feet, begging him for help. When he asks her what she wants, she replies: "O Great and Powerful One, your body!"[74] Of course, this is precisely what Maṇicūḍa, the compassionate bodhisattva, has been waiting for all along—a chance to give away his body in an act of perfect generosity. "O Sister who asks for my body," he thinks to himself with excitement, "now at last I see a supplicant who is daring!"[75]—whereupon Ratnāvalī goes in for the kill:

> O Great and Powerful One . . . If the mere sight of your body can relieve all of the torment suffered by a person, then that person should remain with you! My affectionate friend [Padmāvatī] is suffering from a headache that will [only] go away if she sees you, O Great and Powerful One. There is no other relief![76]

Ratnāvalī, of course, has mischievously tricked Maṇicūḍa, using his own professions of universal compassion to get him to fulfill the particularistic duty of marriage: If he really wants to be compassionate, she suggests, why not start at home? Maṇicūḍa recognizes the trick and continues to resist until the end of act 3, when he is finally forced—both by Ratnāvalī's cruel logic and by his own growing desires—to accept the equivalence between Padmāvatī and other recipients of his compassion. "Since I am greatly compassionate," he says, "I will sacrifice myself for her sake."[77]

The *Lokānandanāṭaka* here is boldly *reversing* the usual line of argumentation, subordinating the universal to the particular rather than the other way around—and deflating its hero's pretences in the process. In fact, Ratnāvalī's trick has the effect of suggesting that the bodhisattva's "universal compassion" is perhaps not so "universal" after all—since it is far more interested in hungry demons and evil brahmins than it is in the members of his own family. Maṇicūḍa's good friend Gautama, fulfilling the typical hero-deflating function of the *vidūṣaka* in a Sanskrit drama,[78] makes this suggestion explicit when he questions Maṇicūḍa—"If you wish to benefit the world of relatives and kinsmen, then why do you stay so far away from it?"[79]—and when he describes Maṇicūḍa, the bodhisattva, as being "without compassion," "lacking even affection," and "devoid of any sympathy" in relation to his own family.[80]

As Gautama's biting remarks make clear, generosity here is not so much a concern with the *other* as it is a concern with *oneself,* for the bodhisattva, in order to display his perfect generosity both to himself and to other beings, relies upon recipients who are pitiful and evil—not beautiful, high-born maidens. Of course one must make note of the fact that this is only act 3; by the end of the play, Maṇicūḍa will succeed twice over in demonstrating that he *can* give his body to lowly creatures and still be the best possible king and husband—and outside of the play stands the final end point of perfect Buddhahood, the ultimate justification for everything. Nevertheless, in regard to the initial question I raised—Can the bodhisattva be all things to all beings?—the *Lokānandanāṭaka* goes a very long way toward saying: "No—at least not until he is a Buddha."

A similar boldness is displayed in a passage from the *Mahāprajñāpāramitā Śāstra,* in its discussion of the six perfections.[81] When the narrator of the text states that each of the bodhisattva's perfections should be practiced in conjunction with the others, his interlocutor points to the possibility of conflict: If someone were to ask the bodhisattva-monk for his monastic robes or alms-bowl, for example, the "perfection of morality" would require him to refuse (since this is forbidden by the Vinaya), but the "perfection of generosity" would require him to assent—so what is he supposed to do? The narrator answers plainly that a "beginner bodhisattva" cannot practice all the perfections at the same time, and he illustrates this point by means of a rather startling reference to the tigress story: When the bodhisattva practiced the "perfection of generosity" by giving his body to the hungry tigress, his mother and father were blinded by grief, and the tigress was karmically punished for killing the bodhisattva. "However," he concludes, "the bodhisattva considers neither the sorrow of his parents nor the punishment reserved for the tigress: He wishes only to accomplish the gift and gain merit."[82] So much for "universal" compassion!

In chapter 5, I return to this theme of the ambiguity surrounding the bodhisattva's "perfect generosity" and the underlying aggression that is perhaps inherent in his gift. For now I raise the issue simply to emphasize once again the willingness of the genre to confront and challenge its own most cherished ideals, and the importance of those conventional characters I have called "opposers" in fulfilling this rhetorical function.

Opposition to the gift is not always so rhetorically explicit, however. In the following section I turn to the treatment of several minor conventional characters who present further obstacles to the gift, thus adding to the dramatic tension of these stories.

Other Conventional Characters

I have already had occasion thus far in my discussion to mention all of the major conventional characters that populate the gift-of-the-body genre—the *bodhisattva,* who gives away his body or is willing to give away his body; the *recipient,* who is the intended target of the bodhisattva's gift (and who is either an ordinary being or the god Śakra in disguise); and those heterogenous characters I have called *opposers* (most often, officials and ministers, women, commoners, and minor deities), who oppose the bodhisattva's intention to give and actively argue against it. I turn now to a brief discussion of three further types of characters that also demonstrate conventional qualities, whom I refer to as the *false donor,* the *envoy,* and the *reluctant helper.* Each of these characters further adds to the dramatic tension of the plot by in some way causing obstacles to the completion of the gift. Each type of character thus plays a particular role in the rhetoric of the genre as a whole.

THE FALSE DONOR

In some stories, the bodhisattva is contrasted with one or more *false donors,* characters who are in the same situation as the bodhisattva himself but behave in a very different manner. Thus in Pāli *Jātaka* 316, as we have already seen, the bodhisattva, who is a hare, has three companions—a monkey, a jackal, and an otter. All four animals are obligated to give food to a wandering brahmin. The monkey, jackal, and otter all give ordinary food to the brahmin, which contrasts sharply with the hare's gift of his own body. Moreover, the text explicitly tells us that the monkey, jackal, and otter all take pride in their own virtue, which again contrasts sharply with the hare's complete selflessness and single-minded concern for the welfare of the recipient. We might call the monkey, jackal, and otter *false donors* who are faced with the same situation as the bodhisattva himself, but who fail to act in the same exalted manner.

Likewise, in the eighteenth chapter of the *Suvarṇabhāsottama Sūtra* the bodhisattva is a prince named Mahāsattva, while the false donors are his two brothers, Mahāpraṇāda and Mahādeva. When all three brothers encounter a starving tigress, Mahāpraṇāda and Mahādeva go off and search for ordinary food, while Mahāsattva gives the tigress his own body. This contrast between Mahāsattva and his brothers is foreshadowed at the beginning of the story, for before entering the great forest where they will encounter the starving tigress, Mahāpraṇāda says that he is afraid of being destroyed by a wild animal, Mahādeva says that he is afraid of being separated from their parents, and Mahāsattva says that he is afraid of nothing at all. Not only does the bodhisattva's fearlessness contrast with the false donors' fears, but the false donors' fears (destruction by a wild animal and separation from parents) are the very fate that the bodhisattva will willingly and gladly undergo.

In *Divyāvadāna* 32, where there are three brahmin ascetics rather than three princely brothers, the situation is much the same: When faced with the starving tigress, two of the ascetics remark, "Who could sacrifice his life for the sake of a mere animal?"—whereupon the third ascetic (the bodhisattva) answers: "I can sacrifice my life for the sake of a mere animal!"[83] In yet other versions of the tigress story, as we have seen, a single false donor is identified as a previous birth of the bodhisattva Maitreya, who fails to consider giving the tigress his own body and thus falls behind Śākyamuni in the race for Buddhahood by nine incalculable eons.

The rhetorical function of such false donors seems fairly obvious: the contrast between their behavior and that of the bodhisattva serves to highlight the uniqueness of the bodhisattva's virtue and the extraordinary nature of his gift. The bodhisattva's excellence is doubly emphasized when set against the background of the other characters' utter failure to meet the same exalted standard; as the false donor in *Jātakamālā* 1 states, "Oh, how his heroic accomplishment sheds harsh light on my own unruliness!"[84] The presence of the false donor thus reinforces the exaltation and idealization of the bodhisattva characteristic of the genre's rhetoric as a whole.

At the same time, however, it is also possible in some cases to see the false donor's role as one of casting doubt upon the bodhisattva's "perfect" conduct by presenting a *more reasonable* reaction to the situation than that pursued by the bodhisattva himself. In the hare story, for example, there is no reason why the brahmin should not be perfectly satisfied with the ordinary food presented to him by the monkey, jackal, and otter—which perhaps suggests to the reader that the hare's urgent desire to immolate himself in a fire is both unreasonable and unnecessary. (As the brahmin wanderer puts it in one version of the hare story, "What is this reckless, excessive, and repugnant deed that you're doing?!")[85]

Thus, whether they are intended to exalt the bodhisattva's conduct or to diminish it, false donors illustrate for the reader the normal, pragmatic response that one might expect in such a situation—which then becomes a background against which to interpret the bodhisattva's extraordinary deed.

THE ENVOY

Earlier I defined the "evil" recipient as one who makes a direct and conscious demand for the bodhisattva's body. In some stories, however, the evil recipient does not himself go to the bodhisattva and ask for his body, but instead sends an *envoy* to do his bidding. In Pāli *Jātaka* 514, for example, it is the evil Queen Subhaddā who constitutes the recipient, since she is the one who demands and ultimately receives the bodhisattva's body (here, an elephant's tusks). However, rather than going to the bodhisattva herself, she sends an *envoy*—the hunter Sonuttara. Likewise, in the *Maṇicūḍāvadāna,* when the evil King Duṣprasaha wants the crest-jewel attached to King Maṇicūḍa's head, he remains in his own kingdom and sends out five brahmins as *envoys* to do the dirty deed.

The functions of such envoys are not entirely clear to me, but several themes seem to be highlighted. The evil recipient often has considerable trouble recruiting an envoy: in the *Sūtra of the Wise and the Fool* 22, for example, an evil king asks all the beggars in his kingdom to go and get King Candraprabha's head, but all of them refuse to do so, citing King Candraprabha's great kindness and compassion; only later does he find a "brahmin from the mountains" who agrees to do the deed in exchange for half of his kingdom and the hand of his daughter. Likewise, in Pāli *Jātaka* 514 Queen Subhaddā at first has difficulty persuading any hunter to go after the tusks of the elephant Chaddanta; as the narrator explains, the hunter Sonuttara eventually agrees to do so only because he had formerly been an enemy of Chaddanta in a previous life. Thus I would say that the problems involved in recruiting an envoy are used to present obstacles to the *recipient's* intentions—just as "opposers" present obstacles to the bodhisattva's intentions—and thus add to the drama and conflict of the story. Moreover, the reluctance of potential envoys to take on the job serves again to highlight the great virtue of the bodhisattva and his widespread power and influence over others—while the very need to use such an envoy at all also suggests the cowardly nature of the evil recipient. The contrast between the bodhisattva and the recipient—and thus the enormity of the bodhisattva's self-sacrifice on the recipient's behalf—is thus intensified by the use of such envoys.

THE RELUCTANT HELPER

Reluctant helpers are those occasional characters who are charged with the actual task of physically mutilating the bodhisattva's body, but who strongly resist doing so, horrified at the very idea or afraid of the consequences of injuring such a virtuous being. In Pāli *Jātaka* 499, for example, King Śibi asks his court surgeon to remove his eyes, but the surgeon is extremely reluctant to do so (although he eventually does). In *Kalpanāmaṇḍitikā* 64 it is a servant who is charged with cutting up King Śibi's flesh, but who begs to be absolved from such a horrific duty. "Have compassion on me," he says,

> I can't do it. I have always received the king's kindnesses; how could I cut with a knife a morsel of flesh from the king's thigh? . . . The king is the savior and protector of all. If I cut the king's flesh with a knife, surely I will be quickly thrown down and fall to the ground.[86]

We might also speak of the "reluctant helper" in a slightly different sense when the bodhisattva has difficulty *recruiting* such a helper (just as the recipient has difficulty recruiting an envoy). In *Avadānakalpalatā* 55 King Śibi offers abundant gold to anyone who will cut up his flesh, but the vast majority of people simply "cover their ears [in horror] and run away"; only a "cruel-minded fellow" with the suggestive name of Kapilapiṅgala ("Reddish-Brown") finally agrees to do the deed.[87] In yet other cases, we might say that it is the *recipient himself* (or his *envoy*) who acts as the *reluctant helper*. That is, though eager to receive the bodhisattva's body, many recipients and envoys display either weakness or cowardliness when it comes to the actual task of physically mutilating the bodhisattva. Thus, in Pāli *Jātaka* 514 the hunter Sonuttara struggles to cut off the elephant Chaddanta's tusks, but is physically unable to do so, just as the tigress in various versions of the tigress story is too weak to devour the bodhisattva. Other recipients and envoys simply refuse to perform the mutilation out of fear and cowardice. The brahmin recipient in *Divyāvadāna* 22 first forces King Candraprabha into a secluded pleasure-park so that the crowds cannot see what is about to occur, and then admits to the king, "I cannot cut off the Lord's head!"[88]—just as the hunter in *Kalpanāmaṇḍitikā* 69 admits to the bodhisattva-elephant, "I fear the fire of your compassion; if I tear out your tusks, certainly my hand will fall dead."[89]

Whether the reluctant helper is a recipient, an envoy, or a separate character, in all cases, his reluctance or fear of performing the mutilation serves to draw out the narrative and make it more dramatic by again delaying the gift and causing further obstacles to the bodhisattva's intention. Moreover, in many cases, this reluctance also serves as a plot-device by means of which the *bodhisattva himself* is eventually forced to injure his own body. These scenes are often milked for as much pathos as they can muster: in Pāli *Jātaka* 514, for example, the elephant, having been shot by the cruel hunter, is so weak from loss of blood that he cannot even lift up his own trunk; nevertheless, he tells the hunter that if the hunter will lift up his trunk for him, he will somehow manage to grasp the hunter's saw and then saw off his own tusks. These pathetic scenes in which the heroic bodhisattva himself mutilates his own body on behalf of those too cowardly, fearful, or incompetent to do so again highlight the great difference between the bodhisattva and other people, for a contrast is drawn between the strength, courage, and heroism of the bodhisattva and the weakness, fearfulness, and cowardliness of those around him. Once again, then, a minor conventional character plays a role that is seemingly insignificant, but that contributes to the rhetoric of the genre as a whole.

Supernatural Occurrences

Another conventional "character" we might speak about is the universe at large—in particular, those responses on the part of the universe that fall into the category of "supernatural occurrences." By "supernatural occurrences" I mean unnatural or abnormal events, events whose occurrence cannot be explained in natural, everyday terms, such as the shaking of the earth or the sudden fall of a shower of heavenly flowers. Such supernatural occurrences appear in many gift-of-the-body stories and are stereotypical in both content and location.

Supernatural occurrences are found almost solely at two locations within the narrative. First, they occur at crucial junctures in the process of giving the gift, such as the moment when the recipient decides to ask for the bodhisattva's body, the moment when the bodhisattva decides to give away his body, the moment when the bodhisattva's body is first harmed, or—most commonly—the moment when the gift is completed. Second, in those stories in which the bodhisattva's body is restored through an Act of Truth, supernatural occurrences very frequently mark the moment of the restoration. In both cases, supernatural occurrences serve to underscore the power of the bodhisattva's virtue by showing how the universe itself reacts to it in spontaneous and unusual ways. Their stereotypical location also makes them important narrative markers that grab the reader's attention at crucial junctures in the story and indicate to him or her that something momentous is going on.

Supernatural occurrences are stereotypical in content as well as location, the same phrases being repeated over and over again. This content seems to suggest to us the most appropriate ways of evaluating the gift and the restoration of the body, contextualizing these events for the reader by demonstrating how the universe itself responds to their occurrence. By far the most common supernatural occurrence is for the earth to shake or tremble violently; very often, a stereotypical cliché is employed in which the earth is said to shake "in six ways" (*ṣaḍvikāraṃ*).[90] The shaking of the earth (and secondarily, of Mount Meru, the oceans, etc.) seems to herald first and foremost the *awe-inspiring power* of the bodhisattva's deed, since the earth and mountains are usually noted for their firmness and immovability.[91] Other supernatural occurrences seem more distinctly *negative* in tone, perhaps heralding the *terrible* nature of the deed. For example, the earth, oceans, and mountains resound with horrible noises, the sun and moon stop shining, the whole world becomes dark, meteors fall, thunder and lightning occur, streams and lakes dry up, trees lose their flowers and fruit, rough winds blow, animals are terrified, and so forth. Such signs are sometimes explicitly referred to as "inauspicious omens," "most dreadful omens," "evil omens," and the like.[92] A third group of supernatural occurrences are undoubtedly more *positive* in tone, and seem to celebrate the *wonderful* or *miraculous* nature of the deed. The most frequently mentioned of these are showers of heavenly flowers, perfumes, and powders, and the sounding of celestial drums. Other "positive" signs are the exact opposites of the "negative" signs mentioned above: instead of not shining, the sun and moon may shine especially brightly; instead of rough winds blowing, a soft and perfumed breeze may blow; instead of losing all their flowers and fruit, trees may spontaneously blossom out of season.

The distribution of "awe-inspiring," "positive," and "negative" supernatural occurrences is also conventional in nature, for all three types seem to occur freely at the moment when the gift is made, but only the "awe-inspiring" and "positive" (never the "negative") occur when the bodhisattva's body is restored. This would suggest that the giving of the gift itself may be both terrible and wonderful in nature, whereas the restoration of the bodhisattva's body is wholly wonderful; both, of course, inspire amazement and awe. In some cases, however, only "negative" signs occur at the moment when the gift is made, and their corresponding "positive" signs occur when the bodhisattva's body is restored; for example, rough winds blow when the gift is made, and a cool, perfumed breeze blows when the bodhisattva's body is restored.[93] This latter scenario perhaps suggests that the bodhisattva's deed, while awe-inspiring in its power, is also a terrible injustice that throws the universe out of whack until the body is restored and the bodhisattva returned to health. In any case, all three types of signs forcefully demonstrate that the bodhisattva's deed has powerful reverberations throughout the cosmos, as well as beginning to suggest to the reader how he or she might evaluate the gift.

The same general categories of *awe-inspiring, negative,* and *positive* are equally well reflected in another large group of supernatural occurrences—the reactions of supernatural beings such as *devas, nāgas, yakṣas, gandharvas, asuras, kinnaras,* and *mahoragas.* Rather than playing a direct part in the narrative, these beings generally constitute a kind of Greek chorus, reacting to and commenting on the action from a distance. The reactions of these beings parallel other types of supernatural occurrences. In some cases, they are simply "amazed" and full of wonder; in some cases, they cry and wail and lament; and in some cases, they sing with joy, play heavenly musical instruments, and otherwise worship the bodhisattva and celebrate his deed. Their occasional proclamations about the gift can again be divided up in a similar way: they either express amazement alone ("It is improbable that such a thing has ever been done before!");[94] or they grieve and lament the bodhisattva's injury or death ("Alas, alas, what a calamity! This noble and great sage has been killed!");[95] or they praise and celebrate the bodhisattva and his deed ("Oh, what nobility! Oh, what compassion! See how great is the purity of his heart!").[96]

In general, however, one feature that seems to distinguish such beings—particularly the higher *devas*—from either ordinary human characters or the natural world is their somewhat greater tendency to recognize and celebrate the "wonderful" nature of the deed. Often, in the midst of terrible earthly omens, wailing people, and frightened animals, the gods alone are busy celebrating, raining down heavenly flowers, and praising the bodhisattva effusively. Moreover, from their lofty position in the skies, they frequently make pronouncements concerning the larger significance of the gift ("By giving away his head, King Candraprabha has completely fulfilled the perfection of generosity!"),[97] or make predictions about the bodhisattva's future ("Soon he will obtain Buddhahood!").[98] Their perspective on the gift is longer and wider than that of the other characters, and their pronouncements have the air of normative statements about how the gift should be interpreted, an effect which is heightened by the distance they maintain from the immediate actions and emotions of the story.

In short, the voice of the higher *devas* sometimes seems to fulfill a largely discursive function within the narrative, temporarily removing the reader from the immediate emotional context of the story and providing him or her with clues as to the true significance of the gift. In terms of rhetoric, it seems to me that the presence of the *devas* and the normative statements they make about the rightness of the gift provide a higher-level frame within which opposition to the gift can be fully elaborated and developed without the reader losing sight of the genre's normative concerns. The profound ambivalence toward the gift so often expressed by the bodhisattva's "opposers," in other words, is perhaps made possible in part by being contextualized within the frame of the higher *devas'* statements in praise of the gift. We will see a similar type of discursive functioning recurring in my final discussion of the conventions of rhetoric—the discursive functions fulfilled by Śakra, lord of *devas*.

Śakra's Discursive Functions

Earlier in this chapter I briefly argued that stories featuring Śakra as the recipient of the gift offer the greatest degree of resolution between the transcendent values embodied in the bodhisattva and the everyday, pragmatic values embodied in the bodhisattva's opposers—not only because the give-and-get-back movement of the gift provides the reader with a concrete image of the conflict's resolution, but also because the character of Śakra fulfills a number of "discursive functions" throughout the narrative that help to develop this resolution in a gradual manner.[99] Once again, it is the distance Śakra maintains from the immediate action of the story that perhaps allows for this kind of discursive functioning. Unlike other *devas,* of course, Śakra does play an active role within the story and is not merely a passive bystander. However, for much of the time he appears in *disguise;* only the reader knows who he really is, which has the effect of distancing Śakra from the story and putting him on a level with the reader.

We might speak of three discursive functions fulfilled by the character of Śakra. First, he constitutes what we might call the *curious reader.* Śakra seems to represent the reader's perspective: From the moment when he is first alerted to the existence of the bodhisattva, Śakra constantly expresses doubt, curiosity, and some skepticism about the bodhisattva's generosity. He is usually the only one who expresses such doubt explicitly; in contrast, the narrative voice of the text always takes the bodhisattva's virtue completely for granted, as well as assuming implicitly that the gift of one's own body is an appropriate course of action. Śakra expresses the doubts and asks the questions that are otherwise forbidden. In this he often seems to echo the reader's own questions about the bodhisattva as he or she reads the story: Will the bodhisattva really give the gift? Why is the bodhisattva giving the gift? Is he crazy?

It is remarkable, in fact, to notice just how often Śakra speaks in the form of questions that might just as easily come from the mouth of a curious reader. Let us look at a few random examples drawn from stories involving King Śibi, all of which are spoken by Śakra, either to himself or to another deity:

> Will he be able to give [his eyes] or not?[100]

> Why does this King Śibi act thus for the sake of beings? Does he [do so] out of compassion?[101]

> How on earth has this king thought up such a thing, his mind carried away by his excessive passion for giving? Is he taking his determination to give to the utmost limit by firmly resolving to give away his own limbs?[102]

> Is it certain that the king will not be shaken from his purpose?[103]

> Will the great king maintain his resolve in the midst of the greatest of sufferings? . . . Will he maintain his resolve if I make him redouble his sufferings?[104]

By means of such musings, Śakra makes explicit the main questions to be answered by the story, and gives the reader a character with whom to identify.

A second discursive function fulfilled by Śakra again largely takes the form of questions, but this time addressed to the bodhisattva himself. We might refer to this as Śakra's role as a *questioner.* Both during the gift itself and when he encourages the bodhisattva to perform an Act of Truth, Śakra frequently questions the bodhisattva about why he is giving the gift, what he hopes to accomplish, whether he has any regret, and so forth. In other words, Śakra is unsatisfied with merely the gift itself; his questions force the bodhisattva to make the logic and motives behind the gift explicit, thus assuring the reader of the true nature of the gift (while exonerating the bodhisattva of any unprompted boasting). In the *Maṇicūḍāvadāna,* for example, when Śakra, disguised as a *rākṣasa,* is drinking Maṇicūḍa's blood, Maṇicūḍa becomes sad for a moment because—as the narrator explains—he sees the stream of blood drying up and is concerned that the *rākṣasa* will be left unsatisfied. However, lest we (or anyone else in the story) find this sadness suspect or do not trust the narrator's explanation, the text uses Śakra—the reader's ally—to make Maṇicūḍa's feelings explicit. Śakra asks Maṇicūḍa, "Do you regret, Great King?"[105]—whereupon Maṇicūḍa makes an explicit denial of any feeling of regret. In many cases, Śakra remains unsatisfied even by statements such as this, and, through further questions, forces the bodhisattva to make a more formalistic statement (such as a vow or an Act of Truth).

This pattern is consistent in story after story, Śakra continually goading the bodhisattva into making the nature of the gift explicit:

Are you beginning to have regrets?[106]

What do you wish to gain by such deeds and by such a strenuous endeavor?[107]

O Great King, what goal do you wish to attain by enduring such torments?[108]

When beggars have reduced you to such a condition, how on earth can you still be concerned with them?[109]

Great King, when you were thinking that you would give up your body, or that you had given up your body, or that you should give up your body, I hope you felt no hesitation or regret. . . . How are we to know this?[110]

Did you not feel grief in sacrificing yourself for a dove? . . . Such words are difficult to believe, and such an act has never been seen before. Who will be able to give it credit?[111]

After giving away your breasts, did you [later] change your mind?[112]

Is it true, Rūpāvatī, that you sacrificed both of your breasts for the sake of a young boy? . . . Rūpāvatī, did your mind feel any regret when you decided to sacrifice, when you were sacrificing, or when you had sacrificed both of your breasts? . . . But who will believe such a thing?[113]

By means of this austerity, do you desire to conquer the station belonging to Indra? Good Woman, I ask you this only out of curiosity.[114]

Not only does Śakra share the reader's initial doubts about the bodhisattva, he also maintains this doubt throughout the giving of the gift and makes sure—on behalf of the reader—that the bodhisattva makes his motives and intentions verbally explicit.

Of course, the same alliance between Śakra and the reader is implicit in the whole motif of the *test* itself: Śakra tests the bodhisattva for the sake of the reader as much as for his own sake, since the narrative voice of the text (as well as most of the other characters) already takes the bodhisattva's virtue for granted. This leads us to Śakra's third discursive function: he constitutes a *reliable witness.* Because Śakra shares all the doubts of the reader, he is a reliable witness to the bodhisattva's generosity; when *his* doubts are finally dispelled, so must ours be. The dispelling of Śakra's doubts is signified not only by his effusive positive praise of the bodhisattva (several examples of which I gave earlier), but also by the fact that he *dispenses with his disguise* and reveals his true identity. Once he becomes a "believer," we might say, he leaves the once-removed, discursive level of the narrative (by shedding his disguise) and seems to meld back into the story itself—hopefully bringing the reader along.

This is why I perceive the character of Śakra to be a mediator between the Buddhist values embodied in the bodhisattva and the everyday, pragmatic concerns embodied in the bodhisattva's opposers. He begins on the side of the opposers (at least in terms of his doubt), and by means of the test, gradually moves over to the side of the bodhisattva, coming finally to fully champion the transcendent ideal represented by the bodhisattva's gift of his body. Moreover, by virtue of his discursive functioning as a *curious reader, questioner,* and *reliable witness,* Śakra guides the reader along the same arc as he himself travels: if only we can identify with Śakra, we too will move from doubt and skepticism to conviction and belief.

Ambivalence Toward the Traditional Rhetoric in Two Chinese Tales

The consistency of the rhetoric characteristic of the gift-of-the-body genre that I have tried to elucidate throughout this chapter can perhaps be brought into greater relief by looking at two Chinese stories that seem distinctly ambivalent toward this rhetoric. Though both stories come from texts that present themselves as Chinese translations of Indic originals (now lost), the rhetoric of each story suggests strongly that a Chinese author was uncomfortable with the traditional version of the story and adapted it to be in greater conformity to his own sensibilities. It is the striking manner in which these adaptations jump to one's attention that convince me of the otherwise consistent nature of the Indian genre's rhetoric.

The *Mohe senzi lu* (T. 1425) contains a story of the bodhisattva's previous birth as an elephant that is familiar to us from Indic tradition as the *Ṣaḍdanta Jātaka* (represented within my corpus, for example, by Pāli *Jātaka* 514 and *Kalpanāmaṇḍitikā* 69).[115] As in the Indian versions, the main character is a magnificent, six-tusked elephant who is shot by the arrow of a cruel hunter and then willingly gives his own tusks to the hunter, refusing to get angry at him out of respect for the religious robes the hunter has deceivingly put on. The *Mohe senzi lu* version, however, distinguishes itself sharply from the other versions in its depiction of the bodhisattva-elephant. Here the bodhisattva-elephant does everything possible to *avoid* having to give away his tusks. Long before he has even encountered the hunter, in fact, the elephant thinks to himself, "Why do men want to kill us? They want to kills us because of our tusks."[116] Thinking this, he prudently stashes away both his grandfather's tusks and his father's tusks when each of them dies, and later uses these tusks to try to avoid giving away his own. When the hunter approaches him and asks for his tusks, the elephant first gives him his grandfather's tusks on the condition that the hunter will never return. The hunter is soon cheated out of the tusks by a wine merchant, however, and returns to the elephant again and asks for another pair of tusks. At this point, the elephant gives him his father's tusks on the condition that he will never again succumb to such debauchery. Once again, the hunter loses the tusks, returns, and shoots the elephant from a hiding place. It is only at this point in the story that the elephant reverts to his more familiar character, refusing to get angry at the hunter out of respect for the religious robes he has put on and freely inviting the hunter to take his own tusks.

The stance of the bodhisattva-elephant here is strikingly different from what we have seen to be so characteristic of the Indian genre. Instead of a bodhisattva who is eager to encounter a supplicant who will ask for his body, offers no hesitation whatsoever in giving his body away, and never dreams of attempting to substitute something else in its place, here we have a bodhisattva who consciously stashes away possible substitute-gifts beforehand, does not offer his own body until these substitute-gifts have been exhausted, and tries in vain to make sure that the supplicant will never return! So inconsistent is this story with the rhetoric I have elucidated above that I cannot help but imagine a Chinese author who was unhappy with the traditional version and thus rewrote it to make it "more reasonable."[117] The rhetoric here is one that promotes a prudent course in which one tries to protect one's own life—but does display virtue if the situation demands it. Frankly, I cannot imagine an original Indic version of such a tale.

Even more striking are the innovations found in another Chinese gift-of-the-body story, this time taken from the *Liudu ji jing* (T. 152).[118] This is clearly a version of the well-known story of King Candraprabha, who gives his own head to an evil brahmin and suffers death as a result. Nevertheless, it again departs radically from other versions of this story (such as *Divyāvadāna* 22 and *Sūtra of the Wise and the Fool* 22) in its depiction of the bodhisattva. In the traditional versions, of course, King Candraprabha is eager to give his body away and overjoyed to encounter a brahmin who asks for his head. In the *Liudu ji jing* version, on the other hand, his reaction is completely different, for as soon as the brahmin asks for his head, he replies: "What advantage could my head be to you that would make you want to have it? I possess all sorts of jewels that I could offer to you in large quantitites."[119] As we have seen, this attempt to substitute material gifts for the gift of the body is usually characteristic of the bodhisattva's *ministers,* not the bodhisattva himself; in fact, it is precisely the *rejection* of this substitution that normally characterizes the bodhisattva himself.

This striking departure from the traditional rhetoric is further underscored later on in the *Liudu ji jing* version when it is *King Candraprabha himself* who offers to the brahmin a head made out of jewels in place of his own head—just as his *ministers* do in the other versions. It is only when the brahmin keeps refusing these material substitutes that King Candraprabha finally agrees to give away his own head. Just as we saw in the elephant-story above, King Candraprabha follows a prudent course in which the gift of his body is a last resort.

The outcome of this story, moreover, is also strikingly different from what we find in the other versions, where, as we have seen, a minor deity becomes angry at the brahmin and tries to obstruct the gift, but is sternly rebuked by the bodhisattva and made to "fall silent" so that the gift can take place, resulting in the bodhisattva's tragic death. In this version, however, the minor deity slaps the brahmin across the face, causing him to fall on the ground and lose his sword, thus sparing King Candraprabha's life! The gift is successfully interrupted by the anger and indignation of a minor, local deity, and the bodhisattva-king offers no protest against this obstruction at all. Instead of the message that Buddhism, as a cosmological and translocal tradition, has authority over the realm of popular, local religious interests, here we seem to get the very different message that the power of a local deity can protect the bodhisattva who chooses to adhere to transcendent Buddhist values. In a sense, the local takes precedence over the translocal rather than the other way around. In several different ways, then, we can detect the Chinese author's discomfort with the traditional rhetoric characteristic of the genre and his significant alteration of this rhetoric—even while maintaining the basic elements of the story in place.

It is against the background provided by these two "alternative" Chinese versions that the project I have engaged in throughout this chapter becomes clear: I have attempted to elucidate some of the conventions of rhetoric that govern the gift-of-the-body genre and make possible its "power to persuade." These conventions are organized around a limited number of character-types who interact with one another throughout the course of the plot, their interactions gradually unfolding the basic argument of the genre in a processual and emergent manner in which the reader is able to participate. It is the narrative form that allows for this process by embodying Buddhist ideals and their antitheses within particular characters who engage in action over time, come into conflict with other characters, resolve their conflicts (to whatever degree and in whatever manner), and experience the various consequences of both conflict and resolution. I follow many scholars here in believing that the type of ethical work performed by narrative literature is not subsidiary to more systematic texts, but absolutely essential.[120] As Hallisey and Hansen have noted in their study of ethics and narrative in Theravāda Buddhism,

> Through narrative we are able to imagine ourselves in the place of another. . . . [W]hen, in reading, we leave aside our own social location . . . and enter imaginatively into the experience of a character in a narrative, we cultivate capabilities that are necessary to all moral agency. . . . In short, narrative prefigures moral life because it cultivates a capacity of imagination that is essential for ethical action.[121]

In addition to such "prefiguring," Hallisey and Hansen also argue that it is narrative, first and foremost, that allows us to think about moral conduct in a manner that fully acknowledges "its conditioning by other values" and the "limitations which 'reality' may impose on our visions of human flourishing"[122] and it is this dimension that I have sought to emphasize here. By subjecting this material to a close and careful reading that takes seriously its complexity and artistry, I have tried to avoid the kind of pat and simplistic judgment of these stories that all too quickly dismisses them as "trivial, didactic fables promoting the virtue of *dāna,*" in favor of an analysis that highlights the conflict and opposition surrounding the gift, the enormous ambivalence such an ideal of generosity engenders in its audience, and the fragile and tenuous nature of the resolution that all such stories ultimately aim to provide.

IV

DĀNA

The Buddhist Discourse on Giving

Now that I have subjected the gift-of-the-body genre to a careful analysis in terms of its "conventions of plot" and "conventions of rhetoric," in this and the following chapters I turn away from a strictly genre-focused approach in order to look more broadly at some of the major conceptual issues that come to the fore within gift-of-the-body tales. Taking a cue from the phrase "gift of the body" itself, chapters 4 and 5 are devoted to the "gift" aspect of these tales, while chapter 6 is devoted to the "body" aspect. I turn now to the subject of the gift.

Over the course of the previous century, the notion of the *gift*—so immediately familiar to us in everyday life—has also become a prominent category of analysis in academic scholarship and critical theory. The genealogy of the gift within modern critical theory begins with the appearance in 1925 of Marcel Mauss' groundbreaking *Essai sur le don* and subsequently meanders through a pantheon of prominent twentieth-century thinkers working from a variety of disciplinary and interdisciplinary perspectives. The wealth and breadth of scholarship now available on the gift has merely confirmed Mauss' original insight that the gift constitutes a "total social phenomenon" in which all kinds of institutions—religious, political, social, economic, and cultural—find simultaneous expression.[2]

This salience of "the gift" within modern academic thought finds a distant parallel in the world of premodern South Asian Buddhism. Indian Buddhist textual discourse pays an enormous amount of attention to the category of the gift. The terms "gift," "giving," and "generosity" are all indicated by the Pāli and Sanskrit term *dāna* (derived from the verbal root *dā*), which is ubiquitous in Indian Buddhist texts. *Dāna* appears on many different standardized lists of highly valued acts and qualities, such as the six or ten "perfections" (*pāramitā*), the three "bases of meritorious action" (*puṇya-kriyā-vastu*), the four "means of conversion" (*saṃgraha-vastu*), and the four "accomplishments" (*sampad*).[3] In the commentarial explanations that so often accompany such lists, Buddhist texts contain extensive discussions of the gift in which the qualities of the giver, the gift, the recipient, and the procedure of giving itself are all exhaustively analyzed and typologies of different gifts are worked out. These discussions are used by the Buddhist tradition to engage in serious and sustained reflection on a variety of different issues: Why is generosity a valued moral quality? Who should give what to whom, and when and how should such gifts be made? What motivates the gift, and how do different motivations relate to each other? The abstract answers to such questions are further illuminated by a voluminous body of *stories about gifts;* gift-giving of various sorts, in fact, may well be the single most popular subject of Indian Buddhist narrative literature, taken as a whole. The gift thus becomes a prominent site for ethical, religious, and ritual reflection. Buddhism here is heir to its South Asian background, as reflection on *dāna* and stories illustrating *dāna* constituted an extensive pan-Indic discourse shared equally by the Hindu and Jain traditions as well.[4]

Discussion of the Buddhist gift, moreover, is not restricted to any single, narrowly defined area, but spreads its tentacles out in virtually every direction. The Buddhist gift manifests itself in a wide variety of different forms—including, for example, the layperson's gift of alms and other material objects to the Saṃgha, the giving of ritual offerings to the Buddha (or to other objects of worship), the status of monks and nuns as "gifts" made to the Saṃgha by their parents (as well as their own "giving up" of the world in an act of renunciation), the bodhisattva's "perfection of generosity" on behalf of others, and the Buddha's and Saṃgha's "gift of the dharma." The gift in Buddhist discourse thus encompasses laypeople, monastics, and religious virtuosos; acts of ritual offering, renunciation, preaching, and self-sacrifice; material gifts, the gift of the dharma, and the ultimate gift of oneself.[5]

Stories featuring the bodhisattva's gift of his body and highlighting the virtue of generosity cannot be taken in isolation, therefore, but must be placed within the larger context of the Buddhist discourse on *dāna*—which is the project I undertake in this and the following chapter. What type of gift is the bodhisattva's gift of his body, and what role does the gift-of-the-body theme play within the larger context of Buddhist ethical discourse on the gift? In the present chapter I first set the background for this discussion by presenting two different conceptual schema for organizing some of the many varieties of *dāna* discussed within Buddhist exegetical texts. The first schema consists of a threefold hierarchy of *reciprocated gifts, unreciprocated gifts,* and *pure gifts,* while the second schema consists of a threefold typology of *giving up, giving down,* and *giving up* in another sense (which I will indicate as *giving up²*). These two schema overlap with each other considerably, but approach the material from quite different perspectives. Together, I hope they will provide the reader with a solid framework for thinking, in some complex ways, about the many Buddhist notions and varieties of *dāna.* Only after this conceptual background has been established will I then turn, in chapter 5, to the gift-of-the-body theme itself and its relationship to this larger discourse.

Reciprocated and Unreciprocated Gifts

At the beginning of his seminal *Essai sur la don,*[6] Marcel Mauss focuses on the practice of gift-giving in "primitive" and "archaic" societies. His primary argument concerning the gift in archaic societies is that although the gift operates under the *illusion* that it is free, voluntary, and disinterested—qualities inherent in the very definition of a "gift"—it is, in fact, obligatory, constrained by social rules, and necessarily reciprocal. Throughout the essay, Mauss emphasizes the reciprocal nature of the archaic gift, not only because he wishes to demonstrate a historical connection between archaic gift-giving and modern economic exchange—which is the fundamental thesis of the *Essai* as a whole—but also because he wants to argue for the gift's social function. It is the gift, according to Mauss, that enables society, for through the constant movement and exchange of goods, honors, and services via the medium of the gift, social networks are established and social ties maintained. Thus Mauss offers a plethora of examples in order to demonstrate that gift-giving in archaic societies is really *exchange;* that gift-giving is always *reciprocal;* that in addition to the "obligation to give" and the "obligation to receive," there is also an "obligation to reciprocate"; and that underneath the disinterested idiom of the "gift" lie the brute social facts of *reciprocity* and *exchange.*

In the middle of the book, however, when Mauss turns to the classical Sanskrit literature of India in order to find "survivals" of the archaic gift, it is only through some subterfuge and obscurity that he is able to use the Indic material in a way that is beneficial to his argument, while he ignores those aspects of the material that fail to cooperate.[7] For while the Brahmanical material Mauss draws on is very useful to him in regard to certain other points he wants to make about the gift, it is not at all useful to him in terms of the "obligation to reciprocate." As several Indologists have subsequently noted,[8] the classical Indian theory of *dāna*—whether Hindu, Buddhist, or Jain—departs radically from Mauss on precisely this point, since *dāna,* as a rule, *must never be reciprocated.* Although there are other forms of gift in South Asian discourse that do involve exchange and reciprocity, the category of *dāna* constitutes a special (and highly valued) case that is defined by its *lack* of such reciprocity. Having begun his career as an Indologist, Mauss was fully aware of this point, but because it didn't support his general argument, he was forced to relegate it to a footnote.[9]

Why did the Indic notion of *dāna* fail to cooperate with Mauss? As Trautmann has most clearly demonstrated,[10] in Buddhism, Hinduism, and Jainism the theory of *dāna* works together with the theory of karma and makes use of a basic Mīmāṃsaka distinction between "seen" and "unseen" "fruits" (*dṛṣṭa-phala, adṛṣṭa-phala*). Any gift that is reciprocated within this world—for example, by a return-gift from the recipient—has a "seen" and visible "fruit" and thereby loses its ability to result in a transcendent karmic reward. Such a gift belongs wholly to the ordinary social realm and is really no different from barter, sale, or purchase. Only the *un*reciprocated gift that has no visible fruit within this world can be presumed to result in an "unseen" and transcendent reward in the form of karmic merit (*puṇya*). The unreciprocated gift thus constitutes an "instrument of salvation":[11] the recipient must not reciprocate the gift because to do so would exhaust the gift's soteriological capacity of resulting in karmic merit for the world to come. The Indic theory thus agrees with Mauss that all ordinary gifts *are* reciprocal in nature—only to reject such gifts in favor of an asymmetrical, *un*reciprocated gift that bears fruit in the transcendent future, beyond the present realm of give-and-take. As Trautmann succinctly puts it, the theory of *dāna* includes no "obligation to reciprocate" because it is "a soteriology, not a sociology of reciprocity."[12]

This leads us to a basic truism about the gift that has been stated by several scholars, both in relation to South Asia and in more general terms. Speaking of several different types of giving among Theravāda Buddhists in Sri Lanka, Parry states: "The reciprocated gift belongs to the profane world; the unreciprocated gift to a quest for salvation from it."[13] Likewise, Michaels notes in relation to Hindu *dāna* that since it is "not normal" for gifts to go unreciprocated, the gift given with no expectation of worldly return must be based on "the giver's search for the abnormal, uncommon, supernatural."[14] And, more broadly, Parry notes of the "world religions" in general that wherever there is a notion of salvation that devalues this profane world in favor of a better world (or better life) yet to come, "the unreciprocated gift becomes a liberation from bondage to [this world], a denial of the profane self, an atonement for sin, and hence a means to salvation."[15] Here then we see one of the fundamental connections between the gift and religion: while the *reciprocated* gift stands as a marker of the purely social, the *unreciprocated* gift often serves to signify the sacred, the salvational, or the soteriological.

This hierarchical distinction between "reciprocated" and "unreciprocated" gifts can be found in many Buddhist passages relating to *dāna*. Indian Buddhist discussions of *dāna* do take notice of the ordinary, "reciprocated" gifts described by Mauss, but tend to accord them a very low status. Thus, in a passage from the *Aṅguttara Nikāya,* the gift given "because he gave to me" and the gift given "because he will give to me" are both found within a list of seven "faulty" gifts and are contrasted with those gifts that do not involve such social reciprocity.[16] Similarly, in the *Bodhisattvabhūmi,* the "pure gift" (*viśuddha-dāna*) of the bodhisattva is defined in part as being "indifferent to payback" in the sense of "not expecting any requital from others."[17] Thus, the kind of reciprocal social exchanges (masquerading as "gifts") described by Mauss are recognized in the Buddhist discourse on *dāna,* but are not highly valued.

"Unreciprocated" gifts of various types, on the other hand, are praised and exalted ad nauseam in Buddhist literature. One classic example of an "unreciprocated" gift in Buddhism is the layperson's gift of alms to the Saṃgha. When a layperson gives alms to a monk, the monk constitutes a nontransactional partner who receives and enjoys the alms but is in no way expected to reciprocate. Though it often seems to the outside observer that the monk "repays" the layperson's gift by preaching a sermon or performing a ritual—the gift of alms and the gift of dharma thus constituting a direct and balanced exchange—the Buddhist tradition itself generally holds that the two gifts are independent of each other, and one is in no way a "repayment" for the other.[18] Indeed, in order to preserve the capacity of the layperson's gift to result in transcendent karmic rewards, the monk should not reciprocate in any explicit manner, not even by an expression of gratitude.[19] In fact, just the reverse obtains: it is the *layperson* who should be grateful to the *monk* for providing him or her with the opportunity to give an "unreciprocated" gift. Contrary to ordinary expectations, then, both gift and gratitude flow in a single direction—from the giver to the recipient—and even the appearance of reciprocity is avoided. The monk in this one-way transaction serves only as a worthy "field of merit" (*puṇya-kṣetra*)—a rich soil in which to "plant" one's good deed—and the layperson's gift is repaid solely by the impersonal karmic mechanism. It is precisely this lack of reciprocity on the everyday social level that defines the gift of alms as a highly valued act of *dāna*—an act set off from the ordinary world of give-and-take by its soteriological power. Thus, the gift of alms is not merely a material or economic transaction that allows the monastic community to survive; it is also a symbolic move by means of which the donor temporarily sets herself apart from ordinary society and expresses her orientation toward the future. Much the same is true of other types of material offerings made to the Saṃgha (such as images, paintings, monasteries, etc.), as well as the "gift" of a son or daughter that parents bestow when they allow their children to join the monastic order. All such gifts are "unreciprocated" in nature—"paid back" only in the form of merit—and are highly praised within Buddhist literature.

Another example of an "unreciprocated" gift in Buddhism is the ritual offering made to the Buddha. If the monk constitutes a nontransactional recipient in the sense that he receives gifts without reciprocating, the Buddha perhaps brings this nontransactional quality to its highest point of perfection. For the Buddha is generally understood to be absent in nirvana and unavailable to his worshipers—incapable even of *receiving* gifts, let alone of reciprocating. Contemporary Buddhists in Theravādin Southeast Asia are fairly insistent on this point, even though other aspects of Buddhist ritual (such as relic worship) seem to suggest that the Buddha is alive and present.[20] In Indian Buddhist discourse, we find something of the same ambiguity. On the one hand, much of the inscriptional evidence suggests that the Buddha was believed to be physically present through his relics and was even conceptualized as a legal owner of property, such that donations made to the Buddha "belonged" to him and were restricted to certain well-defined purposes.[21] But on the other hand, many Indian Buddhist texts are again quite insistent on the technical point that gifts made to the Buddha are not actually "received" by anyone. In the *Abhidharmakośabhāṣya* (hereafter *Kośa*), for example, this lack of a recipient is emphasized. After telling us that ritual offerings made to the Buddha do indeed result in merit, the text has a hypothetical interlocutor raise the objection: "But if no one receives [the gift], then how can there be merit?"[22] The text answers this objection by stating that merit is not solely dependent upon the "favor shown to others"; otherwise, there would be no merit in individual practices such as cultivating meditation or wisdom.[23] Therefore, an actual recipient is not really necessary, and a gift made to the Buddha, "even though he has passed away," still produces merit "through the power of one's intention."[24] One still derives the merit that comes from the "renunciation" (*tyāga*) of the gift—although one does not derive the further merit that comes from the "enjoyment" (*paribhoga*) of the recipient.[25]

Despite significant ambiguity regarding his exact ontological status, then, it is fairly clear that a ritual offering made to the Buddha—or, for that matter, to a *caitya, stūpa,* image, or any other object representing the absent Buddha—is absolutely assured of avoiding any semblance of worldly quid pro quo, since no one actually receives the gift. Having impugned the social ethic of reciprocity through its notion of the unreciprocated gift, the Buddhist tradition now perfects this notion by positing a gift that is given but never received. The orientation of the gift toward the transcendent future could not be more clear: the gift becomes an arrow shot out into space that never quite hits its target, symbolically freeing the giver from this world.

We can further recognize the significance of the Buddha's nontransactional status if we contrast it with the fully transactional status of various other, lesser beings. In the Theravāda Buddhism of Southeast Asia, for example, there is a basic contrast drawn between the reciprocal transactions one makes with the gods and the nonreciprocal transactions one makes with the Buddha.[26] The gods in Theravāda Buddhism are understood to be in charge of worldly goods and benefits. One gives offerings to the gods *in exchange for* their assistance and protection; one haggles and bargains with the gods, just as one haggles and bargains in the marketplace. The Buddha, on the other hand, does not deal in worldly benefits. Therefore, offerings to the Buddha point beyond the present world and should properly be renunciatory in flavor. In the language of Theravāda Buddhism, the gods are *laukika,* or "worldly" in nature, whereas the Buddha is *lokottara*—"beyond the world" or transcendent.

This hierarchical distinction between what is *laukika* and what is *lokottara* is one of the most basic ideological oppositions characteristic of Buddhism as a whole, and is perhaps most concretely materialized through "reciprocated" and "unreciprocated" gifts: "Reciprocated" gifts in Buddhism are classed with barter, sale, or purchase, as well as with the ordinary social world of give-and-take; they bind one to the world and are thoroughly mundane in nature. "Unreciprocated" gifts, on the other hand, bear fruit in the transcendent future; they lead one away from this world and toward one's karmic destiny. The impulse suggested by the "unreciprocated" gift is an impulse to *set oneself apart,* to extricate oneself from the ordinary circuits of exchange, to be temporarily or permanently free from the mundane tyranny of gift and countergift. And this renunciatory impulse—along with the gifts that properly embody it—is highly valued in the Buddhist discourse on *dāna.*[27]

Beyond Reciprocated and Unreciprocated: The Pure Gift

It is also true, however, that what I have been referring to thus far as an "unreciprocated" gift is not wholly "unreciprocated." Mundane, social reciprocity might be rejected in favor of what Trautmann calls "transcendental reciprocity," but reciprocity is involved nonetheless.[28] The layperson who gives alms to a monk or the Buddhist who makes a ritual offering to the Buddha *desires and expects a return* in the form of karmic merit. Though such a gift should ideally be made without focusing on such desires and expectations, everyone knows that giving has its rewards, and Buddhist texts do not shy away from describing these rewards in enormous detail and using them to motivate the giver. To the giver of such "unreciprocated" gifts every form of future worldly felicity is promised: a pleasurable rebirth among humans or gods, along with life, beauty, happiness, strength, intelligence, abundant wealth and riches, the fulfillment of all sensual pleasures, sweet perfumes emanating from the body, and so forth.[29] "He who gives what is dear to him obtains what is dear to him" many times over, for even a small offering "is worth a thousand times as much" in its eventual reward.[30] Indeed, generosity is a prudent investment for the future: giving gifts away is like removing one's riches from a burning house in order to save them for later enjoyment,[31] while that poverty which the miser fears if he gives is exactly what awaits him in the next world if he does not.[32]

Thus even the "unreciprocated" gift is usually motivated by self-interest and calculated to result in the greatest possible return—as the precise "merit account books" kept by Burmese villagers so clearly demonstrate.[33] Buddhist texts recognize this inevitable fact and frequently walk a sort of tightrope between, on the one hand, dangling delicious karmic rewards in front of the giver in order to motivate his giving and, on the other hand, assigning a lower status to any gift that is motivated purely or primarily by the desire for such karmic rewards.

I mentioned before the prevalence of lists containing eight different types of gift, in which seven faulty gifts are contrasted with an eighth gift, which is superior. In one such list from the *Aṅguttara Nikāya,* the gift given "to be reborn in a happy destiny within a heavenly world" is one of the seven "faulty" gifts,[34] while in another such list, the Buddha similarly criticizes the "desirous man who gives a gift while attracted [to its rewards], wishing to store up [its rewards], and thinking, 'I'll enjoy this after death!'"[35]—even though both of these gifts are "unreciprocated" in nature and do indeed result in rebirth as a deity. A passage I previously quoted from the *Dīgha Nikāya* similarly dismisses gifts motivated by the desire for various types of good rebirth as having an "inferior intention."[36] Thus although it is theoretically possible to give an "unreciprocated" gift without hankering after the merit such a gift is known to bestow, it certainly isn't easy. The difficulty of giving such a gift with the proper frame of mind and the automatic nature of such a gift's rewards seem ultimately to taint the "unreciprocated" gift—and suggest that there is something yet higher.

This naturally raises the question of the possibility of what anthropologists (following Malinowski)[37] have often referred to as the "pure" gift—that is to say, the *completely disinterested* gift, the gift given purely out of generosity and altruism, or the gift given with no expectation of return of any kind. Much of the recent theoretical literature on gift-giving has been concerned with the question of the "pure" gift, for this question implicates such fundamental human issues as self-interest versus altruism and the possibility of a truly disinterested human act. Are there any gifts in Buddhism that would qualify as such "pure" gifts? Is "pure generosity" even possible? Beyond the distinction between "mundane reciprocity" and "transcendental reciprocity," is it possible to imagine a gift involving *no reciprocity?*

In the *Dakkhiṇāvibhaṅga Sutta* of the *Majjhima Nikāya,* the Buddha enumerates four types of gifts, those involving: a virtuous giver, a virtuous recipient, neither a virtuous giver nor a virtuous recipient, and both a virtuous giver and a virtuous recipient. Of these four, the last gift is clearly the most superior, its highest example being the gift given by one arhat to another: "When a passionless person gives to another passionless person . . . that gift is the best of all material gifts."[38] This statement is repeated in other Buddhist texts; in the *Kośa,* for example, we are told that "among all gifts, the best is the gift given by one liberated person to another liberated person."[39] An earlier passage in the same text seems to suggest that the reason such a gift is ideal is because the donor is one who can enjoy neither worldly nor karmic rewards—in other words, one who *cannot benefit* in any manner from the giving of the gift. Not only would such a gift lack any worldly rewards—since the recipient is not to reciprocate—but perhaps more importantly, it also lacks any karmic rewards, for the donor (as a liberated person) has "definitively passed beyond the stage where the gift's retribution [would have taken place]."[40] Existing outside of both mundane and transcendental reciprocity, this gift can only be a pure and disinterested gift. Moreover, by specifying that the recipient, too, is a detached and liberated person, this gift has the added benefit of ensuring that even the recipient does not truly "enjoy" the gift (at least in the sense of experiencing attachment or grasping). The ideal gift is not enjoyed or reciprocated by anyone, and nobody enjoys any return, either worldly or transcendent. The ideal gift here stands completely apart, beyond the realm of samsara, passing wordlessly from one liberated person to another.

Jacques Derrida has written eloquently of the *aporia* of the gift: The gift, according to Derrida, is an impossible ideal. As soon as the gift is recognized as a gift, it is implicated in exchange and reciprocal obligation and thereby ceases to be a gift. The gift can be a gift only *when there is no gift at all*—when it is not recognized as a gift, when there is a radical "forgetting" of it, and no remembrance of the gift or obligation to repay it, for either donor or recipient—and this, Derrida maintains, is impossible.[41] But in the Buddhist tradition perhaps we find precisely this impossible ideal expressed in the notion of the gift given by one liberated person to another. Here, the wholly detached and liberated mind of one who has attained nirvana might, in some sense, be seen as equivalent to Derrida's radical "forgetting." Having eradicated all desires, interests, and expectations, the liberated mind can give or receive a gift without recognizing it as such, and without setting into motion the entire cycle of desires and interests that normally accompany all gifts. The gift passed from one arhat to another thus constitutes one example of the perfectly "pure" gift.

A similar sense of absolute desirelessness and radical "forgetting" can also be found in connection with the advanced bodhisattva's "perfection of generosity," or *dāna-pāramitā*. All bodhisattvas should cultivate generosity, of course, but it is only the bodhisattva of a relatively advanced stage that achieves its absolute "perfection." Though the nature of this "perfection" is described in numerous different ways (depending on the context), in many Mahāyāna Buddhist texts it is defined quite specifically as a gift that is "triply pure" because it is given with no conception whatsoever of "donor," "gift," or "recipient."[42] The "perfection of giving," in other words, is any giving that is informed by the "perfection of wisdom" (*prajñā-pāramitā*), or the advanced bodhisattva's thorough realization of the truth of emptiness (*śūnyatā*). The bodhisattva understands that "donor," "gift," and "recipient" are nothing more than conventional notions and are empty of any abiding essence or self—and yet he still gives the gift. Again this might be interpreted in line with Derrida's "forgetting": the ideal gift can exist only when the person who gives it is so thoroughly imbued with an understanding of the emptiness, selflessness, and essencelessness of all things that the very notions of "donor," "gift," and "recipient" are all "forgotten"—he gives without giving, and without expecting anything in return.

Thus the impossible ideal of the "pure" gift exists, but seems to be possible only among Buddhism's most highly exceptional beings. While arhats, Buddhas, and advanced bodhisattvas exist in a strangely desireless world in which they are capable of giving with no conception of giving as such (and thus no expectation of return), the rest of us are mired within Mauss' social world—wholly driven by desires and interests and governed by unwritten rules of obligation, exchange, and reciprocity. The "pure" gift, as Michaels states, is always "a sign of the extraordinary"[43]—or, as Starobinski puts it, only "God, nature and the sun give freely, without asking to be repaid in return."[44] In this sense perhaps we can agree with Derrida about the paradox and impossibility of the "pure" gift.

One manner in which Buddhist texts seem to extend the "pure" gift beyond the realm of such purely desireless beings, however, is by positing a *hierarchy of desires* in which higher and more subtle desires approach the status of being "desireless." We can see this already—if only to some extent—in the first distinction I made above, between "reciprocated" and "unreciprocated" gifts. Both of them are (at least in part) presumably motivated by some kind of *desire*—the desire for a return-gift from the recipient in the former case, and the desire for karmic merit in the latter—but because the latter desire is higher and more subtle in form, its corresponding gift more closely approximates the truly "desireless." In other words (and as Silber has argued with respect to religious donations in medieval Christianity),[45] whatever "return" one receives in the form of karmic "merit" is so abstract, intangible, uncertain—and thus inherently unattractive—that it approaches no return at all and thus partakes in the character of the disinterested gift. (After all, it is the lack of any "seen" reward that one can enjoy here and now that qualifies such gifts as *lokottara* rather than *laukika.*) To a certain extent, then, the gift given in exchange for merit thereby "solves" the problematic of the gift: pure, disinterested generosity and the self-interested expectation of reward are brought together through the inherent *uncertainty* and *intangibility* of the nebulous reward called "merit." Ordinary Buddhists giving alms and making ritual offerings are thus assimilated to arhats, bodhisattvas, and Buddhas.

But while the gift motivated by a desire for merit partakes in the ethic of the "pure" gift only partially, there are other, still higher desires that appear to be accepted by the Buddhist tradition as truly "desireless," in the sense that they do not compromise the status of the perfectly disinterested gift. One such example is the *desire to attain nirvana.* In the lists of eight gifts I mentioned previously (found twice in the *Aṅguttara Nikāya,* as well as in the *Kośa*), the eighth and most superior gift is the gift given "to prepare one's mind [for nirvana]" or "to obtain the highest goal [of nirvana]."[46] This gift is considered to be a "pure" gift and is contrasted with seven "impure" or faulty gifts that are motivated by various lesser desires (such as the desire for reciprocity or the desire for merit). It is only the desire for "desirelessness" itself, one might say, that constitutes a "desireless" desire. The "pure" gift is thus extended from the liberated arhat alone to all those who strive for the goal of arhatship (and give gifts with this motivation).

Much the same is true of gifts given for the sake of attaining Buddhahood. The bodhisattva gives gifts not only out of pure generosity toward others, but also with the desire to attain Buddhahood for himself. Yet "attaining Buddhahood" appears to be the one "self-interested" motivation that does not compromise the purity of the bodhisattva's gift, since Buddhahood—though pertaining to oneself—is desired on behalf of all beings. This is why the *Bodhisattvabhūmi* is able to describe the "pure gift," without contradiction, as one given "with no expectation of reward" but made "seeing Buddhahood [alone] as a benefit."[47] Once again we encounter a paradox: the gift made "with no expectation of reward" is made possible only by aiming for the ultimate reward—the attainment of perfect Buddhahood. It is only at the level of this purest motivation of all that self-interest (*svārtha*) and other-interest (*parārtha*) finally merge together, for the bodhisattva (as the *Mahāyānasūtrālaṃkāra* puts it) "cannot be happy unless others are happy," and "his own happiness is inseparable [from the happiness of others]."[48] Once again, the "pure" gift is extended from the advanced bodhisattva who has attained the "perfection of wisdom" to *all* bodhisattvas (even those who are beginners) who give gifts with a sincere desire for Buddhahood.

In addition to the Buddha (whose ability to give a "pure" gift pretty much goes without saying), then, it seems that arhats, those striving to become arhats, advanced bodhisattvas, and those striving to become advanced bodhisattvas are all capable of giving "pure" gifts—either because they are free of all desire, or because they are motivated by one of the "approved" desires that approach the status of being "desireless."[49] Their gifts thus constitute "pure" gifts standing at the top of the threefold hierarchy I have enumerated here: *reciprocated gifts, unreciprocated gifts,* and *pure gifts.*

Giving Up and Giving Down

The second conceptual schema I will present for organizing the many varieties of *dāna* discussed in Buddhist texts overlaps considerably with the first schema, but approaches the material from a different perspective. This is a threefold typology (rather than hierarchy) among *giving up, giving down,* and *giving up* in another sense (which I will indicate as *giving up*^{2}).

In chapter 2 I briefly mentioned the pan-Indic doctrine of the "worthy recipient" (*supātra*) found equally in the Buddhist, Hindu, and Jain discourses on *dāna.* As I noted, all three religious traditions generally hold that religious gifts should normally be directed upward, toward worthy and superior recipients (such as monks, brahmins, Buddhas, and Jinas), and indeed that the merit accruing from a gift is dependent upon the spiritual worth of the recipient: the more worthy the recipient is—or the better "field of merit" he or she constitutes—the more merit the donor will accrue. Thus in many Buddhist passages we are given a hierarchy of recipients and a corresponding hierarchy of merit: In the *Dakkhiṇāvibhaṅga*

Sutta of the *Majjhima Nikāya,* the Buddha tells Ānanda that giving to an animal produces ten times less merit than giving to an evil human being, which itself produces a hundred times less merit than giving to a virtuous human being, and so on—all the way up to arhats, pratyekabuddhas, and Buddhas as the most "productive" recipients of all.[50] We get another, similar hierarchy in the *Aṅguttara Nikāya,* where offering alms to a hundred people of "right view" produces less merit than offering alms to just a single Once-Returner; feeding a hundred Once-Returners is less meritorious than feeding a single Non-Returner; and so on, through arhats, pratyekabuddhas, and Buddhas.[51] Even better than such gifts made to individuals are gifts made to the Saṃgha, since the Saṃgha includes all virtuous monks from the past, present, and future. In a stereotyped passage that appears throughout the Pāli Canon, the Saṃgha is described as being "worthy of gifts, worthy of hospitality, worthy of offerings, worthy of reverence, the best field of merit in the world."[52] Religious gifts in Buddhism therefore generally flow upward toward worthy and superior recipients, and the Buddha himself advocates choosing one's recipients "with discrimination" in order to maximize one's eventual reward.[53] This is the model of giving I refer to by means of the phrase *giving up*—that is, *giving upward to a worthy recipient in exchange for karmic merit.*

Giving down, on the other hand, is exactly the opposite. For the natural corollary of the worthy-recipient doctrine, as we saw before, is that gifts which flow in the *opposite* direction—that is, *downward* toward *unworthy* recipients—are productive of very little merit, since they are planted within a poor-quality "field." In a passage from the *Aṅguttara Nikāya,* the Buddha says that a gift given to a wicked person bears very little fruit,[54] while the *Kośa* states more explicitly that "because of the faultiness of the field, the result of such a gift will be insignificant or nothing at all."[55] Furthermore, since unworthy recipients (such as animals and beggars) are equally incapable of reciprocating in any worldly manner, gifts directed at them produce neither worldly nor transcendent rewards. Unproductive in any manner, such charitable gifts become the site of pure, unmitigated generosity.[56] This is the model of giving I refer to by means of the phrase *giving down*—that is, *giving downward to an unworthy recipient out of pure generosity and compassion.*

These two models of giving are naturally opposed to one other: gifts given *upward* out of *respect* and for the sake of *merit* are contrasted with gifts given *downward* out of *compassion* and *with no expectation of reward.* This basic distinction can be found within both Buddhist textual discourse and the ethnographic evidence from contemporary Theravāda. It is in this sense, for example, that I interpret the *Kośa*'s statement that the technical term *dāna* should properly be restricted to those gifts given "with the desire to render worship or assistance"[57]—where rendering "worship" (*pūjā*) presumably refers to the upward gift, and rendering "assistance" (*anugraha*) refers to the downward gift. It is these two modes of giving in particular, the *Kośa* suggests, that are the proper subject matter of the discourse on *dāna*. Exactly the same distinction is found among contemporary Theravāda monks in Sri Lanka, who (according to Richard Gombrich) draw a distinction between two kinds of giving: "that with thought of worship (*pūjābuddhiya*), which is motivated by respect (*gaurava*), and that with thought of favor (*anugrahabuddhiya*), which is motivated by pity (*anukampāva*)," with the former being "exemplified by a gift to the Sangha, the latter by a gift to a beggar"[58]—in other words, *giving up* versus *giving down*.

This difference between *giving upward to a worthy recipient* and *giving downward to an unworthy recipient* depends, of course, on the doctrine of the "worthy recipient" itself, and becomes meaningless in the absence of this doctrine. It is important to point out, therefore, that the doctrine of the worthy recipient is not an iron-clad rule; in fact, Indian Buddhist texts are not at all consistent in their upholding of this doctrine. Giving to the sick, for example, is frequently recommended as being especially meritorious, regardless of the spiritual worthiness of the sick person. The *Kośa* itself, in fact, immediately after invoking the worthy-recipient doctrine, includes "those who are sick" among a list of five special recipients who bring about "immeasurable" merit "even though they are ordinary people."[59] A debate recorded in the *Kathāvatthu* even suggests that some schools (such as the Uttarāpathakas) were actively opposed to the worthy-recipient doctrine because of its implication that one person's merit is dependent upon the moral qualities of another (the recipient), thus violating a strict understanding of karma.[60]

In fact, many Buddhist discussions of *dāna* display an ambivalence toward the worthy-recipient doctrine, at one moment upholding the doctrine by asserting that gifts given to unworthy recipients produce little to no reward, and at another moment discounting the doctrine by claiming that *all* gifts result in good rewards, regardless of the status of the recipient. The two passages I quoted above in support of the worthy-recipient doctrine display precisely this ambivalence when we consider their larger contexts. In the *Aṅguttara Nikāya* passage, the statement that a gift given to a wicked person bears very little fruit is immediately preceded by the Buddha's categorical statement of what would seem to be exactly the opposite: "Even if someone were to throw away the dirty rinse-water from washing pots or dishes into a cesspit or other filthy pool with the intention that the living beings dwelling therein might survive on it, I declare, O Vaccha, he would get merit from that act!"[61] Similarly, the *Kośa*'s statement that a "faulty field" results in a reward that is "insignificant or nothing at all" is immediately preceded by the author's reassurance that "even when planted into a bad field, [the gift] bears an agreeable fruit, for there can never be opposition between the seed and its fruit."[62] Such passages seem to want it both ways: on the one hand, the gift given to an unworthy recipient produces little or no merit because the field is bad; on the other hand, the nature of the field is irrelevant, and all gifts produce merit because giving is always good. But how can both claims be true simultaneously?

A historical explanation for these conflicting attitudes toward the worthy recipient has been provided in a recent study by James Egge.[63] Through a careful analysis of the discourse of *dāna* found in Pāli canonical and post-canonical texts, Egge convincingly demonstrates that *dāna* is described and explained in these texts by means of two different discourses, which he refers to as the *sacrificial discourse* and the *karmic discourse.* The *sacrificial discourse,* which Egge sees as the more ancient understanding of *dāna* (and the predominant understanding of *dāna* in the verse-, or *gāthā*-, portions of the earliest Pāli canonical texts), conceives of *dāna*—in particular, the offering of alms to Buddhist mendicants—using the language and imagery of Vedic sacrifice, where Buddhist mendicants replace the sacrificial fire, and alms-offerings replace the Vedic sacrificial oblations. Thus, *dāna* is analogous to a Vedic sacrifice: it is a sacrificial offering made to a worthy recipient, and it results automatically in merit (*puṇya*), which is here nothing more than the good effects of ritual action properly performed. Within this "sacrificial discourse," both the object given and the recipient of the gift are of the utmost importance, for it is only by sacrificing the proper object to the proper recipient that the sacrificial ritual automatically produces its proper reward in the form of merit. *Dāna* is thus a type of giving—sacrificial giving—that is distinct from all other types of giving. It is primarily ritual in nature—rather than moral—and depends for its effects upon having the proper object, procedure, and recipient. It is from this ancient "sacrificial discourse" (inherited from the world of Vedic sacrifice) that the Buddhist emphasis upon the worthy recipient derives. Clearly, from the perspective of this discourse, a gift given to an unworthy recipient would not produce any merit, because without an appropriate recipient, the sacrifice has not been properly performed.

Egge then demonstrates how Pāli literature—beginning with the prose portions of the earliest canonical texts and getting stronger and stronger through later portions of the canon, the commentaries, and medieval story literature—gradually displaces the *sacrifical discourse* of *dāna* with a *karmic discourse* of *dāna*. This *karmic discourse* conceives of *dāna* in primarily moral rather than ritual terms, interpreting it as an act of renunciation, generosity, and mental purification, rather than an act of ritual sacrifice. Within this "karmic discourse," the primary emphasis is on the mental state and ethical intentions of the donor (rather than the appropriateness of the gift or the worth of the recipient)—since karma, in Buddhist discourse, is primarily defined in terms of intention or volition. Emphasis thus shifts from the external factors of *gift* and *recipient* to the internal factor of the *donor's own mind*. The act of giving, when properly performed, still results in merit (*puṇya*), but merit is now conceived as being analogous to "good karma" (the positive results of skillful ethical actions), and not in terms of the automatic effects of properly performed rituals. Almsgiving to Buddhist mendicants is thus no different in nature from any other manifestation of *dāna*—or indeed, from any ethically skillful action that results in the production of merit. It is from the perspective of this "karmic discourse" that the nature of the recipient (whether worthy or unworthy) becomes irrelevant, since giving, as an ethical action, is always ethically good—and its goodness is a function of the donor's own mind.

Egge maintains that as one traces the discourse of *dāna* through different strata of Pāli literature, one sees that the "karmic discourse" becomes stronger and stronger over time, largely displacing the "sacrificial discourse"—but without ever eradicating it completely. The sacrificial understanding of *dāna* remains important, even in later Pāli texts, and nowhere more so than in the continued emphasis such texts place upon the importance of a worthy recipient. Strictly speaking, from the perspective of the "karmic discourse," the worth of the recipient should perhaps be irrelevant, since it is the mental state and ethical intentions of the *donor* that really matter. Nevertheless, we continue to see an emphasis upon giving to worthy recipients, such as Buddhist monks or the Saṃgha. We can see the two discourses uneasily coexisting in those passages (previously mentioned) that give us a hierarchy of recipients and a corresponding hierarchy of merit. On the one hand, such passages adhere to the "karmic discourse," since they maintain that all giving produces merit (even giving to the lowliest animals); on the other hand, such passages also adhere to the "sacrificial discourse" by retaining the notion of the worthy recipient, since the amount of merit acquired in each case is relative to the worth of the recipient. In a similar manner, the ambivalence of the passages I alluded to above can also be seen as resulting from a conflict or tension between sacrificial and karmic understandings of *dāna*.

Why did the "karmic discourse" of *dāna*, though becoming more and more dominant over time, never succeed in eradicating completely the "sacrificial discourse" of *dāna* and its emphasis on worthy recipients? Why did the status of the recipient continue to matter? Why was *dāna* never fully "ethicized"? Egge is surely correct in pointing to economic considerations: in practical terms, the Saṃgha was dependent for its survival upon the material support of the laity and obviously could not afford to discount any doctrine that emphasizes giving to the religiously worthy.[64]

At the same time, however, Maria Hibbets' study of the discourse of *dāna* found in Hindu, Buddhist, and Jain medieval digests suggests equally strongly that the persistence of the worthy-recipient doctrine within all three traditions should not be reduced to economic considerations alone—since this kind of crude and reductive explanation cannot account for the careful theorizing these texts offer on the *ethical effects* of giving to a worthy recipient.[65] Hibbets maintains that medieval discussions of *dāna* from all three traditions promote an "ethics of esteem" which highly values the respect, esteem, and admiration that should arise in the donor when confronted by a religiously worthy person, such as a monk. The unequal and hierarchical relationship between the donor and the worthy recipient is thus crucial, in Hibbets' view, for it encourages the donor to look up to the recipient, admire his moral qualities, use his gift of alms to express a commitment to the religious values the recipient represents, and perhaps gain a greater awareness of his own moral failings. Thus: "The moral excellence of the recipient is vital not only for how much merit or good karma the giver earns by the gift [but also because it] conditions the appropriate intentions and responses expected of the giver. . . . The exalted status of the recipient is the very condition for esteem and respect to rise up in the giver."[66] In contrast, as Hibbets points out, an *unworthy* recipient inspires only a feeling of pity, and "pity may not be far from contempt . . . having pity for others may be akin to despising them at worst and patronizing them at best"—attitudes that are "not particularly ethically valuable."[67] Hibbets hereby demonstrates that the doctrine of the worthy recipient is not incompatible with purely karmic explanations of giving.

It is also important to note that whereas our own culture might consider moral "worthiness" or "unworthiness" to be purely a matter of internal, mental qualities—and thus impossible for the donor to discern—in a South Asian context pervaded by the notions of karma and rebirth, moral worth is at least partially suggested by the particular social position one inhabits, which is clear for all to see. Thus animals, beggars, and lepers are "unworthy" by definition, while monks and ascetics must be presumed to merit one's respect and devotion. In other words (and despite arguments to the contrary by the Uttarāpathakas), the doctrine of the worthy recipient need not strip the donor herself of any ethical agency, since she is free to choose the recipients of her gifts "with discrimination," and fully capable of identifying those who are "worthy." Ultimately, of course, monks and ascetics need not necessarily be good, and the possibility of a corrupt and immoral monk is always there, but Buddhist discussions of *dāna* provide for this as well: whether the individual monk who receives one's alms is moral or immoral, intelligent or stupid—indeed, even if one *knows* he is immoral and stupid—he still constitutes a "worthy recipient" who should be met with respect and esteem, since (as many Buddhist texts make clear) it is the values represented by his religious clothing that one is honoring with a gift, not his qualities as an individual.

This is also the reason a gift made to the Saṃgha is always more meritorious than a gift made to an individual, since the Saṃgha represents an abstraction of all the virtuous qualities that might or might not be realized within any individual monk. The Saṃgha is always a worthy "field of merit," free of the stain of individual faults. In the *Dakkhiṇāvibhaṅga Sutta,* in fact, the Buddha states categorically: "O Ānanda, I say that in no way whatsoever does a gift given to an individual ever have greater fruit than an offering made to the Saṃgha"—even in future times, when the Saṃgha will be full of those who are "immoral and wicked."[68] This is because such a gift is given "on account of the Saṃgha"[69]—in other words, out of esteem for what the Saṃgha *represents* rather than its individual embodiments.

The doctrine of the worthy recipient, in other words, seems to be overdetermined. While economic considerations are of crucial importance, there are also legitimate ethical reasons why a gift given to a worthy recipient might be more salutary (and thus more productive of merit) than a gift given to an unworthy recipient—and why Buddhist monks and the Saṃgha must always be presumed to be worthy recipients. The worthy-recipient doctrine should therefore be seen as an element of the "sacrificial discourse" of *dāna* that continues to persist under the gradual dominance of the "karmic discourse" of *dāna* not only through economic considerations that call up the image of a greedy monkhood, but also because it was compatible with that karmic discourse and capable of being rationalized in karmic terms. The extent of this rationalization varies considerably from one context to another, however, so that the doctrine of the worthy recipient might be upheld, ignored, or opposed altogether, depending on the particular passage: sometimes the merit of the gift derives solely from the worth of the recipient, and an unworthy recipient therefore results in no merit at all; sometimess the merit of the gift derives solely from the intentions of the donor, and the character of the recipient is thus irrelevant; and sometimes we find a curious mixture of the two or another criterion altogether governing the amount of merit produced (such as the excellence of the object given). Hence, the inconsistency and ambivalence.[70]

Having undertaken this lengthy digression in order to explain the ambivalence Buddhist texts sometimes display toward the worthy-recipient doctrine, I now return to the basic contrast I drew above (which seems to coexist unproblematically with this ambivalence): gifts given *upward* to *worthy* recipients out of *respect* and for the sake of *merit* are contrasted with gifts given *downward* to *unworthy* recipients out of *compassion* and with *no expectation of reward.* I refer to these two modes of giving as *giving up* and *giving down,* which together comprise and organize a number of different Buddhist gifts. The rubric of *giving up* covers all those gifts associated with ordinary Buddhists and moving upward with respect and esteem from inferiors to superiors, such as the layperson's gift of alms and other forms of material support to the Saṃgha, the family's gift of their children to be ordained as monks and nuns, or the making of ritual offerings to an image, *caitya,* or *stūpa.* The rubric of *giving down,* on the other hand, covers all those gifts associated with ideal and exalted Buddhist beings and moving downward from superiors to inferiors in spontaneous displays of generosity and compassion, such as the bodhisattva's gift of his body, possessions, or merit, or the Buddha's gift of the dharma.

Historical Origins

What are the historical origins or antecedents of these two prominent modes of giving? If we look beyond the strictly Buddhist discourse on *dāna* to consider its larger Vedic and Hindu background, an argument can be made (based on Vedic, epic, and dharmaśāstric literature) that each mode of giving was associated with one of the two dominant ideological communities of classical Indian society—that is, the brahman and *kṣatriya varṇas,* respectively. Thomas Trautmann long ago pointed out that many Vedic and Hindu textual discussions covering a variety of different topics (such as marriage, caste, and commerce) presume and share in common an underlying "typology of exchange" in which each one of the four *varṇas* is associated with a particular mode of exchange.[71] If we look at Trautmann's typology and compare it to the Buddhist material, it is clear that the Buddhist modes of *giving up* and *giving down* correspond very closely to the modes of exchange associated with the brahman and *kṣatriya varṇas,* respectively.

The *gift given upward for the sake of merit* is closely associated with the brahman *varṇa* because, according to Brahmanical ideology, it is the special privilege of this *varṇa* to be the preordained recipients of all such upward-moving, merit-producing gifts. According to the Dharma Śāstras, while the *giving* of religious gifts (*dāna*) is a strict obligation of all twice-born *varṇas,* only brahmins have the special privilege of earning a livelihood by *receiving* religious gifts (*pratigraha*), since it is the religious position of the brahmins and the spiritual quality of *brāhmaṇya* that make them the exclusive human recipients of such gifts.[72] Religious gifts in the dharmaśāstric conception therefore always flow upward toward superior beings—either the gods or the pure and learned brahmins who are the "gods on earth."

Dharmaśāstric literature seems to restrict the meaning of *dāna* almost exclusively, in fact, to religious gifts given upward to worthy recipients in exchange for merit. Dharmaśāstric definitions of *dāna* (well summarized in P. V. Kane's comprehensive treatment)[73] specify that *dāna* must involve both a material object that is given and a worthy recipient who receives the gift, and that this "receiving" (*pratigraha*) must be done "with the idea that he [the donor] will derive from that act some unseen spiritual result [*adṛṣṭa* or *puṇya*]."[74] Other possible conceptions of *dāna* seem specifically to be excluded. In direct contrast to various Buddhist notions of *dāna,* the dharmaśāstric commentator Medātithi says that the teacher's gift of knowledge to a pupil (in which there is no material object) and the ritual offering made to an image (in which there is no recipient) are called *dāna* only in a secondary sense, and do not constitute the technical meaning of *dāna* as viewed by the Dharmaśāstra.[75] Further demonstrating the absolute necessity of a worthy recipient is the fact that a gift which is lost en route and never reaches its recipient reaps no reward for the donor (regardless of his good intentions),[76] while a gift given to an evil recipient might result in misery for the donor or lead him to hell (in spite of his good intentions).[77] What I have been referring to, in Buddhist discourse, as the mode of *giving up* might therefore be seen as a kind of "brahmanical model" of giving related historically to the brahmanical ideology in which *dāna* refers specifically to *religious gifts given upward to worthy recipients in exchange for merit.*

The Buddhist mode of *giving down,* on the other hand, seems to derive from different historical sources. When Buddhist authors speak not of themselves as members of the Saṃgha accepting the gifts of laypeople, but rather of bodhisattvas and Buddhas compassionately showering extravagant gifts downward upon pitiful and unworthy recipients, they are clearly not drawing upon the dharmaśāstric understanding of *dāna.* (In fact, gifts of compassion are specifically excluded from the dharmaśāstric conception; Kane, for example, observes of the Dharma Śāstras that "when a person makes a gift through compassion it is not the *dāna* and *pratigraha* spoken of by the śāstra . . . [for] a gift made through compassion is made irrespective of caste."[78]) Instead, these magnanimous displays of generosity characteristic of bodhisattvas and Buddhas seem to be drawing on the *kṣatra-dharma* found primarily in the epics, where the *kṣatriya* is repeatedly admonished to acquire goods through noble conquest and the heroic use of arms, and then distribute them indiscriminately to others with complete generosity, thereby rendering him independent of any semblance of direct exchange with other *varṇas.*[79] *Kṣatriyas* are thus the preordained "givers" of the *varṇa* system—particularly in their role as kings, who are repeatedly reminded of their paramount duty to *give, give, give*—while they avoid being "receivers" by acquiring their gifts through noble conquest alone.[80] In sharp contrast to the brahmin, the *kṣatriya* must never accept a gift or make an entreaty, which would be akin to admitting submission and defeat on the battlefield, seriously wounding the *kṣatriya*'s pride.[81]

The Buddhist mode of *giving down* runs parallel to this "*kṣatriya* model" of giving, a parallel that becomes especially clear when we consider the many "*kṣatriya*-like" aspects of that exemplar of magnanimous, downward giving—the bodhisattva. Whether or not one prescribes to the theory that Buddhism represented a radical revolt against brahmanical ideology, there is no doubt that Buddhist thought in India is replete with royal imagery, often seems to regard the *kṣatriya* as being higher in status than the brahmin, and draws a number of distinct parallels—mythical, iconographical, and ideological—between the bodhisattva and the *kṣatriya.* In fact, I would argue that the bodhisattva ideal may, in many respects, be seen as a kind of Buddhist application of a *kṣatriya*-ethic of life. This comes out especially strongly in Mahāyāna texts that deal with the bodhisattva career, such as Śāntideva's *Bodhicaryāvatāra.* Just as courageous battle against one's enemies is perhaps the single most characteristic activity encouraged by the *kṣatra-dharma* of the epics, so Śāntideva's manual on the bodhisattva practice draws quite heavily on the imagery of war and depicts the ideal bodhisattva as a kind of "*kṣatriya* of the human mind" waging a violent battle against the mental afflictions (*kleśa*).[82] Just as the *kṣatra-dharma* attaches special importance to the *kṣatriya*'s quality of *vīrya* (strength, energy, or vigor), and posits it as the underlying root of the *kṣatriya*'s noble qualities,[83] so *vīrya* constitutes the fourth of the bodhisattva's six perfections (*pāramitā*), and is often described as that virtue which informs and activates the other five.

These parallels between the bodhisattva and the *kṣatriya* (which could easily be multiplied in number) extend as well to their ideal modes of exchange. Just as the *kṣatriya* is encouraged to give magnanimously to others but never to receive anything from them in return, so the bodhisattva is exhorted *ad nauseam* to give himself, his possessions, and his merit away to all living beings without distinction, but never to accept any such gifts on his own behalf.[84] In fact, like the *kṣatriya* of the epics, Śāntideva's ideal bodhisattva is loathe to accept gifts or favors of any kind: "Let him be able and energetic, always doing things for himself; he should not let anyone else help him in any task."[85] The *Bodhicaryāvatāra* presents a striking difference, in fact, between the bodhisattva's own means of progressing along the path (through noble endeavor, hard work, and difficult striving) and other people's means of progressing along the path (by receiving everything as a gift from the generous bodhisattva himself). "This world is completely subject to the afflictions and incapable of bringing about its own welfare"—the bodhisattva thinks to himself—"Therefore, I must do it for them, for I am not incapable, as these people are."[86] Like the *kṣatriya,* the bodhisattva should even cultivate an exaggerated sense of pride (*māna*), constantly thinking to himself, "It is I alone who must do it!"[87]—or in other words (as Prajñākaramati's commentary explains), "Whatever good things happen to living beings, I alone should bring all of them about; nobody else should be given any opportunity!"[88] Within such passages, the bodhisattva begins to look very much like the swaggering and self-sufficient *kṣatriya* warrior. In Jan Nattier's felicitious phrasing, the bodhisattva path is here depicted as an especially ambitious and "macho" vocation, appropriate only for "a few good men" or "such people as Olympic athletes ('going for the gold') or Marine Corps recruits ('the few, the proud, the brave')"—in other words, those who are similar in nature to the *kṣatriya* warrior.[89]

What I have been referring to as the mode of *giving down* in Buddhist discourse might therefore be seen as a kind of "*kṣatriya* model" of giving related historically to the *kṣatra-dharma* of the epics, in which *dāna* refers specifically to *royal gifts flowing down a hierarchy of dependence in magnanimous displays of largesse.* Buddhism thus appears to have adapted both the "brahmanical" model of *giving up* and the "*kṣatriya*" model of *giving down.* However, in consonance with Buddhism's general strategy of divorcing religious ideas from the *varṇa* theory (or redefining the *varṇas* in spiritual terms), these two modes of giving are no longer attached to particular *varṇas* determined by birth. Instead they are attached more loosely to religious categories defined by Buddhism: the mode of "giving up" is associated most closely with the Buddhist monastic order (as the preordained recipients of upward-moving gifts), whereas the mode of "giving down" is associated with ideal and exalted beings such as arhats, bodhisattvas, and Buddhas. Thus, when Buddhists act as members of the Saṃgha accepting the gifts of laypeople, they act more like brahmins, but when they imagine their most exalted beings' magnanimous works of compassion, they call up the image of *kṣatriyas*.

It is also pertinent to consider the position of the Buddha himself. The Buddha appears to be equally associated with both models of giving: on the one hand, he is the ultimate monk and a worthy "field of merit" who is the foremost recipient of upward-moving gifts; on the other hand, he is also the exalted, magnanimous being who freely showers his dharma down on his dependents. He is both ultimate (*kṣatriya*) giver and ultimate (brahmin) recipient, the paradigmatic embodiment of both "giving up" and "giving down." By single-handedly attaining perfect Buddhahood and lavishing his dharma upon the world, he partakes in the heroic giving characteristic of the *kṣatriya,* but by establishing a monastic order that can enter into regular relations of patronage with the surrounding lay community, he partakes in the more regularized and institutionalized giving characteristic of the brahmin. His ability to both give and receive with no considerations of relative position is symbolic of his absolute freedom and power.

Giving Up (Again)

But the Buddha constitutes the paradigmatic embodiment of a third mode of giving as well—one that completes my threefold schema of *giving up, giving down,* and *giving up²*. This is "giving up" in quite another sense—the "giving up" of the world in an act of ascetic renunciation. The linguistic slide between "giving" and "giving up" is not limited to the English language alone; in Pāli and Sanskrit, for example, the term *cāga/tyāga* means both "gift" and "renunciation." Buddhist thought acknowledges and often emphasizes this connection: *every gift is a renunciation.* To give a gift to someone else is always to deprive oneself of the same—thus, every "gift" is also a "giving up." Every gift is defined as a moment of cultivating nonattachment, the culmination of which is the monk's renunciation of the world. And just as every gift constitutes a miniature version of world-renunciation, so also world-renunciation itself can be seen as an ultimate variety of "the gift."

This third mode of giving can be conceptualized as the logical culmination of either of the other two—a relationship that is sometimes clarified by the use of narrative. In relation to the "*kṣatriya* model" of giving, for example, there are many Buddhist stories in which the magnanimous generosity of the king easily shades into the ascetic's giving up of the world. The connection between the two is made especially explicit in the famous *jātaka* of Prince Vessantara, whose kingly generosity is so extreme that he eventually gives away his possessions, his royal status, his wife, and his children. Reduced to poverty and exile in the forest, Prince Vessantara begins to look very much like the world-renouncing monk. But rather than becoming a monk in the ordinary way, he renounces the world and becomes a monk as the logical outcome of having given everything away. The royal largesse characteristic of the king, when taken to an extreme, leads Prince Vessantara directly into the renunciation of the world characteristic of the monk.[90] The royal's *giving down* blends into the ascetic's *giving up.*

Much the same is true in regard to the "brahmanical model" of giving as well: the layperson's upward-moving offerings to the Saṃgha, when taken to an extreme, once again blend into the monk's renunciation of the world. This connection is made explicit in the story of another famous king—King Aśoka and the "Great Quinquennial Festival" (*pañcavarṣika*) he holds on behalf of the Saṃgha. During this festival (as described in the *Divyāvadāna*), King Aśoka, acting as a faithful Buddhist layman, engages in

TABLE 3

Two Conceptual Schema for Organizing the Varieties of Buddhist *Dāna*

RECIPROCATED / UNRECIPROCATED / PURE		GIVING UP / GIVING DOWN / GIVING UP^2
(1) RECIPROCATED GIFTS (gifts involving *mundane reciprocity,* i.e. ordinary Maussian social exchanges)	↔	∅
(2) UNRECIPROCATED GIFTS (gifts involving *transcendental reciprocity,* i.e. given for the sake of merit alone)	↔	(1) GIVING UP (giving upward to a worthy recipient out of respect and for the sake of merit) ("brahmanical" model)
(3) PURE GIFTS (gifts involving *no reciprocity,* i.e. either completely desireless or motivated by one of the "approved" desires):		
(a) the gift given by an advanced bodhisattva who has attained the perfection of wisdom, or the gift given by any bodhisattva with the desire to attain Buddhahood	↔	(2) GIVING DOWN (giving downward to an unworthy recipient out of compassion and with no expectation of reward) ("ksatriya" model)
(b) the gift given by an arhat or with the desire to attain arhatship	↔	(3) GIVING UP^2 (giving up the world in an act of renunciation)
(c) the gift given by a Buddha	↔	brings together *giving up, giving down,* and *giving up^2* (as the paradigmatic object of the first and the paradigmatic agent of the latter two)

a frenzy of ritual offerings to the Saṃgha, finally giving away not only his entire kingdom but also his family, his kingship, and his very self—thereby symbolically becoming a monk and joining the Saṃgha. The almsgiving characteristic of the Buddhist layperson, when taken to an extreme, thus leads King Aśoka (if only temporarily) directly into the renunciation of the world characteristic of the monk.[91] The layperson's *giving upward* blends into the ascetic's *giving up.*

World-renunciation, or *giving up*,[2] can thus be related to either the "brahmanical model" of *giving up* or the "*kṣatriya* model" of *giving down.* Perhaps we can relate this to the fact that, historically, scholars have been unable to pinpoint any single, definitive origin for the practices of asceticism and world-renunciation within Indian religions—some scholars seeing them as a natural development from the logic of Brahmanical sacrifice, and other scholars positing a non-Brahmanical and non-Vedic origin. In any case, within the Buddhist discourse on giving this renunciatory aspect ultimately serves to tie together all competing notions of the gift at the level of their logical culmination: whether the gift is given up or given down, out of respect or out of compassion, resulting in abundant merit or none at all, a matter of sacrifice or a matter of charity—all gifts have a renunciatory aspect, and all *giving* ultimately partakes of *giving up.*

• • •

The two conceptual schema I have presented in this chapter for organizing some of the many varieties of *dāna* discussed within Buddhist exegetical texts are summarized in table 3, along with some indication of how the two schema might overlap with one another.

It should be noted, however, that the connections I have drawn in this table between different categories of giving are not intended to be strict or exclusive equivalences but only suggestive parallels. My hope is simply that, taken together, these two schema will offer the reader several different ways of conceptualizing each variety of the gift. The heavy black line that runs across the entire table indicates a more basic distinction between lower (reciprocal) and higher (nonreciprocal) ideals of giving. Using this discussion as a framework, I now turn to a closer consideration of the gift-of-the-body theme.

V

A FLEXIBLE GIFT

How does the bodhisattva's gift of his body relate to the larger discourse on *dāna* I enumerated in chapter 4? In the following discussion I shall be pursuing a double argument: On the one hand, the bodhisattva's gift of his body represents one of the highest ideals of giving to be found in the Buddhist tradition and is commonly depicted and classified as an ideal and nonreciprocal gift—in other words, a gift that falls somewhere *below* the heavy black line in table 3 of the previous chapter. On the other hand, however, gift-of-the-body *jātakas,* through a variety of different narrative strategies, skillfully encompass and invoke various lesser, more ordinary, and more reciprocal models of giving as well—or those that fall *above* the heavy black line in table 3. The gift of the body is thus both ideal and ordinary, simultaneously nonreciprocal and reciprocal. In chapter 2 I invoked the tension between the bodhisattva's "imitability" and his "otherness." The same tension appears here, in the twofold aspect of the gift of the body: as an ideal and nonreciprocal gift, the gift of the body suggests the bodhisattva's "otherness," but as an ordinary and reciprocal gift, it suggests his "imitability." The first demands our admiration and cultic devotion toward the glorious feat of the bodhisattva, while the second demands that we imitate the bodhisattva and engage in *dāna* ourselves. Either one of these aspects may be emphasized at the expense of the other, or a precarious resolution between the two may be attempted.

In what follows, I will examine each of these two perspectives on the gift, as well as demonstrating some of the ways in which they are balanced. I will then turn to another variety of "doubleness" inherent in the gift-of-the-body theme: the double discourse of "self" and "selflessness" that surrounds the notion of "self-sacrifice." In both these discussions, the gift of the body will reveal itself to be highly flexible and multivalent in nature, capable of conveying, at one and the same time, a number of diametrically opposed conceptions of generosity, selflessness, and reward. The artfulness and skill with which the concept's multiple connotations are handled are what make the gift-of-the-body theme such a useful signifier within the Buddhist discourse on *dāna.*

The Ideal Gift

Indian Buddhist textual discourse generally conceives and depicts the gift of the body not as an ordinary act of giving, but rather as the fullest possible manifestation of *dāna* and the ideal form of *dāna.* This high valuation of the gift of the body is conveyed in several different ways. One simple way of indicating its ideal nature is to associate this gift closely, consistently, and almost exclusively with the figure of the bodhisattva. Though gifts of the body are not restricted to bodhisattvas alone,[1] it is no doubt true that within Buddhist literature those who give away their bodies are overwhelmingly described as bodhisattvas. In fact, the gift of the body is even a defining feature of bodhisattvahood, for it is said that all bodhisattvas must make five gifts throughout the course of their careers—those of wealth, children, wife, body parts, and life.[2] Since, as we saw earlier, any gift given by a bodhisattva is by definition a perfectly "pure" gift, closely associating the gift of the body with the figure of the bodhisattva strongly suggests its ideal nature.

This idealization is further reinforced, moreover, by the fact that the gift of the body is often associated more specifically with the bodhisattva's "perfection of generosity," or *dāna-pāramitā.* As I mentioned previously, gift-of-the-body stories are frequently chosen to illustrate *dāna-pāramitā* within narrative collections intended to illustrate the six or ten perfections.

Similarly, gift-of-the-body stories are frequently invoked within exegetical discussions of *dāna-pāramitā.* In the *Mahāprajñāpāramitā Śāstra,* for example, a long section devoted to an explanation of each of the six perfections answers the question "How does the bodhisattva fulfill *dāna-pāramitā?*" by stating: "He gives everything away without restriction, and when he gives even his own body, his heart experiences no regret: for example, King Śibi, who gave his body to a dove."[3] This is followed by a retelling of the story of King Śibi's gift of flesh to ransom a dove, this story itself serving as the complete explanation of *dāna-pāramitā.* Likewise, in the *Pāramitāsamāsa* attributed to Ārya Śūra, the author begins his discussion of *dāna-pāramitā* with eight verses on the gift of the body (mentioning flesh, blood, and limbs), clearly treating this gift as emblematic of *dāna-pāramitā* as a whole.[4] Again, the *Cariyāpiṭaka*'s brief discussion of *dāna-pāramitā* explains that gifts of material goods constitute only the "preliminary requirements for giving," whereas the gift of one's limbs constitutes the "perfection of giving," and the gift of one's entire body or life constitutes the "fulfillment of the perfection [of giving]."[5] These and many other, similar contexts indicate that the gift of the body was conceived not as ordinary giving, but rather as giving's "perfection."

One of the major ways in which this "perfection" is described in Buddhist texts is in terms of the absolute *purity of intention* that accompanies the gift—in other words, the fact that the bodhisattva gives a gift out of pure generosity and compassion and with no ulterior motives whatsoever. In this regard, it is striking to note just how closely and consistently the gift of the body is associated with such purity of intention. Consider again the *Mahāprajñāpāramitā Śāstra*'s definition of *dāna-pāramitā:* "He gives everything away without restriction, and when he gives even his own body, his heart experiences no regret." The definition of *dāna-pāramitā* given here is not merely the act of giving away one's body, but more specifically giving away one's body and *feeling no regret.* It is the purity of intention that is presumed to accompany the gift of the body that is thus highlighted. This is true even when the category of *dāna-pāramitā* itself is not mentioned. In another passage from the same text,[6] gifts are classified as being "inferior," "medium," or "superior," with the gifts of head, eyes, flesh, and blood (as well as kingdom, riches, wife, and children) constituting the "superior" category. But in addition to defining each type of gift in terms of the objects given, the text also defines them as follows: "inferior" gifts are simply given, "medium" gifts come about with one's "progress in the cultivation of giving," and "superior" gifts come about with one's "progress in the intention behind the gift." Gifts of the body are again explicitly linked to the donor's purity of intention.

Much the same is illustrated in yet another section of the same text, this time by means of a humorous story about Śāriputra. Śāriputra, the text tells us, had practiced the bodhisattva path for sixty *kalpas* and was eager to fulfill the perfection of giving. One day a mendicant approached him and asked for his eye. Śāriputra at first hesitated, but then, desiring to fulfill *dāna-pāramitā,* he pulled out an eye and gave it to him. The mendicant took the eye, smelled it, spit up in disgust, threw the eye on the ground, and crushed it with his feet. Angered and resentful, Śāriputra thought to himself:

> People who are so vicious are difficult to save! My eye was truly of no use to him, but he cruelly asked for it, and when he obtained it, he threw it down and crushed it with his feet. What could be more vicious? Such people cannot be saved. Better to tame oneself; one will be liberated from samsara earlier![7]

It was at that very moment, the text explains, that Śāriputra left the bodhisattva path and returned to the Lesser Vehicle.

Notice that Śāriputra makes an immediate connection between the gift of the body and *dāna-pāramitā,* assuming implicitly that the gift of one's own body is the type of gift that will automatically allow one to fulfill the perfection of generosity. This underscores the close association drawn by the tradition between gifts of the body and *dāna-pāramitā.* Notice also, however, what Śāriputra fails to recognize: that gifts of the body constitute a fulfillment of *dāna-pāramitā* precisely because of the great purity of intention that is assumed to accompany such gifts. Śāriputra's failure, after all, is not a failure to give (since he does give the man his eye), but rather a failure to maintain the frame of mind and purity of intention that normally characterize such gifts.

The close association drawn between the gift of the body and the absolute purity of the giver's intention is perhaps explainable by the fact that the former would seem to constitute a stark and obvious signifier of the latter. In other words, whereas the purity of the donor's intention is a purely mental quality—invisible and unverifiable to the outside observer—its existence seems to be vouchsafed by the dramatic spectacle of bodily self-sacrifice, which is clear for all to see. Indeed, one of the underlying assumptions at work here is that *nobody* would give such a difficult and painful gift—such an *extreme* gift—if his intentions were *not* completely pure. The gift of the body thus seems to serve in the Buddhist imagination as a potent external sign or visible marker for the presence of pure generosity.

This presence is further confirmed for us, moreover, by another external sign characteristic of the gift of the body: the spectacle of the unworthy recipient. As we have seen, because the recipient of the bodhisattva's body is either *pitiful* or *evil* (or the deity Śakra pretending to be someone pitiful or evil), we know for certain that the bodhisattva cannot be acting in the interest of gaining merit, but must be acting solely out of pure generosity and compassion. Finally, as if all these external signs still constituted insufficient evidence, the bodhisattva himself, as we have seen, is continually forced to make the purity of his motivations verbally explicit. Through vows, ritualized statements, and Acts of Truth, the bodhisattva repeatedly gives voice to his status as an ideal and perfect giver. When formulated as Acts of Truth, moreover, these verbalized statements often result in yet one more visible marker of the bodhisattva's utter sincerity: the restoration of his injured body to perfect health. Thus, the giver, the gift, the recipient, and the procedure of giving itself—all of these features of the gift-of-the-body genre conspire to prove to us, beyond any suspicion, the status of the gift of the body as a pure and perfect gift, one that adheres to the very highest standards of *dāna.*

Finally, another variety of ultimate and ideal gift, as we have seen, is the *giving up of the world* in an act of renunciation. And once again we find that gift-of-the-body stories sometimes suggest that the gift of one's own body is somehow equivalent to this ultimate gift. This association between the gift of the body and the act of renunciation is never stated explicitly but is suggested in several different ways. For example, if we think of world-renunciation as being equivalent to the *giving up of everything*—one's wealth, possessions, family, and indeed, one's very life (as it was formerly lived)—then it is interesting to note that gift-of-the-body stories often seem to treat the *body* as a signifier for "everything." In other words, the bodhisattva within such stories often implicitly assumes (whether rightly or wrongly) that by giving away his *body,* he is giving away *everything.*

This equivalence is made explicit, in fact, by the consistent association drawn between gifts of the body and the name Sarvaṃdada ("All Giver" or "Giver of Everything"). Sarvaṃdada is a ubiquitous name within gift-of-the-body stories. Although it is most commonly associated with the story of a particular king named Sarvaṃdada who offers his head to a brahmin supplicant,[8] it has a tendency to be invoked within other gift-of-the-body stories as well. Thus King Ambara in the *Karuṇāpuṇḍarīka Sūtra,*[9] King Candraprabha in *Divyāvadāna* 22,[10] and King Śibi in *Avadānakalpalatā* 55[11]—to cite just a few examples—are all referred to using the name Sarvaṃdada or the adjective *sarvaṃdada.* Moreover, in those contexts in which the name is explained, the idea that the gift of one's *body* constitutes the gift of *everything* is always suggested. In *Avadānasārasamuccaya* 3, for example, King Sarvaṃdada asks himself: "How and when could he, whose mind is attached even to his own body, be called 'Sarvaṃdada'?" By giving away his body, he determines, he will "now become one whose name is apt in meaning."[12] Thus it is not until the gift of his body that Sarvaṃdada, the "Giver of Everything," truly "earns" his name. Likewise, in the *Karuṇāpuṇḍarīka Sūtra,* when the gods praise King Ambara for his great generosity and give him the name "Sarvaṃdada," the people of his kingdom are still not convinced and decide to ask him for all of his limbs, noting: "If he gives them, he will be 'Sarvaṃdada,' but if he doesn't give them, he will not be 'Sarvaṃdada.'"[13] Similarly, in *Divyāvadāna* 22, when the evil brahmin Raudrākṣa hears of King Candraprabha's great reputation as an "all-giving" (*sarvaṃdada*) king, he immediately speculates: "If he's really 'all-giving,' then he'll give me his head!"[14] The gift of the *body* thus stands for the gift of *everything*—which is equivalent to renouncing the world.

Perhaps another way of saying much the same thing is to note that the practice of world-renunciation involves not merely the rejection of family or material possessions but also the loss of one's former identity and the giving up of one's *self*—which is aptly symbolized by the gift of one's *body.* As Mauss pointed out long ago, every gift contains something of the giver and represents an abnegation and renunciation of his own self.[15] But this symbolic identity between giver and gift, which is sometimes stronger and sometimes weaker, becomes literal and complete in the gift of one's own body: when the giver himself becomes the gift, the gift loses its flavor as an external object or mere "gift," and becomes a true renunciation, conversion, or giving up of the self. Perhaps this is why gift-of-the-body stories so often take on the structure of "rites of passage" (as described by Van Gennep and Turner), since all such rites involve the loss and stripping of one's former identity in order to take on a new identity, such as that of a monk or renunciant.[16] The gift of the body thus becomes a concrete and visceral image of the kind of eradication of self that is perhaps most fully realized when one renounces the world.

Within Buddhist texts the idea that the gift of the *body* is really the gift of *oneself* finds perhaps its greatest expression in the distinction sometimes drawn between those gifts that are "external" (*bāhira*) and those that are "internal" (*adhyātmika*). Whereas *bāhira* gifts are "external" to the self, consisting of adventitious property or possessions, *adhyātmika* gifts are "internal" to the self, or that which constitutes an integral or inherent part of one's person. In Pāli *Jātaka* 499 King Śibi thinks to himself: "There is not a single external object that I have not given, [yet] external gifts do not satisfy me; I want to give an internal gift."[17] The context clearly suggests that "internal" gifts are of a qualitatively different order than "external" gifts, and cites, as examples of "internal" gifts, the flesh of the heart, the flesh of the body, the blood, and the eyes.

This distinction between material objects as "external" gifts and gifts of the body as "internal" gifts appears in many later Buddhist texts, as well; in the *Bodhisattvabhūmi,* for example, the two types of gifts are defined somewhat technically as follows:

> What is the [bodhisattva's] "gift of everything"? In brief, "everything" refers to the two types of objects that can be given: internal and external. When a bodhisattva gives away his own body—even including the very marrow of his bones—that is referred to as the gift of a wholly internal object. When the bodhisattva ingests food and drink and then regurgitates it for the sake of those beings who eat [only] regurgitated food, that is referred to as the bodhisattva's gift of a partly internal and partly external object. The gift of any object aside from those just mentioned is referred to as the gift of a wholly external object.[18]

While the precise delineation of regurgitated food as "partly internal and partly external" would seem to make the internal/external distinction overly physical or biological in nature, it seems clear from other contexts that what is really at stake here is the *person,* the *identity,* or the *self.* Thus, the *Mahāprajñāpāramitā Śāstra* claims that "the internal gift consists of giving one's life without regret for beings, as is recounted in the *jātakas* and *avadānas*"[19]—thus moving away from an overly physical conception of the *body* and toward a more generalized conception of *self-sacrifice.* Even more tellingly, King Śibi, in the passage from Pāli *Jātaka* 499 alluded to above, includes "doing the work of a slave" (along with more concrete bodily sacrifices) under the category of "internal" gifts.[20] The *adhyātmika* category thus includes any gift that might be interpreted as a *giving up of the self* that is akin to the ascetic's renunciation of the world and that supercedes all ordinary gifts. Giving up the world in an act of renunciation is thus yet another category of ideal and nonreciprocal gift closely associated with the gift of the body.

The Ordinary Gift

The gift of the body thus stands as one of the highest ideals of giving to be found in the Buddhist tradition—the very paradigm of the pure and nonreciprocal gift. At the same time, however, it is my contention that part of the appeal of the gift-of-the-body genre is the manner in which gift-of-the-body stories skillfully encompass and invoke various lesser, more reciprocal, and more attainable models of giving as well—such that the gift of the body becomes an *ordinary* gift, as well as one that is ideal. This occurs in a number of different ways.

One could argue, for example, that it is precisely the *extremity* of the ideal gift that allows it to function as a model of the ordinary—by illustrating, in an exaggerated way, those features that should characterize all acts of giving, no matter how trivial. In other words, the most extreme expression of a phenomenon can serve to clarify those features of the phenomenon that are always present, but might normally be hidden or obscured within its more ordinary manifestations. Thus, if the gift of the body is made akin to renunciation, it is to underscore the point that *every* gift, even the most trivial offering of alms, is ideally an expression of nonattachment to the world and a miniature version of world-renunciation. If the gift of the body is frequently described as being "very difficult, most difficult, for a man to give up"[21] and thus incontrovertible proof of the donor's heroism, bravery, and strength of resolution, it is to underscore the point that *every* gift, even the most mundane, should be given with a firm mind and unwavering resolve, as if one were willingly throwing away one's own life.

In some *jātakas* this ultimate equivalence between extreme and ordinary manifestations of *dāna* is made explicit. In the *jātaka* of King Maṇicūḍa, for example, King Maṇicūḍa is in the process of performing a traditional Vedic sacrificial offering when a demon (who is really the god Śakra in disguise) suddenly rises up from the sacrificial fire and demands his flesh and blood, which Maṇicūḍa then proceeds to give him. Maṇicūḍa's gift of his flesh and blood thus takes place during a Vedic sacrifice and *in the form of an ordinary sacrificial offering*—thus suggesting the idea that every such ritual offering ought to be made with the same seriousness of purpose as if one were willingly taking a knife to one's own flesh. In much the same manner, in *Jātakamālā* 4 a pratyekabuddha looking for alms comes to the door of a generous householder, whereupon Māra conjures up a bottomless hell in between the doorway and the pratyekabuddha. Undeterred, the generous householder steps directly into the hell in his eagerness to give alms, whereupon a lotus magically springs up out of the hell and prevents him from falling in.[22] The point here, of course, is that every mundane gift of alms should be made with the same strength of resolution as if one were willingly stepping into hell itself—an equivalence made clear in the accompanying moral: "Good men will give even at the risk of their own lives—so how can anyone residing in comfort refuse to do so?"[23]

To some extent, then, lower and higher forms of giving are not necessarily incompatible with each other. Higher forms represent the ideal toward which all lower forms should strive and illustrate in an especially clear manner those features of *dāna* that ought to be ever-present. In this sense it is precisely the highly idealized nature of the gift of the body that allows it to serve as a model for more ordinary forms of giving. Nevertheless, I am more interested here in exploring exactly the opposite—in other words, several ways in which the idealism normally associated with gifts of the body is sometimes significantly compromised, so that the gift of the body loses some of its exalted character and moves closer to more ordinary forms of giving and the expectation of giving's rewards. This kind of compromise allows the story to successfully encompass several different notions of *dāna* at once, yet also results in a certain degree of tension and contradiction. Two ways in which this compromise is achieved are by means of plotline and framing.

COMPROMISING THE IDEAL GIFT THROUGH PLOTLINE

In terms of plotline, I am referring, of course, to those stories in which the deity Śakra is the recipient of the gift. As I noted already in chapter 2, stories featuring ordinary beings as the recipients of the gift tend to emphasize the extreme and uncompromising generosity of the bodhisattva, who willingly loses his life on behalf of those who are pitiful or evil. In stories featuring Śakra as the recipient, on the other hand, this extreme and uncompromising generosity cannot help but be weakened to some extent by the fact that the bodhisattva not only *survives* the gift but also *gets his body back.* Though the bodhisattva himself, at the time when he makes the gift, is obviously unaware that his body will ultimately be restored, the reader who is familiar with the conventions of the genre cannot help but recognize the fact that, over and over again, the bodhisattva within such stories is returned to perfect health and suffers no permanent negative consequences as a result of making the gift.

The survival of the bodhisattva and the restoration of his body (often in a better condition than before) significantly weaken the emphasis upon "perfect generosity." At the same time, however, this outcome also allows the reader to vicariously experience the *rewards* of the gift much more so than those stories in which the bodhisattva dies. Consequently, while the bodhisattva's gift of his body remains an extreme gift in nature, it also serves implicitly as a model for more ordinary, reward-based giving, such as the offering of alms to monks and other gifts given for the sake of merit. The balancing act maintained here between reciprocal and nonreciprocal modes of giving is exemplified by the double status of Śakra as the recipient: On the one hand, Śakra is *disguised as someone pitiful or evil*—an "unworthy recipient" whose presence testifies to the great purity of the bodhisattva's generosity. On the other hand, we, the audience, understand that Śakra is *actually a deity*—a classic "worthy recipient" who calls up the image of gifts given for the sake of reward. The confused identity of Śakra as a recipient is a marker of the careful balancing act between competing notions of generosity engaged in by stories of this type.

This strategy raises a number of interesting questions. Can the extremity of the gift be compromised, while still trying to maintain the ideal nature of the gift, which, as we have seen, is in part suggested precisely by its extremity? Does the gift of the body lose its ethical punch when the bodhisattva's body is wholly restored, and the entire episode is revealed to be an elaborate ruse undertaken by Śakra? And why do these stories sometimes strike us as trying to have their cake and eat it too? Within gift-of-the-body stories involving Śakra, I contend, there is indeed some tension between the desire to depict an ideal gift given with no expectation of any reward and the desire to depict this same gift as a model of *dāna* that can speak to the ordinary giver and that includes the expectation and enjoyment of rewards. This tension comes out most clearly, perhaps, in the bodhisattva's Act of Truth.

As we have seen, all Acts of Truth restoring the body invoke the purity of the bodhisattva's intentions when he gave his body away. But such Acts of Truth are inherently contradictory, for while presumably attesting to the bodhisattva's complete lack of regret in making the gift, the obvious purpose of the Act of Truth is to *get his body back;* in fact, such statements display an inordinate concern with payback, return, and reciprocity ("I gave freely, so give it back"; "I gave two eyes when only one was asked for, so give me one back"). The bodhisattva's obvious concern with "payback" stands in stark contradiction to the *lack* of such concern that is enunciated within the Act of Truth itself—and, in fact, that is *required* for the payback to occur—and the reader of such stories thus stumbles when she gets to the Act of Truth and feels a twinge of embarrassment on behalf of the bodhisattva. How do such stories deal with the apparent contradiction?

On the one hand it seems to me that the blatant self-interest inherent in these kinds of statements is permissible precisely because they are framed within the context of an Act of Truth. For the Act of Truth is treated by the tradition not as a declarative statement of one's desires, wishes, and motives, but rather as a performative utterance that ritually draws upon both the power of the truth and the intrinsic connection between moral action and its karmic rewards. In a sense, its performative and ritual status seems to negate whatever declarative value it may have, thus providing a "safe" context in which the bodhisattva is free to make bald statements of his true motives and desires.

On the other hand, however, this ritual sleight-of-hand is perhaps not completely convincing, and the lingering discomfort felt by some bodhisattvas is thus apparent. In Pāli *Jātaka* 499, for example, when Śakra encourages King Śibi to perform an Act of Truth in order to restore his eyes, the king is depicted as being hesitant and uncomfortable, whereas Śakra freely acknowledges the self-interest involved in such gifts: "Great King," he tells King Śibi, "the gift is not only given for the sake of the next world alone; there is also a motive for the sake of this world!"[24] Similarly, in *Jātakamālā* 2, after Śakra offers King Śibi a boon in celebration of his bodily gift, the narrator notes the king's obvious discomfort: "Now, the king was accustomed to giving and was therefore unpracticed in the way of begging and poverty."[25] When King Śibi finally manages to ask for death alone as a boon, Śakra seems to become angry at his overweening humility:

> Enough! Enough of this intention of yours! . . . When beggars have reduced you to such a condition, how on earth can you still be concerned with them? Enough deception! Just tell me, so that you can overcome your condition and at once get on with your life![26]

Thus it is Śakra alone who is willing to face the contradictory character of the Act of Truth, whereas King Śibi, still embarrassed by its blatant nature, complains to Śakra: "Why do you insist on making me boast, Sir?"[27] Only after such hemming and hawing does he finally perform the two Acts of Truth that restore his eyes. These Acts of Truth themselves, however—now rendered "safe" by their ritualized and performative context—freely acknowledge the king's desire to have his eyes restored. Moreover, once the purity of his intentions has been dramatically verified by means of this restoration, the king delivers a sermon in which he now feels free to dwell at length on the enormous *rewards* of giving:

> Who in the world would be lax in favoring supplicants with their wealth, after seeing these supernatural eyes of mine produced from the merit of giving? I can see all visible objects everywhere as clearly as if they were close by, even if they are a hundred *yojanas* away or hidden behind many mountains! What means of prosperity could be better than generosity, born of modesty and compassion for others? For just now, I gave away a human eye and received one that is supernatural and divine! Understanding this, Śibis, make your wealth bear fruit by giving it away and spending it. This is the way to the arising of fame and happiness in this world and the next![28]

In just a few pages, then, King Śibi has moved from hesitation and discomfort at the thought of any reward to enthusiastic promotion of giving-and-getting-back. The tension between these two positions is characteristic of stories that adhere to this plotline.

Stories involving Śakra as the recipient thus walk a sort of tightrope between ideal and ordinary gifts. They use an ideal gift in order to justify and encourage giving in general, yet they must also compromise some of the elements of this ideal in order to bring it closer to the ordinary. Correspondingly, the giver of the gift is something of an enigma: he is *both* the extraordinary bodhisattva who gives away his body with no expectation of reward, *and* the ordinary giver who expects and enjoys the rewards of his meritorious deeds. His confusion over which role he is playing is sometimes manifested as hesitation, embarrassment, or doubt, and the reader of such stories is often struck by the contradictory nature of his words and deeds.

Nevertheless, the movement between these two perspectives on the gift is not completely haphazard, for it is also the case that a consistent pattern can be discerned: the switch from the gift of the body as an *ideal gift* to the gift of the body as an *ordinary gift* seems to be facilitated somewhat by the switch to a *ritualized frame*. In other words, when one is performing a ritualized Act of Truth, or when one is engaging in formal preaching to the public, one approaches the gift of the body *after-the-fact*, from a once-removed distance, and from within a ritualized frame—and it then becomes possible to acknowledge the *rewards* of the gift and to use the gift of the body as a model for more ordinary and reciprocal forms of giving. *At the precise narrative moment when the gift is being made*, in contrast, such an acknowledgment would be impossible. It is through the switching between these two frames that competing conceptions of the gift are carefully balanced.

COMPROMISING THE IDEAL GIFT THROUGH FRAMING

There is a second manner, too, in which the compromise between ideal and ordinary forms of *dāna* is effected by gift-of-the-body stories—one that again relies on a shift to a different frame. This is a compromise that occurs not by means of the story's plotline, but rather by means of its external framing—more specifically, the framing of the "story of the past" within a particular "story of the present."

In chapter 1 I suggested that one possible way of describing the difference between *jātakas* and *avadānas* is to say that *jātakas*, on the whole, illustrate the bodhisattva's cultivation of the moral perfections in an age devoid of Buddhism, whereas *avadānas*, on the whole, take place in a Buddhist devotional context and involve the performance of devotional acts by disciples and layfollowers who take advantage of the presence of Buddhism in the world as a powerful "field of merit." Thus, *jātakas* are about "perfections," whereas *avadānas* are about "devotions," and by means of the two genres' coexistence, moral deeds in a Buddha-less age are both compared to and contrasted with ritual transactions in an age of Buddhadharma.

Now let us observe that the same distinction I have drawn between the *jātaka* and *avadāna* genres is also present *within* many *jātakas* themselves as a distinction between the "story of the past" and the "story of the present." For it is a characteristic feature of the *jātaka* genre that the "story of the past" always involves the bodhisattva within some long-ago life, whereas the "story of the present" always takes place within a Buddhist devotional context centered upon Śākyamuni and explaining the occasion upon which he narrated this particular tale. When the two stories are paired together, it sometimes occurs that an actual life-event undergone by the bodhisattva within the "story of the past" is somehow shown to be parallel to some ritual or devotional situation occurring within the surrounding "story of the present." This framing presents yet another opportunity for contextualizing the bodhisattva's gift of his body within a ritualized frame that makes it akin to more ordinary types of giving.

Let us consider, for example, Pāli *Jātaka* 316. The "story of the present" opens with a landowner inviting the Buddha and his monks to take a sumptuous meal at his house. He invites them back every day for seven days, and on the seventh day he presents the Saṃgha with many material gifts. The Buddha says to him:

> Layman, it is right for you to give joy and satisfaction [to others]. This is called generosity, and it is a tradition of the wise beings of old. For the wise beings of old, upon encountering supplicants, sacrificed their lives for them and gave them even their own flesh.[29]

He then launches into the "story of the past," which is the gift-of-the-body *jātaka* involving a hare who throws himself into a fire in order to feed a hungry brahmin ascetic (whereupon the fire refuses to burn him). Following this, there is a switch back to the "story of the present," where we learn that the landowner, upon hearing the tale of the hare, attained the fruit of stream-entry.

Treating this *jātaka* as a whole and taking seriously its association of these two particular stories, it is clear that the landowner engaging in ordinary *dāna* within the "story of the present" is, in some sense, parallel to the hare engaging in extreme *dāna* (the gift of the body) within the "story of the past"—for the Buddha tells the story of the hare's gift immediately after, and in reference to, the gift offered by the landowner. Moreover, both the landowner and the hare follow a similar arc: the opportunity to make a gift, the giving of the gift itself, and the enjoyment of the gift's rewards. Thus, the bodhisattva's gift of his body remains extreme in nature, yet is subtly made parallel to more ordinary ritual acts of offering, such as the layperson's offering of material gifts to the Saṃgha.

The exalted ideal of generosity represented by the hare's act of bodily sacrifice is weakened and compromised by being associated with a much more mundane form of giving—the upward-moving, merit-producing gift to a worthy recipient. This weakening, however, is also a great strength—for now the ordinary reader can feel good about his gifts and confidently relate his own ritual actions to the heroic deeds performed by the bodhisattvas of old. In fact, he might even be justified in believing that the two gifts are functionally equivalent—for whereas the hare is born in an age devoid of Buddhism and must therefore go to rather extreme lengths, offering his entire body to a passing brahmin, the landowner, fortunate enough to be born in an age of Buddhadharma, can simply offer material gifts to the Saṃgha. Thus, by carefully framing the "story of the past" within a particular "story of the present," the hare's gift of his body is placed within a ritualized context in which it approaches more reciprocal forms of the gift.

Much the same process occurs in Pāli *Jātaka* 499. Here the "story of the present" opens with the king of Kosala entertaining the Buddha and his Saṃgha for seven days straight and then presenting the Buddha with a very expensive robe. When the monks express their amazement at such a wonderful gift, the Buddha states:

> Monks, external possessions are indeed good gifts. [But] the wise men of old made all of Jambudvīpa into a festival every day by giving away gifts of six hundred thousand [gold pieces, yet] they were [still] unsatisfied by these external gifts. Thinking to themselves—"He who gives what is dear [to him] obtains what is dear [to him]"—they [even] tore out their [own] eyes and gave them to the supplicants they encountered.[30]

The Buddha then launches into a "story of the past"—the story of King Śibi's gift of his eyes to a blind old brahmin.

Again it is clear that the king of Kosala engaging in ordinary gifts within the "story of the present" is being in some sense made parallel to King Śibi engaging in extreme gifts within the "story of the past." While the Buddha's comments make it clear that King Śibi's gifts are vastly superior to those of the king of Kosala—for King Śibi is said to be "unsatisfied" by the kind of mere "external gifts" given by the king of Kosala—there is also a sense that the king of Kosala does not *need* to make such superior gifts, for he has access to the potent field of merit represented by the Buddha and his Saṃgha. King Śibi must make the difficult "internal" gift of his eyes, whereas the king of Kosala relies on an ordinary "external" offering of robes. (Perhaps one could go so far as to suggest that "internal" gifts in a Buddha-less age may be replaced by "external" gifts in an age of Buddhadharma.) The bodhisattva's gift of his body is thus associated with—and made functionally equivalent to—the ordinary layman's offering of a robe.

It is also quite striking to note what the Buddha says here about the "wise men of old" who gave their bodies away. Just as the king of Kosala most likely makes his offerings of food and clothing to the Saṃgha with the hope and expectation of receiving merit as a reward, so the Buddha has the "wise men of old" think to themselves (as they give their bodies away), "He who gives what is dear [to him] obtains what is dear [to him]." Since most bodhisattvas in gift-of-the-body stories, as we have seen, are depicted as having no expectation of any reward, the extreme purity of intention normally associated with gifts of the body has here been considerably compromised. By compromising this purity of intention, however, the Buddha's statement allows the king of Kosala to identify himself with King Śibi before the story even begins, since both kings give their gifts based on the expectation of rewards. At the end of the story, moreover, when King Śibi's eyes are not only restored but acquire supernatural powers as well, the king of Kosala gets a foretaste of the kind of worldly rewards he might also expect to enjoy for his more ordinary acts of *dāna*. Thus the extreme ideal of the gift of the body—when compromised to some extent by being motivated by a desire for mundane rewards—is capable of serving as a model for more ordinary forms of giving.

Once again, however, it is interesting to note that this compromise is made possible only by a shift in the story's perspective to a ritualized and "once-removed" frame. In other words, the statement "He who gives what is dear [to him] obtains what is dear [to him]" is attributed to the gift-of-the-body donor only indirectly (by the Buddha), after the fact, and within the confines of the "story of the present." Within the "story of the past," or *jātaka* proper, on the other hand, at the moment when the gift is being made, the bodhisattva himself would never deign to think such a thought. Again, we find the same consistent pattern as before, which hinges on the gift's "framability.": Whenever the gift can be "framed" as something external to oneself and able to be considered from a distance, its interpretation becomes somewhat flexible. But when one is immersed *within the precise narrative moment of its occurrence,* such flexibility becomes untenable, and the perfect purity of the gift must be upheld. It is the careful balancing act between these two perspectives on the gift (through plotline, framing, and other means) that makes the gift of the body such a versatile narrative theme within the Buddhist discourse on *dāna.*

The Slippery Magic of the Gift

The kind of balancing act between higher and lower forms of the gift that I have tried to demonstrate above might perhaps be further elucidated by reference to some of the current scholarly discourse on the gift—for the problematic relationship between the "pure gift" and "reciprocity" has been a major theme of recent gift-related discourse.

If we envision the different types of "reciprocity" that ordinary gift-giving might involve, it is possible to distinguish among several major varieties. Marshall Sahlins, attempting to put forth a purely formal typology of exchange, has identified three different types of reciprocity: *negative, balanced,* and *generalized.*[31] In *negative* reciprocity each person acts purely in his own self-interest and tries to maximize his own personal gain at the expense of the other—for example, through barter or chicanery. *Balanced* reciprocity, on the other hand, works on the principle of a direct and equivalent exchange between two parties: Person A gives to Person B, and Person B reciprocates in an equivalent manner within a finite period of time. Finally, *generalized* reciprocity is indirect and diffuse in nature; here, Person A gives to Person B, who gives to Person C, who gives to Person D . . . until Person A is ultimately "repaid" by someone other than the person to whom he originally gave. Payback is indirect and uncertain in nature and may take a considerable amount of time. Clearly, Sahlins' categories could be placed along a "continuum of reciprocity" that begins with utilitarian self-interest and ultimately culminates in the "pure" gift.

In a similar manner, Lévi-Strauss' work on kinship draws a basic distinction between *restricted exchange* and *generalized exchange* which are equivalent to the "balanced" and "generalized" reciprocities outlined by Sahlins.[32] While *restricted exchange* involves only two parties who are fully aware of the obligatory nature of their gifts and countergifts, *generalized exchange* is theoretically open to an indefinite number of parties; the more diffuse and complicated such a network of reciprocity becomes, the closer we move to the pole of pure *sacrifice,* or the gift given with no expectation of any return.[33] In the formulations of both Sahlins and Lévi-Strauss, then, the "pure" gift represents the idealized end of a continuum of reciprocity—the vanishing point that can never be attained. The "pure" gift seems to fulfill a purely syntactic function and cannot be realized in any particular instance. It is in this sense that we can agree with Derrida that the "pure" gift is an impossible ideal.

And yet . . . many of these reciprocal exchanges are *perceived and experienced as "pure" gifts.* This is the genius, the paradox, the sleight-of-hand enacted by the gift—impossible to realize, yet somehow underlying and informing an entire range of reciprocal exchanges. This paradox of the gift has been commented upon by many. Lévi-Strauss himself, for example, hints at the paradoxical nature of a system of "generalized exchange." In reality, there *is* reciprocity and "payback" within such a system, yet through the indirectness of the returns—which weave their way through a chain of intermediaries not easily observable by the original donor—generalized exchange has the *appearance* of pure sacrifice and is experienced as such by those who partake in it. Once the network of reciprocity is of sufficient complexity, the mechanism of "payback" becomes obscure and impossible to trace, and at least the *illusion* of Derrida's "forgetting" then becomes possible.

Going one step further, much the same can be said even in the case of "restricted exchange" between two parties, where the route of return is completely obvious (A ↔ B). To understand how a direct and obligatory exchange between two parties can nevertheless be experienced through the idiom of the "pure," disinterested gift, it is helpful to consider Lévi-Strauss' critique of Mauss and Pierre Bourdieu's subsequent critique of Lévi-Strauss. In his essay on the gift, Mauss split the act of gift-exchange into three sequential practices—giving, receiving, and reciprocating—and then wondered what it was that held them together, eventually invoking the indigenous Maori notion of *hau* as a kind of "spirit" of the original donor that animates his gift and later compels the recipient to make a return.[34] In his critique of Mauss' argument, Lévi-Strauss accuses Mauss of failing to perceive that "the primary, fundamental phenomenon is exchange itself, which gets split up into discrete operations in social life."[35] In other words, Mauss misses the forest for the trees; instead of examining *exchange as a whole,* he splits this whole up into three sequential parts (giving, receiving, and reciprocating) and must then use *hau* as a glue to put the parts back together again and reconstruct the phenomenon of exchange. Mauss fails to become a true structuralist; his mistake is to see only an empirically given sequence of discrete events, rather than uncovering the simpler, underlying *structure* "to which the given owes its whole reality."[36]

Pierre Bourdieu, on the other hand, has more recently argued that this underlying structure uncovered by Lévi-Strauss does not, in fact, constitute the "whole reality" of gift-exchange. What this structural approach to the gift lacks is any appreciation for the properties of gift-exchange that result from the fact that "it is constructed in time, that time gives it its form . . . and therefore its direction and meaning."[37] In other words, *time and sequence are everything,* and the fact that giving, receiving, and reciprocating *unfold in succession* cannot be excluded from an account of gift-exchange. In particular, Bourdieu emphasizes the crucial importance of the *time-lag* between gift and countergift. A gift can be reciprocated only after an appropriate amount of time; it is the time-lag that most sharply distinguishes gift-giving from ordinary barter, and it is the time-lag that allows the subjective experience of pure generosity to coexist with the objective truth of exchange: "The lapse of time that separates the gift from the counter-gift is what allows the deliberate oversight, the collectively maintained and approved self-deception, without which the exchange could not function. Gift exchange is one of the social games that cannot be played unless the players refuse to acknowledge the objective truth of the game."[38] Though Bourdieu speaks in this and other passages of the "denial," "self-deception," and "illusion" of pure generosity allowed for by this polite lapse of time, he also recognizes that even these labels can be applied only retroactively, *after* the entire sequence has been completed. For *at the time when a gift is given,* it is no illusion to suppose that there may not be any return—the gift, after all, may fall flat. Time, in other words, introduces uncertainty and unpredictability into the mechanical model put forth by Lévi-Strauss, and thus allows for the subjective experience of generosity.

Pure, disinterested generosity therefore coexists with reciprocity and exchange—not only within a complicated network of "generalized exchange," but even within the most direct and seemingly transparent relationship of "restricted exchange." The continuum of reciprocity I proposed above thus collapses, and leads to a paradox in which the "pure" gift is an unattainable ideal—yet all gifts somehow partake of the character of the "pure" gift. Derrida's "forgetting" may be impossible, yet it is also that which enables all gifts.

If we now return to the case of Buddhism, we can see that much the same paradox obtains. While perfect generosity and the "pure" gift may well be restricted to arhats, bodhisattvas, and Buddhas alone, there is also a sense in which the many gifts and offerings made by ordinary Buddhists in exchange for karmic merit equally partake in the ethic of the "pure" gift. For *at the time when such a gift is given,* merit, as its reward, is nebulous, intangible, and uncertain in nature, and clearly involves a time-lag between the gift and its recompense. In fact, not only does this recompense frequently extend beyond death and into a future lifetime, but it can even be described as repaying a "different" person altogether—thus sharing in the indirectness characteristic of "generalized exchange."

To take the argument one step further, even those wholly *laukika* exchanges that would fall into the category of "restricted exchange"—such as offerings made to the gods in direct exchange for worldly benefits—also share some of the features that would allow them to be experienced as "pure" gifts. For example, the outcome of such a gift is exceedingly uncertain—nor is the physical presence of the recipient wholly clear—and once again involves a time-lag between the gift and its recompense. Thus, such gifts can be given—in the moment—with a spirit of pure generosity, even though—after the fact—what we see is exchange. As Jan Gonda has remarked in regard to the exchanges between men and deities characteristic of the *Ṛg Veda,* "it would . . . be incorrect to regard this reciprocity as a mere matter of barter."[39] Instead, we might rather say that the worshiper's initial gift opens up a stream of beneficence and generosity within its divine recipient, and his or her return-gift does the same within the giver, so that "both god and worshipper give and receive."[40] Thus:

> The old formula *do-ut-des*—[or in the Sanskrit texts,] *dehi me dadāmi te,* 'give me, I give thee'—often quoted to indicate that man sacrifices to the gods in order to persuade them into reciprocating should therefore be replaced by *do-ut-possis-dare,* 'I give in order that thou mayest be able to give': man adds to the god's power, that he may have power to reciprocate and that life may not stagnate because of any lack of potency.[41]

This more charitable view of reciprocal gift-exchange as an ever-flowing stream of good will and generosity that spontaneously unfolds over time and ultimately benefits everyone is perhaps truer to the gift-giving experience than the cold, market rationalism implied by the notion of "exchange."

Through the slippery magic of the gift, then, pure generosity informs even the most self-interested, *laukika* exchange. By the same token, however, the reverse is perhaps equally true: the logic of self-interest informs even the purest, most *lokottara* gift. Once again it is the category of *time* that seems to mediate between these two perspectives. When the bodhisattva is immersed *within the precise narrative moment of the gift's unfolding,* he can and must adhere to the perfect ideal of pure, one-sided generosity. But once the gift is framed *from a distance* and *after-the-fact,* it moves closer to more ordinary forms of giving that freely acknowledge reciprocity and exchange. It is this slippery magic of the gift that is taken full advantage of by the gift-of-the-body genre.

Self and Selflessness in the Buddhist Discourse on Giving

I would like to turn now to another fundamental paradox or "slippery magic" that lies at the heart of the gift—one I have hinted at several times already but not yet treated at any length. This is the tension between "self" and "selflessness" that is inherent in the concept of generosity. Although generosity is presumably an expression of *selflessness,* it often seems to involve a very strong assertion of *self.* On the surface a gift is given wholly for the sake of the other, but underneath this surface lies a deeper concern with oneself—not, this time, in the sense of a self-interested expectation of reward, but rather in the subtler sense of using the gift as an expression of oneself, or to convey a certain message about oneself, in the guise of aiding another. In fact, this tension seems to become increasingly worse as the gift itself becomes increasingly altruistic: the more the giver insists on the "selflessness" of his or her generosity, the more suspect this "selflessness" seems to become. We are all familiar with the modern stereotype of the zealous do-gooder who altruistically devotes his or her entire life to a variety of enlightened and charitable causes, but whose personality is that of a self-aggrandizing egomaniac making everyone around them miserable. What role does this paradox play within the Buddhist discourse on giving—especially considering Buddhism's overriding emphasis on the importance of cultivating *nonself?*

Many of the Buddhist ideals of giving I described in the previous chapter do indeed contain suggestions of an underlying *assertion-of-self.* In the initial distinction I drew between "reciprocated" and "unreciprocated" gifts, for example, we saw that the "unreciprocated" gift (which is given only for the sake of karmic merit) rejects and repudiates the kind of social give-and-take represented by the "reciprocated" gift described by Mauss, instead allowing the donor to set herself apart from ordinary society and express her own soteriological aspirations and orientation toward the transcendent future. There is a paradoxical sense, then, in which the ordinary, reciprocated gift—which might appear to be wholly calculating and "self-interested" on the surface—actually expresses one's *involvement in society* and *commitment to maintaining social bonds;* whereas the unreciprocated gift—which appears to be a "purer" expression of generosity precisely because it is not reciprocated—really expresses one's *independence from other people* and *rejection of social bonds*. Thus, the more "selfless" the gift is, the more it involves an assertion of one's "self" and a separation from the "other." This paradox only becomes stronger when we consider what is perhaps the most "selfless" and "other-directed" gift of all—the bodhisattva's gift of his body.

We saw in chapter 2, for example, that those who oppose the bodhisattva's intention to give away his body represent a variety of different realms of interest, such as worldly political interests, familial and affective interests, and the interests of popular, local religious tradition. It might be said that all such interests represent a man's entanglements in the social world—the constitution of his personality through his mutual obligations with others and his involvement within ever-widening networks of interdependence. Thus, when the bodhisattva resists his opposers, he rejects this definition of himself and instead asserts his right to act *as an autonomous and free individual*—even to the point of giving his body away. Here we encounter a paradox: whereas giving up one's body and life for the sake of another would seem on the surface to be the ultimate *denial of self*, it is, at the same time, an ultimate *act of self-will*—an aggressive assertion of the self's right to dispose of himself as he pleases (others be damned). This is why the bodhisattva's "selfless" act encounters so much opposition. It is in the arguments of his opposers, perhaps, that we see which "self" the bodhisattva really wishes to deny—the self entangled within and defined by its obligations and duties to others, the self that must engage in reciprocity. Whereas the bodhisattva's gift is presumably given wholly for the sake of the other, it also declares his independence from others in a way that is perhaps inherently self-aggrandizing.

Indeed, gift-of-the-body stories, which are touted as paradigmatic examples of selflessness—and which even seem to materialize this selflessness through visceral images of self-mutilation—are consistently characterized by an underlying *assertion-of-self* through which the bodhisattva is depicted (and perceives himself) as a completely unique and autonomous being capable of doing what no one else can do, and giving a unique and unprecedented gift, a gift that surpasses all other gifts. This is a common conceit within these stories: the bodhisattva frequently prides himself on giving the "excellent gift never given before"[42] and often contrasts himself favorably with other, more lackluster givers. "Ah, how good is this, my gift of an eye!"[43]—King Śibi thinks to himself, while Prince Mahāsattva notes that he is giving up his body, "which is so difficult for others to sacrifice."[44]

The elephant Ṣaḍdanta calls himself a "prince of generosity,"[45] while King Puṇyabala proudly notes that only *eight other bodhisattvas in the whole of time* made such a gift as he.[46]

In addition to asserting a strong sense of himself, moreover, the "selfless" bodhisattva also evinces a certain repugnance at the idea of reciprocity with others. Far be it from him to ask anyone else to share in his compassionate works or to help him in any manner whatsoever. Totally self-sufficient and self-dependent, the bodhisattva *must do it alone.* "You alone . . . are called to be the savior of all," King Śibi reprimands himself,[47] while King Maṇicūḍa resolves: "For the sake of all beings, I will endure all suffering by myself alone!"[48] Once again we are reminded of the *kṣatra-dharma* of the epics, and the way in which the *kṣatriya*'s magnanimous liberality only masks his extreme fear of becoming dependent upon others. Much like the *kṣatriya,* the bodhisattva aggressively asserts his autonomy and independence from others—even in the very act of self-sacrifice on their behalf.

This "terror of reciprocity" that is characteristic of the bodhisattva's practice of *dāna* is equally discernible in another of his paradigmatic gifts as well—the "gift of merit" (*puṇyadāna*). The bodhisattva gives away not only his material possessions, his family, and himself, but also the *merit* that results from each of these acts of giving. He engages in gifts of all types that result in transcendent karmic rewards, but out of pure generosity and compassion he refuses these rewards for himself by making them into further gifts and passing them on to other beings. This is surely the very height of other-directed generosity—and yet, once again, one often senses an underlying concern with the *self* and a defensive fear of the self being "tainted" by any suggestion of reciprocity or reward. Thus, in an especially intriguing passage from the *Mahāyānasūtrālaṃkāra,* the bodhisattva celebrates the karmic fruitfulness of his gift and its power to produce karmic rewards on behalf of its beneficiaries[49]—while at the same time he seems to exhibit a peculiar *distaste* for the karmic reciprocity represented by the gift, for at one point in the passage he takes pains to compare his own penchant for one-sided giving with the gift's penchant for "repayment" (*pratikāra*), actually taunting the gift with the following words: "You do not bear fruit for one who doesn't deal with you. Since you expect repayment, you are not like me! I do not expect repayment; I freely give to others the fruit which comes from you!"[50] The bodhisattva here wants to *out-gift the gift itself,* and he scornfully suggests that even that which we call a "gift" is actually devoid of the pure, one-sided generosity of which *only he,* the bodhisattva, is capable. The boasting and prideful tone in this passage suggests, once again, that the gift given with no expectation of reward is not only a manifestation of "pure generosity," but also an expressive strategy the giver uses to *set himself apart* from others—to turn his back on the world and categorically state: "I expect nothing in return!" It is perhaps less about the other than it is about oneself.

Indeed, in many passages on the bodhisattva's *dāna* one can sense a kind of *fear* of accumulation or retention of any kind—every gift (or reward from a gift) is like a "hot potato" that must relentlessly be "passed on" before it scalds one's "perfect generosity." Thus, in the *Bodhisattvabhūmi* the "pure gift" of the bodhisattva is described as being "unaccumulated," meaning that the bodhisattva never accumulates or stores up gifts before giving them away, but rather gives them the moment they arise. He cannot see any reason to hang on to any potential gift, and he "cannot bear" to refuse any supplicant.[51] The bodhisattva of the *Mahāyānasūtrālaṃkāra* likewise states that any gift whose fruit is not *immediately rejected* is unsatisfactory because "to remain without giving for even an instant is to be unsatisfied with the gift."[52] He realizes that every gift only brings back to him "more numerous and more wonderful pleasures" in reward, but assures himself: "I don't have to worry about such pleasures, since I [also] give them away unceasingly!"[53] The fear and insecurity suggested by such passages serve as the flip side of the exaggerated pride and self-confidence exemplified by some of the passages cited earlier. Perhaps most disturbingly, this same fear or insecurity is sometimes vulnerable to being projected outward and manifesting itself in the form of submerged hostility toward the *recipient*. In fact, as Hibbets has reminded us, this is one of the dangers inherent in the use of the "unworthy recipient": compassion for those who are "pitiful" or "unworthy" sometimes borders on hateful contempt, as the bodhisattva lords it over those who are clearly inferior.[54] (As David Shulman has remarked in another context, "here, as elsewhere in Indian myth, the coinage of aggression is compassion."[55])

This paradoxical self-aggrandizement and aggressiveness toward others that is perhaps an inherent element of "pure generosity" is not simply my own (rather uncharitable) view of the bodhisattva's *dāna*, but is a danger well recognized within Buddhist literature itself. In fact, we often find warnings against precisely this danger in manuals and treatises on the bodhisattva path. The *Bodhisattvabhūmi*, for example, pointedly reminds its readers that the "pure gift" of the bodhisattva should be an "unarrogant gift" (*anunnata-dāna*), meaning that the bodhisattva "has a humble mind when he gives," "does not give out of rivalry with others," and "does not think that because of that gift, he alone is a giver and a master of generosity, while others are not"[56]—a statement that seems almost as if it might be addressed to the heroes of many gift-of-the-body *jātakas.* Similarly, in the *Bodhicaryāvatāra,* Śāntideva takes pains to remind the bodhisattva that he is utterly dependent upon sentient beings in order to attain Buddhahood; therefore, those pitiful sentient beings he is intent upon saving are equal to the Buddha himself—and equally deserving of his respect and worship.[57] Arrogance, pride, self-aggrandizement, and contempt for others were thus well-recognized dangers that might arise in the very midst of the bodhisattva's selfless generosity and compassion.[58]

There is even some evidence for the view that out of all gifts, the gift of the body in particular was especially prone to this kind of self-aggrandizement and therefore could not possibly constitute an "ideal gift." This is because the gift of the body appears to be susceptible to a particularly vexing form of the paradox I have been discussing. Self-sacrifice, one could argue, depends for its very existence upon a reified *self to be sacrificed*—thus paradoxically rendering self-sacrifice a clear indication of one's clinging to the concept of a "self" and one's lack of the perfect wisdom that realizes "nonself."

Several textual discussions seem to suggest such a notion. In the ninth chapter of Buddhaghosa's *Visuddhimagga,* for example, there is a long discussion of the four *brahmavihāras*—four beneficial states of mind the Buddhist practitioner is supposed to cultivate in meditation and direct outward toward all living beings, including benevolence (*mettā*), compassion (*karuṇā*), sympathetic joy (*muditā*), and equanimity (*upekkhā*).[59] Beginning with the cultivation of "benevolence," Buddhaghosa advises the meditator to develop a feeling of "benevolence" first toward himself, then toward a friend, then toward a neutral person, and finally toward an enemy—thus moving from the easiest state of mind to achieve to the most difficult. Once all four states of mind are well established, however, the meditator should then strive to "break down the barriers"[60] between them—that is, to develop a feeling of "benevolence" toward all four categories so equally that no distinctions among them are possible. As an illustration of the "breaking down of barriers," Buddhaghosa says that if oneself, a friend, a neutral person, and an enemy were all being attacked by a robber who wished to kill one of them, the one who has "broken down the barriers" would be completely unable to choose which of the four people should be killed.

What is crucial here is that Buddhaghosa explicitly rules out the option of the meditator *sacrificing himself* to the killer in order to save the other three—since that would indicate a preference for the *others over himself*, and thus a clinging to the notion of separate and discrete selves and a lack of the even-mindedness that treats all beings the same. In other words, one should cultivate benevolence until it is truly universal in nature and directed equally toward all beings—*including oneself*—and self-sacrifice is incommensurable with this goal. This necessity of "breaking down the barriers" is then repeated in connection with each of the remaining three *brahmavihāras:* compassion, sympathetic joy, and equanimity. Naturally, "equanimity" comes last in the list of *brahmavihāras* because it represents the highest of the four and the level to which all of the others should be cultivated. Equanimity suggests that one's benevolence, compassion, etc., are so thoroughly informed by the truth of nonself that they are applied equally to all beings, including oneself—again excluding the possibility of self-sacrifice. Though Buddhaghosa's discussion deals only with the meditative cultivation of the *brahmavihāras* and does not directly address the *jātakas* dealing with the bodhisattva's self-sacrifice, his discussion is at least capable of suggesting that the bodhisattva was at a relatively low stage of progress when he performed such deeds and had not yet developed equanimity or a realization of the truth of nonself.

For a stronger version of this suggestion, and one that explicitly invokes the bodhisattva's gift of his body, we can turn to yet another intriguing discussion found in the *Mahāprajñāpāramitā Śāstra.* Whereas previously we saw that two other passages within this text cited King Śibi's gift of his flesh to ransom a dove as a paradigmatic example of *dāna-pāramitā,*[61] and classified all gifts of the body as "superior" gifts,[62] in the present discussion the text contradicts these sentiments and puts forth a quite different classification, according to which King Śibi's gift of his flesh (and other gifts of the body) are merely "medium" gifts, whereas any gift given with utter "detachment" (*niḥsaṅga*) is a "superior" gift.[63] As for why King Śibi's gift of his body could not have been a "superior" gift (or one given with "detachment"), the text records three different opinions. The first is that King Śibi perceived both himself and the dove as *real selves;* thus, his gift lacked perfect wisdom and was merely a "medium" gift. The second opinion recorded states more boldly that gifts of the body can *never* constitute the fulfillment of *dāna-pāramitā* because they are always motivated by intense compassion for the recipient and thus lack the "detachment" essential to "superior" gifts. The third opinion is that King Śibi's gift was necessarily "impure" because he was still attached to the three notions of "donor," "gift," and "recipient"—in other words, a notion of self.

Though stated in slightly different ways, all three of these opinions seem to agree with the *Visuddhimagga*'s suggestion that self-sacrifice is incommensurable with the wisdom that realizes absolute selflessness and the resulting equanimity that treats all beings the same. In fact, one can perhaps go even further and say that self-sacrifice is actually suggestive of an underlying *clinging to the notion of a self*—of which the kinds of arrogance and self-pride sometimes displayed by the bodhisattva are only the most overt manifestations. Thus Buddhist discourse itself seems to recognize the same "assertion-of-self" underlying the rhetoric of "selflessness" that I have posited above.

Worthy Self, Unworthy Other

One final paradox involved in the strong sense of "selfhood" that underlies the bodhisattva's "selfless" gift of his body is the fact that this selfhood is completely dependent upon the presence of a particular *other*. I would like to demonstrate this reliance of the Buddhist hero upon a particular type of transactional other by comparing our gift-of-the-body stories featuring the bodhisattva as the *donor* with another set of gift-giving stories featuring an idealized Buddhist figure—this time, as the *recipient* of the gift rather than as the donor.

In an interesting article,[64] Liz Wilson has examined a set of related narratives involving the "selective begging practices" of the Buddha's disciple Mahākāśyapa. In stories taken from several Pāli and Sanskrit texts (such as the *Udāna,* the *Vimānavatthu Commentary,* and the *Mūlasarvāstivāda Vinaya*), Mahākāśyapa—a venerable monk and master of asceticism, and thus a very good "field of merit"—goes out of his way to receive alms-food from highly disadvantaged donors (such as poor people, lepers, and low-caste weavers), while avoiding or outright refusing the alms offered by highly advantaged donors (such as a group of five hundred *apsarases* or, most commonly, the deity Śakra). The reasoning behind these selective begging practices is clear: Mahākāśyapa is full of compassion and therefore favors those unfortunate donors who are most in need of the abundant merit they will receive from "sowing" their gifts within such a productive "field." Thus in a narrative from the *Vimānavatthu Commentary,* he goes out of his way to receive a gift of leftover rice-water from an old and poverty-stricken woman, thereby allowing the woman to escape from her impending fate of being reborn in hell and instead attain rebirth in heaven—an act that he himself describes as "the exercise of the highest compassion."[65]

In contrast, he avoids or directly refuses the alms-food offered to him by highly advantaged donors such as Śakra or the *apsarases* because (as he says to the latter in a narrative from the *Udānaṭṭhakathā*): "You've earned merit, you have great enjoyment because of it. I'm going to act in sympathy with those who are badly off!"[66] Though refusing to accept an offering of alms may not seem appropriate to such a paragon of compassion, we must remember that Mahākāśyapa, as an ardent practitioner of fasting, does not eat very much alms-food to begin with; therefore, any merit obtained by a highly advantaged donor such as Śakra has, in a sense, been "stolen" from one who is more unfortunate. Indeed in several of these narratives Śakra attempts to deceive Mahākāśyapa by disguising himself as a disadvantaged donor and thus obtaining for himself the merit intended for somebody else—a ruse Mahākāśyapa generally sees through.

Though Wilson is interested in examining Mahākāśyapa's transactions in terms of a particular interpretation of *dāna,*[67] I am interested in them from quite another perspective: these narratives involving the monk Mahākāśyapa as a "choosy recipient" offer a fascinating parallel to gift-of-the-body stories involving the bodhisattva as a "choosy donor," for in both cases we have a Buddhist hero who relies on a particular type of transactional "other" in order to convey a certain message about himself. In gift-of-the-body stories, as we have seen, the bodhisattva is a *donor* who specifically chooses to give his gifts to "unworthy" recipients rather than "worthy" ones. He avoids "worthy" recipients because giving gifts to such recipients would result in the acquisition of merit for himself, thereby suggesting that his gift was not given out of pure generosity and compassion. Thus, although the bodhisattva should ostensibly be a *universal giver*—giving gifts to everyone—the fact is that he *relies on the unworthy recipient* in order to display, to both himself and others, his own exalted status as a paragon of perfect generosity. In the narratives examined by Wilson, on the other hand, we have a perfect reversal of this scenario: Mahākāśyapa is here a *recipient* (not a donor) who specifically chooses to receive his gifts from "unworthy" donors rather than "worthy" ones. He avoids "worthy" donors (such as Śakra) because accepting gifts from such donors would mean that he was favoring them and their welfare over those who were more unfortunate, thereby suggesting that he was not accepting gifts out of pure compassion. Thus, although Mahākāśyapa should ostensibly be a *universal recipient*—graciously accepting alms from everyone—the fact is that he *relies on the unworthy donor* in order to display, to both himself and others, his own exalted status as a paragon of perfect compassion.

The two situations are exact reversals of each other, yet they are also structurally parallel—for whether the Buddhist hero is the donor or the recipient, in both cases he relies on a particular type of transactional "other." More specifically, this "other" must be *unworthy* rather than worthy in order to display something about the Buddhist hero himself—perhaps even to exalt the "worthy Buddhist hero" against the background of his "unworthy other." Both cases militate against the *universal giving and receiving* that should presumably characterize true generosity and compassion: after all, why shouldn't the perfect bodhisattva give equally to everybody, and why shouldn't the perfect monk be a "field of merit" for all? The fact that both scenarios rely on particular transactional relationships that are visibly hierarchical and unequal in nature suggests to me that both types of stories are fundamentally concerned with the matters of social *display* and *prestige,* and not purely with generosity and compassion. In other words, the concern of each hero is not merely to *be* generous or to *be* compassionate, but to have this generosity or compassion visibly displayed to the world through the particular nature of the recipient.

Perhaps this is one reason why *anonymous* or *hidden* gifts do not seem to be highly valued in the Buddhist discourse on *dāna*—because they lack this crucial element of *display.* Rather than exalting the humble generosity of one who gives a gift anonymously, the Buddhist discourse on giving seems to celebrate openhanded liberality as a way of visibly displaying to the world one's power, rank, and prestige and forcing them to be acknowledged by others, who are perceived as being weaker than oneself. Here we are reminded once again not only of the *kṣatra-dharma* of the epics, but also of Mauss' discussion of the institution of the potlatch and, more generally, the entire prestige-aspect of the gift:[68] the more one gives away in the form of material goods, the more one receives in return in the social currencies of rank and prestige—yet this exchange is always agonistic in nature and relies upon rivalry with others. Despite the bodhisattva's protestations of absolute autonomy and independence, then, the *worthy self* he constructs through generosity is finally dependent upon the presence of the *unworthy other.*

Contradictory Discourses and the Rise of Buddhism

The gift-of-the-body theme thus seems to hang precariously between *selflessness* and *assertion-of-self.* On the one hand, the bodhisattva is completely selfless and altruistic, acting wholly for the welfare and benefit of the other; on the other, the bodhisattva asserts a particularly aggressive type of self—one that ignores all social obligations and acts exactly as it pleases, and one whose rank and prestige are won out of rivalry with "unworthy others." How can we place this contradictory discourse of "self" and "selflessness" within a larger historical context?

One way to move forward is by considering the fact that "selfhood" itself is not a unitary concept but can have several different connotations. In an analysis of Marcel Mauss' seminal essay on notions of the "person" (*personne*) and notions of "self" (*moi*), Michael Carrithers has attempted to systematize Mauss' loose and poetic language by making a clear conceptual distinction between *personne* and *moi.*[69] In brief, *personne* for Carrithers is a conception of the self defined as the member of a specific social collectivity and characterized by specific rights and obligations, whereas *moi* is a conception of the individual and autonomous self who relates to others as an individual moral agent and not as the embodiment of a particular social role.

Though Carrithers, for various reasons, denies that ancient India had any conception of *personne,* Patrick Olivelle has subsequently expanded Carrithers' understanding of *personne* and argued convincingly that the male head-of-household in ancient Vedic society was very much a *personne*-type of self—a relational personality largely defined by his position within various social orders defined by caste, class, and gender.[70] Furthermore, he contrasts this *personne*-type of self characteristic of the Vedic worldview with the *moi*-type of self represented by the ideologies of Buddhism, Jainism, and the Upaniṣads. In Olivelle's view, the dramatic socioeconomic, political, and cultural changes occurring throughout North India during the sixth century B.C.E.—such as the rapid development of trade, increasing urbanization, political consolidation into large kingdoms, and greater individual freedom and mobility—significantly weakened the traditional communal structures characteristic of older, Vedic society and gave rise to various new ideologies that promoted the concept of individual selfhood, or the self divorced from social relationships.[71]

This general thesis—that "individualism" was born in ancient India only in the mid-first millennium B.C.E. and concomitant with the rise of *śramaṇa* movements such as Buddhism—has been stated by many scholars before. Louis Dumont asserted long ago, for example, that whereas there was no such thing as an autonomous individual within the Vedic worldview, the world-renouncer within Buddhism and Jainism, in contrast, was "invested with an individuality" that was "the distinctive trait . . . oppos[ing] him to the [Vedic] man-in-the-world."[72] We have already witnessed something of the historical clash between these two conceptions of the self in the conflict between the bodhisattva and his opposers—with the opposers promoting the interdependent, *personne*-type of self characteristic of the Vedic worldview, and the bodhisattva promoting the independent, *moi*-type of self characteristic of new ideologies such as Buddhism.

We can also contrast their attitudes toward salvation. In the Vedic worldview, salvation is brought about through the joint sacrifices offered to the gods by the male head-of-household, whom Orlan Lee has described as a kind of *pater familias* or "pharaonic personality" that stands for the household as a whole and performs sacrifices on their collective behalf.[73] In the Buddhist and śramaṇic worldview, on the other hand, salvation is brought about through an individual act of world-renunciation that cleaves one from family and society and asserts one's individual instrumentality in one's own salvation.

Historically, then, the social and cultural context in which Buddhism arose was characterized by a weakening of traditional social networks and a new conception of the self as an individual and autonomous agent fully capable of acting on its own behalf—a new and confident "selfhood," as it were. Yet at the same time perhaps the primary emphasis in Buddhist teaching is on renunciation of one's individuality and detachment from the notions of "I" and "mine." Here we encounter a larger version of the paradox I have been dealing with: the rise of Buddhism is witness to a new and powerful *self*, yet the primary goal of its teachings is to *eradicate the self*.[74] As the *Dhammapada* puts it: "For the self is the refuge of the self; the self is the destiny of the self; therefore, restrain the self."[75] This paradox makes a certain amount of logical sense, for *in order to deny the self, one must have a self to begin with*. But though explainable, this paradox inevitably results in a continuing tension in Buddhist thought between the *assertion* of one's individuality and its *denial*. It is these larger historical forces surrounding the rise of Buddhism, I contend, that perhaps contributed to the contradictory discourse of "self" and "selflessness" characteristic of the gift-of-the-body theme.

These same tumultuous forces, moreover, might also be invoked to explain the other major balancing act I have dealt with above—that between the "pure" gift and more reciprocal forms of giving. If we wish to consider this contradictory discourse again in terms of the historical context of the rise of Buddhism, then perhaps we should take note of the argument put forth by Jonathan Parry that the ideology of the "pure" gift is made possible only by the development of a capitalistic marketplace.[76] In other words, the "pure" gift is everything the market is *not*—disinterested, altruistic, etc.—and therefore depends on the market for its very existence. Historically, it is only when a highly developed marketplace based wholly on the notion of utilitarian self-interest becomes progressively disembedded from the rest of society that a space is left open for the *utterly free and disinterested gift.* (In Mauss' "archaic" or "primitive" societies, on the other hand, the two realms are inextricably woven together.) Parry thus speculates that perhaps "it is not . . . coincidental that the ideology of the 'pure gift' is accorded such prominence among groups—such as the Jews and Jains—which have a particularly close historical association with market trade."[77]

The Buddhists, too, should be added to this list, since the social and historical context in which Buddhism arose was characterized (among other things) by rapid industrialization and increasing trade, the growth of mercantile classes, and the development of money and a market economy—all trends with which Buddhism is closely associated.[78] These historical conditions perhaps fostered the development not only of an ideology of pure, economic self-interest, but also of an ideology of "pure generosity"—both of which then coexisted in some tension with the traditional norms of reciprocity more characteristic of older, Vedic society. Again, it is this historical tension that perhaps contributed to the contradictory discourse of reciprocal and nonreciprocal forms of giving characteristic of the gift-of-the-body theme.

Of course, the two contradictory discourses I have dealt with above (self-vs.-selflessness and pure-gift-vs.-reciprocity) are historically related to each other. The "pure gift," the market economy, and the autonomous, *moi*-type of self that is presumed by them both all arise together—and all stand in opposition to the relational personality and mingled realms of interest and disinterest characteristic of Mauss' "archaic" gift-exchange. What we find in the gift-of-the-body genre is thus not merely a skillful use of narrative strategies to convey and balance multiple, contradictory notions of *dāna,* but also a reflection of some of the wider historical forces and conflicts surrounding the rise of Buddhism itself.

VI

BODIES ORDINARY AND IDEAL

> The Buddhist attitude towards the body has been summed up as follows: (1) the body, whether of men or of higher beings, can never be the abode of anything but evil; (2) final deliverance from all bodily life, present and to come, is the greatest of all blessings, the highest of all boons, and the loftiest of all aims.
>
> —J. H. Bateson, "Body (Buddhist)" (1908)

I turn, in this final chapter on the gift-of-the-body genre, from the "gift" aspect of these tales to their "body" aspect. For despite the bodhisattva's apparent willingness to throw his "worthless" body away, and despite the opinion expressed by J. H. Bateson (in the quote given above[1]) that there is little more to say about the matter, gift-of-the-body stories do, in fact, have much to say about the body—about the ordinary body, about the ideal body, and about the ways in which one is transformed into the other. Such stories give voice, in fact, to a rich and complex discourse on the body—a discourse that does *not* depict all bodies as "abodes of evil," nor preach "final deliverance from all bodily life" as the ultimate goal.

The denigration of the body so strongly emphasized by Bateson does, of course, constitute one prevalent trend of thought within Buddhism itself and is not merely an invention of Western perceptions. Nevertheless, to focus so singularly upon this denigration in one's depiction of Buddhist attitudes as a whole is to ignore the extraordinary attention also paid in Buddhist literature to the care and maintenance of the human body, its use within religious practice, and the various pleasures it can afford. It is also to ignore the fact that Buddhist literature of all kinds depicts various types of "ideal bodies" that stand in direct opposition to the "ordinary body" and that are exalted rather than degraded—such as the perfectly controlled and decorous body of a monk, the unusual and supernatural bodies that often result from the performance of meritorious deeds within the *jātakas* and *avadānas,* the golden-colored and irresistibly attractive body of the Buddha, or the "bodies" involved in the worship of relics, images, or *stūpas.* How do such "ideal bodies" relate to the "bag of excrement" so often scorned in Buddhist texts?

Not only have such positive views of the body been relatively ignored in the history of Buddhist studies, they have also been artificially separated from the negative view espoused by Bateson above. This is in line with the historical tendency of Buddhist studies as a discipline to depict "Buddhism" itself as an ethereal, disembodied, and wholly rational philosophy, preserved and conveyed primarily through doctrinal and philosophical texts, and only gradually debased and corrupted by grosser, more material concerns (such as ritual, devotion, and cult)—concerns which themselves are often depicted as mere concessions to "lay," "Tantric," "Hindu," or "substratum" pressures.[2] "Negative" body topics such as meditations on the foulness of the body or statements concerning the body's impurity and impermanence have been artificially emphasized because they are in perfect accord with the historical tendency of the discipline to conceive "true" Buddhism as an austere path for the world-renouncing, nirvana-seeking monk, whereas "positive" body topics such as relic-worship or the beauty of the Buddha's body have been relegated to the realm of "lay" or "popular" religion and thus discussed within a different context, if at all.

The fact that "negative" and "positive" views of the body are mutually related and constructed is not recognized; instead these views have been falsely located within completely different interpretive contexts. At the same time, "positive" views of the body are further obscured by the modern Western dualism between mind and body. The split between "mind" and "body" automatically demands a hierarchical relationship in which one is elevated and the other is degraded; as soon as "mind" is elevated and "body" degraded, positive views of the body and "ideal bodies" tend to drop out of sight. Dualistic Western assumptions thus bring to the Buddhist material a question of mind *versus* body, and therefore fail to see that the material's own concern may sometimes be a question of *one type of mind/body complex versus another* or even *one type of body versus another.*[3] These biases characteristic of the discipline as a whole are what result in such sweeping generalizations.

During the last twenty-five years, however, the discipline of Buddhist studies—like the discipline of religious studies as a whole—has undergone some profound and significant shifts in the direction of "rematerialization."[4] The scholarship of Gregory Schopen has been particularly influential, overturning our understanding of Indian Buddhism by making unprecedented use of material sources (such as inscriptions), demonstrating conclusively that "materialistic" concerns (such as the image cult, the *stūpa* cult, and rituals surrounding death) were all high, monastic preoccupations, and "rematerializing" Buddhist texts themselves by pointing to their status as cultic objects of devotion.[5] Following Schopen's lead, recent scholarship in Buddhist studies has shown a growing tendency to focus on the local, the vernacular, the ritual, and the material, in favor of the universal, the disembodied, and the ideal. Thus the titles of several recently published anthologies of Buddhism consciously invoke Buddhism's "practice," "life," and "experience"—in contrast to an older cohort of anthologies and their focus upon "texts," "translations," "scriptures," and "teachings."[6]

This same trend toward "rematerialization" has also resulted in increasing attention paid to Buddhist conceptions of the body and a gradual dispelling of the image of Buddhism as a dualistic system that denigrates the body and holds complete bodily emancipation—"nirvana-without-remainder"—as its ultimate goal. Scholars are now paying more attention to the topics of relic worship, the glorious bodies of Buddhas and bodhisattvas, the bodies created through Buddhist monastic practice, the gendered body, and the various types of bodily transformation so often encountered in Buddhist literature. Moreover, they are beginning to overcome the persistent framing of these issues in terms of mind *versus* body (with all its attendant hierarchies),[7] as well as the tendency to artificially separate "ordinary" bodies from those that are "ideal."[8] We will encounter some of their conclusions throughout the rest of this chapter. In exploring Buddhist conceptions of the body as they are manifested within gift-of-the-body *jātakas,* I hope to demonstrate the complexity of this body discourse, the importance of perspective and point of view, and the sophisticated ways in which a Buddhist "ideology of the body" is conveyed through the narrative form.

The Worthlessness and Worth of the Ordinary Body

Gift-of-the-body *jātakas* exhibit at least two traditional lines of Buddhist thinking about the ordinary human body. We might refer to one line of thinking as the *worthlessness* of the body: the body is impure, foul, and disgusting (commonly described as a "wound," a "boil with nine openings," and a "bag of excrement"); the body is afflicted by old age, disease, suffering, and death; the body is transient and impermanent (like a "bubble" or "foam")—yet the body's deceptive wholeness leads to delusions of selfhood, sexual passion for others, and other undesirable consequences that entrap one in the round of rebirth. Such negative attitudes toward the human body appear in a wide variety of Buddhist texts; since they have been well documented before,[9] I will here restrict myself to citing a few verses from the *Dhammapada* that encapsulate them succinctly:

> Behold [the human body]—a dressed-up image, a collection of wounds, an accumulation [of bones], diseased, full of intentions but lacking any permanence or duration! This decaying form, [the body], is a frail nest of diseases. This putrid body [finally] disintegrates, for life ends in death. [This body is] a city of bones, plastered over with flesh and blood, wherein lie hidden decay, death, pride, and hypocrisy.[10]

Negative views of the body thus center around its impurity, its impermanence, its fragility, and its significant role in reinforcing one's passions and delusions. Given these negative qualities, attachment to the body is worthless and futile, and the Buddhist monk is encouraged to overcome such attachment through a variety of body-focused meditations, such as meditation on the thirty-two loathsome parts of the body, meditation on the nine stages of decomposition undergone by a corpse, or meditation on the ten varieties of dead bodies found in the cremation ground.[11] Negative statements about the nature of the body and admonitions to practice various types of meditation focusing on the body's many unsatisfying qualities both suggest the body's inherent *worthlessness.*

In contrast to this *worthlessness,* however, we might refer to the second line of thinking as the *worth* of the body. First and foremost, the body is a necessary locus of enlightenment; as Bernard Faure has said: "Despite its transcendental claims, awakening is always localized: it needs a locus to 'take place,' and this locus is the body."[12] More than just a passive locus where enlightenment "takes place," however, the body is also a necessary instrument for the attainment of enlightenment. Without the physical body one could not engage in religious practice of any sort; meditation, worship, ritual, and acts of devotion and merit-making would all be impossible to perform. Thus the human body, as both the vehicle for one's spiritual progress and the locus of its ultimate goal, should be adequately cared for and maintained.

This second line of thinking finds expression in many different contexts. In the Buddha's own life story, for example, true spiritual progress was made only when he renounced severe mortification of the body and came to understand that the body needed adequate food and maintenance in order to serve as a locus of enlightenment. Proper care for the body was thus an essential element of the Middle Way propounded by the Buddha and distinguished the Buddha's teaching from some other *śramaṇa* groups who engaged overzealously in asceticism. Similarly, the human body is often celebrated for the rare opportunity it provides to engage in religious practice, while suicide is frowned upon as a wasteful squandering of this opportunity; [13] food is recommended in moderation; health and physical vitality are extolled; the bodily pleasures of meditation are praised; and so on. In a variety of such ways, the essential *worth* of the human body and the necessity of caring for it properly are clearly recognized and extolled.

These two lines of thinking—both well attested throughout Buddhist literature—tend to be invoked in different contexts, the *worthlessness* of the body being emphasized when the motivation is to overcome one's attachment to self, and the *worth* of the body being emphasized when the motivation is to inculcate proper care for the body in the pursuit of higher religious goals. Nevertheless, there is a sense in which the two notions taken together might appear to be contradictory. In the *Visuddhimagga,* for example, Buddhaghosa, invoking the foulness and impurity of the body, scorns the manner in which people continually attend to it, "scouring the filth from their teeth by using toothpicks and rinsing the mouth and so on, concealing their genitals with all types of clothing, smearing [themselves] with sweet-smelling ointments of various colors, adorning [themselves] with flowers and ornaments and so on"—all in a vain attempt to "make it fit to be grasped as 'I' or as 'mine.'"[14] Such care for the body is depicted as nothing but the futile efforts of fools who do not understand the body's intrinsic nature. This might lead one to surmise that those who are wise and *do* understand the body's intrinsic nature would not bother to expend such care on the body, knowing it to be futile. Yet, as several scholars have pointed out,[15] Buddhist monastic discipline itself is greatly preoccupied with minutely detailed matters of dress, etiquette, and bodily deportment, and places a high value on such qualities as cleanliness, health, and decorum. The scorn heaped on ordinary people's care for their bodies and the monastic preoccupation with carefully controlling the bodies of monks and nuns are on some level contradictory.

At the same time, of course, the *worthlessness* and *worth* of the body can also be explained in such a way that they become complementary rather than contradictory. One could argue, for example, that ordinary people care for their bodies because they misperceive them as truly existing and satisfying *selves* that are worthy of such elaborate attention, whereas monastics (ideally) are under no such delusions and only care for their bodies because they recognize the body's practical worth as a vehicle for attaining enlightenment. Much of the care that ordinary people lavish on their bodies, moreover, is intended to make these bodies more sexually attractive, whereas monastic care of the body minimizes sexuality and seeks to detract attention rather than attract it. Finally, one might add, monastic attention to the body is detached and analytical in nature and contrasts with the ordinary person's slavish devotion. Within such an explanation, the *worthlessness* and *worth* of the body are logically related to each other rather than standing in contradiction.

An explanation of this type does in fact occur in a discussion in the *Milindapañha,* in which King Milinda asks the monk Nāgasena why Buddhist monks "cherish and take pride in" the body if it is not "dear" to them.[16] Nāgasena answers by comparing the body to a wound received in battle: although it is not "dear" to the one who receives it, it is nevertheless "rubbed with ointment, smeared with oil, and wrapped in a fine cloth bandage."[17] In just the same way, the body is not "dear" to monks, but they care for it "for the benefit of the religious life."[18] In Nāgasena's answer, too, the worthlessness of the body as a "wound" and the necessity of caring for it because of its worth in practicing the dharma are not necessarily in conflict.[19] Similarly, in his own variation on the *Milindapañha* dialogue, Steven Collins has argued that the monk's positive nurturing of his body—though superficially in opposition to the negative views of the body he is supposed to cultivate in meditation—"creates the actual behavioural space in which the 'subjectivized' interiority inculcated by meditative practices can take place."[20] In other words, the monk's decorous and controlled behavior—which would seem to imply a faulty overvaluing of the body—actually serves to mark him off from other people (physically, behaviorally, and psychically) and thus gives him the "room" in which to attain a truly internalized realization of the body's worthlessness. In various such ways, then, the *worthlessness* and *worth* of the body may be interpreted as complementary.

Nevertheless, it is perhaps inevitable that an element of contradiction and paradox always remains: How could the impure, foul, and disgusting body also serve as a necessary locus for the *summum bonum* of enlightenment? How could such a worthless entity turn out to be an object of such incalculable worth? The degree to which this paradox is highlighted may vary from one context to another: in some instances, the body's "worthlessness" or "worth" alone might be emphasized; in other instances, the logical relationship between them might be demonstrated; while in yet other instances, the paradox between them might be heightened and celebrated without providing any explanation of their relationship. An entire range of possibilities exists—and all of them make an appearance in the gift-of-the-body genre.

Worthlessness and Worth in Gift-of-the-Body Tales

In some passages—often from stories involving the feeding of hungry beings—the bodhisattva depicts the "worthlessness" of his body in stark and uncompromising terms, using standard Buddhist images of the body's foulness and impermanence, while the only "worth" invoked is the minimal worth others might draw from the abandoned carcass left behind. Because the body is totally worthless and doomed to destruction anyway—the bodhisattva reasons—it might as well be abandoned and put to use in feeding others:

> This body is devoid of individual existence. It is insubstantial and breaks apart. It is miserable, ungrateful, and always impure. He who would not rejoice upon its being useful to another is a fool.[21]

> Since my body is perishable and a source of unhappiness [anyway], even deliberating [this gift] would be base.[22]

> The body is a corruptible instrument; how can it be protected? Everything living must die; who is there who could preserve himself for all eternity? If you don't take [my body], it will return to dust [anyway].[23]

All living beings must perish; the body is a corruptible instrument. Since it has to be abandoned anyway, it is better to give it away as food.[24]

Eat fearlessly! I will not stop you. The body is worthless and repulsive, attended by misfortune and wasting away in an instant. [Only] when it gives the slightest benefit to others does it attain [any] worth in samsara. How could anyone so inappropriately love the filthy human body—a despicable abode of evil that oozes with discharges and emits little snorts with every step? The only thing desirable about it is that having seen someone, somewhere, sometime, in a time of trouble, it is prepared through meritorious deeds to help them just a little bit.[25]

It is not merely the worthlessness of one's *present* body that is invoked, in fact, but also its *perpetual* worthlessness—in one life after another, throughout the entire round of samsara, whether in a good station or a bad. The worthlessness of the body here takes on almost cosmic proportions—an unbearable burden the bodhisattva is only too happy to abandon and throw away:

Even when one's intentions are innocent, many miseries are experienced in samsara over and over again—in the hells, among the animals, in the world of Yama, and in the world of men. The cutting off of the hands, of the feet, of the ears, of the nose, of both the ears and the nose, and many other similar types of misery are experienced. What good am I to gain from that, when I might [instead] generate power, strength, and energy within myself, satisfy this woman with my own flesh and blood, and [thus] set free her son?[26]

This putrid body has been maintained for an exceedingly long time with very expensive beds, clothing, food, drink, and vehicles. Characterized by decay and death, finally breaking apart and ending in misery, this [certainly] isn't the first time this ungrateful [body] will relinquish its own nature.[27]

For all eternity, this body has been circling around in samsara. For a long time, when it was a being in hell, transmigrating many times even in a single day, this body was consumed by lye, iron dogs, boiling hot water, vomit, chariots of fire, pits of fire, and so on, and as a hell-being, it underwent suffering for a very long time. But even though this body was consumed countless times by being boiled, burned, and so on, it did not produce even the slightest merit. When born in the womb of animals, who bite and devour one another, [this body] was killed by others and eaten by all, and having died, it decomposed and rotted away over

> and over again. But even though it was consumed in this way, it did not produce any merit. When born in the realm of hungry ghosts, fire burned in this body; its head was split open by a wheel, only to recover again immediately, and this happened over and over again. But even though this body was consumed in this way, it did not produce any merit. Even when born as a human being, [this body's] eyes gaped wide open with anger and greed due to wealth and women. This body was consumed by [people] hurting and killing each other, meeting in battle and murdering each other. But even though this body was thrown away countless times through desire, hatred, and delusion, it still did not make any merit. I completely reject this body![28]

Despite the occasional reference to making merit, it seems fairly clear that such passages are concerned, first and foremost, with the body's "worthlessness." Because the body is completely and utterly worthless, it might as well be abandoned, and the only "worth" of the body invoked is the "leftover" or "remaining" worth of the carcass, which is usually nothing more than its status as potential *food.* The emphasis here is on *abandoning* the foul and worthless body, rather than on *using* the body to achieve some kind of goal; the body is not an instrument, but merely a burden to be unloaded. The sentiments expressed here might perhaps be compared to some of the most negative statements about the body's loathsome nature found elsewhere in Buddhist literature—passages concerned solely with eradicating one's attachment to the body and convincing one of its foul and disgusting nature rather than considering the body's practical worth.

Such passages as the above are relatively few in number, however, and do not constitute the perspective on the body characteristic of the genre as a whole. For outside of such isolated passages, these stories generally make it clear that this "unloading of the burden of the body" is not merely a passive occurrence; it is also instrumental in nature—a positive moral deed that generates enormous merit and furthers one's spiritual progress. To *abandon* the worthless body is also to *use* the worthless body in a particular way—and if done in the proper manner and in pursuit of the proper ends, such abandonment carries its own, significant rewards. We thus begin to move from the "worthlessness" of the body to a realization of its "worth," and to see that these two qualities are complementary and logically related rather than standing in contradiction. This movement can be traced in many gift-of-the-body tales.

My first example is an interesting passage from *Jātakamālā* 6, in which the bodhisattva is a hare who offers his body to a wandering brahmin (see

FIGURE 5 Gift-of-the-body *jātakas* from India continue to be retold in popular formats in many Buddhist cultures today. Osamu Tezuka (grandfather of *manga* in Japan and creator of *Astro Boy* and many other series) opens his magnificent, eight-volume *Buddha* (originally serialized in Japanese in the 1970s) with the story of the hare. In this series of panels, the hare has thrown himself into a fire in order to feed a brahmin wanderer, and the brahmin wanderer lifts his corpse up toward the sky, whereupon his image comes to adorn the moon. Image reprinted with permission from Vertical, Inc.

figure 5). This passage, I believe, attempts to demonstrate the causal and logical relationship between the body's *worthlessness* and its *worth* by having the ruminations of the hare move *sequentially* from the former to the latter. Pondering what food he might offer to supplicants he encounters on the fast-day, the hare begins by berating the absolute *worthlessness* of his body in procuring adequate food for a guest, and then—in a kind of "a-ha!" experience—has a sudden realization of its *worth:*

There is no possible way I can give to a guest the very bitter blades of grass I nibble off with the tips of my teeth. What a curse is my helplessness! What use do I have for such a weak and miserable life, when a guest who should bring me joy thus becomes a matter of sorrow? When will this wretched body—worthless in its ability to attend on a guest—be of use to someone by being abandoned? . . . I've got it! Indeed, I myself possess something that is suitable for honoring a guest, blameless, easy to obtain, and at my own disposal—the treasure of my body! So why should I despair? I have found something that is proper for a guest. Therefore, heart, let go of your despair and misery! I will honor the requests of guests as they arise with this wretched body![29]

The sequential ordering of the ideas of *worthlessness* and *worth* within the context of a sudden realization on the part of the hare serves to clarify the fact that the body's worth *derives from one's realization of its utter worthlessness.* That is, it is only because the hare realizes how worthless his body is that, in a moment of frustration, he suddenly hits upon the idea of abandoning it completely—which then leads him to see that it might, in fact, derive some worth in the very act of being abandoned, enough worth, in fact, so that the "worthless" and "miserable" body is paradoxically transformed into a "treasure." In that moment of sudden realization, the negative worth involved in merely *abandoning* the body is transformed into the positive worth involved in *using* the worthless body in a religious act, one which paradoxically transforms the body into a precious "treasure."

In the hare's monologue, of course, the *worthlessness* and *worth* of the body are invoked in terms of a specific narrative situation: the body is worthless because it cannot procure adequate food for a guest, and it is worthy because it itself constitutes adequate food for a guest. Clearly, however, the *worthlessness* and *worth* of this particular body in this particular situation can be taken to stand for the *worthlessness* and *worth* of the body in general—that is, the body's *worthlessness* as characterized by impermanence, impurity, and suffering, and its *worth* as a locus and vehicle for attaining enlightenment. Therefore, I believe that what *Jātakamālā* 6 is trying to demonstrate by means of the structure of this monologue is the double-edged role of the body in relation to bondage and freedom. Miserable and wretched, the body is a major cause of bondage for deluded beings, yet one need only *recognize* this awful truth about the body (and about old age, disease, suffering, and death) in order to be free—with the body itself serving as the ground for this realization—and in that sense the body is also the cause of freedom. The body encompasses bondage in samsara, the freedom of nirvana, and the path leading from one to the other. As the Buddha puts it in the *Saṃyutta Nikāya:* "Moreover, monk, it is precisely within this fathom-long cadaver that I make known the world, the arising of the world, the cessation of the world, and the path leading to the cessation of the world."[30] Thus, *worthlessness* and *worth* here are not merely compatible, but mutually entail one another, with the latter deriving from the former.

In other passages, we can see the same movement compressed into a single, brief statement. In the story of the tigress found in the *Suvarṇabhāsottama Sūtra,* for example, the bodhisattva, upon seeing the hungry tigress ready to devour her own young, thinks to himself:

> There is no use to this [body] because it is nothing but piss, [so] I will now employ it in a virtuous act. Thus, it will be like a boat carrying me across the ocean of birth and death.[31]

Once again we move from the *worthlessness* of the body (which is "nothing but piss"), to the *use* of the worthless body in the performance of "a virtuous act," which then paradoxically transforms the worthless body into a "boat carrying me across the ocean of birth and death"—all within the confines of a single, brief passage. In *Avadānasārasamuccaya* 2, we have exactly the same movement (although, in this case, the grammar of the sentence presents the ideas in a slightly different order):

> If I do not use this body in such a way to acquire merit, which will result in incomparable happiness, of what use will it be when it is a corpse, shunned [by everyone] and as feeble as a bubble being whirled about in the ocean by the wind?[32]

Implicit in this statement is the same basic movement—from the worthlessness of the "feeble corpse," to the "use" of this corpse "to acquire merit," which then paradoxically brings about a state of "incomparable happiness."

In all of these passages, then, we move through a logical sequence of ideas linking the body's "worthlessness" to its "worth." If we wanted to enumerate these ideas as explicitly as possible, they might look something like the following:

1. The body is worthless.
2. I realize that the body is worthless.
3. Because I realize that the body is worthless, I am willing to abandon it for others.
4. Yet my *abandoning* of the body (because it is worthless) is also a particular *use* of the body.
5. This use of the body (when done in the proper manner and with the proper motivation) is positive in nature and results in desirable rewards.
6. These rewards thus paradoxically turn my worthless body into something of incalculable worth.
7. However, my body never would have attained this "worth" without the original realization of its "worthlessness."

Through their implicit suggestion of this sequence of ideas, these passages demonstrate for their readers the double-edged nature of the body in relation to bondage and freedom and the causal and logical relationship between its "worthlessness" and its "worth."

At the same time, however, the fact that such passages are either more or less explicit in their enumeration of this sequence of ideas also points to the possibility of one final option available to the authors of gift-of-the-body tales—that of painting the "worthlessness" and "worth" of the body in starkly contradictory terms and celebrating the paradox between them without clarifying how they might be related. This is perhaps a more poetic strategy, one of reveling in the paradox instead of resolving it. In *Jātakamālā* 8, for example, King Maitrībala, in a single verse, refers to his body as "a noxious sore" and a "corpse" that is "perpetually ill and the cause of disease," but also notes that he will use this corpse in "an extraordinary deed" and thus exact upon it an "exceedingly sweet revenge."[33] In the *Maṇicūḍāvadāna* Maṇicūḍa exclaims that his "putrid body" is, at one and the same time, a "requirement for [attaining] unsurpassed, perfect enlightenment."[34] And in *Jātakamālā* 30 the bodhisattva (as an elephant) refers to his body as an "asylum for many hundreds of diseases" but also "a raft for crossing [the ocean of] misfortune for these men afflicted by suffering."[35] Finally, a particularly striking example can be found in *Avadānasārasamuccaya* 3, where the simultaneous invocation of *worthlessness* and *worth* occurs in each of three consecutive verses spoken by King Sarvaṃdada:

> Today, at last, with your help, this *evil called the body, which despairs at the sudden attacks of countless miseries,* will now be of use to me in *fulfilling the side of virtue!* O Best of Brahmins! The *wish that I have longed for* for such a long time—may it be fulfilled today, through your power, and in dependence on *this body, a parade of decay, disease, and death.* The king will have joy, you will attain great wealth, and I will have *superior perfection.* See what *extraordinary joy* has befallen each of us through the abandonment of *a single body filled with misfortune!*[36]

The continual oscillation here between *worthlessness* and *worth* elicits a reaction of amazement at the paradox of the body without attempting to draw attention to the ways in which this paradox might be resolved. Within such passages we leave the realm of coherent doctrine behind and enter a more aesthetic and emotional realm, one in which the foul and loathsome body is suddenly—almost alchemically—transformed into a precious and highly valued object.

Although for the purposes of description I have distinguished and treated separately several different ways of invoking the "worthlessness" and "worth" of the ordinary human body, many gift-of-the-body stories pursue all of these strategies simultaneously. In fact, the richness of the gift-of-the-body genre's discourse on the body lies precisely in the fact that its perspective is constantly shifting. One story that is particularly rich in this regard is *Avadānasārasamuccaya* 2, in which the bodhisattva is a merchant who tries to convince his one hundred drowning companions to accept the gift of his body. Throughout the course of a long monologue, all of the strategies enumerated above are represented in a constantly shifting pattern. Thus at one moment he emphasizes the body's utter worthlessness, telling his companions that if he does not abandon this "weak and putrid body," then "powerful Death, which is intent upon destroying the world, will make me abandon it [anyway]."[37] Since "the body's end is already near," he reasons, "what is so difficult about [giving it away]?"[38] At another moment, however, this same worthless body that can only be thrown away in disgust is also, paradoxically, "an occasion of great joy" that "should be celebrated for the excellence of its merit";[39] indeed, it is like "moonlight out of season" and "an eternal remedy for misfortune."[40] And at other moments the reasoning behind such contradictory evaluations is made explicit: "[By using it] to achieve the welfare of my friends," he explains, "I will make this body an abode of joy"[41]—thus transforming "this strife called the body from an enemy into a friend."[42] Several different perspectives on the body are presented simultaneously, in a constantly shifting pattern, leaving the reader with a rich and complex discourse on the body's "worthlessness" and its "worth."

Extracting the Essence from This Essenceless Body

My description of the bodily discourse found in gift-of-the-body *jātakas* in terms of the two perspectives of "worthlessness" and "worth" finds a very close parallel within the stories themselves, through the use of a particular cliché repeated over and over again. In many gift-of-the-body stories, it is said that the bodhisattva, by giving away his body, will "extract the essence from this essenceless body." This statement is usually spoken by the bodhisattva, and often addressed to the recipient:

> I will [now] extract the essence from my body.[43]

> Today, having met you, I wish to draw the essence from this essenceless body.[44]

> Today, having gained you as my friend, I am ready to extract the essence from this putrid corpse, destined to decay.[45]

> I must extract the essence from this crumbling, essenceless body, as if I were plucking a piece of fruit from a tree hanging on to a river bank, just as its roots are being torn by the current and giving way.[46]

The idea of "extracting the essence from the essenceless body" seems to be closely associated with the bodhisattva's self-sacrifice outside the gift-of-the-body genre as well. The phrase is used several times, for example, in the first chapter of Śāntideva's *Śikṣāsamuccaya,* which deals at length with the bodhisattva's gift of his body.[47] Later in the same text the wilderness-dwelling bodhisattva who is attacked and devoured by snakes and ferocious beasts is also told to remind himself that because of this self-sacrifice, "I have met with great profit, for I will [now] grasp the essence from my essenceless body."[48] Though this cliché is invoked in regard to other types of meritorious deeds as well, and is by no means limited to contexts involving the bodhisattva's gift of his body, it does seem to have a particularly close association with this context.

In all of these passages, the words used for "essence" and "essenceless" are *sāra* and its negative, *asāra*. The term *sāra* has a wide range of related meanings; it refers to the "core," "pith," "sap," "heart," or "essence" of something and, by extension, its "essential part," "best part," "value," or "worth."[49] Thus the terms *sāra* and *asāra* could legitimately be translated as "worth" and "worthless," and the bodhisattva described as one who "extracts the worth from this worthless body." This expression gives voice to the inherent paradox involved in getting "worth" out of a body that is "worthless," yet also hints at the way in which the two qualities might be related—the body's "worth" being derived (or "extracted") from one's realization of its utter "worthlessness." The cliché thus encapsulates the two major lines of Buddhist thinking about the body I have discussed above within the confines of a single phrase: to "extract the essence from the essenceless body" is to realize the body's *worthlessness* and thus make use of the body in pursuit of higher religious goals, thus creating the body's *worth*.

The fact that *sāra* and *asāra* are almost always translated as "essence" and "essenceless" (or "substance" and "insubstantial") rather than the more abstract "worth" and "worthless" is due, I believe, to the fact that the term *sāra* seems to have chiefly physical connotations, referring primarily to the "core," "pith," or "sap" of something, and only by extension to its "value" or "worth."[50] It is perhaps because of these substantialist connotations that John Strong, in his discussion of this cliché (as it appears in the *Aśokāvadāna*), states that Aśoka's talk about extracting the body's "essence" is "somewhat reminiscient" of the Brahmanical concept of *ātman*, the Jain concept of *jīva*, and the Sāṃkhya concept of *puruṣa*, as well as aligning it closely with the later Mahāyāna concepts of *tathāgatagarbha* and *dharmadhātu*.[51] Like the *tathāgatagarbha* or *dharmadhātu*, according to Strong, the "essence" one must rescue from the essenceless body is the "ultimate reality to be understood in enlightenment" and is one of several concepts used to emphasize "the immanence of the Unconditioned."[52]

Though Strong himself observes that the *Aśokāvadāna* here "is not concerned with doctrine per se but with stressing the immediate possibilities of soteriological action,"[53] he nevertheless interprets the term *sāra* in a manner that I believe veers too far in the direction of turning it into some kind of substantial, metaphysical entity extracted from the body.[54] Though the extraction of *sāra* is often described in terms of vivid, concrete images (such as rescuing a treasure chest from a sinking ship or removing the pith from a palm tree), this language is strictly poetic and metaphorical in nature. The "essence" of the body itself, I believe, is indeed nothing more and nothing less than "the immediate possibilities of soteriological action"—in other words, the body's basic ability and potential to engage in religious action of every sort. In fact, it seems to me that this strictly functional (rather than ontological or metaphysical) status of *sāra* is made exceedingly clear within the *Aśokāvadāna* itself. Explaining the idea of the body's "essence" to his minister Yaśas, Aśoka states (from Strong's own translation):

> When my body lies in the ground,
> discarded like the pulp of sugarcane,
> it will be of no use for merit making;
> it won't be able to perform strenuous activities:
> getting up, bowing down, and making añjalis.
> Therefore, right now, I should endeavor to save
> my meritorious essence from perishing in the grave.
> Those who do not extract the essence
> from this body that must inevitably perish
> are like those who fail to save a chest of jewels
> from a burning house or a ship sinking at sea.
> Unable to distinguish essence from non-essence,
> they never see the essence at all
> and are totally distraught
> when they enter the jaws of Death.
> Once one has enjoyed curds,
> ghee, fresh butter, and buttermilk,
> the best part of the milk—its essence—is gone.
> If the jar is then accidentally broken,
> it is hardly something to get upset about.
> So too there should be no sorrow at death
> if one has already extracted from one's body,
> its essence—good conduct.
> . . . The wise in this world make merit
> by getting up, bowing down, and performing
> other acts of obeisance,
> relying on this most vile body,
> hoping for the essence.[55]

Within this passage, it seems to me, the "essence" of the essenceless body is not a substantial or metaphysical entity akin to *dharmadhātu;* instead, it is simply one's ability to make *use* of the body within religious acts—"getting up, bowing down, and performing other acts of obeisance."

My interpretation here is in accord with that of Jonathan Silk, who has also discussed the meaning of this cliché.[56] Noting that "the idea of a body which has a transcendent essence seems to be rather common in the *Tathāgatagarbha* literature"—but that he remains unconvinced that this has anything to do with the meaning of *sāra* within this cliché—Silk then cites a passage from the *Ugraparipṛcchā Sūtra* which he believes makes the meaning of the expression explicit. The passage in question runs as follows:

> [The bodhisattva] thinks in terms of extracting the essence from his essenceless body. . . . What is "thinking in terms of extracting the essence from one's essenceless body"? It is taking pleasure in doing all that is to be done for others; speaking respectfully to one's teachers, doing homage to them, rising up, pressing one's palms together, and bowing to them—this is "thinking in terms of extracting the essence from one's essenceless body."[57]

Once again, the "essence" of the body here is nothing more and nothing less than its ability to be *used* to engage in acts of a religious nature. It is functional in nature rather than metaphysical.

And yet—it is no doubt true that the concreteness of the imagery still remains. Because *sāra* retains its physical connotations, the idea of "extracting the essence from this essenceless body" seems almost alchemical and magical in nature and is associated with vivid, physical images of jewels rescued from a burning house, delicious ghee extracted from thin and watery milk, or ripe and luscious fruit plucked from a barren, windswept tree. By means of extracting this "essence," moreover, the foul and loathsome body—the "noxious sore" and the "putrid corpse destined to decay"—is quite suddenly and inexplicably transformed into "moonlight out of season," "an eternal remedy for misfortune," and "a raft for crossing the ocean of birth and death." Clearly, such images begin to point beyond the mere *potential* of the ordinary body toward a different kind of body altogether—one that is *already* perfect and ideal, and one that paradoxically overcomes all of the "worthlessness" whose realization is precisely what brings it about. It is perhaps this poetic and paradoxical use of imagery, then, that ultimately makes possible the Buddhist tradition's leap from the *ordinary* body to the *ideal.*

The Ideal Body Achieved

Susanne Mrozik (again in connection with the "essence" cliché) has spoken of this as a "productive paradox" lying at the heart of Buddhist conceptions of the body. She describes this paradox in the following terms:

> The person who cultivates detachment from his body, even to the point of sacrificing his body and life for the sake of others, is the very person who gets the best body of all—the irresistibly beautiful body of a Buddha. Paradoxically, the realization that one's body is inherently disgusting, impermanent, and without abiding essence creates an altogether different kind of body. Likewise, the ability to regard all bodies as alike in their foulness, impermanence, and lack of abiding essence produces a body that is quite different from all others.[58]

This paradox is fully evident in the gift-of-the-body genre, for in spite of their frequent condemnation of the ordinary body's worthlessness, gift-of-the-body *jātakas* share with other genres of Buddhist literature a tendency to celebrate various types of "ideal bodies" that stand in stark contrast to the ordinary body and overcome all its deficiencies and limitations. These statements move beyond the mere "worth" of the ordinary body to celebrate—often in literal and concretely physical terms—a body that is *already* perfect and beautiful to behold. Let me enumerate four different contexts in which the conception of such an "ideal body" occurs.

1. The first and most prevalent context consists of statements made about the bodhisattva's body by *others*—for despite the bodhisattva's own tendency to dwell on his body's impurity and repulsiveness, this same body is almost always described by others (and by the authorial voice itself) as one that is *already ideal.* In *Avadānasārasamuccaya* 3 King Sarvaṃdada describes his own body as "a parade of decay, disease, and death" that is "afflicted by many misfortunes," yet this same body is hyperbolically extolled by the narrative voice of the text as "having the gait of an elephant in rut, shiny as gold, tall as Mount Sumeru, with brilliant jewel-like features."[59] In *Kalpanāmaṇḍitikā* 64 the body that King Śibi himself describes as being "a seat of old age and disease, numerous dangers and repugnant substances" is

nevertheless praised by the narrator for being "as blue as a lotus-leaf" and "shining with a pure brilliance."[60] And in *Jātakamālā* 8 King Maitrībala's body—which, according to him, is a "noxious sore" and a "corpse"—is described by one of his subjects in the following terms:

> His chest is as broad as a rock on Mount Meru; he is handsome, with a face as lovely as the clear moon in autumn; his arms are long and thick like bars of gold; he has the look and stride of a bull.[61]

In fact, not even the gory act of mutilation can make this body unattractive. For even when his body is cut open and "his blood [is] being lapped up by the demons," King Maitrībala is still described as having "a body shining like gold, as if Mount Meru were being embraced by clouds heavy with the weight of rain and reddened by twilight"[62]—just as the woman Rūpyāvatī, after severing her own breasts and arriving home with her clothing drenched in blood, still manages to look like "a golden image worshipped with saffron powder."[63]

In addition to physical beauty, moreover, these bodies are often characterized by supernatural powers that belie the weak and fragile image often painted by the bodhisattva himself. In Pāli *Jātaka* 514 the elephant's tusks emit six-colored rays of light and have magical powers.[64] In the *Maṇicūḍāvadāna* King Maṇicūḍa's crest-jewel lights up the entire city of Sāketa every night, appeases all misery (such as disease, fire, and floods), and turns everything it touches into pure gold;[65] whereas King Candraprabha of *Divyāvadāna* 22 derives his name (meaning "Moonlight") from the fact that "neither jewels nor lamps nor torches were led in front [of him], but light went forth from his own body, like rays from the disk of the moon."[66] In numerous such ways, then, these stories indicate that—at least according to those around him—the bodhisattva's body, far from sharing the foul nature that is supposed to be characteristic of *all* bodies, is already perfect and ideal.

2. Secondly, in those stories in which the bodhisattva dies, much the same can be said of the corpse he leaves behind. Because these stories often involve descriptions of the body's impermanence and impurity and its mutilation and dumping in the charnel ground, they strongly evoke the image of the meditative practice of *aśubha-bhāvanā,* in which one meditates on dead, rotting, and mutilated corpses in the charnel ground in order to realize the body's foul and loathsome nature. In fact, the bodhisattva's body, after being mutilated or devoured, is often described in such a way

so as to match up perfectly with one of the nine or ten varieties of corpses focused on in the cemetery meditations, such as the "corpse pecked at by crows, vultures, dogs, and worms," the corpse that is reduced to "bones scattered in all directions," or the "hacked and scattered" corpse.[67] We might therefore expect the bodhisattva's mutilated corpse to be evaluated in equally negative terms, and perhaps used as a meditative object illustrating the foul and transient nature of the body for those he leaves behind. Yet this is just the opposite of the reaction to the corpse that occurs in story after story.

In the first place, the bodhisattva's lifeless corpse—even when headless, bloody, or otherwise mutilated—is still described as an object of great beauty. In *Jātakamālā* 30, even after the elephant has thrown himself off a mountain, the weary travelers who find his corpse extol its great beauty in three long verses, comparing its various parts to lotus-stalks, moonbeams, the graceful curve of a bow, and other poetic images.[68] In *Jātakamālā* 6 the rabbit's corpse, even after being burnt in a fire, is still "as beautiful as lotus petals and adorned with radiant jewels."[69] In *Suvarṇabhāsottama Sūtra,* chapter 18, Prince Mahāsattva, having been devoured by the tigress, is reduced to nothing more than "bones devoid of blood, flesh, and sinews, with hair scattered in all directions"—but for the onlookers this has the appearance of delicately scattered lotus petals.[70] And finally, in *Avadānasārasamuccaya* 2 the merchant-leader's dead body is described as being "pleasing although devoid of life" and "having a beautiful complexion like polished gold, as if it had been willingly stroked by Lakṣmī."[71] Even as a dead corpse it is contrasted with the living bodies of ordinary beings, who are "immersed in the filth and excrement of birth, full of large, quivering worms of affliction."[72]

Rather than being meditated on or allowed to rot further, moreover, the bodhisattva's corpse is almost always made the object of elaborate ritual treatment. In Pāli *Jātaka* 514 the elephant's corpse is ceremonially cremated in a sacred enclosure by the other elephants, while five hundred pratyekabuddhas recite texts all night long.[73] In *Divyāvadāna* 22 the king's headless and bloody corpse is cremated on a pile of fragrant wood, interred in a *stūpa* at a great crossroads, adorned with flags and banners, and worshiped with various types of offerings.[74] In *Jātakamālā* 1, after the bodhisattva is devoured by the tigress, his disciple says of his remains: "Oh! How his body, which was not lacking in goodness, has now suddenly become worthy of the greatest adoration!"[75] Joined by *gandharvas, yakṣas, nāgas, devas,* and other men, he worships the remains with garlands, jewels, and unguents.

And in *Jātakamālā* 30 the gods themselves honor the elephant's corpse by showering down flowers, singing hymns of praise, making cloud canopies for him in the sky, and causing trees to bloom out of season.[76]

Finally, the holy sites resulting from such ritual treatment are sometimes depicted as having a lasting—almost permanent—duration. In *Suvarṇabhāsottama Sūtra*, chapter 18, Prince Mahāsattva's parents, the king and queen, remove all of their ornaments, pay homage to the relics of their son, and then erect a beautiful *stūpa* made of jewels, gold, and silver. This *stūpa* lasts throughout the eons and is later made to reemerge from the earth by the Buddha himself, who explains to Ānanda: "By means of these bones, Ānanda, I quickly awoke to unsurpassed, perfect enlightenment."[77] Perhaps the most enduring treatment is accorded to the hare's body in *Jātakamālā* 6: though the hare himself dies, his body lives on in an image of cosmic proportions, for Śakra inscribes his image on the disk of the moon, and thus "even today, when the moon is full, the image of the hare shines in the sky, like a reflection in a silver mirror"[78]—elsewhere described as one of the "four marvels" of the present eon.[79]

In short, we see that over and over again the same body that the bodhisattva denigrates as foul and impure even when alive is treated by others—even as a mutilated corpse—as a sacred and physically beautiful object worthy of the highest adoration and most elaborate ritual treatment. Moreover, in many stories the corpse itself, instead of rotting away and thus illustrating impermanence, seems to be physically transmuted through the bodhisattva's deed into relics, *stūpas,* or holy sites that sometimes take on cosmic dimensions and have an almost permanent duration.

3. A similar process occurs on a smaller scale in those stories in which the bodhisattva survives. As we have seen, despite the bodhisattva's sincere willingness to give away his impure body, it is inevitable in these stories that he later performs an Act of Truth intended to get his body back. In the *Maṇicūḍāvadāna,* for example, King Maṇicūḍa, who speaks so eloquently of the "putrid body" *before* giving away his flesh and blood, later performs an Act of Truth asking for his "perfectly beautiful" body to be restored.[80] Moreover, many such stories manifest a bizarre brand of bodily alchemy wherein the limb offered as gift is not only restored, but becomes greater and more powerful than before. For instance, the light emitted by King Maṇicūḍa's crest-jewel doubles in size when later restored.[81] Likewise, in Pāli *Jātaka* 499 King Śibi's restored eyes can see through walls, rocks, and mountains, and for a hundred *yojanas* on every

side (as he himself states, "I gave away a human eye and obtained one that is supernatural!").[82] Although neither Maṇicūḍa nor Śibi *asks* for such increases in power, such passages at least imply that the bodhisattva gives away his impure and "worthless" body in order to acquire one that is *better* and *more powerful.*

4. Whereas the above three contexts all involve the statements made about, and the treatment accorded to, the bodhisattva's body by *others* (or by the voice of the text), a fourth context—relatively rare by comparison—consists of the bodhisattva's own statements about what type of "ideal body" he hopes to attain in the future (often in exchange for the ordinary one he is giving away). This *desire for a better body* can take a number of different forms. In the story of the woman Rūpāvatī, for example, it is specifically cast in terms of gender, for Rūpāvatī vows that by means of the gift of her breasts, "may the bodily faculties of a woman disappear from me, and may I appear with the bodily faculties of a man!"[83]—since manhood is "the basis of virtue in this world."[84] This physical transformation does indeed come to pass, with the resultant male body (in Haribhaṭṭa's version of the story) being celebrated for its "moon-like face," "manly chest," and "beard as dark as collyrium."[85] In this case it is the *male body*—perhaps a trope for Buddhahood itself?—that constitutes the desired ideal, while the female body is cast as ordinary and imperfect.

In *Divyāvadāna* 22, on the other hand, King Candraprabha's desire for a better body seems to be focused on the corpse's post mortem transformation into powerful relics and holy sites, for as he is giving away his head, he vows:

> And when I have attained nirvana, may there be relics the size of mustard seeds. And in the middle of this Maṇiratnagarbha pleasure-park, may there be a great *stūpa,* more excellent than any other *stūpa.* And may those beings who go with pure bodies to the great *caitya,* wishing to worship it, having seen that [*stūpa*], full of relics and more excellent than any other *stūpa,* feel at ease. And when I have attained nirvana, may crowds of people come to my *caityas,* perform acts of worship, and be destined for heaven or liberation.[86]

Although King Candraprabha's vow in regard to his *stūpa* does involve the soteriological effects it will have upon others, it also includes an unabashed desire for physical beauty and "oohs" and "aahs" from the adoring crowds.

The same type of desire takes on a particularly grotesque form in those stories involving the theme of the "flesh-mountain." In the story of King Ambara found in the *Karuṇāpuṇḍarīka Sūtra,* King Ambara vows:

May this body of mine become a mountain of flesh! May whatever beings have flesh for food and blood for drink come eat my flesh and drink my blood! And, by the power of my vow, may my body grow enough [to accommodate] as many beings as may eat my flesh and drink my blood, until it is a hundred thousand *yojanas* in height and five thousand *yojanas* in width![87]

Following this vow, he further explains that he satiated the beings there with his flesh and blood for one thousand years and also gave away numerous tongues to be devoured by the birds and beasts, "yet by the power of my vow, one after another of them appeared [until] there was a heap of them as big as Vulture Peak Mountain."[88] King Durdhana in the same text also becomes a "flesh-mountain" by means of a vow—a mountain that subsequently grows to a thousand times its original size, with "human heads appearing everywhere, with hair, ears, eyes, noses, lips, teeth, tongues, and many hundreds of thousands of mouths."[89] Here the ideal body seems almost to translate into sheer *quantity* and *multiplicity* of body parts.

In yet other cases, the ideal body the bodhisattva wishes to attain by giving away the body he presently has is the *body of a Buddha.* The exact nature of the Buddha-body he hopes to attain, however, is somewhat open to question. In some cases, such as the following two passages, this body is referred to rather abstractly as a "dharma-body" (*dharma-kāya*):

By abandoning my body, a boil, impelled through hundreds of existences, full of excrement and urine, as insubstantial as foam, full of hundreds of worms, driven forward by its acts, I will obtain a dharma-body, free of grief, free of change, free of [all] attachments, pure and stainless, full of hundreds of virtues, fully endowed with virtues such as meditation and so forth.[90]

[By giving away my body,] I will obtain a dharma-body that cannot be split apart, cut up, or carried away, that is imperishable, unscarred, and unsurpassed.[91]

It is difficult to interpret the exact sense of *dharma-kāya* within these passages; as research on the various bodies of the Buddha has shown,[92] the meaning of *dharma-kāya* varies from text to text, and the word itself has fluid connotations. Here the adjectives used to describe it ("free of grief," "free of change," "imperishable," "unscarred," "cannot be cut up," etc.) obviously imply something that escapes all of the limitations of ordinary physical existence without making it clear whether this something itself is also a physical body in nature. Therefore, the bodhisattva's wish to exchange his ordinary body for a "dharma-body" *could* be interpreted as a wish for transcendence beyond the physical condition into a completely immaterial existence. Nevertheless, there are other passages that make it clear that it is the *physical* body of a Buddha that the bodhisattva desires. In the *Karuṇāpuṇḍarīka Sūtra* King Ambara gives away his genitals in the hope of acquiring the "mark of hidden genitals" and his flesh and blood in the hope of acquiring the "mark of a golden complexion"[93]—which are two of the thirty-two marks characteristic of the physical body of a Buddha (the so-called *mahāpuruṣalakṣaṇa*).

Finally, as the last two examples make clear, it is also common for the bodhisattva to give away an individual part of the body (rather than the body as a whole) in exchange for its idealized counterpart. Thus King Śibi gives away his physical eye in hope of acquiring the "eye of omniscience,"[94] just as the elephant Ṣaḍdanta gives away his physical tusks in hope of acquiring the "tusks of omniscience."[95] Likewise, King Puṇyabala gives away the "ordinary eye of flesh" in hope of acquiring the "unsurpassed eye of dharma,"[96] King Maṇicūḍa gives away the jewel attached to his head in hope of acquiring the "jewel of enlightenment,"[97] and King Ambara gives away his hands and feet in hope of acquiring the "excellent hands of faith" and the "excellent feet of morality."[98] The process is the same as we have seen in regard to the whole body, but is here limited to individual parts of the body. In fact, both elements—the individual body parts and the dharma-body as a whole—are brought together in a passage on the bodhisattva's self-sacrifice from the *Vajradhvaja Sūtra* (as preserved in the first chapter of the *Śikṣāsamuccaya*). This passage states that the bodhisattva sacrifices his head, "longing for the most excellent knowledge, which is the foremost head of all the world"; he sacrifices his hand, "using the hand of faith to act for the welfare [of all beings]"; and he sacrifices his foot, thus "stepping with the soles [of his feet] upon the great foundation [of Buddhahood]." The passage then concludes that as he sacrifices all of these individual body parts, he bears in mind "the idea of a body that is uncut, unbroken, and undiminished—the *dharma-body* consisting of knowledge without any obstacles."[99] The specific qualities attained in exchange for individual body parts (such as hand, foot, and head) thus come together to form the "dharma-body" as a whole.

Morality and Physicality Intertwined

The citations given above should suffice to demonstrate that gift-of-the-body *jātakas,* in spite of their frequent rhetoric concerning the body's utter worthlessness, also hold out the hope of attaining a different kind of body altogether—an *ideal body,* one that escapes the negative qualities attributed to all physical bodies while still remaining resolutely physical in nature. Moreover, this ideal physical body is not merely the body of a Buddha that will be attained by the bodhisattva in the future, it is also the body he *already possesses.* Despite the frequent Buddhist claim that *all* human and animal bodies are foul and disgusting by nature—and despite his own enthusiastic assent to this claim—the bodhisattva's body, whether human or animal, is seen and treated by others as being already perfect and ideal. Clearly, as I have noted before, there is something of a paradox involved in the very existence of such an ideal body. If *all* bodies are supposed to be equally unsatisfactory, how can *some* bodies escape from this condition and be perfect and ideal? Moreover, how can it be the case that one attains such an ideal body precisely through one's realization of the body's worthless nature? And how can others see a perfect body where the bodhisattva himself sees only a decrepit and impure form?

One way of resolving the apparent paradox is by overcoming our inherited tendency toward mind/body dualism and instead keeping in mind the absolute interpenetration of the moral and the physical characteristic of the Buddhist worldview. As recent scholarship has increasingly come to show, the world depicted in traditional Buddhist texts is one in which the moral and physical orders are completely intertwined.[100] Moral virtues such as compassion or wisdom are not exclusively "mental" or "spiritual" in nature, but also have concrete physical embodiments such as a golden complexion or a mellifluous voice. Characters in Buddhist literature (as Susanne Mrozik has noted) "literally reek with sin or are made fragrant with virtue . . . are disfigured by vice and adorned with morality."[101] Positive moral status manifests itself in an idealized body—just as negative moral status is reflected in a foul and impure form.

Perhaps the most obvious example of this intertwining is the figure of the Buddha himself, for each of the thirty-two "marks of a great man" (*mahāpuruṣalakṣaṇa*) that adorn his physical body is described as the karmic result of particular moral virtues cultivated during his former lives. The correlation between moral deed and physical mark is made explicit in sources such as the *Lakkhaṇa Sutta* of the *Dīgha Nikāya.* He has soft and delicate skin because he approached ascetics and Brahmins for moral advice; he has a bright and golden complexion because he lived without anger and never showed hostility; he has a perfect sense of taste because he avoided harming beings by hand, stones, stick, or sword; and so forth.[102] The same is true of less exalted beings as well, such as the ordinary monks and laymen who populate the *Avadānaśataka* and are described as acquiring specific physical features (such as a golden body) as a result of performing specific moral deeds (such as worshiping a *stūpa*).[103] Moral deeds thus result in physical marks, and these physical marks themselves then go on to have profoundly moral effects, for both oneself and others—such as one's ability to practice religion at all (which, after all, requires a certain minimum type of body) or the ability of one's body to morally inspire others (as we see with the moral conversions undergone by so many characters in Buddhist literature merely as a result of catching a glimpse of the Buddha's physical body, being touched by him, or hearing his beautiful voice).

In other words, this is a world in which *physical features are always indicative of moral status,* and *moral attainments must be reflected by their corresponding physical effects.* Of course, this correspondence between the moral and physical orders is an absolute necessity in a worldview dominated by the theory of karma, which holds that all morally significant deeds must inevitably bear fruit—including fruit of an obviously physical nature, such as the type of body one inhabits or one's realm of rebirth. Perhaps this correspondence is *so* obvious, however, that it is easily lost from view—and not only among ourselves but even among those who inhabit the world depicted in Buddhist texts, who must often be reminded of this fact. In *Avadānaśataka* 31, for example, the monks of Jetavana are "stricken by illness, yellow and pale, their bodies emaciated and their limbs weak," while the Buddha is "free from disease, free from illness, strong and healthy."[104] In explanation for this bodily difference, the Buddha relates his previous birth as a king who sacrificed his own body in order to cure an epidemic among his subjects, and then notes that it was precisely because of this compassionate moral deed that he is now "endowed with a stomach whose digestion is regular, by means of which everything I eat, drink, chew, and enjoy is digested with perfect ease, and I am free of disease and have left illness behind."[105] Thus, the gift of the body does not merely lead one to spiritual enlightenment, it also improves one's digestion! The reason for this is simple and clear; as the Buddha himself patiently explains to his monks: "The acts that [a person] performs and accumulates, monks, do not bear fruit outside [of that person]. . . . Rather, the acts that [a person] performs—whether pure or impure—bear fruit in the *skandhas, dhātus,* and *āyatanas* that [he] receives."[106]

Here then is a logical way of resolving the paradox of the ideal body: realization of the body's worthlessness constitutes a positive moral deed that *must* have its corresponding physical effect—in this case, the attainment of a body of great worth. The body is indeed worthless by nature, yet a true realization of this worthlessness is not purely a mental achievement; it is also one which manifests itself in the physical realm through a body that overcomes the very worthlessness whose realization helped bring it about. We must remind ourselves again that there is no question here of the "spiritual" mind transcending the "vulgar" body, but rather of *mind-and-body transforming together.* King Śibi trades in his physical eyes for "eyes of the perfection of truth"[107]—yet these same eyes are also superior physical eyes that can see through walls and for a hundred *yojanas* on all sides. Likewise, Prince Mahāsattva's inferior body is physically transmuted into a beautiful and long-enduring *stūpa* full of relics—yet these same relics are also "fragrant with [the bodhisattva's] morality and virtue."[108] The moral and physical orders mutually implicate one another and are always transformed in tandem. Perhaps nowhere is this absolute interpenetration of the moral and the physical made clearer than in an interesting motif sometimes found in the gift-of-the-body genre—a motif I will refer to as "tasty flesh."

Tasty Flesh

Let me begin my discussion of the "tasty flesh" motif with a remarkable quote from the *Śikṣāsamuccaya,* a Mahāyāna compendium compiled by Śāntideva in perhaps the late seventh or early eighth centuries C.E. As Richard Mahoney has demonstrated through a close and careful analysis,[109] the *Śikṣāsamuccaya* presents the bodhisattva-path wholly in terms of the virtue of generosity. The entire text, in fact, is structured around the following line of argument:

1. One attains perfect enlightenment by "giving away everything."
2. One "gives away everything" by giving away one's "body," "enjoyments," and "merit."
3. However, in order to make the gift of one's body, enjoyments, and merit into a truly worthy gift that will most effectively benefit others, one must constantly

work to "preserve," "purify," and "increase" each of these things by means of moral conduct.[110]

For Śāntideva, in other words, it is the activities of *preserving, purifying,* and *increasing* one's body, enjoyments, and merit that logically come first, and *giving* them that comes later. Within this schema, the bodhisattva's gift of his body to benefit all beings thus stands at the very *end* of the bodhisattva-path, whereas most of the path is more properly concerned with "preserving," "purifying," and "increasing" this body through moral conduct in order to make it into a worthy gift. Throughout the text, Śāntideva therefore makes several comments arguing *against* premature and ill-considered self-sacrifice.[111]

It is in this context that we find the following passage at the beginning of chapter 8, where Śāntideva explains why it is so important for the bodhisattva to "purify" his person *before* giving it away:

Now I will speak about purification. And why is that? Because once the body is purified, it will be like clean and well-prepared rice, and its consumption will be salutary for embodied beings. As it says in the noble *Tathāgataguhya Sūtra:* "In the great cities, there are large cremation-grounds filled with many hundreds of thousands of living beings. Even there, when his time has come and he has died, the bodhisattva-mahāsattva displays his great body. And the beings there who have been reborn as animals eat as much of his flesh as they desire. And at the end of their lifespans, when their time has come and they have died, they are reborn in a happy destiny, among the gods in heaven. And he alone is the cause of their [rebirth there, or any other good destiny they attain], even up to [their attainment of] *parinirvāṇa*—that is, [it occurs] through the purity of that bodhisattva's former vow. [The bodhisattva] who has vowed for a long time—'When my time has come and I have died, may [beings] enjoy my flesh!'—he alone would be the cause of their [happy destiny]. The aspiration of that virtuous [bodhisattva] is accomplished, his wish is accomplished, his vow is fulfilled."

. . . Moreover, I will also tell you what is wrong with *not* purifying [the body]: Just as a crop overcome by weeds fails to prosper and wastes away with disease, so also a Buddha-sprout, when overcome by the afflictions, never grows.[112]

In other words, the bodhisattva's gift of his body is not merely an act of generosity and compassion, it is also the serving of a physical meal that morally transforms those diners who consume it. The bodhisattva's high moral attainments actually *infuse his physical body* (like "well-prepared rice"), and it is directly by means of consuming the bodhisattva's flesh that lowly beings in the cemeteries attain rebirth in heaven or even achieve nirvana. If the bodhisattva sacrifices his body prematurely, on the other hand, his flesh is likened to "a crop overcome by weeds," and no matter how generous his intentions might be, the meal will not have the desired effect. Though we tend to think of the bodhisattva's positive moral effects upon other beings purely in terms of the example he sets in regard to virtues such as generosity and compassion, this text states emphatically that it is equally a matter of his *physical flesh.* Through constant moral practice and cultivation of virtue, the bodhisattva gradually "seasons" his flesh and transforms it into a magical elixir capable of saving all beings—if only they will *eat.* Perhaps nowhere is the total interpenetration of moral and physical qualities so pronounced as in this ability to depict the moral conversion of beings through the purely physical idiom of *eating the right food.*

It is equally important to take note of the fact that, in addition to its salvific qualities, this flesh also *tastes good,* its delicious taste being a direct result, of course, of the bodhisattva's moral virtue. Emphasis is often placed on its wonderful taste, which seems to rival in importance its positive soteriological effects. The moral power of the bodhisattva is thus inseparable from the wonderful taste of his flesh, and spiritual salvation is indistinguishable from the physical satiety one experiences after eating a good meal. The bodhisattva's self-sacrifice is both a heroic deed of generosity and the serving of a fine gourmet meal that satiates the recipient (and gives the Buddha good digestion).

This motif of the bodhisattva's "tasty flesh" occurs in several gift-of-the-body stories involving the feeding of hungry beings, though it is more explicit in some cases than in others. In *Jātakamālā* 8, for example, it constitutes an undercurrent that never quite comes to the surface but is at least implicitly present. In this story, five cannibalistic *yakṣas* disguise themselves as brahmins and ask the virtuous King Maitrībala for food. He gladly offers to them a "pleasing meal fit for even a king," whereupon they explain that "we don't eat this kind of food."[113] When he asks what kind of food they *do* eat, they resume their terrifying *yakṣa*-forms and reply: "Warm and fresh flesh and blood from human beings—this is what *yakṣas* eat and drink."[114] Full of joy at the arising of this opportunity, King Maitrībala then decides to give them, from his own body, some "thick, solid lumps of flesh, dripping with blood."[115] When his ministers object to this gift, King Maitrībala argues that this meal of flesh must come from a living being, "for the flesh of those who have died a natural death is bloodless and cold, and will not please these [*yakṣas*],"[116] and that it is he alone who should give it because his body is "big, solid, and distinguished by its masses of flesh."[117]

Implicit in this exchange is the notion of "tasty flesh": by having the *yakṣas* refuse a "pleasing meal" in favor of King Maitrībala's flesh, the text suggests that the king's body constitutes a *better-than-pleasing* meal (at least for those who are *yakṣas*). Moreover, King Maitrībala clearly takes pride in providing the *yakṣas* with flesh they will find delicious—not flesh that is "bloodless and cold," but flesh that tastes good to them and fills their stomachs to satiety. *Only he* can give them this meal, not his ministers—and not merely because he is more virtuous than they are, but also because he has a *better body,* one that is "big, solid, and distinguished by its masses of flesh." Thus, while much of the story is preoccupied with ethical arguments both for and against the gift, this sprinkling of passages constitutes an undercurrent of concern focused instead on the merits of delicious flesh, yummy bodies, and physically satisfying meals.

The same scenario is also characteristic of the story of King Maṇicūḍa, who makes a gift of his flesh and blood to feed a hungry *rākṣasa* (who is really the god Śakra in disguise). In the *Maṇicūḍāvadāna,* once again, this *rākṣasa* first refuses the "large heap of delectable foods" offered to him and informs the king that he eats only "the flesh and blood of the recently killed," whereupon King Maṇicūḍa, full of joy, decides to give him "fresh" flesh and blood from his own body.[118] Once again, he takes peculiar pride in the taste of his flesh, for as he slices it from his body, he indicates to the *rākṣasa* the particular gastronomic qualities of each piece (almost as if he were a waiter describing the daily specials): "This flesh is rich in blood, this is rich in fat, and this is very tender."[119] The obvious pride the bodhisattva takes in the deliciousness of his flesh stands in stark contrast to the statements he makes elsewhere in the text describing his body as a "putrid corpse, destined to decay," and so on.[120] It is almost as if the idiom of food-and-feeding provides the bodhisattva with a roundabout way of acknowledging and taking pride in his own generosity, compassion, and moral virtue—qualities he cannot recognize explicitly, but can attest to in terms of their consequences for the taste of his flesh.

It is in the version of the Maṇicūḍa story found in the *Lokānandanāṭaka,* however, that this motif of the bodhisattva's "tasty flesh" reaches its highest culmination, becoming the object of an extended dialogue among several characters. Here, the *rākṣasa* first explains that the only food acceptable to *rākṣasas* is "glistening flesh, freshly cut by the blade of a sword, abundant in quantity, warm and red in color,"[121] whereupon Maṇicūḍa tells him that "this body is the kind of food you desire!"[122] When Maṇicūḍa's brahmin priest argues that the *rākṣasa* should instead be given an animal slaughtered in sacrifice, Maṇicūḍa answers angrily: "O Brahmin, why are animals [alone] suitable for a *rākṣasa* in a sacrifice? After all, once you've refused ambrosia, what are you going to do with something tasteless?"[123] Maṇicūḍa here compares his own body to "ambrosia" and contrasts it with the "tasteless" flesh obtainable from the bodies of others—once again, perhaps a roundabout way of trumpeting his own moral virtue and contrasting it with the moral inferiority of others. Maṇicūḍa's wife Padmāvatī then jumps into the fray, offering her own body to the *rākṣasa,* since "this body, too, is divine, is it not?"[124] The *rākṣasa* refuses this equivalence, however, through an extended excursus on the gastronomic qualities of the flesh characteristic of different types of people, depending on their moral qualities:

> The flesh of a sorrowful person tastes bitter, astringent, and salty. That of a passionate person is like liquid and goes down easily. That of a very fearful person is dry. That of an angry person is sour, very salty, pungent, bad-tasting, and gives you heartburn. [But] the body of one who is greatly benevolent in nature tastes sweet, and completely satisfies all the senses.[125]

Maṇicūḍa is clearly pleased at the implication of the *rākṣasa*'s remarks, for he states, "After all this time, only now do I see a supplicant who is endowed with higher knowledge!"[126]—and immediately begins slicing up his own flesh. Clearly, the bodhisattva's virtue throughout this extended exchange is more than just an abstract "spiritual" quality; it also manifests itself in the concrete, physical world through the very taste of his flesh. This taste provides the *rākṣasa* with a delicious, pleasing meal, yet it also does much more—providing concrete, physical proof of the pure generosity that motivates the bodhisattva's gift. In the final analysis, the act of self-sacrifice alone is not enough, for this act might be motivated by grief, fear, greed, or other negative emotions. What *proves* the sincerity of the bodhisattva's deed is the resultant taste of his flesh.

The motif of the bodhisattva's "tasty flesh" is thus a potent indicator of the absolute interpenetration of the moral and physical orders characteristic of the world depicted in Buddhist narrative. Moral status is always inscribed upon the physical body one inhabits, and it is this which accounts for the bodhisattva's already-ideal body. The compassion and generosity that drive the bodhisattva's deed are not merely "spiritual" qualities; they are also materially embodied through his beautiful appearance, his pure corpse, and his delicious, tasty flesh. The gift of the body is not merely a moral act; it is also the serving of a gourmet meal that has a salutary effect upon its diners. From this perspective, we can also begin to understand how this ideal, beautiful body coexists with denunciations of the body's worthlessness, and why the bodhisattva sometimes characterizes his body in such profoundly contradictory ways: when the bodhisattva denounces his "putrid" and "impure" body, the concern is with demonstrating his wisdom and his level of realization into the true nature of things; when, on the other hand, he praises his "fresh" and "ambrosia-like" flesh, the concern is with demonstrating how this wisdom necessarily manifests itself within the physical world. In other words, statements about the nature of the body cannot be taken in isolation but must always be interpreted *within context.*

Opposing Ideologies of the Body and the Importance of Perspective and Point of View

In his work on the Chan Buddhist tradition, Bernard Faure has discerned two opposing ideologies of the body, the first of which he refers to as an "ideology of absence/transcendence" and the second of which he refers to as an "ideology of presence/immanence."[127] The first ideology denigrates the body and the physical universe, assigns an ontological primacy to mind, emphasizes the direct and unmediated nature of enlightenment ("sudden awakening"), and is characterized by a radical antinomianism and an iconoclastic denial of the cultic mediations of traditional Buddhism. All such views are aspects of the "rhetoric of immediacy" that Faure finds to be characteristic of the orthodox discourse of "classical" Chan. Within such a discourse we should expect to find a denigration of the physical body in favor of some kind of immaterial goal, as well as a rejection of cultic mediations (such as relics and icons) that embody and instantiate this immateriality for others.

As Faure demonstrates, however, behind this orthodox ideology lies another, unspoken ideology—an ideology of *body,* of *presence,* and of *immanence.* This second ideology is manifested, for example, in the Chan preoccupation with funerary ritual, relic-worship, mummification, and the production of various other types of "substitute bodies" for the deceased (such as icons, portraits, patriarchal robes, and mortuary tablets)—all perceived as a means of transforming the mortal body of the deceased Chan master into an immortal and permanently incorruptible body that can be harnessed for its power by the world of the living. As Faure notes, all of these concerns "imply a *mediation* with the invisible realm, that seems at first glance to contradict the Chan emphasis on immediacy, i.e., the sudden and unmediated character of awakening."[128] The "ideology of absence" enunciated in Chan's rhetorical discourse, in other words, is everywhere belied and contradicted by the "ideology of presence" that clearly motivates so much of Chan practice. "Here again," he states, "we are confronted with the limits of ideology, the inverted relation between the doctrine and the values underlying practice."[129]

It is precisely because classical Chan discourse puts forth such an uncompromising "rhetoric of immediacy"—a rhetoric that is just as obviously subverted in actual practice—that Faure is able to draw this sharp distinction and to speak of the two ideologies as being inherently contradictory (with the ideology of presence "lurking behind" the ideology of absence). As we have already seen, however, within the context of Indian Buddhism (with its notions of a more "gradual" enlightenment) such was never the case. With regard to our gift-of-the-body stories, for example, the physical transmutations and glorifications of our bodhisattvas do not "lurk behind" a more orthodox wish for transcendence; instead, they display themselves unabashedly and repeatedly throughout each tale. Thus, to whatever extent it might be possible to distinguish between Faure's two "ideologies" in the Indian case, for the most part these stories (and the Indian Buddhist tradition as a whole) seem to view them as completely complementary: denunciations of the body's worthlessness and the wish for "nirvana-without-remainder" coexist unproblematically with the idealization and glorification of the wonderful bodies of Buddhas and bodhisattvas. Yet how can this be so?

In the effort to overcome the tendency toward mind/body dualism and "rematerialize" our understanding of Indian Buddhism, I believe there is a danger of going too far in the other direction—in other words, emphasizing the interpenetration of the moral and physical orders to such a great degree that any notion of an "ideology of absence" within Indian Buddhism becomes impossible. In fact, I believe that Faure's categories *are* analytically useful, even in the case of Indian Buddhism, and that a limited distinction between the two ideologies *can* be drawn in the Indian case. With regard to our gift-of-the-body stories, for example, I would point to the importance of considering *perspective* and *point of view* when evaluating statements concerning the body.

There is a basic distinction to be drawn, I believe, between the point of view taken by the bodhisattva and the point of view taken by those around him. This distinction results, once again, from the differing time perspectives involved in the logic of the *jātaka*—that is, the *pre-Buddha past* in the "story of the past" and the *post-Buddha present* in the "story of the present." From his *own* perspective in the pre-Buddha past, the bodhisattva himself—as a king, prince, hare, etc.—is an ordinary being (with an ordinary body) struggling on the long path to enlightenment. This perspective would naturally involve a denigration of the body and the desire for an "upward" movement—for transcendence over ordinary physical existence (without any explicit conceptualization of what form such transcendence might take). But from the perspective of the *reader* in the post-Buddha present—and by extension, the characters in the story who react to the bodhisattva's deed—the bodhisattva is a future Buddha, one whose ultimate perfection is *already* assured. This perspective would naturally involve the desire for a "downward" movement—for presence and immanence in the form of relics, *stūpas,* or an ideal being with supernatural powers, and correspondingly, a glorification of the resultant body.[130]

Although this distinction is never absolute (as we saw in the discussion of "tasty flesh"), it seems to me that the bodhisattva is *more likely* to denigrate his body and to speak from the perspective of the "ordinary body" alone, whereas other characters are more likely to focus on the "ideal body" they *know* becomes a reality in the future. In Faure's terms, the bodhisattva generally gives voice to an "ideology of absence," whereas those around him give voice to an "ideology of presence." Or, to rephrase the same idea in terms I have made use of throughout this book, the bodhisattva speaks from the perspective of the "ethos of the *jātaka,*" or the long moral career leading to Buddhahood in the far distant future, while those around him speak from the perspective of the "ethos of the *avadana,*" or the great field of merit (including sacred relics and salutary bodies) that becomes available once Buddhahood has been achieved. Contradictory statements concerning the nature of the body thus fit into a larger set of contrastive relations between the past and the present, the ordinary being and the ideal Buddha, moral deeds and ritual transactions, the ethos of the *jātaka* and the ethos of the *avadāna.* In this way, competing ideologies of the body are balanced and harmonized through the help of the narrative form and its shifting use of perspective and point of view. Either perspective taken alone is partial and limited in nature, and it is only through both perspectives in combination that the *true* "ideal body" comes into view—one that *encompasses* an understanding of the "ordinary body" and how the two are connected.

Another way of stating the same thing is in terms of the various bodies of a Buddha discussed throughout Buddhist doctrinal literature. From the bodhisattva's own perspective, we might say, there is a wish to exchange the debased *rūpa-kāya* of an ordinary being for the eternal *dharma-kāya* of the Buddha. From the perspective of the reader and those who react to the bodhisattva's deed, there is a wish to celebrate the way in which the *dharma-kāya* of the Buddha manifests itself in the world in the form of a glorified *rūpa-kāya,* which we might perhaps speak of as *nirmāṇa-kāya.* And finally, if we combine both perspectives together, the overall conception of the "ideal body" depicted within these stories as a whole is perhaps suggestive of *saṃbhoga-kāya.* As Nagao has pointed out, *saṃbhoga-kāya* has a "double character," paradoxically partaking of both the transcendence of *dharma-kāya* and the immanence of *nirmāṇa-kāya.* It thus "occupies the central position in the triple-body doctrine" and may be called "the Buddha *par excellence.*"[131]

Technically, of course, *saṃbhoga-kāya* is defined as a specific body of a specific Buddha, such as Amitābha or Śākyamuni when he preaches the Mahāyāna *sūtras.* But the essence of the *saṃbhoga-kāya* idea, it seems to me, can be extended to relics, *stūpas,* holy sites, and the bodies of special beings such as bodhisattvas—all those glorified yet physical "substitute bodies" that paradoxically embody, instantiate, and concretize the immaterial without losing their quality of transcendence. In fact, the same themes we have encountered in regard to the bodhisattva within gift-of-the-body stories have also been encountered by scholars in relation to other such "substitute bodies." In speaking of the Chan tradition's production of relics and mummies, for example, Faure states that relics and mummies "result in a somewhat paradoxical bifurcation: an upward movement of spiritualization, leading to *nirvāṇa,* the achievement of immutability; and a downward movement of materialization, a return to the realm of change, to the world of cults."[132] Likewise, several scholars, speaking of the significance of the *stūpa,* have interpreted it as a symbol that paradoxically mediates between the *absence* of the Buddha in transcendent nirvana and his *presence* in the world through the power of his relics.[133] And finally, Steven Collins has sought to demonstrate much the same thing about the decorous and highly controlled bodies of monks, arguing that the monk's negative attitudes toward his body and positive nurturing of his body work together in such a way that the practitioner becomes able to "embody in imagination the immateriality posited in the doctrines of Buddhism."[134] Thus, relics, mummies, *stūpas,* and the bodies of well-disciplined monks all serve to mediate the immaterialist conception of nirvana for believers—and might all be loosely described as versions of the Buddha's *saṃbhoga-kāya.* To this list of "substitute bodies" we can now add the bodhisattva's body in stories of self-sacrifice.

The Body That Tends Toward Non-Body

The special character of these "substitute bodies," of course, is that although they are physical, they are very peculiar bodies, bodies that escape all of the shortcomings of ordinary embodiment. In conceiving of such a body, I have found Jean-Pierre Vernant's description of the bodies of the gods in pre-Socratic Greece to be especially suggestive.[135] In pre-Socratic Greek thought, Vernant argues, there was no sharp distinction between divinity and corporeality. The gods were *not* "pure spirit"; rather, they were endowed with divine "super-bodies" that perfected and brought to fulfillment all that was imperfect and diminished in the bodies of men:

> Roughly, the problem consists of deciphering all the signs that mark the human body with the seal of limitation, deficiency, incompleteness, and that make it a sub-body. This sub-body cannot be understood except in reference to what it presupposes: corporeal plenitude, a super-body, the body of the gods. . . . By pushing to an extreme all the qualities and bodily values that are present in an always diminished, derivative, faltering and precarious form in man, one is led to endow the divinities with a set of traits which, even in their epiphanic manifestations here below . . . locates them in an inaccessible beyond and causes them to transgress the corporeal code by means of which they are represented in their relation to humans.[136]

Thus, the divine super-bodies of the gods were conceived by "subtract[ing] from the human body all those traits that bind it to its mortal nature and betray its transitory, precarious and unfulfilled character," and by magnifying and multiplying "all values which appear by comparison on the human body as diminished, paltry and laughable."[137]

It seems to me that this is a cogent way of interpreting at least some of the odder descriptions of the divine "super-body" of the bodhisattva engaged in self-sacrifice. In regard to the story of King Ambara mentioned earlier, for example, we might pose the problem as follows. If one's tongue is unsatisfactory because it is single, impermanent, and unable to feed more than one hungry being, one can overcome these physical limitations in either one of two ways: either get rid of physicality altogether in favor of some kind of "transcendence," *or* (as King Ambara chooses to do) replace the single, faulty tongue with an ever-replenishing *mountain of tongues* that will never run out or diminish. The mountain of tongues is represented in a "corporeal code" (the everyday code of faulty, impermanent tongues), yet through its ever-replenishing and permanent nature, it also transgresses this code and locates itself "in an inaccessible beyond"—the *same* "beyond" that one would achieve by ridding oneself of physicality altogether, which means that the two options are really the same (just as the tradition holds the various bodies of the Buddha to share an essential unity).[138] Exchanging one's *rūpa-kāya* for the eternal *dharma-kāya* of the Buddha and exchanging it for an *ever-replenishing mountain of flesh* thus become fully compatible. Though the motif of the "flesh-mountain" is a particularly striking example, the same argument can be advanced in more prosaic cases as well. The impermanent and unsatisfactory nature of King Śibi's eyes is resolved *both* by throwing these worthless eyes away in favor of the "eye of omniscience," *and* by magically replenishing them with supernatural eyes that can see through walls and for a hundred *yojanas* on every side.

Ultimately, of course, this notion of a "super-body" is inherently contradictory and must lead to paradoxical statements. The *saṃbhoga-kāya* of the Buddha, for example, is said to be corporeal and physical in nature, yet also to fill up the entire universe and suffer no limitations in space. As Vernant notes, such a "super-body" is "a body that is not a body," a body that "evokes and touches upon the non-body" yet "never merges with it,"[139] or what I prefer to call "a body that tends toward non-body." It represents the dilemma of human beings, stuck "somewhere between angel and animal,"[140] and only able to conceptualize something greater than themselves by drawing on their own, imperfect forms. In the gift-of-the-body genre, however, this process is facilitated by the conventions of the *jātaka* genre and the manipulation of perspective and point of view. Unlike such "sudden," paradoxical symbols as the *stūpa* or the *saṃbhoga-kāya,* the "ideal body" in gift-of-the-body stories emerges in a more "gradual" manner through the unfolding of a narrative plot and the constantly shifting perspectives of different characters.

The Importance of Pain

Throughout this chapter I have attempted to demonstrate how gift-of-the-body stories use the narrative form to give expression to a complex ideology of the body—one that recognizes both the "worthlessness" and the "worth" of the ordinary body, as well as the simultaneous coexistence of the ordinary body with one that is already perfect and ideal. I now conclude my discussion with some remarks on the importance of the bodhisattva's *pain* in mediating between these various conceptions. Pain within these stories is far more than just a narrative embellishment; in fact, it is crucial, I believe, for effecting the transition between one conception of the body and another.

The presence of pain within our stories can first be highlighted by contrasting it with the *absence* of pain in stories of a closely related type. In 1963 Jean Filliozat published an article on "autocremation" in the Indian Buddhist tradition in which he subjected to close analysis a number of passages from the Mahāyāna *sūtras* in which bodhisattvas set themselves on fire to pay homage to the Buddha—such as the story of Kṣemadatta from the thirty-third chapter of the *Samādhirāja Sūtra* and the story of Sarvasattvapriyadarśana from the twenty-second chapter of the *Lotus Sūtra.*[141] Throughout his analysis of these episodes Filliozat repeatedly emphasizes the *absence of any pain.* In his view, the hero who performs such a deed is always an advanced bodhisattva whose mind is firmly set on the dharma, or "true nature of things," alone. He has an absolute conviction in the emptiness of all things, including the body; he understands that the mutilation of the body is, in truth, nothing more than a playful, sham appearance (since the body does not truly exist anyway); he carries out the mutilation in a yogic state of *samādhi;* and because of his yogic training, complete detachment, and understanding of the body's emptiness, *he does not feel any pain.* Though Filliozat's analysis is restricted to episodes of autocremation in the Mahāyāna *sūtras,* he also aligns these episodes with other forms of "voluntary death" in the Hindu, Buddhist, and Jain traditions, suggesting that all such forms of "voluntary death" can be interpreted in a similar manner—including the bodhisattva's self-sacrifice in gift-of-the-body *jātakas.*

But while Filliozat's interpretation does seem to hold for the Mahāyāna episodes he focuses on, I do not think it applies in the least to most gift-of-the-body *jātakas.* The heroes of our tales are usually detached from their bodies, but they generally do not make any explicit philosophical statements about the emptiness of the body or its status as an illusory appearance; though they may describe the body as being *worthless,* they do not characterize it as being *unreal.* Moreover, although they always demonstrate great courage and unwavering resolution in submitting to the mutilation of their bodies, in many cases it is made abundantly clear that they are indeed experiencing suffering and pain. The violence inflicted upon their bodies and the resulting physical pain are frequently emphasized in great detail. There is no yogic state of *samādhi* that anesthetizes the pain; in fact, in many cases the pain is so excruciating that the bodhisattva loses consciousness altogether—perhaps the very opposite of a focused, yogic trance. In short, Filliozat interprets the bodily-mutilation theme wholly in terms of the type of philosophical playfulness and manipulation of appearance-versus-reality that is typical of bodhisattvas in the Mahāyāna *sūtras,* but which I believe is inapplicable to most heroes in gift-of-the-body *jātakas.* The *jātakas* wish to draw us into a world of reality, a world where the hero is a real being cutting open a real body in excruciating pain—a world of high stakes rather than playful, sham performances.[142]

But why is there so much emphasis on the bodhisattva's pain? While such stories seem to delight in long and graphic descriptions of the painful act of self-mutilation, I believe that pain within this context is far more than just a concession to the vulgar appetite for blood and gore. Instead, the bodhisattva's pain is fundamental to the *transformation* of his body achieved through self-sacrifice and thus allows these stories to mediate between the ordinary, worthless body and the glorified, ideal form. The problem with an advanced bodhisattva who carries out the act of self-mutilation in a yogic state of *samādhi,* sees the entire act as an illusory performance, and feels no pain is that, within such a case, *no transformation is involved,* and thus no link between the ordinary body and the ideal. It is only *pain* that can bridge these two conceptions and thus allow these stories to balance several different lines of thinking about the body.

The role pain plays in religious rituals around the world has been recently analyzed by Ariel Glucklich in *Sacred Pain: Hurting the Body for the Sake of the Soul,*[143] and his analysis is quite suggestive for understanding the link between *pain* and *transformation,* even in the case of purely literary representations of pain such as we find in gift-of-the-body *jātakas.* Glucklich's aim is to offer an explicitly reductionistic account of "sacred pain"—in other words, to elucidate the neurodynamic and psychological effects of ritualized pain on human consciousness and identity, regardless of the specific religious or cultural context in which the pain occurs. In briefest terms—and no succinct summary can possibly do justice to the complex and meticulously detailed analysis he offers—Glucklich demonstrates that pain has the effect of "progressively weaken[ing] the body-self template, resulting in the diffusion of the self or its complete disappearance." "In other words," he states,

> if you scourge your body repeatedly, the sensory over-stimulation would not eradicate your thoughts, sense perceptions, and so forth. But your experience of being a self, an agent who undergoes these perceptions and thoughts would gradually disappear, until it seemed that these belonged to someone or something else.[144]

This is what he refers to as "disintegrative" or "telic-decentralizing" pain—pain experienced as an overwhelming *threat to the self,* a strong signal "to the conscious steering mechanism (ego) of the whole organism that the functional purpose of a subsystem is jeopardized . . . [or] that the overall function of the entire system is threatened, perhaps by death."[145]

Now, if one's ego is the highest system or "center of telos" with which the individual identifies, this weakening or destruction of the ego will be experienced as a devastating *loss*—such as might be the case, for example, for an ordinary person who suffers a devastating accident and then struggles with agonizing, chronic pain. Glucklich also points out, however, that there can be many different "centers of telos" involved in the human organism, ranging from organic subsystems, to the ego as a whole, to systems higher than the ego. Thus, if the person in pain identifies with a "center of telos" that is *higher* than the ego, then the weakening or destruction of the ego (through ritualized and modulated pain) can actually *strengthen* and make more real his identification with that higher center of telos. In this way, "disintegrative" or "telic-decentralizing" pain is transformed into "integrative" or "telic-centralizing" pain: "bad" pain becomes "good" pain—a pain that transforms and empowers the self at a higher level of being, rather than diminishing and destroying it. It is religion that most often provides the higher "center of telos" that allows pain to become transformative for the self. The exact nature of this higher "center of telos" will, of course, differ from one religious context to another—"union with God" for the Christian mystic, for example, or "becoming a Buddha" for the Buddhist—but the process itself, Glucklich maintains, is based on neurological and psychological principles common to all human beings. This is pain that has been transformed into *sacrifice:* "A pain-induced subservience to a greater telos turns the torture into a ritual of self-sacrifice."[146]

Glucklich's comments are quite suggestive for the gift-of-the-body theme and seem to run parallel to some of the language of the stories themselves. When King Puṇyabala gives away the "ordinary eye of flesh" in hope of acquiring the "unsurpassed eye of dharma," when the elephant Ṣaḍdanta gives away his physical tusks in hope of acquiring the "tusks of omniscience," or when Prince Mahāsattva abandons his body "full of excrement and urine [and] as insubstantial as foam" in hope of acquiring a "dharma-body, free of grief, free of change, pure and stainless"—they all appear to be partaking in the type of sacrificial logic that Glucklich has found to be characteristic of the religious use of pain, using pain both to weaken and diminish the ordinary self and to redefine this self in relation to the higher "center of telos" constituted by full Buddhahood. Likewise, when our various bodhisattvas speak of "extracting the essence from this essenceless body," perhaps they are referring (in religious language) to the process of transforming "bad" pain into "good" pain, using the destruction and disintegration of the "essenceless" self to ritually incorporate within themselves the highest and most precious "essence."

Similarly, in chapter 5 I addressed the contradictory discourse of "self" and "selflessness" that underlies the gift of the body, or the manner in which self-sacrifice seems to constitute both the ultimate *denial of self* and the ultimate *act of self-will.* Glucklich's analysis helps us to see that this paradox is resolvable by reference to two different selves: a *lower* self is willfully denied and destroyed through a violent act of pain, in favor of empowering a *higher* self that is constituted by the aspiration to perfect Buddhahood.

But it is the presence of *pain,* I contend, that is crucial to signifying this process of self-transformation. The very image of "extracting" the essence from the essenceless body seems to recognize the importance of pain, suggesting that this essence cannot simply be "realized" or "created," but must rather be "extracted" through the violent and painful act of self-sacrifice. In *Kalpanāmaṇḍitīka* 64, in which King Śibi mutilates and sacrifices his body on behalf of a hungry hawk (who is really Śakra in disguise), Śakra justifies this cruel test of the bodhisattva by stating: "When one chooses an excellent jewel, one examines it several times in order to make sure that it is not fake. The means of examining a jewel are to cut it, shatter it, expose it to fire, and strike it; then alone can one know that it is not fake."[147] The painful torture undergone by the bodhisattva's body during self-sacrifice is thus compared to the cutting, burning, and rubbing of a jewel in order to ensure that it is genuine—or, perhaps, to *make* it genuine through the very act of the torture itself. Pain and transformation go together, and the presence of the latter is vouchsafed by reference to the former. This transformative pain still *hurts,* of course, but its hurt has become meaningful and thus delicious. Thus, in *Avadānakalpalatā* 51, such bodhisattvas "are joyful as their lives are being extinguished," the "wounds made on their bodies by extremely sharp weapons feel like blows from the lotuses that wanton women wear behind their ears," and they are "happily amused to be ornamented by hairs that stand on end [from the pain]."[148] By giving voice to the delicious pain of self-transformation, gift-of-the-body stories provide the fulcrum between the ordinary body and the ideal, thus further ensuring their ability to balance several contradictory lines of thinking about the body.[149]

VII

KINGSHIP, SACRIFICE, OFFERING, AND DEATH

Some Other Interpretive Contexts

In this final chapter I move beyond both the "gift" aspect and the "body" aspect of the gift-of-the-body theme to consider a number of other interpretive contexts that might be brought to bear on this discussion—contexts I have not been able to deal with in the remainder of the book, but wish to discuss at least briefly before I conclude. These discussions revolve around the topics of kingship, sacrifice, offering, and death: Why is the bodhisattva within gift-of-the-body *jātakas* so frequently a king, and what do these stories have to tell us about kingship and its legitimation? How is the bodhisattva's gift of his body related to the category of sacrifice? How is it related to the category of the ritual offering? How is it related to the Buddhist discourse on death? And how might one characterize the bodhisattva's stance toward death, as manifested by his self-sacrifice?

Gift and Kingship

It is striking to observe that a preponderance of gift-of-the-body stories revolve around the figure of the generous king, and that many of these stories share a similar pattern: The king begins with material gifting, which reaches a climax of some kind and results inevitably in the gift of his own body. The king survives this gift, and the story ends with the king undertaking what is clearly a kingship that has been renewed and legitimated through the gift of the body.

The basic logic of this pattern is not so difficult to understand: it is the foremost duty of the Indian king to be generous, and the kings in gift-of-the-body stories are always generous from the very beginning. But to give away wealth and material goods is easy for a wealthy and powerful king and thus gives no real proof of his virtue. By giving away his *body*, however, the king demonstrates the sincerity of his generosity and his willingness to give away his very person. The gift of the body thus legitimates all future royal gifts, and more generally, the kingship itself. The gift of the body, though not explicitly enacted as a ritual, functions within these stories almost as if it constituted a ritual of consecration, renewal, or legitimation in regard to the kingship of the hero. In fact, as I briefly noted before, such stories often bear a loose resemblance to the structure of "rites of passage," as described by Van Gennep and Turner.[1] Just as Van Gennep and Turner describe the rite of passage as a process involving the loss and stripping of one's former identity, a liminal period of ambiguity and transition, and the reincorporation into a new identity, so gift-of-the-body stories often involve a preliminary period leading up to the gift; the gift itself, which is symbolic of a total giving up of oneself or one's identity; and the aftermath of the gift, which often places the bodhisattva in a new and rejuvenated status—in this case, that of kingship.

In much more concrete ways, as well, however, many gift-of-the-body stories involving kings play themselves out like magnificent rituals of royal consecration. The confluence between the gift of the body and royal consecration will require some background discussion concerning the structure of such stories and their ties with classical Indic conceptions of the king's royal authority. In particular, we must focus on the movements of the king and the physical spaces in which he acts.

It is a striking feature of gift-of-the-body stories involving kings that they often exhibit a basic structural pattern characteristic of Indian thought and widely found throughout Buddhist and Hindu literature. This pattern involves the movement of the king from the kingdom to the forest and back to the kingdom. The forest provides the setting for an ultimate test of some kind, and the king's successful passing of this test results in a triumphant return to the kingdom and a renewed and legitimated kingship.

The salience of this pattern in Indian literature is remarkable. Within the Buddhist tradition we might cite what are perhaps the two most famous "life stories" in the Indian Buddhist world—that of Prince Vessantara and that of Śākyamuni Buddha himself. Prince Vessantara, of course, takes refuge in the forest with his wife and children after being exiled from the kingdom for his excessive generosity. The forest provides the setting for an ultimate test of generosity—the gift of his wife and children—whose successful completion results in a restoration of royal status and a triumphant return to the kingdom. Likewise, the life story of the Buddha can also be interpreted along the same lines. Prince Siddhārtha renounces his royal status, goes forth into the forest, is severely tested by Māra, succeeds in passing this test (in part by invoking his own previous birth as Prince Vessantara), and then regains a renewed form of "kingship"—in his case, the spiritual sovereignty of Buddhahood. The story is given a radical twist with the concepts of enlightenment and Buddhahood, yet the same pattern still holds.

Moving from the Buddhist to the larger Indian context, we find this pattern repeated in many Hindu myths, as well as forming the basic structure of the two great epics of India, the *Mahābhārata* and the *Rāmāyaṇa*. Both the Pāṇḍava brothers and Rāma are royal figures who are exiled and endure many trials in the forest before returning triumphantly to the kingdom; in fact, it is precisely this basic pattern that holds these voluminous works together and gives them some semblance of unity. The king's movement from the kingdom to the forest, his passing of a test in the forest, and his resultant return to the kingdom and legitimation of his kingship thus constitutes a dominant theme in Indian myth and literature.[2]

The same pattern is strikingly characteristic of many gift-of-the-body stories involving generous kings. The pattern appears most clearly in the story of King Sarvaṃdada,[3] who renounces the kingship and leaves the kingdom when an enemy king comes to attack him, taking exile in the forest as an ascetic. The forest provides the setting for an ultimate test of his generosity: a brahmin's demand for his head. King Sarvaṃdada freely offers his head, and although this gift is never actually completed, the offer itself results directly in his return to the kingdom and the restoration of his kingship. Moreover, his kingship is clearly empowered by this gift; in *Mahajjātakamālā* 45, for example, the fame resulting from his magnificent gift spreads throughout the whole world and has a beneficial effect on all other kings as well.[4] The same pattern appears again in the story of King Maṇicūḍa:[5] after his excessive generosity gets him into trouble with another king, King Maṇicūḍa renounces his kingship, leaves the kingdom, and enters the forest as an ascetic. The forest provides the setting for the gift of his crest-jewel, and after completing the gift and restoring his body, King Maṇicūḍa is brought back to the kingdom in great pomp and glory and reconsecrated into the kingship.

In the story of King Śibi's gift of his eyes,[6] the pattern is slightly different. Here it is the two Acts of Truth restoring his body rather than the initial gift of his eyes that seem to constitute King Śibi's ultimate "test." For the gift of the eyes takes place in one of King Śibi's alms-halls, but shortly after completing the gift of the eyes, King Śibi moves from the palace to the royal pleasure-park. The pleasure-park provides the setting for the two Acts of Truth restoring the body, which is followed by a triumphant and glorious return to the palace. If we interpret the Acts of Truth as being the ultimate "test" of King Śibi rather than the gift of his eyes, we have a pattern moving the king from the *palace* to the *pleasure-park* and back to the *palace*. This is merely another version of the movement from *kingdom* to *forest* to *kingdom*—a point that becomes clear when we consider the significance in Buddhist literature of the pleasure-park.

The pleasure-park (*ārāma*) in Buddhist literature is closely associated with the *caitya,* or woodland shrine, and both spaces appear to constitute a kind of "reserve" or "residue" of the forest contained within the kingdom.[7] Both the *caitya* and the *ārāma* consisted minimally of a tree (or grove of trees) and a stone seat or bench. According to Jeannine Auboyer, the tree(s) represented the forest, the seat or bench represented the mountains, and the *caitya* and *ārāma* as a whole were both doubles of the forest out of which the settled kingdom had been carved. Thus King Śibi, by moving from palace to pleasure-park to palace, in a sense also moves from "kingdom" to "forest" to "kingdom," with the "forest" providing the setting for the test that legitimates and renews his kingship. Moreover, we can now begin to see how this pattern is related to royal consecration. Auboyer has shown that the stone seat or bench located within the *caitya* or *ārāma* was a prototype of the Indian throne, and appears to have been considered a powerful—almost magical—source of the king's royal authority.[8] In several Buddhist *jātakas,*[9] for example, a man wanders into a royal pleasure-park and sits down on its stone seat; meanwhile, the king dies with no male heirs. The funeral procession goes by the park, and the people immediately consecrate the man sitting on the stone seat as the new and rightful king, merely by virtue of his being seated on the "throne." The king's royal authority was thus vested in the stone seat or "throne" within his pleasure-park, and the pleasure-park itself was a double of the forest—which further suggests that the king's royal authority was somehow derived from or located in the forest. In line with this, Nancy Falk has demonstrated that there existed a complex relationship between kingship and the forest in ancient India, with the forest acting in numerous ways as the source and support of the king's royal authority.[10] It now makes sense that gift-of-the-body donors who are kings must perform the gifts that legitimate their kingship within the forest or a "residue" of the forest, such as a pleasure-park.

Without going into excessive detail, let me briefly note that many other gift-of-the-body stories involving kings also show this pattern, though in more altered and truncated forms. In *Suvarṇabhāsottama Sūtra* 18 a prince moves from the kingdom to the forest before making his gift; however, because the gift kills him, there is no question of returning to the kingdom. In a story found in the *Karuṇāpuṇḍarīka Sūtra* a king renounces his kingship and enters the forest as an ascetic; while in the forest, he makes a gift of his body, but instead of returning to the kingdom, he becomes a "flesh mountain" that feeds hungry beings for thousands of years. In *Divyāvadāna* 22 a king goes into his pleasure-park to give away his head, but again the gift kills him; in *Sūtra of the Wise and the Fool* 22, the same gift takes place in the forest. Though these tales do not fit the kingdom/forest/kingdom pattern so evident in the stories of Sarvaṃdada, Maṇicūḍa, and Śibi, and do not involve the legitimation of kingship, nevertheless fragments of the same pattern are still evident.

More than just a narrative pattern, however, the kingdom/forest/kingdom structure of gift-of-the-body stories involving kings also mimics the structure of the Indian royal consecration ritual itself. Heesterman has discussed the fundamental opposition drawn in Indian thought between the settled, agricultural community (*grāma*) and the alien, outside sphere of the forest (*āraṇya*), as well as the use of this opposition within rites of royal consecration.[11] In his view the Vedic ritual texts dealing with royal consecration utilize the opposition between *grāma* and *āraṇya* to symbolize a basic and insoluble conflict between the king's embeddedness within society and his need to find a source of authority outside of it:

> The dilemma of kingship can then be expressed in terms of this basic paradigm: the king must belong to the *grāma,* but his authority must be based in the alien sphere of *āraṇya.* . . . The necessary complementarity of the two spheres can then be ritually expressed as alternating phases in a cycle connecting the two opposites.

Since the opposition as well as the complementarity is there all the time and cannot be overcome, the cycle has to go on forever.[12]

Analyzing closely the Vedic ritual texts dealing with royal consecration, Heesterman illustrates this use of the *grāma/āraṇya* opposition. For example, in the *rājasūya* rite the king's unction is followed by a "chariot drive," which is then followed by his enthronement. Though the "chariot drive" is ritualized, the symbolism involved clearly shows that it is representative of a true war expedition or cattle raid. We thus have a pattern in which the king is consecrated within the *grāma,* goes out on a heroic journey into the *āraṇya,* and is enthroned only upon his triumphant return to the *grāma.* The *rājasūya* also contains many larger cycles that follow exactly the same pattern of *grāma/āraṇya* alternation.

Like Heesterman, Ronald Inden, working with later texts, has recognized a potential conflict between the king's need to transcend society and his need to be immanent within it, maintaining that this conflict is "stated in royal rituals and resolved in them by the device of alternation or oscillation between [*grāma* and *āraṇya*] on a cyclic, periodic basis."[13] Analyzing the *rājyābhiṣeka* rite as found in the *Viṣṇudharmottara Purāṇa* (eighth century C.E.), Inden notes that the ritual is binary in structure, the first half taking the king out of the kingdom and infusing him with royal authority, and the second half returning him to the kingdom, where his authority once again becomes immanent within the world. This alternation between *grāma* and *āraṇya* is repeated yearly, and is conceptually tied to other cyclic oscillations, such as that between day and night. Ritual as well as myth, then, suggests that the forest is the source of the king's royal authority, and the king needs to venture into the forest (or a forest-like setting) to acquire and renew that authority before returning triumphantly to the kingdom.

None of this is made explicit within our stories, of course. In our stories, I would argue, the gift of the body legitimizes the king's kingship by demonstrating the sincerity of his generosity and his willingness to give away everything—especially that which cannot be reacquired through the power and wealth of his office. His successful passing of this ultimate test of generosity proves the king to be a worthy embodiment of virtuous Buddhist kingship, and justifies the obedience and devotion of his subjects. This is the moral message of the stories, and it is this message that is highlighted. In the background, however, worked into the very structure of the tale, this message is reinforced and strengthened by several other ideas: the forest as a source of royal authority, the power of the pleasure-park's stone throne, the oscillating structure of rites of royal consecration, and the king's need to renew his authority at regular intervals. These themes are not explicitly presented, but they contribute to the overall effect of the tale and reinforce the intended message. Because of the associations and connotations they convey, the king's gift of his body leaves the realm of mere "gift" and plays itself out as a magnificent ritual of royal consecration.

At the same time it is also well to recall that the king is not only a king trying to legitimate his kingship, but also a bodhisattva on his way to the attainment of Buddhahood. And, in fact, these same ideas surrounding the legitimation of kingship are also invoked more broadly by the Buddhist tradition as a whole in its discourse on the Buddha's Buddhahood—which is itself, of course, a type of "kingship." The Buddha himself, as noted before, follows the same basic pattern: he begins in the kingdom, renounces kingship and goes forth into the forest, is tested by Māra in the forest, and returns triumphantly to the kingdom to deliver his first sermon as the Buddha. The Bodhi Tree and the Seat of Enlightenment are doubles of the tree and stone seat that minimally constitute a *caitya,* and the Buddha's confrontation with Māra over the Seat of Enlightenment may thus be interpreted as a king's heroic battle for possession of a *caitya*'s stone throne and the world-sovereignty such possession would confer.[14] The forest is thus the source of the Buddha's authority, and throughout his life he regularly renews this authority by oscillating between wandering and settled life on a seasonal and cyclical basis—a practice that was continued by the early Saṃgha and appears to have contributed to the regular renewal of their spiritual authority as well. We might also note that all major events in the Buddha's life—such as his birth, enlightenment, first sermon, and death—take place in the forest or in forest-like settings. The Buddhist monastery (*ārāma*) is assimilated to the forest and the royal pleasure-park, while the Buddhist monastic concern with rules about seats and sitting mirrors the social code of propriety surrounding the seats and thrones of royalty.[15]

Finally, we might also note that the same pattern holds not only in regard to the Buddha's final life, but in regard to his extended biography as well. Over and over again, throughout the *jātakas,* Śākyamuni is reborn as a king who renounces the kingdom to live as an ascetic, or otherwise spends time in the forest. In one sense, each of these tales demonstrates how Śākyamuni "practiced" the Great Renunciation in numerous former lives.

But in another sense, when taken as a whole such tales imply a continuous pattern of life-in-the-kingdom and life-in-the-forest—an oscillating pattern that legitimates not only each of Śākyamuni's previous lives as a king, but his present "kingship" as well.

Gift and Sacrifice

Although thus far I have not paid much attention to the category of *sacrifice,* the themes of bodily mutilation, blood, and death obviously suggest that the bodhisattva's gift of his body might be interpreted as a *sacrificial ritual* in which the bodhisattva plays the double role of both *sacrificer* and *sacrificial victim.* This interpretation has indeed been advanced several times before, particularly in relation to the many connections that can be drawn between some gift-of-the-body stories and the practice and theory of Vedic sacrifice.

In her analysis of the story of King Maṇicūḍa,[16] for example, Phyllis Granoff points out that Maṇicūḍa's gift of his flesh and blood to a hungry *rākṣasa* takes place in the middle of an actual sacrifice: Maṇicūḍa is performing a traditional sacrifice on behalf of his father-in-law Bhavabhūti when Śakra takes on the guise of a *rākṣasa* and emerges from the sacrificial fire to demand the king's flesh and blood; moreover, in another, similar story about a king who gives his flesh and blood to hungry demons (the story of King Maitrībala), this gift is explicitly compared to the blood sacrifices made to the gods.[17] Thus we might see Maṇicūḍa's gift of his flesh and blood not so much as a compassionate gift made to a *rākṣasa,* but rather as a traditional sacrificial offering made to a Vedic deity (albeit one in disguise). Later on in the story Maṇicūḍa makes another gift of his body, this time giving away the healing crest-jewel embedded in his head to another king whose kingdom is suffering from an epidemic. Although this gift does not take place during an actual sacrifice, it again seems to contain distant echoes of ritual sacrifice, for as Granoff points out, in the very similar Hindu story of Aśvatthāman from the *Mahābhārata,* the crest-jewel given away is referred to as *ucchiṣṭa,* or the "fructifying, life-giving remainder of the sacrifice"—while in another version of the same tale Aśvatthāman is said to be bound just as one binds the sacrificial beast.[18] The Buddhist episodes involving Maṇicūḍa and Maitrībala, as well as the Hindu episode involving Aśvatthāman, might therefore all be seen as involving *sacrifice* rather than gift.

In answer to the question of what *kind* of sacrifice is being invoked, Granoff interprets these gift-giving episodes primarily as *sacrifices of expiation.* She points out that not only do several of the episodes seem to involve a situation of *sin that needs to be eradicated*—the epidemic for which Maṇicūḍa's crest-jewel is needed, for example, has been brought about by the sins of a particular king—but the Buddhist tradition itself offers this explanation for *all* gifts of the body performed by the bodhisattva. According to a story found in the *Samādhirāja Sūtra,*[19] the Buddha, in one of his previous births, was a wicked king who viciously ordered an innocent monk's execution, and it was in order to expiate this heinous sin of killing a monk that the Buddha, through countless subsequent lives, had to suffer the great pain of giving away his head, eyes, flesh, and blood. The bodhisattva's gift of his body can thus be seen as a *sacrifice of expiation*—one that accords well, in fact, with the rituals of expiation outlined, for example, in Hindu dharma texts such as the *Apastambadharma Sūtra,* which states that "the proper expiation for the sin of murder was for the sinner to cut off his hair, skin, and flesh and offer them into the sacrificial fire."[20]

In Hubert's and Mauss' still-classic account of the mechanism and varieties of sacrifice, this is a so-called *sacrifice of desacralization,* in other words, a sacrifice whose aim is to make the sacrificer *less sacred* by transferring his sacredness (here, in the form of sin or impurity) to a victim and then destroying the victim.[21] In our case, of course, the bodhisattva alone is both sacrificer *and* victim—but this only makes explicit a condition that is characteristic of all Vedic sacrifice, in which the sacrificer is always identified with the victim. In fact, Hubert and Mauss themselves, generalizing from the Vedic case, make this identification one of the fundamental features of *all* sacrifice: "Indeed, it is not enough to say that [the victim] represents [the sacrificer]: it is merged in him. The two personalities are fused together."[22] Even without a separate victim the same logic can apply to our stories as well: the bodhisattva who gives away his body performs a classic *sacrifice of expiation,* purifying himself in the long run by sacrificing his impure and worthless body in the present.

Hubert and Mauss, however, also emphasize the "fundamental complexity of sacrifice" that makes each individual sacrifice combine elements of several different types and accomplish a number of different, often contradictory ends at the same time[23]—and much the same is true of the bodhisattva's gift of his body. In their typology of the various types of sacrifice, the *sacrifice of desacralization* can be contrasted with the *sacrifice of sacralization*—in other words, a sacrifice whose aim is to make the sacrificer *more sacred* by identifying him with a consecrated victim and then destroying the victim to release its sacred power, which then redounds upon the sacrificer himself.[24] This again is a useful category in interpreting the gift-of-the-body theme.

To put this in an Indic context, we can refer to Edith Parlier's very thorough analysis of the story of King Śibi's gift of his flesh to ransom a dove (from either a hawk or a hunter) and its numerous connections with the life-giving, order-restoring variety of Vedic sacrifice.[25] Though I cannot do justice here to the wealth of details contained in her article, Parlier demonstrates how virtually every element of the story—including the dove, the hawk, the hunter, and even the fact that the dove lands upon the right thigh of King Śibi—has rich and detailed resonances with the theory and practice of Vedic sacrifice, particularly with the *soma* sacrifice and the altar-building ritual known as the *agnicayana.* Ultimately, she demonstrates that the story of King Śibi uses these parallels and resonances to suggest that just as the Vedic sacrifice renews and sanctifies both the sacrificer and his cosmos through the consecration and destruction of a victim (which is identified with the sacrificer himself), so also does the bodhisattva's gift of his body. As we have already seen, the bodhisattva sacrifices his present state in order to gain the more sacred state of Buddhahood, he sacrifices his ordinary body in order to gain the body of a Buddha, or he sacrifices an individual body part (such as the "eye of flesh") in order to gain its more sacred counterpart (such as the "eye of the dharma")—and in all such cases the larger cosmic order he inhabits is likewise sanctified and renewed. As Hubert and Mauss observe to be characteristic of the sacrifice of sacralization, "the changes effected [by such sacrifices] are more or less of long duration"; in fact, "they are sometimes constitutional and imply a real metamorphosis."[26]

The bodhisattva's gift of his body might therefore be seen as either a sacrifice of *desacralization,* in the sense of eradicating his sin or impurity, or a sacrifice of *sacralization,* in the sense of sanctifying the bodhisattva and moving him one step closer to perfect Buddhahood. In the first case the victim accepts sin and impurity *from* the sacrificer, while in the second case the victim imparts sacred power *to* the sacrificer—and since in our case the bodhisattva himself is the victim, this accords nicely with the double character of the bodhisattva's body as both a worthless and impure carcass and an already-ideal form. Ultimately, of course, the bodhisattva's gifts of his body are not *literal* sacrifices, but they do share with literal sacrifice the destruction of a victim and the profound surge of sacred energy that seems to be released by such destruction. They might therefore be seen as *metaphorical* sacrifices or, perhaps, as "spiritualizations" or "ethicizations" of sacrifice.

The general kinship between Vedic sacrifice and Buddhist renunciatory ideals has been noted many times before. Carol Meadows has interpreted the bodhisattva's perfection of giving as a "metaphorical or spiritual sacrifice,"[27] and Granoff, citing Meadows, observes that "a metaphorical interpretation of the actual ritual sacrifice to extend the concept to a spiritual sacrifice is central to classical India."[28] Hubert and Mauss themselves, in their pioneering work on sacrifice, noted the essential connection between Vedic ritual sacrifice and the type of spiritual "sacrifice" embodied in Buddhist renunciation and detachment. One of the consistent features of sacrifice they enumerated, for example, was the preliminary sacralization of the sacrificer through ascetic and purificatory rituals such as the Vedic consecration ritual known as *dīkṣā.* Connecting such rituals directly to the rise of Buddhism and Jainism, they state: "These preparatory actions often become the type for the sacrifice of oneself. The asceticism preliminary to the sacrifice became, in many cases, the whole sacrifice."[29] The idea that renunciatory and ascetic traditions in India represent an "internalization" of the Vedic sacrifice is common, of course:[30] the renunciant is one who internalizes the sacrificial fire within his own body as *tapas,* or the "heat" of his ascetic austerities, and who performs the sacrifice within himself by means of his renunciation and detachment.[31] Perhaps we might argue that this hereditary connection between Vedic sacrifice and Buddhist renunciation is enacted in a *reverse* direction in gift-of-the-body stories, in which Buddhist renunciation is embodied by a deed that once again bears some resemblance to Vedic sacrifice.

While the bodhisattva's gift of his body might well be interpreted as a metaphorical Vedic sacrifice, however, it is also crucial to note that the manner in which it adapts the sacrificial motif contains within itself an implicit *critique* of Vedic sacrifice—a point made most effectively in the discussion of Parlier. In her analysis it is strictly the *theory* of Vedic sacrifice that posits a complete identification between the sacrificer and the victim—an identification made most explicit in the famous *Puruṣa Sūkta* hymn of the *Ṛg Veda* (10.90), in which the cosmic man Puruṣa sacrifices *himself* in order to create the universe. When it comes to the *practice* of Vedic sacrifice, on the other hand, we find that the sacrificer always *relies on a substitute;* he substitutes a *victim* in place of himself, thus leaving himself free to enjoy the many benefits of the sacrifice while the innocent victim is destroyed in his place.

There is a rupture, in other words, between the theory and the practice of Vedic sacrifice—a rupture that results directly in *violence* unleashed upon the victim. According to Parlier, this violence inherent in the practice of Vedic sacrifice was intolerable for both Buddhism and epic Hinduism because of their adherence to the new, renunciatory ideal of perfect *nonviolence* (*ahiṃsā*). The story of King Śibi—in both its Buddhist and *Mahābhārata* versions—offers us at least one solution to this problem: by having King Śibi sacrifice *himself* rather than the dove, the mechanism of substitution is rejected, violence is avoided, the rupture between theory and practice is healed, and the new values of selflessness, detachment, and nonviolence are dramatically affirmed (see figure 6). In repudiating the mechanism of substitution upon which the practice of Vedic sacrifice is based, there is a return to the original mythological ideal represented by Puruṣa: true sacrifice is revealed to be nothing other than renunciation.

Moving beyond the strictly Indian context, much the same point is made by Hubert and Mauss in their discussion of the phenomenon of the "self-sacrificing god." Contrasting the self-interest inherent in ordinary sacrifice with the total selflessness of the self-sacrificing god, they state:

> In any sacrifice there is an act of abnegation since the sacrifier deprives himself and gives. . . . But this abnegation and submission are not without their selfish aspect. The sacrifier gives up something of himself but he does not give himself. Prudently, he sets himself aside. This is because if he gives, it is partly in order to receive. Thus sacrifice shows itself in a dual light. . . . Disinterestedness is mingled with self-interest.
>
> There is, however, one case from which all selfish calculation is absent. This is the case of the sacrifice of the god, for the god who sacrifices himself gives himself irrevocably. . . . [But this] is possible only for mythical, that is, ideal beings. This is how the concept of a god sacrificing himself for the world could be realized, and has become, even for the most civilized peoples, the highest expression and, as it were, the ideal limit of abnegation, in which no apportionment occurs.[32]

The self-interest involved in making use of a substitute victim is thus contrasted with the absolute disinterest involved in sacrificing oneself. As we have seen from our stories, however, the contrast between these two poles is not always so clear-cut—and once again, we can draw some general differences between our two basic plotlines: when the recipient

FIGURE 6 The story of King Śibi's gift of his flesh to ransom the life of a dove continues to be popular in contemporary India today. This is a page from a popular children's comic book in India ("Indra and Shibi," *Amar Chitra Katha,* vol. 254) originally published in 1978 and reprinted in 2001. It depicts a Hindu version of the story, taken from the *Mahābhārata* epic.

of the gift is an ordinary being and the bodhisattva dies as a result of making his gift, this is perhaps the most perfect exemplification of the self-sacrificing god—for not only does the bodhisattva lose his life, but the emphasis within these stories is on what the *recipients* gain through the sacrifice, rather than on what the bodhisattva gains. It is *they* who are sacralized, often through direct ingestion of the bodhisattva's flesh—direct consumption of the victim being identified by Hubert and Mauss as the most common means of sanctification used within sacrifices of sacralization. Thus, if we do choose to see the bodhisattva's gift of his body as a "sacrifice of sacralization," then these stories perhaps advocate being the *victim* of such a sacrifice rather than the one who sacrifices. On the other hand, when the recipient of the gift is the deity Śakra in disguise and the bodhisattva restores his body by performing an Act of Truth, the situation is more complicated: the bodhisattva himself still constitutes the self-sacrificing god who acts with complete disinterest and refuses to use a substitute. Nevertheless, the fact that he survives the gift and then gets his body back (often in a better form than before) makes a nod, at least, toward the idea of substitution; it is *as if* there were a substitute victim. These stories thus temper the ideal notion of the self-sacrificing god with intimations of ordinary, acquisitive sacrifice.

One final point remains to be made. While gift-of-the-body stories effectively manipulate the tension between using and not using a substitute, it is also worth asking whether even the rejection of substitution really goes far enough in adhering to the principle of perfect nonviolence. After all, even in the absence of a substitute victim, the basic *mechanism* of sacrifice—in which a violent act of destruction leads to sanctification and the reestablishment of order—still remains in place. Charles Orzech, in an article that attempts to relate several varieties of Buddhist self-sacrifice to René Girard's theory of violence and the sacred,[33] offers just such an analysis of Pāli *Jātaka* 316, the story of the hare who immolates himself in a fire in order to feed a brahmin supplicant. In Orzech's interpretation, the hare's eager willingness to make a sacrifice of himself may seem exemplary on the surface, but in fact it is nothing more than the "oppressive internalization of the process of victimage" elucidated by Girard. It glorifies the mechanism of sacrificial violence and has the unfortunate effect of mimetically motivating others to engage in similarly violent deeds.[34] In this sense, he contrasts the hare-story with the equally famous *Kṣāntivādin Jātaka,* in which an ascetic calmly and passively endures the horrific mutilation inflicted upon him by an angry king, refusing to give rise to any anger himself.[35] In Orzech's analysis, the ascetic here *is* a victim, but he doesn't go out and *make himself* a victim—and this distinction is important. In this way, the ascetic puts a stop to the cycle of reciprocal violence and demonstrates the "perfection of forbearance" (*kṣānti-pāramitā*) in a way that is enlightening and transformative for others. Orzech thus contrasts the "violent course of the sacred victim" with the "nonviolent transformative course of the exemplary victim,"[36] and maintains that these two types of victimage should be distinguished from each other, for the former "fuels the process of reciprocal violence" while the latter "stops it."[37]

In Orzech's Girardian analysis, the Buddhist tradition contains both nonviolent and violent (sacrificial) strands—with gift-of-the-body *jātakas* being perhaps the primary exemplification of the latter. It is perhaps this lingering sense of sacrificial violence surrounding the bodhisattva's gift of his body that ultimately results in some of the ambivalence we have seen in previous chapters.

Gift and Offering

The dialectical tension between *using* and *not using* a substitute examined above in connection with the category of "sacrifice" can also be discussed, of course, in terms of the related category of "ritual offering." As we saw in chapter 1, it is precisely the issue of *substitution* that constitutes the fundamental difference between the bodhisattva's gift of his body within the past and the ordinary Buddhist's ritual offerings within the present. The bodhisattva within gift-of-the-body stories exists in a Buddha-less past in which there is no "Buddhism" in the world to function as a powerful "field of merit." He therefore has no choice but to manifest his generosity in an extreme and unmediated manner—giving *himself* away rather than relying on any substitute. His deeds make it possible for *others,* however, to offer substitutes in place of themselves. By becoming a Buddha and establishing "Buddhism" as a powerful "field of merit," he creates a situation in which it is *no longer necessary* to give oneself away. Instead one can give away various substitutes (such as alms)—for once these substitutes are multiplied by the great "field of merit" in which they are bestowed, they become equivalent, in some sense, to the original gift of oneself. We thus move from the bodhisattva's gift of his body to the ordinary Buddhist's devotional offering, from the "ethos of the *jātaka*" to the "ethos of the *avadāna*," from the life of the Buddha to the ritual of the Buddhist—in other words, from *not using* to *using* a substitute.

What are we to make, then, of forms of self-immolation that seem to collapse these two categories together? In the famous "Medicine King" chapter of the *Lotus Sūtra,* for example, the bodhisattva "Seen With Joy By All Living Beings" sets his own body on fire as a devotional offering to the Buddha "Pure and Bright Excellence of Sun and Moon," and—in his subsequent rebirth—burns both of his forearms for seventy-two thousand years as a devotional offering to this same Buddha's relics.[38] Similarly, in other Mahāyāna *sūtras,* bodhisattvas, in a frenzy of Buddhist devotion, write out the *sūtras* using their skin as parchment, their bones as pens, and their blood or marrow as ink.[39] Episodes such as these proved to be of great inspiration to ordinary Buddhists in China, where, beginning from the fourth century C.E. and extending into relatively recent times, both individual, private instances and mass, public spectacles of bodily self-mutilation very often occurred in conjunction with the worship of relics or *stūpas.*[40] In 873 C.E., for example, when the emperor Yizong of the Tang had a segment of one of the Buddha's bones brought into the capital in a magnificent procession, there were spectators who cut off their arms, sprinkled the relic with their blood, walked on their elbows and knees, bit off their fingers, pulled out their hair, and set their heads on fire.[41] (It was precisely such spectacles of mass chaos, in fact, that inspired the scholar-official Han Yu's famous invective against Buddhist relic-worship in 819 C.E.)[42] Self-immolation of many different varieties was also popular among individual Chinese monks—so much so that "self-immolation" constitutes one of the basic organizing categories of most of the "Biographies of Eminent Monks" collections[43]—and although motivated by many different concerns, was quite often associated with the worship of relics, images, or *stūpas.*

All of these acts take place within a Buddhist devotional complex, and the devotees who perform them have full access to Buddhism as a powerful field of merit. Nevertheless, they *refuse to make use of any substitute,* choosing instead to turn *themselves* into the offering. We might say that although the Buddha—through his *jātaka*-like deeds—has brought about for them an *avadāna*-like setting, they choose to respond to this setting in the most devotional manner possible by once again acting in a *jātaka*-like manner, thereby collapsing the the former and the latter ethos together. The message suggested by such episodes, perhaps, is that once one recognizes the profound debt of gratitude owed to the Buddha for *making the mechanism of substitution possible,* one realizes that the best way to pay honor to this debt is by *forgoing the mechanism itself.* In China, moreover, many self-immolators who chose this route themselves left behind further relics and *stūpas*—which then made the same choice available to yet others: either make use of substitution or reject it.

A polemic that favors the route of dispensing with any substitute rather than using one is discernible in many Buddhist texts. In the "Medicine King" chapter of the *Lotus Sūtra,* for example, when the bodhisattva "Seen With Joy" uses his own body as a devotional offering, the Buddhas of innumerable world-spheres congratulate him by favorably comparing the offering of one's own body to any other material offering:

> Excellent! Excellent! Good man, this is true perseverance in vigor! This is called a true Dharma-offering to the Thus Come One. If with floral scent, necklaces, burnt incense, powdered scent, paint-scent . . . and a variety of such things one were to make offerings, still they could not equal this former [act of yours]. Even if one were to give realm and walled cities, wife and children, they would still be no match for it. Good man, this is called the prime gift. Among the various gifts, it is the most honorable, the supreme. For it constitutes an offering of Dharma to the Thus Come Ones.[44]

The highest form of worship, then, is one that rejects the mechanism of substitution upon which *all* worship presumably depends. It is called a "dharma-offering" in the sense that it constitutes the very dharma itself, rather than an act of worship in honor *of* the dharma.

In the Theravāda tradition a similar polemic is perhaps discernible in the tradition of the bodhisattva's "thirty perfections" (found, for example, in the *Buddhavaṃsa, Jātaka,* and *Dhammapada* commentaries), where each of the ten Theravādin "perfections" is said to be fulfilled by the bodhisattva in three different degrees, resulting in thirty perfections altogether. As the commentary to the *Buddhavaṃsa* explains, when one sacrifices external possessions, this is merely a "lower perfection" (*upapāramī*); when one sacrifices one's limbs, this is a "perfection" (*pāramī*); and when one sacrifices one's life, this is an "ultimate perfection" (*paramatthapāramī*).[45] While it is difficult to understand how the distinctions among sacrificing external possessions, limbs, and life could be applied to any perfection other than *dāna* (and perhaps *kṣānti*), the significance of the distinction itself is fairly clear: using a *substitute* makes the act in question a "lower" perfection, using *oneself* (rather than a substitute) makes it an "ultimate" perfection, and using one's *limbs*—which might be said to occupy an intermediate position between using and not using a substitute—occupies the middle ground between the other two. Implicit within these distinctions is a value judgment about the logic of substitution itself—a judgment in which *immediacy* is ranked more highly than *mediation.*

We thus move in a dialectical manner from the *immediacy* characteristic of the Buddha to the *mediation* made available to the ordinary Buddhist follower, and back once again to the *immediacy* freely chosen by the fervent Buddhist devotee. Nevertheless, it is perhaps inevitable that pure immediacy is impossible to sustain and must inevitably give way to mediation. This is apparent even in the "Medicine King" chapter itself, if we pay careful attention to its sequence of events. For it is significant, I believe, that in his first life, the bodhisattva "Seen With Joy" burns his entire body as an offering and suffers death as a result, whereas in his second life, he burns only his forearms and then restores them through an Act of Truth. We thus move from the *entire body* to the *major limbs,* from *death* to *survival,* and from *permanent loss* to *restoration.* The pure immediacy of the offering is thus gradually domesticated—and by the time we get to the end of the chapter and its recommendations for the ordinary Buddhist follower, we are down to a single finger or toe:

> If there is one who, opening up his thought, wishes to attain anuttarasamyaksaṃbodhi, if he can burn a finger or even a toe as an offering to a Buddhastūpa, he shall exceed one who uses realm or walled city, wife or children, or even all the lands, mountains, forests, rivers, ponds, and sundry precious objects in the whole thousand-millionfold world as offerings.[46]

The immediacy characteristic of exalted Buddhas and bodhisattvas is thus domesticated just enough that it becomes a viable possibility for the ordinary Buddhist devotee. Perhaps we might locate the ultimate end point of this process of "domestication" in the common East Asian Buddhist practice of burning incense, or moxa, on the crown of the head (or the forearm) at the time of Buddhist monastic ordination.[47] Here, the practice of self-sacrifice has been thoroughly ritualized, routinized, and institutionalized. It stands at the beginning of the Buddhist path rather than its end, and constitutes a standard procedure applying to everyone rather than an option freely chosen by the heroic few.

Gift and Death

In a recent essay on "death" as a "critical term" for the study of Buddhism,[48] Jacqueline Stone identifies two interrelated issues that should stand in the foreground of any attempt to study death-related discourses and practices across Buddhism as a whole. These two issues are *mastery over death* and the *legitimation* such mastery confers. As Stone puts it, "This promise [held out by Buddhism] of control over that most mysterious and terrifying realm—death—has been a chief source of Buddhism's attraction as a lived religion, and the perceived possession of such control has been one of its major sources of legitimation."[49] Both issues—the mastery itself and the legitimation it confers—can be related to the gift-of-the-body theme.

While the high value that Buddhism places on mastery over death is fairly obvious—being manifested by such things as the Buddha's defeat of Māra, the God of Death, on the night of his enlightenment, the definition of nirvana itself as a conquest of death, and the many exemplary stories told about Buddhist heroes who displayed such mastery—it is worth asking the question of *how one knows* that such mastery has been achieved. If "mastery over death" can be displayed in several different ways, then it might be possible to construct a continuum ranging from the "least visible" to the "most visible" displays of such mastery. Standing on the "least visible" end of the continuum might be the common Buddhist phenomenon of "voluntarily giving up the life-force"—such as the Buddha himself is said to have done three months before he actually died. While this is certainly an impressive achievement, it is also a phenomenon that is invisible to the outside observer (ignoring, for the moment, the earthquake that is said to occur every time a Buddha does this), it can be widely separated from the moment of death itself (as it was in the case of the Buddha), and it can result in a wholly ordinary-looking death (as the Buddha is said to have died from a stomach illness). This mastery, in other words, is wholly internal in nature, impossible for the outside observer to see, and leaves few traces upon the actual death itself—which is perhaps the very reason the tradition felt it necessary to supplement it with external signs such as earthquakes. In the absence of such external signs, this mastery is perhaps somewhat suspect.

Further down on the continuum of visibility, we might place something like the *Kṣāntivādin Jātaka,* in which the ascetic Kṣāntivādin willingly submits to being murdered by a king, without giving rise to any anger, thus fulfilling the "perfection of forbearance." Here the mastery over death consists of submitting to one's death with perfect calm and utter detachment—states of mind which are present at the moment of death itself and leave visible traces on the face, body, and demeanor of the one who possesses them. In comparison to "voluntarily giving up the life-force," this mastery over death is perhaps easier for an external observer to discern. Nevertheless, since somebody else does the actual killing and the ascetic's "mastery" consists only of the proper *response*, even this mastery is perhaps not completely clear.

It is from this perspective that we can see some of the appeal of the gift-of-the-body theme. For the bodhisattva who actively *brings about his own death* takes control of the reins, as it were; he exerts his mastery over death in an active and heroic manner, he leaves no question about this mastery—it is clear for all to see. The gift of the body thus constitutes the most visible marker of one's mastery over death (just as we earlier saw that it constitutes the most visible marker of the presence of pure generosity). Perhaps this is why the bodhisattva who gives his body away is so often depicted as a *king*, for as Graeme MacQueen has noted, Buddhist texts give voice to two different types of mastery: *internal mastery*, which is symbolized most potently by the *ascetic*, and *external mastery*, which is symbolized most potently by the *king*.[50] If the king is one who exercises his mastery in an outward and visible manner, then the king who heroically takes his own life is perhaps the most potent and external symbol of the mastery over death so highly valued by the Buddhist tradition.

At the same time, of course, such mastery can never be completely assured by external signs alone. Even the person who brings about his own death and seems to submit to it with utter calm and detachment could well be afflicted by passion and delusion and thus committing an ordinary act of suicide, which is generally looked down upon by the Buddhist tradition. Ultimately, true mastery over death is determined solely by internal mental factors which can never be wholly visible; as Charles Hallisey has noted, "[the] good death [in Buddhism] is distinguished by one's state of mind, by volitional and affective factors, at the moment of death, and not by outward circumstances."[51] In fact, it might even be the case that the more "actively" and externally such a death is pursued, the more suspect the presence of the correct mental factors becomes. Perhaps this is why there is also so much emphasis within Buddhism upon *post-mortem visibility:* What signs are left over from the death that indicate the mastery of the one who has died? In the case of the Buddha and other venerated disciples, such signs take many different forms: spontaneous combustion of the cremation fire, the body's refusal to rot and decay, various post-mortem actions of the body, or the post-mortem production of relics. And in our stories as well we see a consistent concern with such signs: after the death itself has occurred, heavenly flowers fall from the sky, the gods shout with glee, relics are produced, *stūpas* are erected, flesh-mountains spring into existence, the bodhisattva comes back to life, other people undergo moral conversions, and so forth. Even in the face of the bodhisattva's active enactment of his own death, such further signs are needed to legitimate the presence of the mastery that brought it about.

In the Chinese Buddhist tradition, in fact, it was precisely the visibility of such pre- and post-mortem signs that reassured authors such as Huijiao, Daoxuan, and Zanning that all of the cases of self-immolation they were reporting on within their "Biographies of Eminent Monks" collections were, indeed, legitimate expressions of the self-immolator's mastery over death.[52] As James Benn has demonstrated,[53] all three compilers were concerned to draw a distinction between the advanced bodhisattva, whose mastery over death legitimizes his act of self-immolation, and the ordinary person, who has no such mastery and would only be breaking the Vinaya's prescription against suicide if he were foolishly to decide to kill himself. And for all three compilers, we see a consistent need to rely on external signs in order to make this distinction. Thus, Huijiao states confidently that if the act of self-immolation is legitimate, this will be indicated by "auspicious omens" and "a myriad of good signs"; Daoxuan notes that illegitimate self-immolators often betray themselves by a "groan of pain" at the moment of death; and Zanning points to a number of legitimating signs common in Chinese practice, such as the unburned tongue, the body that drowns but doesn't sink, and the cremation fire that spontaneously combusts.[54]

The concerns expressed by Huijiao, Daoxuan, and Zanning are quite reminiscent of the discourse surrounding the Hindu practice of *sati,* in which a virtuous wife immolates herself on the cremation pyre of her husband. This discourse, too, is often characterized by an anxious need to distinguish "legitimate" from "illegitimate" cases through the use of various external signs. As Lindsey Harlan has noted, for example, because Rajput women consider the wifely virtue that leads to *sati* to be a trait characteristic of themselves alone, all non-Rajput cases of *sati* require "additional evidence" in order to be considered legitimate. The woman must vow to commit *sati* with no hesitation whatsoever, for example, and the flames that consume her body—which should properly arise directly from the heat of her own wifely virtue—must be "visibly distinct" from the fire used to light the cremation pyre itself.[55] The anxious need for such signs that characterizes both Chinese Buddhist self-immolation and the Hindu practice of *sati* is perhaps inevitable in the face of such gruesome forms of death. Death is disturbing enough when it happens in a natural manner, but the self-inflicted death is disturbing in the extreme. The anxious desire for visible signs that might vindicate such disturbing deeds is perhaps indicative of the human anxiety surrounding death.

All of this reveals that the relationship between *mastery over death* and the *process of legitimation* is something of a vicious circle. Perceived mastery over death does, indeed, legitimate the one who displays it—yet this mastery itself stands in need of constant legitimation.

Giving to Gain or Giving to Save?

In further considering the active and heroic—perhaps almost *too blatant*—manner in which the bodhisattva within gift-of-the-body stories confronts and tackles death, it seems to me that we can characterize his basic stance toward death in one of two contradictory ways. On the one hand, he is a braggart and a rogue who taunts the very gods themselves and purposefully gambles everything away in the hope of winning back an even greater return. He recklessly courts death and disaster itself in the hope of winning back a renewed and eternal life. Underneath their surface structure, gift-of-the-body stories suggest to me the vague ideas of risk and gambling, courting disaster and wagering with destiny.

One of the earliest occurrences of the Act of Truth in Indian literature occurs in the *Ṛg Veda* and involves the trials and tribulations of a gambler.[56] A gambler has lost everything through his compulsion to gamble—his possessions, his home, his wife, and himself. All he has left are his ten empty fingers. He extends his ten fingers to Savitṛ, the god of dice, performs an Act of Truth, and asks to be released from his compulsion. Though the Act of Truth is not explicitly stated, Brown surmises that it consists of the simple statement that, as the complete and ultimate gambler, he has gambled away all his possessions and has only his ten empty fingers left.[57] Savitṛ restores all his possessions and commands him to stop gambling.

The story has a strange resemblance to many gift-of-the-body *jātakas*. In both cases the initial dispensing of material goods escalates to a critical point; the hero refuses to retreat or back down; he confronts destiny itself by staking his own *body;* and because he can truthfully attest to the sheer audacity of his move, the gods are forced to make an even greater return. The giver and the gambler are really not so different. The gift-of-the-body bodhisattva is the ultimate gambler: by staking his own body, he poses the ultimate challenge and takes the ultimate risk, yet he does so in the hope of winning back the ultimate prize.

In agricultural harvest rituals from around the premodern world, grain is exorbitantly displayed and recklessly destroyed in order to ensure the fertility of the next year's crop. Since life comes from death, the life of the new crop can be assured and guaranteed by recklessly killing the old. Instead of waiting for fate to intervene, a proactive stance is taken and fate is brazenly challenged:

> Fertility is born of excess. . . . In a sort of wager with destiny, ruinous consequences are courted in the attempt to be the one who will give away the most, so that destiny is obliged to return with compound interest what it has received. . . . Economy, accumulation, and moderation define the rhythm of profane life, while prodigality and excess define the rhythm of the festival.[58]

We are reminded here, too, of the institution of the potlatch, in which the conspicuous and extravagant gifting of accumulated wealth is engaged in with the hope and expectation of eventual return, and wealth may be recklessly destroyed in the attempt to outdo a rival chief. The gift-of-the-body bodhisattva, too, as we have seen, has some of the same reckless and agonistic quality about him.

A similar type of logic, however, also governs religious actions that are less brazen and more defensive in nature. Instead of boldly gambling everything in order to gain a greater return, in some cases one suffers a "tolerable loss" in order to save the whole. Trapped in a rocking boat during a storm, one throws dollar bills into the ocean in order to spare oneself. In many fairy tales, the hero escapes from a pursuing monster by throwing his possessions (and sometimes body parts) behind him to stall the monster's pursuit. In the second century C.E., when a man named Aristeides was destined to die in three days, Asclepius, the god of healing, told him to "cut a piece of his body for the sake of saving the whole." Finger-sacrifice often has the same logic: "Pursuing demons are pacified by the act of severing a finger from the body; the partial loss is to save the whole man."[59] On the level of groups, as well, one person may constitute the partial loss suffered, such that his self-sacrifice ensures the survival of all. Even celibacy may be interpreted along the same lines: by renouncing one's role in creating life, one hopes to escape from the jaws of death. Life is ransomed away from death through the suffering of a manageable loss.

In Burkert's illuminating discussion, from which all these examples are drawn,[60] all such actions embody a kind of *pars pro toto,* or "part for whole," logic that is a common feature of religion and cult, and that is frequently enacted in situations of panic or despair. In such a way, religion functions to reduce and manage the anxiety brought about by illness, pain, and fear. I bring up this context of ideas not in order to suggest that it bears directly on the gift-of-the-body theme, but only to emphasize the double character of the bodhisattva who gives his body away. On the one hand, he is a braggart who challenges destiny, tempts fate, and gambles everything away in the hope for a greater return; on the other hand, he is a being reacting in panic and despair, escaping from the jaws of death by suffering a manageable loss. He gives to gain, and he gives to save—yet another variety of "doubleness" built into the theme itself.

CONCLUSIONS

Throughout this book I have focused upon the plotlines, characters, rhetorical strategies, and religious conceptions characteristic of a particular genre of stories involving the bodhisattva's gift of his body. Though many different points have been treated and discussed, several of them converge around a single, consistent, underlying dialectic. By way of summarizing my discussion and highlighting this dialectic, let me return to an idea that I presented in chapter 1 and that has served as a *leitmotif* throughout the remainder of this book.

In chapter 1 I made a wide-ranging distinction between the "ethos of the *jātaka*" and the "ethos of the *avadāna*"—the former involving "perfections" and the latter involving "devotions." *Jātakas* feature the heroic and inimitable moral exploits performed by a worthy and superior being in a difficult, Buddha-less age of the past, while *avadānas* feature the commonplace ritual and devotional transactions performed by ordinary Buddhists in an age of Buddhadharma. By reading the two genres together, we can see how pre-Buddha "perfections" are contrasted with post-Buddha "devotions," or how the *life of the Buddha* is contrasted with the *ritual of the Buddhist.* Within the context of this contrast, I argued, gift-of-the-body stories might be seen as "super-*jātakas*," or those *jātakas* that exemplify the ethos of the *jātaka* most strongly and provide the greatest contrast of all with the ethos of the *avadāna*. Nevertheless, I also argued that despite the particularly paradigmatic way in which the gift-of-the-body theme exemplifies the ethos of the *jātaka*, the ethos of the *avadāna* is never far away. Through a variety of narrative strategies, gift-of-the-body *jātakas* repeatedly invoke the *avadāna*-type ritual deed and strive to suggest that the two ethoses can, in fact, be made equivalent through the existence of Buddhism itself.

In chapter 2's examination of conventional plotlines I began to elucidate some of these narrative strategies. The contrast between the ethos of the *jātaka* and the ethos of the *avadāna* is reflected somewhat in the gift-of-the-body genre's use of two major conventional plotlines. Stories featuring ordinary beings as the recipients of the gift exemplify the ethos of the *jātaka* in a particularly stark manner by depicting pitiful, evil, and unworthy recipients who cannot, in any sense, "repay" the bodhisattva's gift, as well as having the bodhisattva die as a result of giving this gift, thus highlighting the theme of extreme, disinterested generosity. Stories featuring Śakra as the recipient of the gift, on the other hand, while still exemplifying the ethos of the *jātaka*, implicitly invoke the ethos of the *avadāna* as well by depicting a *deity*—the classic "worthy" recipient—as the recipient of the gift. In addition, by allowing the bodhisattva to survive the gift and restore his body to perfect health, such stories also depict the rewards of the gift and implicitly align it with more ordinary ritual offerings. Different aspects of the bodhisattva's character are highlighted by each plotline. If *otherness* and *imitability* are the two contrasting elements of "sainthood," then stories of the first type clearly err on the side of "otherness," while stories of the second type make a nod toward "imitability." The reader's response also varies in accordance, the first plotline inviting a response of ritual, worship, and devotion, and the second plotline demanding that we imitate the bodhisattva and engage in giving ourselves. Finally, the third (and more minor) plotline I enumerated, in which the *gift is interrupted once the bodhisattva's willingness to give has been established*, perhaps represents one strategy for bringing together the ethos of the *jātaka* and the ethos of the *avadāna:* by suggesting that the *intention to give* is really equivalent to the gift itself, such stories collapse the enormous distance between heroic bodily self-sacrifice and ordinary ritual offerings, suggesting that the two are, in fact, equivalent—as long as the underlying motivation is pure.

In chapter 3's examination of rhetoric I suggested that the basic rhetorical purpose of the gift-of-the-body genre is to pose and then resolve the fundamental conflict between the universalistic demands of "perfect generosity" (as embodied by the bodhisattva) and the particularistic claims of family, community, and kingdom (as embodied by the bodhisattva's opposers). As we might expect from the discussion in chapter 2, stories featuring ordinary beings as the recipients of the gift generally offer the least resolution to this conflict, since the tragic death of the bodhisattva and the grief of those he leaves behind suggest that the two sides are, in fact, irreconcilable. Stories featuring Śakra as the recipient of the gift, on the other hand, generally offer the greatest resolution to the conflict—bringing the two sides together through the *give-and-get-back* movement of the gift, and using Śakra as a mediator between the transcendent Buddhist values adhered to by the bodhisattva and the everyday, pragmatic concerns adhered to by those who oppose him. Once again, this is in keeping with my basic distinction between the *jātaka* and the *avadāna:* the ethos of the *jātaka* (characteristic of the former stories) is an ethos of absolute and transcendent values that can brook no concession or compromise and might clash tragically with the ordinary, mundane world, whereas the ethos of the *avadāna* (characteristic of the latter stories) is an ethos of effective ritual action that reflects universal Buddhist values but can be fully incorporated into everyday life.

In addition to these general tendencies characteristic of our two major plotlines, however, I hope that chapter 3 has also demonstrated the enormous variety of different strategies for relating the universal and the particular displayed across the genre as a whole. In some cases, for example, the *particular is fully subordinated and made subservient to the universal*—such as when the bodhisattva sternly rebukes a minor deity by drawing on the full authority and grandeur of the Buddhist cosmos and demonstrating the deity's purely local concerns to be trivial. In some cases, the *universal and the particular are placed in a proper, hierarchical relationship*—such as when the higher *devas* above applaud the gift and understand its true significance, whereas human beings below consider only the gift's immediate consequences and are therefore deeply opposed. In some cases, the *universal wholly encompasses the particular*—such as when a king's strict adherence to perfect generosity spreads inexorably to everyone around him, eventually obviating any need to distinguish between his own subjects and all other beings. And in some cases, the *particular becomes a valid expression of the universal*—such as when Maṇicūḍa becomes convinced that to marry Padmāvatī *is* a legitimate expression of the bodhisattva's compassion for all beings. The conflict between universal and particular values is fundamental to the Buddhist tradition, and rather than providing any single, straightforward resolution, the gift-of-the-body genre offers to its readers the full range of creative resources needed to grapple with the conflict themselves.

The basic distinctions of plotline enumerated in chapter 2 (and made use of in chapter 3) appear again in chapters 4 and 5, but this time in connection with the Buddhist discourse on *dāna.* In line with their exemplification of the ethos of the *jātaka,* stories featuring ordinary beings as the recipients of the gift depict the bodhisattva's gift of his body as an ideal and nonreciprocal form of *dāna*—a gift given downward to an unworthy recipient out of pure generosity and compassion, and a gift that perhaps ultimately derives from a "*kṣatriya* model" of exchange. In contrast, in line with their movement toward the ethos of the *avadāna,* stories featuring Śakra as the recipient of the gift suggest that the bodhisattva's gift of his body can also be interpreted as an ordinary and reciprocal form of *dāna*—a gift given upward to a worthy recipient with a desire for karmic rewards, and a gift that perhaps ultimately derives from a "brahmanical model" of exchange.

In enumerating this basic distinction, however, I have been particularly interested in the category of *time* and the role time plays in balancing between these two conceptions. As we have seen, *at the precise narrative moment when the gift is being given,* it *must* be depicted as a pure and nonreciprocal gift. It is only later on and *after-the-fact*—once the bodhisattva's body has been restored and his generosity proven sincere, for example, or even many eons later, when the Buddha himself recounts the tale of a previous life—that this same gift can then be celebrated as a reciprocal exchange that brings the giver enormous rewards. In stories featuring Śakra, these two categories of time are signified, in part, by the *donning* and *dispensing* of Śakra's disguise: when Śakra is disguised as an "unworthy" recipient, the bodhisattva's gift is wholly pure, but once Śakra is revealed to be the classic "worthy" recipient—a deity—the gift becomes relatable to more ordinary ritual offerings. It is the passage of *time*—and with it, the gift's increasing "framability"—that serves to balance these two depictions, and it is only within the Act of Truth (such an appropriate name!) that this careful balancing act falls apart. For within the Act of Truth, time is collapsed: the ideal and the ordinary forms of *dāna* are brought together within a single ritual moment, leading inevitably to contradictory and disconcerting statements in which the bodhisattva's *utter lack of regret* at giving away his body is combined with his driving desire to *get this body back.* A more satisfactory strategy for collapsing time, on the other hand, can perhaps be found in the standard *jātaka* practice of pairing a particular "story of the present" with a particular "story of the past." As we have seen, in some cases, ordinary ritual offerings in the "story of the present" are implicitly equated with heroic bodily self-sacrifices in the "story of the past." On the one hand, "past" and "present" are kept apart from each other; on the other hand, by pairing the two stories together and framing one inside the other, *time is collapsed*—and the ethos of the *jātaka* and the ethos of the *avadāna* become equivalent through the ritual magic worked by Buddhism as a powerful "field of merit."

In chapter 6's examination of the discourse on the body characteristic of the gift-of-the-body genre, the same distinction between *jātaka* and *avadāna* once again came into play, but this time in terms of character and point of view rather than in terms of plotline. The bodhisattva himself usually speaks from the perspective of the ethos of the *jātaka*—seeing himself as an *ordinary body* struggling on the long moral path that ultimately leads to Buddhahood in the far-distant future and often emphasizing this body's worthlessness. Those around the bodhisattva, on the other hand, usually speak from the perspective of the ethos of the *avadāna*—celebrating the bodhisattva as an *already-ideal body* that manifests itself in the world in a glorified form and makes itself ritually available to others as a powerful field of merit. The first is an "ideology of absence," while the second is an "ideology of presence." Once again, we see a distinction in terms of *time,* for the first is placed squarely in the *pre-Buddha past,* while the second seems to assume the *post-Buddha present.* In this way, two entire sides of the Buddhist tradition are brought together—the *ascent* away from this world and the *descent* that brings one back out of compassion. It is, at least in part, the *pain* of the bodhisattva's body that serves as a fulcrum for these different conceptions by signifying the possibility of *transformation,* or movement from one side to the other. Different perspectives on the body are thus brought together and balanced, so that the *true* "ideal body" depicted across the genre as a whole constitutes a middle way between transcendence and immanence—a *sambhoga-kāya* or "substitute body" that paradoxically materializes the immaterial.

Finally, in several of the discussions contained in chapter 7, the same contrast between the ethos of the *jātaka* and the ethos of the *avadāna* is implicit in my treatment of the logic of substitution: when seen in relation to the category of *sacrifice,* the bodhisattva's gift of his body represents a sacrifice in which one forgoes the mechanism of substitution and sacrifices oneself in place of a victim. Similarly, when seen in relation to the category of the *ritual offering,* the bodhisattva's gift of his body represents the offering of oneself rather than any material substitute. Yet in both cases the gift-of-the-body genre effectively manipulates the tension between *not using* and *using* a substitute—the first being reflective of the ethos of the *jātaka* and the second being reflective of the new ritual situation brought about by the ethos of the *avadāna.*

The "ethos of the *jātaka*" and the "ethos of the *avadāna*" have thus served throughout this book as imprecise yet suggestive labels for two entire sides of the Buddhist tradition and complexes of thought and practice that seem to be brought together, over and over again, by the gift-of-the-body genre. How are we to explain the multiplicity of the gift-of-the-body theme and its ability to suggest a number of opposing conceptions simultaneously? I would like to suggest that this ability depends, at least in part, upon the very structure of the theme itself—more specifically, on the complete identification it achieves between the giver and his gift. Merely by virtue of the fact that *the gift and the person who gives it are not normally one and the same thing—but in this case they are,* the gift-of-the-body theme is inherently suggestive of the *two-that-are-really-one-but-that-can-be-strategically-separated-back-into-two.* Symbolically, in other words, the very theme itself embodies a dialectic between *immediacy* and *mediation,* between the *two-that-are-fused-together* and the *two-that-are-separated-through-some-form-of-mediation.* And what is this dialectic other than the tension that exists between the "ethos of the *jātaka*" and the "ethos of the *avadāna*"? Between the pre-Buddha past and the post-Buddha present? Between becoming a Buddha oneself and worshiping the Buddha through offerings? Between the life of the Buddha and the ritual of the Buddhist? This "double character" is built into the very structure of the theme itself, and it enables the theme to bear multiple connotations and conceptions at the same time.

By itself and in isolation, however, the gift-of-the-body theme cannot automatically function in this multifaceted way. Though the gift-of-the-body theme has the *potential* for symbolizing numerous opposing conceptions, the playing-out of those conceptions always takes place within the context and structure of a *story.* It is the *story* that is able to develop multiple lines of thought simultaneously and balance their interests against each other. The multivalency and successful functioning of the theme thus depend not only on the nature of the theme itself, but also on the narrative context through which it is conveyed. This is why I have insisted throughout this book on treating the gift-of-the-body theme within the context of the stories themselves. Stories involving the gift-of-the-body theme are not randomly constructed; they are structured in particular ways that enable them to bear particular meanings, and an understanding of their structures illuminates the manner in which those meanings are conveyed. Theme and story thus work seamlessly together and are dependent upon each other for their functioning. The connotations and suggestions of the gift-of-the-body genre are born only through this perpetual interaction.

APPENDIX

A CORPUS OF GIFT-OF-THE-BODY *JĀTAKAS*

This appendix contains basic information about each of the gift-of-the-body *jātakas* that collectively constitute the corpus of material on which this book is based. I make no claims whatsoever to comprehensiveness—either in terms of which gift-of-the-body stories are included within the corpus, or in terms of what kind of information is provided below for those stories that are. The corpus itself is highly idiosyncratic in nature, its contents determined by all kinds of different factors (such as whether I was aware of the story beforehand, its easy accessibility in a published edition, its inherent interest, its inclusion of a particularly striking passage, whether my library was able to obtain a particular volume, or just pure chance), and I am aware of many gift-of-the-body stories (and individual versions of such stories) that are not included here.

Each of the entries below includes such basic information as the title of the story, its language, its location within a larger collection, the published editions and translations I have made use of (not necessarily all that exist), a brief summary of the plot, citations of any relevant discussions, and ancillary comments that I thought might be helpful to the reader. Again, none of this information is necessarily complete. For many of the stories, more thorough bibliographical citations are already available in Leslie Grey's *A Concordance of Buddhist Birth Stories* (2nd ed., 1994); I have included citations to Grey wherever applicable. I have organized the corpus in terms of basic plotlines (arranged in no particular order), with the exception of the final two categories.

A. King Śibi Gives His Eyes to a Brahmin

1. Pāli *Jātaka* 499: *Sivijātaka*

Pāli. Ed. Fausboll 1875–1897:4, 401–412. Trans. Cowell 1895–1913:4, 250–256. King Śibi gives both of his eyes to an old, blind brahmin (the deity Śakra in disguise) and later restores them through two Acts of Truth.

2. *Cariyāpiṭaka* 1.8: *Sivirājacariyaṃ*

Pāli. Ed. Jayawickrama 1974: pt. 2, 7–8. Trans. Horner 1975: pt. 2, 7–8. King Śibi gives both of his eyes to an old, blind brahmin (the deity Śakra in disguise); their later restoration is not related. The account is told in the first-person voice by the Buddha himself.

3. *Jātakamālā* (of Āryaśūra) 2: *Śibijātaka*

Sanskrit. Ed. Vaidya 1959a:7–15 and Kern 1891:6–14 (emendations in Khoroche 1987:15–17). Trans. Khoroche 1989:10–17 and Speyer 1895:8–19. King Śibi gives both of his eyes to an old, blind brahmin (the deity Śakra in disguise) and later restores them through two Acts of Truth.

4. *Mahajjātakamālā* 44: *Śibirājacakṣuḥpradānāvadāna*

Sanskrit. Ed. Hahn 1985:514–531. King Śibi gives both of his eyes to an old, blind brahmin (the deity Śakra in disguise) and later restores them through two Acts of Truth. Borrows substantially from no. 3 above.

5. *Avadānaśataka* 34: *Śibyavadāna*

Sanskrit. Ed. Speyer 1958:1, 182–186 and Vaidya 1958:83–85. Fr. trans. Feer 1891:124–127. Three episodes: King Śibi gives his blood to insects, has his eyes plucked out by a bird (the deity Śakra in disguise), and offers his eyes to a brahmin (the deity Śakra in disguise), but the final gift is not completed.

See also: Grey 1994:361–365 (s.v. Sivi); Lamotte 1944–1980:1, 255, n. 1; Cummings 1982:75–83.

B. King Śibi Gives His Flesh to Ransom a Dove

1. *Kalpanāmaṇḍitikā* (of Kumāralāta) 64

Chinese translation from Sanskrit (T. 201). Fr. trans. Huber 1908:330–341. King Śibi gives his flesh to ransom a dove (the deity Viśvakarman in disguise) from a hawk (the deity Śakra in disguise) and later restores his body through an Act of Truth.

2. *Avadānakalpalatā* (of Kṣemendra) 55: *Sarvaṃdadāvadāna*

Sanskrit. Ed. Vaidya 1959b:2, 334–337 (emendations in De Jong 1979:93–94). King Sarvaṃdada (rather than Śibi) gives his flesh to ransom a dove from a hunter (the deity Śakra in disguise) and later restores his body through an Act of Truth.

See also: Grey 1994:361–365 (s.v. Sivi); Grey 1994:337–338 (s v. Sarvaṃdada); Schlingloff 1988:86–92; Cummings 1982:75–83; Parlier 1991.

C. King Candraprabha Gives His Head to a Brahmin

1. *Divyāvadāna* 22: *Candraprabhāvadāna*

Sanskrit. Ed. Cowell and Neil 1970:314–328 and Vaidya 1959c:195–203. Trans. Ohnuma 2004b. King Candraprabha gives his head to a brahmin and dies.

2. *mDzangs bLun zhes bya ba'i mdo* (Skt. *Damamukha Sūtra,* or *Sūtra of the Wise and the Fool*) 22

Tibetan translation from Chinese. Ed. Schmidt 1845:132–146. Trans. (from Mongolian version of same) Frye 1981:105–114. King Candraprabha gives his head to a brahmin (sent by another king) and dies.

See also: Grey 1994:49 (s.v. Candraprabha); Lamotte 1944–1980:1, 144, n.; Hartmann 1977; Matsumura 1980.

D. King Maitrībala Gives His Flesh and Blood to Five Yakṣas

1. *Jātakamālā* (of Āryaśūra) 8: *Maitrībalajātaka*

Sanskrit. Ed. Vaidya 1959a:43–54 and Kern 1891:41–51 (emendations in Khoroche 1987:23–26). Trans. Khoroche 1989:47–57 and Speyer 1895:55–71. King Maitrībala gives his flesh and blood to five yakṣas and later has his body restored directly by the deity Śakra.

2. *mDzangs bLun zhes bya ba'i mdo* (Skt. *Damamukha Sūtra,* or *Sūtra of the Wise and the Fool*) 12

Tibetan translation from Chinese. Ed. Schmidt 1845:53–54. Trans. (from Mongolian version of same) Frye 1981:46–47. King Maitrībala gives his flesh and blood to five yakṣas; the later restoration of his body is not related.

See also: Grey 1994:231 (s.v. Maitrībala); Schlingloff 1988:139–142.

E. King Maṇicūḍa Gives His Flesh and Blood to a Rākṣasa *and His Crest-Jewel to a Group of Brahmins*

1. *Maṇicūḍāvadāna*

Sanskrit. Ed. Handurukande 1967:1–105. Trans. Handurukande 1967:106–146. A long biography of King Maṇicūḍa containing two gift-of-the-body episodes: King Maṇicūḍa gives his flesh and blood to a *rākṣasa* (the deity Śakra in disguise) and later restores his body through an Act of Truth. Then he gives the crest-jewel embedded in his head to a group of brahmins (sent by another king) and later restores it through an Act of Truth.

2. *Lokānandanāṭaka* (Tib. *'Jig rten kun tu dga' ba'i zlos gar*) of Candragomin

Tibetan translation from Sanskrit. Ed. Hahn 1974. Transliterated in Handurukande 1967:209–291. Trans. Hahn 1987. Ger. trans. Hahn 1974. Detailed synopsis in Handurukande 1967:292–298. See also: Hahn 1979. A five-act Sanskrit drama containing two gift-of-the-body episodes: King Maṇicūḍa gives his flesh and blood to a *rākṣasa* (the deity Śakra in disguise) and is later restored to health directly by the earth-goddess. Then he gives the crest-jewel embedded in his head to a group of brahmins (sent by another king) and later restores it through an Act of Truth.

See also: Grey 1994:239–240 (s.v. Maṇicūḍa, Ratṇacūḍa); Granoff 1990; Handurukande 1975.

F. King Sarvaṃdada Offers His Head to a Brahmin

1. *Avadānasārasamuccaya* 3: *Sarvaṃdadajātaka*

Sanskrit. Ed. Handurukande 1984:54–87. Trans. Handurukande 1984:54–87. King Sarvaṃdada offers his head to a brahmin to bring to another king for a reward, but the gift is not completed. This story has been attributed by Michael Hahn (1992) to Gopadatta's *Jātakamālā*.

2. *Mahajjātakamālā* 45: *Sarvaṃdadābhidhānamahārājāvadāna*

Sanskrit. Ed. Hahn 1985:532–550 and Handurukande 1984:196–206. King Sarvaṃdada offers his head to a brahmin to bring to another king for a reward, but the gift is not completed. Borrows substantially from no. 1 above.

3. *Kalpanāmaṇḍitikā* (of Kumāralāta) 71

Chinese translation from Sanskrit (T. 201). Fr. trans. Huber 1908:416–421. An unnamed king offers himself (not specifically his head) to a brahmin to bring to another king for a reward, but the gift is not completed.

See also: Handurukande 1984:20–23; Lamotte 1944–1980:2, 714, n. 2; Matsumura 1980.

G. King Padmaka Becomes a Fish and Gives His Flesh and Blood to His Subjects

1. *Avadānaśataka* 31: *Padmakāvadāna*

Sanskrit. Ed. Speyer 1958:1, 168–172, and Vaidya 1958:78–80. Trans. Ohnuma 2004a. Fr. trans. Feer 1891:114–117. King Padmaka sacrifices his life to transform himself into a fish, gives his healing flesh and blood to his subjects to cure an epidemic, and dies.

2. *Avadānakalpalatā* (of Kṣemendra) 99: *Padmakāvadāna*

Sanskrit. Ed. Vaidya 1959b:2, 544 (emendations in De Jong 1979:250–251). King Padmaka sacrifices his life to transform himself into a fish, gives his healing flesh and blood to his subjects to cure an epidemic, and dies.

3. *mDzangs bLun zhes bya ba'i mdo* (Skt. *Damamukha Sūtra,* or *Sūtra of the Wise and the Fool*) 26

Tibetan translation from Chinese. Ed. Schmidt 1845:171–173. Trans. (from Mongolian version of same) Frye 1981:133–134. King Śudolagarne (not Padmaka) sacrifices his life to transform himself into a fish, gives his flesh and blood to his subjects during a drought (not an epidemic), and dies.

See also: Grey 1994:277 (s.v. Padmaka > Rohita).

H. A Merchant Gives His Body to Save His Drowning Companions

1. *Mahāvastu: Pañcakānāṃ Bhadravargikānāṃ Jātakaṃ*

Sanskrit. Ed. Senart 1977:3, 353–356 and Basak 1963–1968:3, 470–475. Trans. Jones 1949–1956:3, 350–354. A merchant kills himself in the ocean so that his drowning companions can use his body to get to shore.

2. *Avadānasārasamuccaya* 2: *Sārthavāhajātaka*

Sanskrit. Ed. Handurukande 1984:34–57. Trans. Handurukande 1984:34–57. A merchant kills himself in the ocean so that his drowning companions can use his body to get to shore. This story has been attributed by Michael Hahn (1992) to Gopadatta's *Jātakamālā.*

3. *Sambhadrāvadānamālā* 4: *Sārthavāhajanmāvadāna*

Sanskrit. Ed. Handurukande 1984:187–195. A merchant kills himself in the ocean so that his drowning companions can use his body to get to shore. Borrows substantially from no. 2 above.

See also: Handurukande 1984:16–20.

I. Three Gift-of-the-Body Episodes Together: (1) A Woman Gives Her Breasts to Another Woman Who Is Starving; (2) A Merchant's Son Gives His Eye and Flesh to Some Birds; (3) A Brahmin Gives His Body to a Starving Tigress

1. *Divyāvadāna* 32: *Rūpāvatyavadāna*

Sanskrit. Ed. Cowell and Neil 1970:469–481 and Vaidya 1959c:307–313. Three episodes: (1) The woman Rūpāvatī gives her breasts to another woman who is starving, and later has them restored through her husband's Act of Truth. Then she performs her own Act of Truth by which she becomes a man named Rūpāvata. (2) Rūpāvata, after dying, is reborn as the merchant's son Candraprabha, who gives his eye and his flesh to a flock of hungry birds and then dies. (3) Candraprabha is reborn as the brahmin Brahmaprabha, who gives his body to a starving tigress and dies.

2. *Avadānakalpalatā* (of Kṣemendra) 51: *Rukmavatyavadāna*

Sanskrit. Ed. Vaidya 1959b:2, 316–319 (emendations in De Jong 1979:80–82). Trans. Das 1893. Three episodes: (1) The woman Rukmavatī gives her breasts to another woman who is starving and then performs an Act of Truth and becomes a man named Rukmavān. (2) Rukmavān is reborn as the merchant's son Sattvavara, who gives his eye and his flesh to a flock of hungry birds and then dies. (3) Sattvavara is reborn as the brahmin Satyavrata, who gives his body to a starving tigress and dies.

3. *Jātakamālā* (of Haribhaṭṭa) 6: *Rūpyāvatījātaka*

Sanskrit. Ed. Hahn 1992:51–57. Trans. Ohnuma 2004c. One episode: The woman Rūpyāvatī gives her breasts to another woman who is starving, and later has them restored through her husband's Act of Truth. Then she performs her own Act of Truth, by which she becomes a man named Rūpyāvata.

See also: Grey 1994:305–306 (s.v. Rukmavatī, Rūpāvatī); Ohnuma 2000.

J. A Prince or an Ascetic Gives His Body to a Starving Tigress

1. *Jātakamālā* (of Āryaśūra) 1: *Vyāghrījātaka*

Sanskrit. Ed. Vaidya 1959a:1–6 and Kern 1891:1–6 (emendations in Khoroche 1987:15). Trans. Khoroche 1989:5–9 and Speyer 1895:2–8. A brahmin ascetic gives his body to a starving tigress and dies.

2. *Suvarṇabhāsottama Sūtra* 18: *Vyāghrīparivarta*

Sanskrit. Ed. Nobel 1937:201–240. Trans. Emmerick 1970:85–97. Prince Mahāsattva gives his body to a starving tigress and dies.

3. *Avadānakalpalatā* (of Kṣemendra) 95: *Vyāghryavadāna*

Sanskrit. Ed. Vaidya 1959b:2, 538–539 (emendations in De Jong 1979:240–242). Prince Karuṇarekha gives his body to a starving tigress and dies.

See also: citations for episode 3 in item I above; Grey 1994:222–224 (s.v. Mahāsattva, Vyāghrī); Schlingloff 1988:145–146; Cummings 1982:85–93; Feer 1899.

K. A Hare Gives His Body to a Wandering Supplicant or Ascetic

1. Pāli *Jātaka* 316: *Sasajātaka*

Pāli. Ed. Fausboll 1875–1897:3, 51–56. Trans. Cowell 1895–1913:3, 34–37. A hare throws himself into a fire to feed a wandering supplicant (the deity Śakra in disguise), but the fire refuses to burn him.

2. *Cariyāpiṭaka* 1.10: *Sasapaṇḍitacariyaḥ*

Pāli. Ed. Jayawickrama 1974:2, 12–13. Trans. Horner 1975:2, 14–16. A hare throws himself into a fire to feed a wandering supplicant (the deity Śakra in disguise), but the fire refuses to burn him. The account is told in the first-person voice by the Buddha himself.

3. *Jātakamālā* (of Āryaśūra) 6: *Śaśajātaka*

Sanskrit. Ed. Vaidya 1959a:30–35 and Kern 1891:27–33 (emendations in Khoroche 1987:19–21 and Hahn 1986–1992). Trans. Khoroche 1989:32–38 and Speyer 1895:37–45. A hare throws himself into a fire to feed a wandering supplicant (the deity Śakra in disguise) and dies.

4. *Avadānaśataka* 37: *Śaśāvadāna*

Sanskrit. Ed. Speyer 1958:1, 206–212 and Vaidya 1958:93–95. Trans. Feer 1891:138–142. A hare throws himself into a fire to feed an ascetic who lives with him in the forest, but the ascetic immediately pulls him out.

5. *Avadānakalpalatā* (of Kṣemendra) 104: *Śaśakāvadāna*

Sanskrit. Ed. Vaidya 1959b:2, 556–557 (emendations in De Jong 1979:262–264). A hare throws himself into a fire to feed an ascetic who lives with him in the forest, but the ascetic immediately pulls him out.

See also: Grey 1994:338–341 (s.v. Sasa); Grey 1994:341 (s.v. Śaśaka); Schlingloff 1988:123–129.

L. *The Elephant Ṣaḍdanta Gives His Tusks to a Hunter*

1. Pāli *Jātaka* 514: *Chaddantajātaka*

Pāli. Ed. Fausboll 1875–1897:5, 36–57. Trans. Cowell 1895–1913:5, 20–31. The elephant Ṣaḍdanta gives his tusks to a hunter (sent by an evil queen) and dies.

2. *Kalpanāmaṇḍitikā* (of Kumāralāta) 69

Chinese translation from Sanskrit (T. 201). Fr. trans. Huber 1908:403–411. The elephant Ṣaḍdanta gives his tusks to a hunter (sent by an evil queen) and dies.

See also: Grey 1994:50–52 (s.v. Chaddanta, Ṣaḍdanta); Grey 1994:109 (s.v. Hastaka, Ṣaḍdanta); Lamotte 1944–1980:2, 716–717, n. 1; Foucher 1917; Feer 1895.

M. *An Elephant Gives His Body to Lost Travelers*

1. *Jātakamālā* (of Āryaśūra) 30: *Hastijātaka*

Sanskrit. Ed. Vaidya 1959a:209–216 and Kern 1891:200–207 (emendations in Khoroche 1987:66–68). Trans. Khoroche 1989:213–220 and Speyer 1895:281–291. An elephant gives his body to a group of hungry and lost travelers and dies.

2. *Avadānakalpalatā* (of Kṣemendra) 96: *Hastyavadāna*

Sanskrit. Ed. Vaidya 1959b:2, 539–540 (emendations in De Jong 1979:243–244). An elephant gives his body to a group of hungry and lost travelers and dies.

See also: Grey 1994:109–110 (s.v. Hastin); Schlingloff 1988:149–150; Cummings 1982:69–73.

N. *Three Stories from the (Mahāyāna)* Karuṇāpuṇḍarīka Sūtra

1. King Ambara gives away many body parts and eventually becomes a flesh-mountain.

Ed. Yamada 1968:2, 376–384. Summarized in Yamada 1968:1, 112–117. See also: Grey 1994:11 (s.v. Ambara).

2. King Durdhana sacrifices his life to become a flesh-mountain.

Ed. Yamada 1968:2, 360–368. Summarized in Yamada 1968:1, 108.

3. King Puṇyabala gives his eyes and skin to an Ajīvaka and dies.

Ed. Yamada 1968:2, 348–355. Summarized in Yamada 1968:1, 105–107. See also: Grey 1994:290–291 (s.v. Puṇyabala).

O. Supporting Stories from the Chinese Buddhist Canon

In addition to the stories that constitute my corpus (given above), I have sometimes drawn additional details from the following thirteen stories translated from Chinese into French in Édouard Chavannes' two-volume *Cinq cents contes et apologues extraits du Tripiṭaka chinois* (Paris: Ernest Leroux, 1910–1934). All of them come from Chinese Buddhist canonical texts presumably translated from lost Indic originals, and most of them run parallel to one or more stories within my corpus (though individual names and details are often different). I have used Chavannes' numbers to designate each story.

1. Story no. 2 (Chavannes 1910–1934:1, 7–11), translated from *Liudu ji jing*, or *Sūtra on the Collection of Six Perfections* (T. 152): A king gives away his flesh to ransom a dove from a hawk (the deity Śakra in disguise), and later has his body restored by a celestial doctor (equivalent to plotline B above).

2. Story no. 4 (Chavannes 1910–1934:1, 15–17), translated from *Liudu ji jing*, or *Sūtra on the Collection of Six Perfections* (T. 152): An ascetic gives his body to a starving tigress and dies (equivalent to plotline J above).

3. Story No. 5 (Chavannes 1910–1934:1, 17–19), translated from *Liudu ji jing*, or *Sūtra on the Collection of Six Perfections* (T. 152): A king offers his head to a brahmin but the gift is not completed (equivalent to plotline F above).

4. Story no. 10 (Chavannes 1910–1934:1, 38–45), translated from *Liudu ji jing*, or *Sūtra on the Collection of Six Perfections* (T. 152): A king offers his head to a brahmin to bring to another king for a reward and dies (similar to plotline F above).

5. Story no. 11 (Chavannes 1910–1934:1, 46–49), translated from *Liudu ji jing*, or *Sūtra on the Collection of Six Perfections* (T. 152): A king offers his head to a brahmin to bring to another king for a reward; he cuts his own head off and dies (similar to plotlines F and C above).

6. Story no. 19 (Chavannes 1910–1934:1, 71–72), translated from *Liudu ji jing*, or *Sūtra on the Collection of Six Perfections* (T. 152): A female swan tries to feed her own flesh to her young during a drought, but they refuse to eat it. The gods respond by granting all of their wishes.

7. Story no. 21 (Chavannes 1910–1934:1, 75–77), translated from *Liudu ji jing*, or *Sūtra on the Collection of Six Perfections* (T. 152): A hare throws himself into a fire to feed an ascetic who lives with him in the forest, but the fire refuses to burn him (equivalent to plotline K above).

8. Story no. 28 (Chavannes 1910–1934:1, 101–104), translated from *Liudu ji jing*, or *Sūtra on the Collection of Six Perfections* (T. 152): An elephant gives his tusks to a hunter (sent by an evil queen) and dies (equivalent to plotline L above).

9. Story no. 67 (Chavannes 1910–1934:1, 245–247), translated from *Liudu ji jing*, or *Sūtra on the Collection of Six Perfections* (T. 152): A merchant kills himself in the ocean so that his drowning companions can use his body to get to shore; Śakra later restores his life (similar to plotline H above).

10. Story no. 139 (Chavannes 1910–1934:1, 411–12), translated from *Jiu za piyu jing* (T. 206): A hare throws himself into a fire to feed an ascetic who lives with him in the forest, but the fire refuses to burn him (equivalent to plotline K above).

11. Story no. 191 (Chavannes 1910–1934:2, 59–61), translated from *Za piyu jing* (T. 207): A king offers his head to a brahmin to bring to another king for a reward, but the gift is not completed (equivalent to plotline F above).

12. Story no. 197 (Chavannes 1910–1934:2, 70–72), translated from *Zhong jing xuan za piyu jing* (T. 208): A king gives his flesh to ransom a dove (the deity Viśvakarman in disguise) from a hawk (the deity Śakra in disguise); his body is later restored by Śakra (equivalent to plotline B above).

13. Story no. 344 (Chavannes 1910–1934:2, 289–293), translated from *Mohe senzi lu* (*Mahāsaṃghika Vinaya* [T. 1425]): An elephant gives his tusks to a hunter and dies (equivalent to plotline L above).

NOTES

Introduction

1. The Buddha's journey to northwest India is not found in any of the standard Buddha-biographies, but does appear, for example, in the *Mūlasarvāstivāda Vinaya.* On this legend, see Strong 1992:23–37, Lamotte 1966, and Przyluski 1914.

2. On this point, see Strong 2004:52–55, Snellgrove 1987:311, and Lamotte 1988:332–337.

3. For translations of this account (T. 2085), see Li 2002, Legge 1965, Giles 1956, and Beal 1884: xxiii–lxxxiii.

4. Trans. Li 2002:169–170.

5. Trans. Li 2002:170.

6. Trans. Li 2002:170.

7. Trans. Li 2002:170.

8. Trans. Li 2002:170.

9. For translations of this account (T. 2087), see Li 1996, Watters 1904–1905, and Beal 1884. See also Wriggins 1996 and Grousset 1932.

10. Trans. Li 1996:78.

11. Trans. Li 1996:95.

12. Trans. Li 1996:94–95.

13. Trans. Li 1996:99.

14. See Foucher 1974 for a detailed account of Xuanzang's travels through the northwest and an attempt to identify the sites he describes with current-day archaeological remains.

15. Trans. Li 1996:86.

16. Trans. Li 1996:86–87.

17. Trans. Li 1996:87.

18. Trans. Li 1996:88.

19. See Foucher 1917: pl. XXX(1).

20. This story is also depicted at Bhārhut, Amarāvatī, Sāñcī, and Ajaṇṭā Cave 10. For a comparison of textual and visual versions of this story, see Cummings 1982:68–73 and Foucher 1917.

21. The same story is also depicted at Amarāvatī, Nāgārjunikoṇḍa, and Mathurā. For a comparison of textual and visual versions of the various stories involving King Śibi, see Parlier 1991, Schlingloff 1988:86–92, and Cummings 1982:74–83.

22. Fr. trans. Lamotte 1944–1980:1, 143. The *Mahāprajñāpāramitā Śāstra* (or *Da zhi du lun,* T. 1509) is attributed to Nāgārjuna, but exists only in a Chinese translation done by Kumārajīva in 404–405 C.E.; moreover, there is scholarly consensus on the fact that the attribution to Nāgārjuna is incorrect, and the text most likely constitutes a Chinese or Central Asian compilation. Nevertheless, since this massive text clearly borrows much from the Indian Buddhist tradition and contains an abundance of interesting material relating to the bodhisattva's bodily self-sacrifice, I will be treating it loosely throughout this book as if it were indeed an Indian Buddhist text.

23. Trans. Bays 1983:1, 249–256; Ensink 1952:22–27; and Shackleton Bailey 1954.

24. Trans. Shackleton Bailey 1954:26.

25. As quoted in Śāntideva's *Śikṣāsamuccaya* (ed. Bendall 1957:21; trans. Bendall and Rouse 1990:23).

26. As quoted in Śāntideva's *Śikṣāsamuccaya* (ed. Bendall 1957:25–26; trans. Bendall and Rouse 1990:28).

27. *dānavarṣaṃ kṛtayugamegha iva vavarṣa* (from *Jātakamālā* 2, ed. Vaidya 1959a:7).

28. *dānaśauṇḍaḥ* (from *Jātakamālā* 2, ed. Vaidya 1959a:8).

29. From *Jātakaṭṭhakathā* 499 (ed. Fausboll 1875–1897:4, 402).

30. *mama ito akkhito satagunena sahassagunena sabbaññutañāṇakkhiṃ eva piyaṃ tassa me idaṃ paccayo hoti 'ti* (from *Jātakaṭṭhakathā* 499, ed. Fausboll 1875–1897:4, 407).

31. Ed. Vaidya 1959b:2, 538, vv. 15–18.

32. Ed. Vaidya 1959b:2, 317–319, vv. 28b–50. I have retained the verse-form of some of the verses.

33. Contained in the eighteenth chapter of the (Mahāyāna) *Suvarṇabhāsottama Sūtra.*

34. Contained in the thirty-second chapter of the *Divyāvadāna.*

35. Ed. Jayawickrama 1974: pt. 2, 12–13, vv. 125–143.

36. *pārami pūrayiṃ* (ed. Jayawickrama 1974: pt. 2, 13, v. 147).

37. Ed. Vaidya 1959b:2, 556–57, vv. 10–17 (in v. 12, reading *-pāśaṃ* rather than *-pāśa-* and *bhṛtyākulaṃ* rather than *-bhṛtyākulā* [see De Jong 1979:262–263]).

38. See the discussion further below and note 50.

39. Ed. Schmidt 1845:171–173.

40. Ohnuma 1998.

41. Given the problems involved in dating early Buddhist texts, it is difficult to say precisely how early in the Buddhist tradition such stories can be placed, but the elephant story (*Ṣaḍdanta Jātaka*), for example, is depicted in art as early as Bhārhut and Sāñcī (second to first centuries B.C.E.).

42. Trans. Horner and Jaini 1985.

43. The *Vessantara Jātaka* is Pāli *Jātaka* 547 (trans. Cowell 1895–1913:6, 246–305 and Cone and Gombrich 1977). For the speculation that the *Vessantara Jātaka*'s enormous popularity may have come at the cost of the gift-of-the-body theme, I am indebted to John Strong (personal communication, September 28, 2004).

44. It is doubtful whether the *Divyāvadāna* can really be classified as a "relatively early" collection. Although it is common to place it in around the fourth or fifth century C.E. (see, for example, Winternitz 1933:284–290 and Weeraratne 1989), Michael Hahn believes that the collection as a whole cannot predate 1000 C.E. (personal communication, March 29, 2005). Nevertheless, substantial portions of the collection are undoubtedly significantly earlier. (On the sources of the *Divyāvadāna,* see Huber 1904, Huber 1906, and Lévi 1907.) It is also important to note that the *Divyāvadāna* exists in several widely varying manuscripts, and the edition published by Cowell and Neil (1970) represents only one version of what seems to have been a somewhat fluid textual tradition.

45. Sanskrit fragments of the *Kalpanāmaṇḍitikā* have been edited in Lüders 1926, and Kumārajīva's Chinese translation of the complete *Kalpanāmaṇḍitikā* has been translated into French by Huber (1908), who mistakenly identifies it

as the *Sūtrālaṃkāra* of Aśvaghoṣa. On the identification of Kumārajīva's text as Kumāralāta's *Kalpanāmaṇḍitikā,* see Hahn 1982. Throughout this book, I rely on Huber's translation.

46. These two texts, whose original Sanskrit contents appear to have come down to us as scattered portions of various anonymous *avadāna* collections, have been painstakingly reconstructed by Michael Hahn (in the case of Haribhaṭṭa, with the help of an existing Tibetan translation). Among his many publications, see especially (in English) Hahn 1992 and 1993. Hahn tentatively dates Haribhaṭṭa to the early decades of the fifth century, and places Gopadatta some time after Haribhaṭṭa but before 800 C.E.

47. The *Mahajjātakamālā* was composed in late medieval Nepal (fourteenth to seventeenth centuries C.E.); half of its contents paraphrase an earlier Mahāyāna *sūtra,* the *Karuṇāpuṇḍarīka Sūtra* (see Tatelman 2000:10). It has been edited by Michael Hahn (1985).

48. Throughout this book, I make use of Paul Harrison's term "Mainstream Buddhism" to refer to traditional, non-Mahāyāna Buddhism. See Harrison 1992:77–78, n. 2.

49. I am drawing on this text (relying on the French translations available in Chavannes 1910–1934) because of the many interesting gift-of-the-body stories it contains, most of which seem closely related to stories existing in Sanskrit or Pāli.

50. Throughout this book, I refer to this text as the *Sūtra of the Wise and the Fool* and rely only on the Tibetan translation, as edited in Schmidt 1845 (I am aware of Takahashi 1969 but was unable to obtain a copy). The Mongolian version has been translated into English in Frye 1981. For the many historical uncertainties surrounding this text, see Mair 1993, Lévi 1925, and Takakusu 1901. Despite the difficulties in making use of it, I have freely drawn on this text because of the several interesting gift-of-the-body stories it contains, most of which seem closely related to stories existing in Sanskrit or Pāli.

51. Dayal 1970:181–187.

52. Dayal 1970:175.

53. Dayal 1970:181–182.

54. Ramanujan 1991:46.

1. "The 'Gift-of-the-Body' Genre"

1. *sarvaṃdadaḥ sarvaparityāgī niḥsaṅgaparityāgī ca mahati tyāge vartate* (ed. Cowell and Neil 1970:316).

2. *rājakrīḍayā krīḍitum ārabdhāḥ* (ed. Cowell and Neil 1970:317).

3. Ed. Cowell and Neil 1970:320.

4. Pāli *Jātaka* 316 and *Cariyāpiṭaka* 1.10.

5. Khoroche 1989:xvii–xviii.

6. My discussion of genre has been influenced by many works, including the following: Duff 2000, Fowler 1991, Rosmarin 1985, Kent 1986, Fowler 1982, Dubrow 1982, Culler 1981, Fowler 1979, Todorov 1976, Jameson 1975, Culler 1975, Guillén 1971, and Fowler 1970.

7. The death of genre has been heralded by everyone from (most famously) the early-twentieth-century Italian philosopher Benedetto Croce (2000) to (more recently) Jacques Derrida (2000).

8. Guillén 1971:109.

9. Jauss 1974. Jauss borrows this phrase from Karl Popper but adapts it to the reading of literature.

10. Propp 1958; see also Propp 1983. The English title *Morphology of the Folktale* is somewhat misleading, since the object of analysis in Propp's work is the fairy tale (types 300–749 in the Aarne-Thompson Tale-Type Index).

11. See Culler 1975 and 1981.

12. See Fowler 1970.

13. Fowler 1982:47.

14. See Rosmarin 1985:3–51 (quoted phrases taken from 25, 46, and 43).

15. I am referring here to the *Sūtra of the Wise and the Fool;* see Introduction (and note 50 therein).

16. I would cite Ajaṇṭā as one such possibility. The caves of Ajaṇṭā contain paintings that depict scenes from Āryaśūra's *Jātakamālā,* with captions that seem to come directly from the text (see Schlingloff 1988). Thus, we can say with some confidence that this text (and its version of these stories) was known by the community of this particular place and time. Moreover, since the dating of Ajaṇṭā's caves is relatively certain, and since inscriptions and other types of evidence give us some indication of the social, historical, and political context of the Ajaṇṭā community, we could perhaps say something about the reception and interpretation of the *Jātakamālā* within this particular context, and also reconstruct its potential readers.

17. Strong 1992:xii.

18. Strong 2004:xv.

19. Collins 1998:78. He also, of course, gives a lengthy theoretical and methodological explanation of this concept and its relationship to historical change (72–89).

20. Hallisey and Hansen 1996:311.

21. Occasionally, however, this does occur. *Mahajjātakamālā* 45, for example, refers to itself as a *dehadānāvadāna,* or "gift-of-the-body *avadāna*" (ed. Hahn 1985:550, v. 173).

22. Pāli *Jātaka* 316, *Jātakamālā* 6, and *Avadānaśataka* 37.

23. Fowler 1982:158.

24. Etymologically, all scholars are in agreement that the term *jātaka* is formed from *jāta* + *ka,* with *jāta* being derived from the Sanskrit verbal root *jan* ("to be born," "to happen," "to occur") and *ka* being an affix—*jātaka* thus indicating "of or relating to birth."

25. The term can also be applied to other Buddhas or advanced bodhisattvas, but is much more commonly associated with the historical Buddha Śākyamuni. Thus Winternitz (1908:491) defines the *jātaka* as "a story in which the Bodhisattva, i.e. the Buddha in one of his former births, plays some part, either that of the hero or of some other character, or sometimes only that of a looker-on." Similarly, various Pāli and Sanskrit dictionaries define the word as "the story of any previous birth of the Buddha" (Rhys Davids and Stede 1989), "a story of a previous birth of the Buddha" (Edgerton 1985), and "the story of a former birth of Gautama Buddha" (Monier-Williams 1979).

26. On the systems of nine and twelve *aṅgas,* see Lamotte 1988:143–147, Kalupahana 1965, and Lamotte 1944–1980:5, 2281–2286.

27. For canonical accounts concerning the "three knowledges" (*trividyā*) obtained by the Buddha during the three watches of the night of his enlightenment, see Bareau 1963:75–91.

28. For the *Jātakanidāna*'s version of this episode, see Jayawickrama 2000:3–35; for the *Buddhavaṃsa*'s version, see Horner 1975: pt. 1, 9–25.

29. In the later Theravādin tradition of Sri Lanka and Southeast Asia, however, the situation is slightly different. Medieval-period Theravādin narrative texts such as the *Mahāsampiṇḍanidāna, Sotaṭṭhakīmahānidāna,* and *Jinakālamālī* stretch the *jātaka* backward in time by up to sixteen more "innumerable eons" to include six lives that occurred before the Buddha's birth as Sumedha. But here too the movement into the past is not infinite; instead these lives begin with the very first life in which the Buddha made a firm vow to attain Buddhahood—but did not yet receive a prediction of his future success. Thus, although these additional lives do not technically deal with the Buddha as a bodhisattva, they do deal with a being who has formally aspired to become a bodhisattva in the future. Beyond this point, the *jātakas* do not extend. On this "extended biography," see Strong 2001:23–27, Derris 2000:1–11, and Gombrich 1972; and for a sensitive analysis of the additional lives recounted in one such text (the *Sotaṭṭhakīmahānidāna*), see Derris 2000:26–123.

30. *Jātakamālā* 5, 12, and 28 (trans. Khoroche 1989:26–35, 84–87, 193–204).

31. Speyer (1958:2, ii–iv) derives *avadāna* from the verb *ava* + *dā*, in the sense of "to cut off, to select," with *avadāna* suggesting "something cut off, something selected," and thus, "notorious facts, *fascinora*," and eventually, "illustrious, glorious achievements." He notes that non-Buddhist writers regularly use the word *avadāna* in the sense of "glorious achievement," and even the *Jātakamālā* itself, in two instances, uses the word in the same way. Thomas (1933:35) and Vaidya (1958:ix) largely concur, with the former defining *avadāna* as "glorious achievement" or "heroic story," and the latter as "good, illustrious, heroic or noble act." While these definitions seem to ignore those *avadānas* that involve wicked deeds (such as those in the fifth section of the *Avadānaśataka*), Winternitz' definition (1933:277–278) does take these into account: "The word *avadāna* means a 'noteworthy deed,' sometimes in a bad sense, but generally in the good sense of 'a heroic deed,' 'a feat,' with the Buddhists a 'religious or moral feat' and then also the 'story of a noteworthy deed, or feat.'" However, an alternative etymology adhered to by Müller (1881:50, n.), Monier-Williams (1979: s.v. *avadāna*), and Takahata (1954:xxi–xxiv) derives *avadāna* from the verb *ava* + *dai*, in the sense of "to cleanse, to purify." Thus, Müller defines *avadāna* as "a legend, originally a pure and virtuous act . . . afterwards a sacred story, and possibly a story the hearing of which purifies the mind," while Takahata claims that it is "beyond doubt that the central idea underlying *avadāna* literature is . . . the purification of mind." In Chinese, however, *avadāna* was rendered as *pi yu*, a word meaning something akin to "parable," "simile," "metaphor," or "illustration"—and in various Buddhist *śāstras*, *avadāna* is explained in similar terms, described as being synonymous with *dṛṣṭānta* ("example"), *upamā* ("simile"), and *aupamyodāharaṇa* ("illustration by way of a simile") (see Matsumura 1980: xiv–xvii for the relevant references). Many Japanese scholars have followed these interpretations, sometimes also proposing an etymological derivation from *ava* + *dā*, in the sense of "to unfasten, to unravel," and thus, "to show clearly or explain by way of illustration."

32. Oldenburg (1893:301), for example, says that *avadāna* is applied to "legends" in general; Burnouf (1844:64) says that the true sense of *avadāna* is "légende, récit légendaire"; and the Pāli Text Society's *Pāli-English Dictionary* defines *apadāna* as "legend, life-history" (Rhys Davids and Stede 1989: s.v. *apadāna*).

33. For example: "[*Avadānas*] usually revolve around two subjects, the explanation of present actions through past actions, and the prediction of rewards or sufferings reserved for the future through present actions" (Burnouf 1844:64); "An *avadāna* is a tale which establishes a relationship between current events and conditions, on the one hand, and past or future events and conditions, on the

other, by reason of the merit or demerit of the acts of a specific individual—the current state being a reward or punishment for past actions, the future state being a reward or punishment for present actions" (Feer 1879:147); "[The main tendency of the *avadāna* is,] on the one hand, to show the irresistible and all-pervading power of Karma towards determining for each creature the course and the fortune of his existences within . . . Saṃsāra, and on the other, to convince the minds of the audience of the individual power of every creature to gather, by means of the performance of good actions, stores of *śuklaṃ karma* [positive karma] which shall have precious results . . . in time to come" (Speyer 1958:2, iv); "The word *apadāna* . . . means 'heroic deed, glorious deed' . . . [The *Apadānas*] are 'tales of the heroic deeds,' i.e., the pious works of the saints (which often consist of very commonplace actions performed in adoration of a Buddha). . . . These stories are, therefore, legends of saints" (Winternitz 1933:157); "The general characteristic of all *avadānas* is that an *avadāna* primarily discusses the consequence of some act good or bad . . . directed towards the Buddha, the Dharma or the Saṅgha, or some other object of religious significance, such as *stūpas*" (Weeraratne 1967:396); "An *avadāna* is a narrative of the religious deeds of an individual and is primarily intended to illustrate the workings of karma and the values of faith and devotion . . . the main protagonist of the *avadāna* is usually . . . [an] ordinary individual, often a layman" (Strong 1983a:22); "[An *avadāna* is] a biography which depicts the workings of karma in the life of an individual or individuals" (Tatelman 2000:5).

34. See, for example, Weeraratne 1967:396–398 and Feer 1891:xii–xiv.

35. See note 27 above.

36. See note 26 above.

37. That is, *avadānika* and *avadānārthakovida* (ed. Vaidya 1958:272 and 275; see the discussion in Strong 1985).

38. Weeraratne 1967:397.

39. Speyer 1958:2, vii–viii.

40. Strong 1977:62.

41. Fr. trans. Feer 1891; trans. Horner 1975: pt. 1.

42. Strong 1977:53–64; see also Strong 1985. The four texts in question are the *Kalpadrumāvadānamālā, Ratnāvadānamālā, Aśokāvadānamālā,* and *Ratnamālāvadāna.* Excluding a few exceptions and irregularities, the *Kalpadrumāvadānamālā* retells stories 1 and 2 from each *varga* of the *Avadānaśataka* (except the fourth); the *Ratnāvadānamālā* retells stories 3 and 4 from each *varga* (except the fourth); the *Aśokāvadānamālā* retells story 10 from each *varga* (except the fourth); and the *Ratnamālāvadāna* retells twenty-one remaining stories that have not already been treated (and excluding any from the fourth *varga*).

43. See, for example, Hibbets 1999a:216–239, and its criticism of Gombrich 1984 and 1996; see also the discussion in Egge 2002:124–125, n. 39.

44. Some of the points I have made in this discussion are echoed in an unpublished paper by John Strong that I received only belatedly. Strong observes, for example: "Avadānas are about acts done in the presence of the Buddha or some other meritorious field; jātakas are about acts done in the absence of such. Another way of putting this, perhaps, is to say that avadānas provide the devotee with models for religious action in a Buddhist milieu, while jātakas provide the devotee with models for religious action in a non-Buddhist milieu. This does not mean that in the jātakas there is no field of merit. Rather, in them, the field of merit and the merit-maker are merged; they are, in fact, one and the same. In the jātakas, the bodhisattva's actions reflect his own glory, while in the avadānas the same actions reflect another's" (Strong 1983b:17).

45. Consider, for example, the aforementioned narratives of the *Buddhavaṃsa* and the *Avadānaśataka*'s second *varga.* If the heroic moral deeds performed by the bodhisattva in the *jātakas* stand in sharp contrast to the ordinary ritual deeds performed by commonplace Buddhists in the *avadānas,* then narratives such as these in which the *bodhisattva worships former Buddhas* serve to bring these two realms together. For it is in these narratives that we suddenly discover that the austere bodhisattva of the *jātakas*—performing moral feats we can only worship but never hope to imitate ourselves—is *also* the ordinary Buddhist who himself made simple offerings of flowers or almsfood to a former Buddha, who himself took advantage of a powerful field of merit. Thus, in this group of stories, the ethos of the *jātaka* is conjoined with the ethos of the *avadāna:* he is us, and we are him. The same point is made in a slightly different way in stories such as those appearing in the first *varga* of the *Avadānaśataka,* in which an ordinary Buddhist makes a ritual offering to the Buddha and receives a prediction of his own future Buddhahood. These stories communicate the message that even when we engage in commonplace, ritual, *avadāna*-type offerings, we become like Sumedha himself and initiate a path that will eventually encompass those *jātaka*-type moral deeds we can only stand in awe of at the present time. Both types of stories mix, in some manner, the ethos of the *jātaka* and the ethos of the *avadāna*—thus ensuring that the life of the Buddha and the ritual of the Buddhist do not become too estranged from each other.

46. "Real *jātakas*" (Speyer 1958:2, v); "unequivocal *jātakas*" (Speyer 1958:2, v); "true *jātakas*" (Speyer 1958:2, xvi); "*jātakas* proper" (Weeraratne 1967:396); "classical *jātakas*" (Feer 1891:xv); "distinctly Buddhist *jātakas*" (Norman 1983:81); etc.

47. Barua 1939:vi; Morris 1882:xv; Horner 1975: pt. 2, vi; Rhys Davids 1880:liv.

48. For example, Khoroche 1989:xi.

49. Trans. Jayawickṛama 2000:58.

50. Trans. Li 2002:206.

51. Notice that much the same is true in the quote by Speyer I gave above (cited in note 39), where a contrast is drawn not between *avadānas* and *jātakas in general,* but between *avadānas* and *jātakas involving gifts of the body.* It is these *jātakas* in particular—what Speyer calls the "world-famed heroic performances" of the bodhisattva—that are called upon to emphasize the stark *contrast* between *jātakas* and *avadānas.*

52. Fowler 1982:37–44.

53. Pāli *Jātaka* 12 (trans. Cowell 1895–1913:1, 36–42).

54. Ed. Fausboll 1875–1897:1, 151.

55. *Divyāvadāna* 27 (trans. Strong 1983a:268–286); *Therīgāthā* 71 (trans. Norman 1971:38–40).

56. However, for an analysis that brings together the story of Subhā and the story of King Śibi's gift of his eyes, see Trainor 1993.

57. Versions of this story include Pāli *Jātaka* 313 (trans. Cowell 1895–1913:26–29) and *Jātakamālā* 28 (trans. Khoroche 1989:193–204).

58. For an interesting discussion of this genre, see Granoff 1991–1992.

59. Trans. Jones 1949–1956:2, 240–242.

60. Trans. Hurvitz 1976:293–302. For a discussion of this theme and its ritual elaborations in China, see Benn 2001, Jan 1965, Filliozat 1963, Gernet 1960, and Kieschnick 1997:35–50.

61. See citations in Lamotte 1944–1980:1, 143–145, n. 1, and 2, 975, n. 1.

62. Durt 1998.

63. In a more recent article, however, Durt (2000) has discussed a somewhat similar story that does feature the bodhisattva as its hero. This is the story (preserved in four Chinese texts) of a seven-year-old boy named Sujāti (a previous birth of the Buddha) who feeds his flesh to his parents when they have no other food, thus demonstrating the virtue of filial piety.

2. *"Conventions of Plot"*

1. Although the *jātakas* themselves are full of wise and noble animals who are capable of making complex moral choices (especially when such animals are previous births of the Buddha himself), the more common view of the animal rebirth in Buddhist literature is that such an existence is full of suffering and wholly governed by the concerns of physical survival. This is the view that ap-

pears to predominate in the depiction of animal recipients within gift-of-the-body *jātakas*.

2. *paritrāyasva mahārāja asmā[n asmā]d vyādheḥ prayaccha jīvitam iti* (ed. Speyer 1958:1, 170).

3. *śastravyagrakaraḥ piṭakān ādāya . . . jīvata eva māṃsāny utkartitum ārabdhaḥ* (ed. Speyer 1958:1, 171).

4. *Sūtra of the Wise and the Fool* 26.

5. In some cases, in fact, epidemic and famine seem to reduce human beings to something well *below* the animal state. In a story from Haribhaṭṭa's *Jātakamālā*, for example, when a woman, dying of starvation during a horrible famine, decides to eat her own newly born son, the bodhisattva compares her unfavorably with a lowly animal, the crow: "Even when afflicted with hunger, a mother crow cares for and nourishes her young, who follow her around with their faces lifted up and their beaks wide open, longing for food and uttering a harsh cry. So how much more should a human woman do so!" (*vyākoṣatuṇḍakam udānanavīkṣamāṇam āhārakāṅkṣiṇam udīritarūkṣaśabdam / puṣṇāti śāvam anugāminam ādareṇa kākī kṣudhā parigatāpi satī kim u strī //;* ed. Hahn 1992:53, v. 16).

6. *mūrtas . . . āśvāsa; śaraṇaṃ; no bandhur abandhūnāṃ; yathā vetsi . . . tathā nas trātum arhasi* (ed. Vaidya 1959a:210–211).

7. Ed. Vaidya 1959a:215.

8. Referred to as the *Pañcakānāṃ Bhadravargikānāṃ Jātakaṃ*.

9. Michael Hahn (1992) believes that this story derives from Gopadatta's *Jātakamālā*.

10. Ed. Handurukande 1984:36–38, vv. 11–14, 16–17.

11. *abhiprasāritamānasāḥ; śaṅkāvyathitahṛdayā; viṣādadainyavidheyāś; cintāviṣayātītagocaram aviṣahyam ativismayanīyaṃ* (ed. Handurukande 1984:44).

12. Ed. Handurukande 1984:44, vv. 32–33.

13. Ed. Handurukande 1984:191–192, vv. 98–111.

14. *Divyāvadāna* 22.

15. *kleśānāṃ daurātmyam* (ed. Handurukande 1967:54).

16. *gyo sgyu; gyo thabs* (ed. Hahn 1974: 188).

17. Two typical examples: In *Avadānaśataka* 31, when King Padmaka becomes a healing fish on behalf of his subjects who are suffering from a terrible illness (i.e., pitiful recipients), the gods cry out with glee: "This great fish has appeared like ambrosia in the sandy river for beings long tormented by great illness!" (*eṣa dīrghakālamahāvyādhyutpīḍitānām amṛtakalpo nadyāṃ vālukāyāṃ mahān rohitamatsyaḥ prādurbhūta iti;* ed. Speyer 1958:1, 171). In contrast, in *Divyāvadāna* 22, when the cruel brahmin Raudrākṣa asks for King Candraprabha's head (i.e., an

evil recipient), the gods have a very different response: "O Sinful Brahmin," they yell at him, "how can you now cut off the head of King Candraprabha, who is irreproachable, non-injurious, affectionate toward many people, and endowed with many virtues?" (*katham idānīṃ tvaṃ pāpabrāhmaṇa rājñaś Candraprabhasyādūṣiṇo 'napakāriṇo mahājanavatsalasyānekaguṇasampannasya śiraś chetsyasīti;* ed. Cowell and Neil 1970:325).

18. For example: *karuṇāsahagataṃ maitracittam utpādya* (from *Divyāvadāna* 22, ed. Cowell and Neil 1970:327); *bhūyasī karuṇā teṣu samabhūt* (from *Jātakamālā* 8, ed. Vaidya 1959a:46); *tīvrakāruṇyaś cintayām āsa* (from *Maṇicūḍāvadāna,* ed. Handurukande 1967:75); *maitracittam upasthāpya* (from *Maṇicūḍāvadāna,* ed. Handurukande 1967:82); *kṣāntiṃ maitrīṃ karuṇāṃ ca vardhayām āsa* (from *Maṇicūḍāvadāna,* ed. Handurukande 1967:84).

19. *rājaiśvaryamadamatto; jīvita . . . tṛṣṇayā vyāmohito; dṛṣṭadhārmikaṃ sāṃparāyikaṃ cānarthaṃ manasi kṛtvaivam ātmano nāśāya pratipannas* (ed. Handurukande 1967:55–56).

20. *udyataśastre 'pi vadhake* (ed. Handurukande 1967:55).

21. Fr. trans. Huber 1908:405.

22. It should be noted, however, that this is not always so easy for the bodhisattva to do. The bodhisattva-elephant in *Kalpanāmaṇḍitikā* 69, for example, actually pauses for a brief moment before giving the hunter his tusks. When the hunter asks him why he is pausing, he replies: "I waited a moment in order to calm down my heart and make my sufferings cease, so that I could recover toward you a heart full of veneration and faith. . . . I do everything with a pure intention. So wait for my heart to be free of all hesitation, so that my reward may be vast and grand" (Fr. trans. Huber 1908:410). This suggestion of inner struggle is a rather remarkable admission on the part of the bodhisattva.

23. See, for example, two verses from Śāntideva's *Bodhicaryāvatāra:* "Like a treasure found in my own house and acquired without any effort, my enemy is one who helps me in the practice that leads to enlightenment; therefore, I should long for him" (*aśramopārjitas tasmād gṛhe nidhir ivotthitaḥ / bodhicaryāsahāyatvāt spṛhaṇīyo ripur mama //* [v. 6.107]; ed. Vaidya 1960:109); "It is precisely as a result of his evil intentions that I give rise to forbearance. Therefore, he alone is the cause of my forbearance; I should worship him as if he were the true dharma" (*tadduṣṭāśayam evātaḥ pratītyotpadyate kṣamā / sa evātaḥ kṣamāhetuḥ pūjyaḥ saddharmavan mayā //* [v. 6.111]; ed. Vaidya 1960:110).

24. *kalyāṇamitraṃ; arthataḥ śikṣayate; kalyāṇam evāstv anayo 'py ato 'sya sabandhumitrasya śaracchatāni* (ed. Handurukande 1984:64). This passage comes from *Avadānasārasamuccaya* 3, which has been attributed by Michael Hahn (1992) to Gopadatta's *Jātakamālā.*

25. *eṣāṃ vadhakānām satvānāṃ raudracittānāṃ nirghṛṇahṛdayānāṃ pāpakāriṇāṃ tyaktaparalokānāṃ akṛtajñānāṃ niṣkāruṇikānām* (ed. Handurukande 1967:91); *cintāmaṇayo bhadraghaṭā dhenavaś ca kāmaduhā guruvac ca devavac ca* (ibid., 92).

26. *yid bzhin nor ni nor tsam ster byed kyi // slong ba'i skye bo yon tan kun 'byung ngo //* (ed. Hahn 1974:174).

27. *'di ni sbyin bdag 'dir bdag slong mo pa // grogs po phyin ci log tu ci phyir byed //* (ed. Hahn 1974:174).

28. See the introduction to Kieckhefer and Bond 1988.

29. To cite just one example: "Due to the radiant power of [the bodhisattva's] virtue, Śakra's marble stone throne became hot" (*tassa sīlatejena sakkassa paṇḍukambalasilāsanaṃ uṇhākāraṃ dassesi;* from Pāli *Jātaka* 316, ed. Fausboll 1875–1897:3, 53).

30. This happens, for example, in *Jātakamālā* 2 (ed. Vaidya 1959a:8), *Jātakamālā* 6 (ibid., 32–33), and *Mahajjātakamālā* 44 (ed. Hahn 1985:517, vv. 43–45).

31. For example: "Śakra, understanding his intention . . ." (*sakko tassa ajjhāsayaṃ viditvā;* from Pāli *Jātaka* 499, ed. Fausboll 1875–1897:4, 403); "Śakra, understanding my intention . . ." (*mama saṅkappam aññāya sakko;* from *Cariyāpiṭaka* 1.8, ed. Jayawickrama 1974: pt. 2, 6, v. 3); "Śakra, understanding my intention . . ." (*mama saṅkappam aññāya;* from *Cariyāpiṭaka* 1.10, ed. Jayawickrama 1974: pt. 2, 12, v. 10).

32. *śakrasya devendrasyādhastāj jñānadarśanaṃ pravartate* (from *Avadānaśataka* 34, ed. Speyer 1958:1, 185); *devatānāṃ cādhastāj jñānadarśanaṃ pravartate* (from *Avadānaśataka* 37, ed. Speyer 1958:1, 210).

33. For example: "I will give a boon to the great king and restore his eye" (*mahārājassa varaṃ datvā cakkhu paṭipākatikaṃ karissāmīti;* from Pāli *Jātaka* 499, ed. Fausboll 1875–1897:4, 408); "Since such a wonderful being should not be made to experience such hardship for long, I will endeavor to restore his eye by showing him how to do it" (*tan nāyam āścaryasattvaś ciram imaṃ parikleśam anubhavitum arhati / yataḥ prayatiṣye cakṣur asyopāyapradarśanād utpādayitum;* from *Jātakamālā* 2, ed. Vaidya 1959a:12); "I should act now in such a manner that this Great Being might obtain excellent, divine vision and [again] be able to see" (*tadyathāyaṃ mahāsattvo labdhvā divyaṃ sudarśanam / paśyet tathā prayatnāni kartum arhāmi sāṃpratam //;* from *Mahajjātakamālā* 44, ed. Hahn 1985:526, v. 164); "The great king has shown his compassion for all beings; it would be right for his body to be rendered as it was previously" (from *Kalpanāmaṇḍitikā* 64, here spoken by Viśvakarman to Śakra, Fr. trans. Huber 1908:339); "This wonderful being should not have to endure such hardship for very long. Is there any way that his body can be restored to its former condition?" (*nārhaty ayaṃ mahātmā ciram imaṃ parikleśam anubhavitum / tat ko 'sāv upāyaḥ syād yenāsya yathāpaurāṇaṃ śarīraṃ syād iti;* from *Maṇicūḍāvadāna*, ed. Handurukande 1967:44).

34. On the Act of Truth, see Brown 1968, 1963, 1940, and Burlingame 1917.

35. Ed. Handurukande 1967:45.

36. Ed. Vaidya 1959a:13.

37. From *Kalpanāmaṇḍitikā* 64 (Fr. trans. Huber 1908:338).

38. From *Avadānaśataka* 34 (ed. Speyer 1958:1, 185–186).

39. From *Jātakamālā* 6 (ed. Vaidya 1959a:35).

40. For example: "I will test the royal hare" (*sasarājaṃ vimaṃsissāmiti;* from Pāli *Jātaka* 316, ed. Fausboll 1875–1897:3, 53); "[Śakra came] in order to test my generosity" (*dānaṃ vimaṃsanāya;* from *Cariyāpiṭaka* 1.10, ed. Jayawickrama 1974: pt. 2, 12, v. 10); "[Śakra came] in order to test him" (*tassa vimaṃsanatthāya;* from Pāli *Jātaka* 499, ed. Fausboll 1875–1897:4, 403); "I will test him" (*vimaṃsayāmi taṃ;* from *Cariyāpiṭaka* 1.8, ed. Jayawickrama 1974: pt. 2, 6, v. 5); "[Śakra,] wishing to test the bodhisattva . . ." (*bodhisattvasya mimāṃsanārthaṃ;* from *Maṇicūḍāvadāna,* ed. Handurukande 1967:28); "Suppose I were to test her?" (*yan nv aham enāṃ mimāṃseyam;* from *Divyāvadāna* 32, ed. Cowell and Neil 1970:473); "I will just test him" (*tam mimāṃsiṣye tāvad enam iti;* from *Jātakamālā* 2, ed. Vaidya 1959a:8); "[Śakra,] wishing to test [the bodhisattva's] character . . ." (*sattvaṃ jijñāsuḥ;* from *Avadānakalpalatā* 55, ed. Vaidya 1959b:2, 334, v. 13).

41. Trans. Khoroche 1989:119–125.

42. *samāpūryamāṇavismayakautūhalena manasā tasya mahāsattvasya bhāvajijñāsayā* (ed. Vaidya 1959a:33).

43. *rājñā dānātirāgeṇa kiṃ svid idaṃ vitarkitam / etat satyam asatyaṃ vā draṣṭuṃ gaccheya tanmanaḥ* (ed. Hahn 1985:517, v. 47).

44. Fr. trans. Huber 1908:330–341.

45. *yesaṃ samādinnattā sakko sakkattaṃ ajjhagā; muttacāgo payatapāṇi vossaggarato yācayogo dānasaṃvibhāgarato* (ed. Feer 1960:1, 228).

46. *pure pure dānaṃ adāsi; sakkacchaṃ dānaṃ adāsi; āvasathaṃ adāsi* (ed. Feer 1960:1, 229).

47. *dānaṃ hi loke sakkasampattiṃ deti* (ed. Rhys Davids and Carpenter 1968–1971:2, 472).

48. *chattiṃsakkhattuṃ kho panāhaṃ bhikkhave sakko ahosiṃ devānam indo* (ed. Morris 1955–1961:4, 89).

49. *mā haiva sā rūpāvatī strī ataḥ śakraṃ bhavanāc cyāvayet* (from *Divyāvadāna* 32, ed. Cowell and Neil 1970:473); *rūpyāvatī mām amarapurāt pracyāvya svayaṃ eva devādhipatyaṃ kartukāmā syād iti* (from *Jātakamālā* [of Haribhaṭṭa] 6, ed. Hahn 1992:55).

50. This story comes from the *Liudu ji jing* (T. 152) (Fr. trans. Chavannes 1910–1934:1, 7–11 [story no. 2]).

51. Fr. trans. Chavannes 1910–1934:1, 10 (story no. 2).

52. Pāli *Jātaka* 523 (trans. Cowell 1895–1913:5, 79–84). Isisiṅga is more commonly known in Indic tradition by his Sanskrit name Ṛṣyaśṛṅga; for a discussion of several different Hindu and Buddhist versions of his story, see O'Flaherty 1981:42–50.

53. The depiction of Śakra within gift-of-the-body stories that I have elucidated here is consistent with his depiction throughout Indian Buddhist literature as a whole. As Charles Godage has noted (1945), Śakra appears in Indian Buddhist texts as a humanized, moral, and beneficient character who respects the Buddha, recognizes his inferiority to him, and is interested in hearing his teachings, but who is also "not in any way free from general human weaknesses" such as ignorance and fear (60).

54. *mahābrāhmaṇa gṛhytāṃ yad abhirucitaṃ na me 'tra vighnaḥ kaścit astīti* (ed. Speyer 1958:1, 185).

55. *adhīratayā cakampe; sādhvasākulitamatiś* (ed. Handurukande 1984:78).

56. Ed. Handurukande 1984:80, vv. 68–69.

57. *tyaktvā . . . krodhābhidhānaṃ viṣam* (ed. Handurukande 1984:84, v. 82).

58. Fr. trans. Huber 1908:421.

59. *so pana aggi bodhisattassa sarīre lomakūpamattam pi uṇhaṃ kātuṃ nāsakkhi* (ed. Fausboll 1875–1897:3, 55).

60. *sītodakaṃ . . . sameti . . . pariḷāhaṃ* (ed. Jayawickrama 1974: pt. 2, 13, v. 17). The commentary glosses *sameti* as *vūpasameti.*

61. From the *Jiu za piyu jing* (T. 206) (Fr. trans. Chavannes 1910–1934:1, 411–412 [story no. 139]).

62. From the *Liudu ji jing* (T. 152) (Fr. trans. Chavannes 1910–1934:1, 71–72 [story no. 19]). I have not encountered an Indic version of this story.

63. Fr. trans. Lamotte 1944–1980:2, 662.

64. *phalena saha sarvasvatyāgacittāj jane 'khile / dānapāramitā proktā tasmāt sā cittam eva tu //* (v. 5.10, ed. Vaidya 1960:53).

65. *cetanāhaṃ bhikkhave kammaṃ vadāmi; cetayitvā kammaṃ karoti kāyena vācāya manasā* (ed. Morris 1955–1961:3, 415). In relation to *dāna,* however, this was apparently not an uncontested point. In the *Kathāvatthu* (7.4), for example, in relation to the proposition that "*dāna* is a mental state rather than the object given," the text has the Rājagirikas and Siddhatthikas agreeing with this point, while the Theravādins disagree (trans. Aung and Rhys Davids 1915:198–200).

66. *saccabalena mahārāja avatthumhi dibbacakkhu uppajjati saccaṃ yeva tattha vatthu bhavati dibbacakkhussa uppādāya* (ed. Trenckner 1880:120; emphasis added).

67. For example: in Pāli *Jātaka* 499, in company with the Act of Truth, Śakra tells King Śibi to "choose a boon," and the resulting eyes are later said to have been "given by Śakra" (*varaṃ varassu; sakkabrāhmaṇassa . . . dinnacakkhuṃ;* ed.

Fausboll 1875–1897:4, 409 and 410); in *Jātakamālā* 2, Śakra again tells King Śibi to "choose a boon," and later tells him, "these eyes of yours were given by me" (*varaṃ vṛṇīṣva; pratidatte te mayeme nayane;* ed. Vaidya 1959a:12 and 14); and in the *Maṇicūḍāvadāna,* King Maṇicūḍa's restoration of his body by means of an Act of Truth is immediately preceded by Śakra's administration of "quickly strengthening and stimulating medicines" (*sadyobalābhis saṃjīvanībhir auṣadhībhir;* ed. Handurukande 1967:44).

68. This is the case, for example, in two Chinese versions of the story of King Śibi's gift of flesh to ransom a dove (one from the *Liudu ji jing* [T. 152], Fr. trans. Chavannes 1910–1934:1, 7–11 [story no. 2], and one from the *Zhong jing xuan za piyu jing* [T. 208], Fr. trans. Chavannes 1910–1934:2, 70–72 [story no. 197]), as well as in the Tibetan *Lokānandanāṭaka,* where King Maṇicūḍa's flesh is restored directly by the earth goddess.

69. Granoff 1991–1992.

70. Granoff 1991–1992:168.

71. See, for example, Van Gennep 1960 and Turner 1995, 1987, 1977, and 1974.

72. Ed. Yamada 1968:2, 381–382.

73. *nidhikoṭīnayutaśatasahasrāṇi nidhānānāṃ* (ed. Yamada 1968:2, 382); *saptasaptavarṣakoṭīnayutaśatasahasreṣv* (ibid., 383); *gaṅgānadīvālikāsameṣu* (ibid., 383).

74. *svastyayanena . . . mahatā* (ed. Vaidya 1959a:44).

75. Ed. Vaidya 1959a:45.

76. Ed. Vaidya 1959a:48–49.

77. As Khoroche (1989: xviii) has pointed out, the superiority of Buddhist morality to the *realpolitik* or *nīti* of the *Arthaśāstra* is a consistent theme throughout the *Jātakamālā.* See also Meadows (1986:9–10), who summarizes numerous passages in the *Jātakamālā* in which the dharma proper to a good Buddhist king is explicitly contrasted with *nīti.*

78. *paraṃ prasādaṃ vismayaṃ copajagmuḥ* (ed. Vaidya 1959a:51); *hiṃsā bhavadbhir viṣavad vivarjyā / lobhaḥ paradravyaparigraheṣu vāg garhitā madyamayaś ca pāpmā* (ibid., 53).

3. "Conventions of Rhetoric"

1. Collins (1998) usefully emphasizes what is sometimes easy to forget: the non-obviousness of transcendent religious values. "A transcendental vision is not one of the immediate givens of everyday life; rather, it sets the everyday in a larger, and consciously critical (because not obvious) frame" (1998:39). Elsewhere, he reminds

us: "the overall intolerable condition responded to by a spiritual conception of salvation, a soteriology, is not necessarily, indeed is not usually an ailment or form of distress . . . in any immediate physical or psychological sense" (107).

2. My interpretation here is slightly different from that of Edith Parlier (1991). In her comparison between Hindu and Buddhist versions of the story of King Śibi's gift of his flesh to ransom the life of a dove, Parlier observes that the Hindu versions of this story (specifically, those found in the *Mahābhārata*) demonstrate "the total equation between general interests and particular interests which characterizes Hindu dharma" (143), whereas the Buddhist versions, in stark contrast, "emphasize the radical opposition between mundane preoccupations and the search for bodhi, between universal welfare and particular interests" (145). I agree with Parlier that the Buddhist versions of this story do set up and emphasize this opposition—at least initially. Nevertheless, the outcome of the story as a whole, in my opinion, performs much the same sort of reconciliation between worldly and spiritual goals as we find in a more obvious form in the Hindu versions. Parlier herself, in fact, later observes that even within the Buddhist versions, King Śibi appears to be able to resume his royal functions once he has given the gift (153).

3. Collins 1998:38–40.

4. Collins (1998) argues that the "syntactic" (rather than semantic) function of nirvana has previously been ignored—the fact that the concept of nirvana acts as "a narrative closure-marker, both in narrated time and in the time of narration" (234) and "provides the sense of an ending in the Buddhist master text" (117). See Collins 1998, esp. 121–133 and 234–281.

5. MacIntyre 1981:221.

6. It should further be noted that A-B-C in all of the above formulas is very often (though not always) a version of the standard bodhisattva vow for Buddhahood, whose consistent usage within these formulas further lends to their conventional quality.

7. *śīghraṃ śiraḥpradānād dhi labheya bodhim* (from *Divyāvadāna* 22, ed. Cowell and Neil 1970:324).

8. *andhe loke anāyake apriṇāyake buddho bhūyāsam atīrṇānāṃ sattvānāṃ tārayitā amuktānāṃ mocayitvā anāśvastānām āśvāsayitā aparinirvṛtānāṃ parinirvāpayiteti* (from *Avadānaśataka* 37, ed. Speyer 1958:1, 210–211).

9. *na vāham etaṃ yasasā dadāmi na puttam icche na dhanaṃ na raṭṭhaṃ* (from Pāli *Jātaka* 499, ed. Fausboll 1875–1897:4, 406).

10. *na prāpyam asti me kiṃcil loke 'smin kiṃ tv annuttarām / hitāya sarvajagatāṃ samyaksaṃbodhim arthaye //* (from *Avadānakalpalatā* 55, ed. Vaidya 1959b:2, 337, v. 52).

11. From *Kalpanāmaṇḍitikā* 64 (Fr. trans. Huber 1908:337–338).

12. From *Sūtra of the Wise and the Fool* 22 (ed. Schmidt 1845:144–145).

13. From *Maṇicūḍāvadāna* (ed. Handurukande 1967:43–44).

14. From *Jātakamālā* 30 (ed. Vaidya 1959a:212).

15. From *Divyāvadāna* 32 (ed. Cowell and Neil 1970:478).

16. From *Jātakamālā* 1 (ed. Vaidya 1959a:5).

17. Speyer 1895:6, n. 1.

18. Ed. Rhys Davids and Carpenter 1975–1982:3, 258–260; ed. Morris 1955–1961:4, 239–241.

19. *tassa taṃ cittaṃ hīne 'dhimuttaṃ uttariṃ abhāvitaṃ tatr' upapattiyā saṃvattati* (*Dīgha Nikāya*, ed. Rhys Davids and Carpenter 1975–1982:3, 258–260, passim). The *Aṅguttara Nikāya* passage is identical except that it substitutes *vimuttaṃ* for *adhimuttaṃ* (ed. Morris 1955–1961:4, 239–241, passim).

20. *dānaṃ cittālaṃkārārthaṃ dānaṃ cittapariṣkārārthaṃ yogasaṃbhārārtham uttamārthasya prāptaye dānaṃ* (*Abhidharmakośabhāṣya* 4.117, ed. Pradhan 1975:270).

21. *cittālaṅkāracittaparikkhāratthaṃ*, found first in a list enumerating eight "types of gift" (*dānāni*) (ed. Morris 1955–1961:4, 235–236), and then in a list enumerating eight "occasions for giving" (*dānavatthūni*) (ibid., 236–237).

22. Fr. trans. Lamotte 1944–1980:2, 664.

23. *bodhisattvasya ca . . . dānaṃ . . . sarvasattvahitahetos tad . . . 'bhyādānam agram* (*Abhidharmakośabhāṣya* 4.117, ed. Pradhan 1975:270).

24. *tad dhi samyaksambodhyarthaṃ sarvasattvārthañ ca* (ed. Śāstrī 1998: 744–745).

25. Fr. trans. Lamotte 1944–1980:2, 677.

26. More specifically, the gift that is "indifferent to reward" (*vipākānapekṣa*) is first listed as one of the ten different forms of the bodhisattva's "pure gift" (*viśuddhaṃ dānaṃ*) and subsequently defined as follows: "The bodhisattva, having given a gift, does not expect in the wake of that gift either material or bodily good fortune as a reward. He sees all conditioned states as being worthless, and supreme Buddhahood [alone] as a blessing" (ed. Dutt 1978a:94).

27. *dānapāramitā . . . mūrtimatī* (from *Jātakamālā* [of Haribhaṭṭa] 6, ed. Hahn 1992:53, v. 27).

28. It is interesting to note that Edith Parlier's analysis of visual depictions of the story of King Śibi (as they appear at Amarāvatī and Nāgārjunakoṇḍa) also emphasizes two of these groups, those of *royal ministers* and *women*. She first notes that these depictions emphasize "the profound opposition between the supreme gift and the temporal order, between the universal welfare that the Bodhisattva has in view and the interests of the kingdom." As evidence for this opposition, she notes that within these depictions: "The king is generally surrounded by sev-

eral assistants. Among them, one can sometimes recognize one of the ministers who, according to the texts, tried to restrain the king . . . but it is especially the fear manifested by the assistants or the women of the palace . . . which demonstrates to what degree the gesture of the king impacts upon his entourage. Even more so than in the sculpture of Gandhāra, the women incarnate better than any other figure, the temporal order that is compromised by the sacrifice of the king" (1991:153).

29. Ed. Hahn 1985:522, vv. 105–107, 109a.

30. *cakṣuṣā kiṃ daridrasya parābhyudayasākṣiṇā / dhanam eva yato dehi deva mā sāhasaṃ kṛthāḥ //* (ed. Vaidya 1959a:10).

31. Ed. Cowell and Neil 1970:323.

32. The *dāna* appropriate to an Indian king, as well as many other aspects of the dharmaśāstric notion of *dāna,* are summarized in Kane 1941:837–888.

33. Collins 1998:414–496.

34. Collins 1998:420.

35. Collins 1998:420.

36. Collins 1998:422.

37. The importance of giving whatever object is asked for is frequently emphasized in our stories. As King Śibi puts it (in *Jātakamālā* 2), "One should give exactly what has been asked for, for unwanted gifts are not pleasing. What use is water to one being carried off by a flood? Therefore, I will give him what he wants!" (*yad eva yācyeta tad eva dadyān nānīpsitaṃ prīṇayatīha dattam / kim uhyamānasya jalena toyair dāsyāmy ataḥ prārthitam artham asmai //;* ed. Vaidya 1959a:11).

38. The beneficial effects of good kingship on the natural world are a common theme within our stories. They are evocatively portrayed, for example, in *Jātakamālā* [of Haribhaṭṭa] 6: "Then the rain clouds gave them water, seasonably and to their hearts' content, and no natural disasters ever gave them trouble. With that Lord of the Earth ruling the earth through good government, people no longer heard even the word 'suffering.' The rice grew abundantly without being cultivated, and the trees were always laden with flowers and fruit. With that good king ruling the kingdom, as if he were [the first ruler] Pṛthu, the water-buffalo gushed forth such abundant milk, they virtually milked themselves" (ed. Hahn 1992:56, vv. 39–40).

39. Ed. Handurukande 1967:35.

40. Ed. Vaidya 1959a:48.

41. Ed. Hahn 1985:549, vv. 155, 160.

42. *taddharmasatyaprabalānubhāvāt sarvatra rājyeṣv api maṅgalāni* (ed. Hahn 1985:530, v. 211).

43. Trans. Johnston 1984: pt. 2, 123–140.

44. Ed. Hahn 1985:518, vv. 54–56 (emphasis added).

45. *sevakā hi prabhor dharma utsāhaṃ vardhayanty api* (ed. Hahn 1985:520, v. 83 [emphasis added]); *deva . . . dharme 'nusaṃraktāś carāmahe 'nujīvinaḥ* (ibid., v. 86 [emphasis added]).

46. . . . *sahasā kāryasādhanam / samīkṣya sādhayet kāryaṃ saddharmasukhasiddhaye //* (ed. Hahn 1985:520, v. 90 [emphasis added]).

47. Ed. Hahn 1985:521, vv. 96–97, 99.

48. Ed. Hahn 1985:523–524, vv. 128–137, 141–143.

49. *divi devādhipaḥ sudhīḥ* (ed. Hahn 1985:514, v. 6); *sarvatrāpi mahītale sarve sattvā durācārāḥ* (ibid., v. 5); *tān samuddhartuṃ samutsāhaṃ samādadhau* (ibid., v. 8); *martyān dharmaratān kartuṃ* (ibid., v. 9); *śibirājakule janma labdhvā* (ibid., v. 10).

50. *sa jagaddhitārthaṃ saṃbodhicittaḥ pracaraṃś* (ed. Hahn 1985:530, v. 213).

51. *sukṛtaṃ karma* (ed. Hahn 1985:514, v. 2).

52. *prākarod dharmasādhanam* (ed. Hahn 1985:530, v. 215); *prajāṃś . . . śāstuḥ saddharmasādhanam / śrāvayan bodhimārgeṣu niyujya pātum arhati //* (ibid., v. 217).

53. *etatpuṇyānubhāvena sarvadā te śubhaṃ bhavet / krameṇa bodhisaṃbhāraṃ pūrya bodhiṁ avāpnuyāḥ //* (ed. Hahn 1985:531, v. 218).

54. It should be noted here that the external framework involving a dialogue between Upagupta and King Aśoka is not unique to this story alone; it is characteristic, in fact, of many later *avadāna* collections (including all of the *Avadānamālās*); on this point, see Strong 1985. Nevertheless, this does not negate the specific form in which the framework appears and the significance it plays within this particular story.

55. See, for example, Wilson 1994.

56. Ed. Handurukande 1967:40–41. Despite the pathos of Padmāvatī's lament, one wonders whether the epithets "Hero in Generosity," "Protector of the World," and "Sinless One" don't carry a hint of sarcasm here. In fact, later on, when Maṇicūḍa has agreed to give both Padmāvatī and their son Padmottara away (in an act reminiscent of Vessantara), Padmāvatī's remarks in the *Lokānandanāṭaka*'s version of the story almost seem to drip with sarcasm, for she tells her son matter-of-factly: "Take a good look at your father, for His Majesty has completely abandoned us" (*'phags pa'i bus bdag cag yongs su btang zin gyis yab la legs su ltos shig;* ed. Hahn 1974:146).

57. Trans. Johnston 1984: pt. 2, 104–122. The hurt, suffering, and indignation experienced by the Buddha's wife Yaśodharā (also called Bimbā) after he re-

nounces the world are emphasized in a particularly effective manner in a popular northern Thai text known as "Bimbā's Lament"; see Swearer 1995.

58. Trans. Cone and Gombrich 1977:65–74.

59. *Mahābhārata* 2.27.62 (trans. van Buitenen 1975:148–149).

60. Turner 1995:94–130.

61. One could again compare this to Vessantara's behavior in the *Vessantara Jātaka* after giving away his children. Though Vessantara's wife Maḍḍi spends the entire night lamenting, searching for her children, and repeatedly pleading with Vessantara to tell her of their fate, Vessantara says nothing to her for many hours (other than a brief and particularly cruel exchange in which he accuses her of sexual infidelity). In the Cone and Gombrich translation (1977), she begins lamenting to him on page 69, and he doesn't inform her of the children's fate until the bottom of page 73.

62. *hā kaṣṭaṃ katham idānīṃ yūyaṃ pāpabrāhmaṇa imaṃ rājarṣiṃ paramakāruṇikaṃ sarvasatvavatsalam adūṣiṇam anapakāriṇaṃ praghātayateti* (ed. Handurukande 1967:81).

63. *raudracitta pāpabrāhmaṇa mā praviśeti* (ed. Cowell and Neil 1970:322).

64. Throughout this discussion of minor deities, I use the masculine pronouns "he," "him," and "his" as a matter of convenience, but within the texts themselves, the gender is not clear, since the feminine noun *devatā* (the term most commonly used) can refer to masculine deities as well as feminine ones.

65. Ed. Handurukande 1967:81–82.

66. Ed. Schmidt 1845:145.

67. *mamottamāṅgayācanakasyāntarāyaṃ mā kuru / eṣa eva devate sapṛṣṭhībhūto maitrīyo yo vyāghryā ātmānaṃ parityajya catvāriṃśatkalpasaṃprasthito Maitreyo bodhisattva ekena śiraḥparityāgenāvapṛṣṭhīkṛtaḥ /* (ed. Cowell and Neil 1970:326). The correct interpretation of the second sentence is somewhat problematic. Jaini (1988:58) takes both *pṛṣṭhībhūto* and *avapṛṣṭhīkṛtaḥ* as "turned his back on [imminent Buddhahood]" and translates the passage as follows: "This is [the spot], O guardian deity, where Maitreya had turned away. [How?] Maitreya the bodhisattva, who had [once] abandoned himself to a tigress and had proceeded [on the bodhisattva course] for forty *kalpas,* had been compelled to turn his back upon [his career because of a similar obstruction] in once giving away his head." The same interpretation is suggested by Edgerton (see Edgerton 1985: s.v. *pṛṣṭhībhūta, avapṛṣṭhīkṛta,* and *Maitrīyo*). When translated in this way, the idea seems to be that Maitreya had practiced the bodhisattva path for a long time, and had even sacrificed himself to a tigress, yet because he was once hindered in giving away his head, his attainment of Buddhahood was significantly delayed. (On the general

idea that Maitreya should have become a Buddha before Śākyamuni, but at some point was placed on a "slow track" to Buddhahood, see La Vallée Poussin 1928 and Strong 1992:54–55.) However, I am not convinced that this is the correct translation. It seems to me that the passage may be somewhat garbled, and that its real intent may be to say that Śākyamuni himself (not Maitreya), as a bodhisattva, sacrificed himself to a tigress at that very spot and thus outdistanced Maitreya by a single gift of his head. In fact, Śākyamuni's surpassing of Maitreya does play a role in various versions of the tigress story, for Maitreya is sometimes identified as the companion who went in search of food while Śākyamuni, the bodhisattva, was giving his body to the tigress. In *Divyāvadāna* 32, for example, the Buddha says of his gift to the tigress: "And thus, Monks, Maitreya Bodhisattva, who had set out on a journey [for Buddhahood] forty eons before, was outdistanced by a single gift of my throat" (*tadā me bhikṣavaś catvāriṃśatkalpasaṃprasthito Maitreya Bodhisattva ekena galaparityāgena paścānmukhīkṛtaḥ;* ed. Cowell and Neil 1970:481). Thus I would interpret *pṛṣṭhībhūto* and *avapṛṣṭhīkṛtaḥ* in the prior passage in the same passive sense as *paścānmukhīkṛtaḥ* in this passage, and translate: "Maitreya was outdistanced [by me] . . ."

68. On this general process, see Decaroli 2004.

69. *sahajā vṛttir* (ed. Vaidya 1959b:2, 334, v. 14); *nisargasiddham* (ibid., 335, v. 15).

70. *mayi pārāvataprītyā na dveṣaṃ kartum arhasi / . . . yathaivāyaṃ tathaivāhaṃ ko viśeṣas tavāvayoḥ / sarvabhūtasamāḥ santaḥ kṛpāṃ naikatra kurvate //* (ed. Vaidya 1959b:2, 335, vv. 18–19). In another version of the story (involving a hawk rather than a hunter), the hawk similarly says to King Śibi: "O King, how can you be benevolent toward others while denying me my nourishment?" (from *Liudu ji jing* [T. 152], Fr. trans. Chavannes 1910–1934:1, 9 [story no. 2]). Likewise, in a third version, he says: "O King, if you want to save all living beings, I am among these beings. How can I be the only one not to have pity taken upon him . . . ?" (from *Zhong jing xuan za piyu jing* [T. 208], Fr. trans. Chavannes 1910–1934:2, 70 [story no. 197]).

71. *cintāmaṇiḥ kila vicintitavastudātā kalpadrumaś ca parikalpitam eva sūte* (ed. Vaidya 1959b:2, 334, v. 1); *śuśrāva pṛthivīkāryam asaṃkhyair iva vigrahaiḥ* (ibid., 334, v. 8).

72. Fr. trans. Huber 1908:333.

73. *sman med pa'i nad* (ed. Hahn 1974:68).

74. *mthu chen po khyod kyi lus so* (ed. Hahn 1974:78).

75. *lus rab tu slong ba sring mo de srid nas spobs pa can gyi skye bo slongs mo pa bdag gis mthong ngo* (ed. Hahn 1974:80).

76. Ed. Hahn 1974:80.

77. *ci'i phyir shin tu snying rje bas // de'i phyir bdag ni yongs su spong //* (ed. Hahn 1974:112).

78. It is interesting to note that in the *Maṇicūḍāvadāna* Gautama is a minor character (a sage Maṇicūḍa encounters in the forest) who offers only weak opposition to Maṇicūḍa's actions and is soon won over by his arguments. In the *Lokānandanāṭaka,* on the other hand, Candragomin has rather brilliantly turned Gautama into a *vidūṣaka* (the comical friend of the male hero in a Sanskrit drama), who opposes Maṇicūḍa's actions, deflates Maṇicūḍa's pretences, and becomes the strongest voice of opposition and moral conscience throughout the entire play. This is in keeping with the role of the *vidūṣaka;* see, for example, the following statements from G. K. Bhat's (1959) thorough study of the *vidūṣaka:* "The Vidūṣaka enjoys another privilege: His tongue is free. He can make fun of everybody, including the king and the queen" (65); "The jokes which the Vidūṣakas cut in the presence of the king, particularly those that are directed against the hero himself, have often the quality of wisdom inspired by the knowledge of the world" (99); "the Vidūṣaka assumes the role of a critic, symbolising, as it were, the 'conscience of the play'" (139); "[the Vidūṣaka's wit] manifests itself very often as innocent nonsense; but occasionally it is crammed with practical wisdom. In fact, the Vidūṣaka often becomes the mouthpiece of sound commonsense" (167).

79. *gnyen 'dun 'jig rten rnams kyi don mdzad pa la de las ci'i phyir ring du sdod par byed* (ed. Hahn 1974:76). Later on in the play Maṇicūḍa himself is forced to admit, "I am making my relatives suffer!" (*nye du'i skye bo sdug bsngal bar bya'o;* ibid., 164).

80. *snying rje med pa* (ed. Hahn 1974:70); *mnyes gshin pa 'ang . . . mi 'dug* (ibid.); *snying rje ba yang med* (ibid., 74).

81. Fr. trans. Lamotte 1944–1980:2, 979–981.

82. Fr. trans. Lamotte 1944–1980:2, 980.

83. *ka utsahate tiryagyonigatasyārthāya jīvitaṃ parityaktum . . . aham utsahe tiryagyonigatasyārthāya jīvitaṃ parityaktum* (ed. Cowell and Neil 1970:478).

84. *aho madīyā gamitā prakāśatāṃ khaṭuṅkatā vikramasaṃpadānayā* (ed. Vaidya 1959a:6).

85. *kim etat sāhasaṃ tīvraṃ viruddhaṃ bhavatā kṛtam* (from *Avadānakalpalatā* 104, ed. Vaidya 1959b:2, 557, v. 19).

86. Fr. trans. Huber 1908:335.

87. *pidhāya śravaṇau yayuḥ* (ed. Vaidya 1959b:2, 336, v. 39); *dāruṇamatir nāmnā kapilapiṅgalaḥ* (ibid., v. 40).

88. *nāhaṃ śakṣyāmi devasya śiraś chettum iti* (ed. Cowell and Neil 1970:325).

89. Fr. trans. Huber 1908:408.

90. See, for example, *Suvarṇabhāsottama Sūtra* 18 (ed. Nobel 1937:214); *Maṇicūḍāvadāna* (ed. Handurukande 1967:46, 78, and 94); *Sūtra of the Wise and the Fool* 22 (*rnam pa drug tu gyos;* ed. Schmidt 1845:145); *Sūtra of the Wise and the Fool* 14 (*rnam pa drug tu gyos te;* ed. Schmidt 1845:85); *Kalpanāmaṇḍitikā* 64 (Fr. trans. Huber 1908:338); etc.

91. One of the Sanskrit words for "mountain" is *acala,* and one of the Sanskrit words for "earth" is *acalā*—both terms literally meaning "immovable."

92. *aśivāni nimittāni* (from *Divyāvadāna* 22, ed. Cowell and Neil 1970:321); *paramadāruṇāni nimittāni* (from.*Maṇicūḍāvadāna,* ed. Handurukande 1967:90); *apraśastāni nimittāni* (ibid.).

93. Compare, for example, two passages from the *Maṇicūḍāvadāna:* the moment when Maṇicūḍa gives away his crest-jewel (ed. Handurukande 1967:88–89) and the moment when the crest-jewel is restored (ibid., 94–95).

94. Spoken by *devas, nāgas, yakṣas, gandharvas, asuras, kinnaras,* and *mahoragas* when King Śibi first begins cutting off his flesh in *Kalpanāmaṇḍitikā* 64 (Fr. trans. Huber 1908:336).

95. *hā hā kaṣṭaṃ praghātito 'yaṃ mahātmā maharṣir* (from the *Maṇicūḍāvadāna;* spoken by *devas* when King Maṇicūḍa gives away his crest-jewel; ed. Handurukande 1967:89).

96. *aho bataudāryam aho kṛpālutā viśuddhatā paśya yathāsya cetasaḥ* (from *Jātakamālā* 2; spoken by "flocks of great supernatural beings" [*maharddhibhir bhūtagaṇaiḥ*] when King Śibi's eyes are restored; ed. Vaidya 1959a:14).

97. *rgyal po zla 'od kyis mgo sbyin pa byas pas / sbyin pa'i pha rol tu phyin pa yang yongs su rdzogs par gyur to* (from *Sūtra of the Wise and the Fool* 22, ed. Schmidt 1845:145).

98. From *Kalpanāmaṇḍitikā* 64 (Fr. trans. Huber 1908:341).

99. Though I am concerned in this discussion only with the discursive functions fulfilled by Śakra within the gift-of-the-body genre, I should note that Śakra fulfills many such discursive functions throughout Buddhist narrative literature in general. In the *Avadānakalpalatā,* for example, it is Śakra's questioning of the Buddha that is used to set many of the stories into motion.

100. *sakkhissasi nu kho dātuṃ udāhu no ti* (from Pāli *Jātaka* 499, ed. Fausboll 1875–1897:4, 403). Although Śakra is here speaking to himself, the question actually translates as "Will *you* be able to give them or not?"—as if he were imagining himself speaking to King Śibi.

101. *kim ayaṃ śibi rājā sattvānām artham evaṃ karoti uta karuṇayā* (from *Avadānaśataka* 34, ed. Speyer 1958:1, 185). The *uta* is problematic (see Speyer's note 2 on the same page).

102. *dānātiharṣoddhatamānasena vitarkitaṃ kiṃsvid idaṃ nṛpeṇa / ābadhya dānavyavasāyakakṣyāṃ svagātradānasthiraniścayena //* (from *Jātakamālā* 2, ed. Vaidya 1959a:8).

103. From *Kalpanāmaṇḍitikā* 64 (Fr. trans. Huber 1908:331).

104. From *Kalpanāmaṇḍitikā* 64 (Fr. trans. Huber 1908:336–337).

105. *mahārāja mā haiva te vipratisāro bhūd iti* (ed. Handurukande 1967:37).

106. From *Kalpanāmaṇḍitikā* 64 (Fr. trans. Huber 1908: 337).

107 *karmabhis tvam īdṛśair aho suduṣkareṇa vyavasāyena ca kiṃ prārthayasa iti* (from *Maṇicūḍāvadāna*, ed. Handurukande 1967:43).

108. From *Liudu ji jing* (T. 152) (Fr. trans. Chavannes 1910–1934:1, 10 [story no. 2]).

109. *imām avasthāṃ gamitasya yācakaiḥ kathaṃ nu te saṃprati teṣu mānasam* (from *Jātakamālā* 2, ed. Vaidya 1959a:12).

110. *mahārāja mā haiva te śarīraṃ tyakṣāmiti vā parityajito vā parityājyo vā bhūt cetaso 'nyathātvaṃ vipratisāro veti . . . katham etad jñāyate iti* (from *Maṇicūḍāvadāna*, ed. Handurukande 1967:44–45).

111. From *Kalpanāmaṇḍitikā* 64 (Fr. trans. Huber 1908:339–340).

112. *api te stanadānena mano vikṛtim āyayau* (from *Avadānakalpalatā* 51, ed. Vaidya 1959b:2, 316, v. 14).

113. *satyaṃ te rūpāvati dārakasyārthāyobhau stanau parityaktau / . . . evaṃ te rūpāvati ubhau stanau parityajāmīti parityajantyāḥ parityajya vābhūc cittasya vipratisāraḥ / . . . atra kaḥ śraddhāsyati /* (from *Divyāvadāna* 32, ed. Cowell and Neil 1970:473).

114. *kim aindram amunā sthānaṃ tapasā vijigīṣase / kutūhalavaśād bhadre pṛcchāmi bhavatīm aham //* (from *Jātakamālā* [of Haribhaṭṭa] 6, ed. Hahn 1992:55, v. 33).

115. Fr. trans. Chavannes 1910–1934: 2, 289–293 (story no. 344).

116. Fr trans. Chavannes 1910–1934:2, 290.

117. The only link between the *Mohe senzi lu* version's innovations and the extant Indic originals is a brief statement made by the elephant in Pāli *Jātaka* 514. In this version, the hunter has been sent for the tusks by an evil queen, and the elephant muses at one point that perhaps the queen has done this because she knows that "I have many excellent pairs of tusks, which I got from my fathers and ancestors" (*bahū hi me dantayugā uḷārā / ye me pitunnam pi pitāmahānaṃ;* ed. Fausboll 1875–1897:5, 51). Nevertheless, he never makes any attempt to substitute these tusks in place of his own.

118. Fr. trans. Chavannes 1910–1934:1, 17–19 (story no. 5).

119. Fr. trans. Chavannes 1910–1934:1, 18.

120. There is a large body of scholarly literature on narrative, ethics, and theology. For one useful anthology, see Hauerwas and Jones 1997.

121. Hallisey and Hansen 1996:314–316.

122. Hallisey and Hansen 1996:316–317.

4. "Dāna: *The Buddhist Discourse on Giving*"

1. The theoretical scholarship on gift-giving is voluminous, but see, for example, the following: Diprose 2002, Godelier 1999, Godbout and Caillé 1998, Coles 1997, Starobinski 1997, Derrida 1995 and 1992, Mauss 1990, Cheal 1988, Strathern 1988, Hyde 1979, and two edited collections that bring together a number of programmatic pieces, Schrift 1997 and Komter 1996.

2. Mauss 1990.

3. See Dayal 1970:172 for an enumeration of lists including *dāna.*

4. The scholarship on gift-giving in South Asia is again voluminous, but see, for example, the following. For South Asian Buddhism: Egge 2002, Falk 1990, Strong 1990, Endo 1987, Weeraratne 1984, Strenski 1983, Strong 1979, Dayal 1970:172–193, Ames 1966, and Findly 2003 (in regard to the last source mentioned, I regret that I became aware of this book too late to incorporate many of its insights). For Vedism and Hinduism: Michaels 1997, Parry 1994:119–148, Acharya 1993, Raheja 1988, Nath 1987, Parry 1986, Trautmann 1986 and 1981:77–93, Gonda 1975, Hara 1974, Gonda 1965, and Kane 1941:837–888. For discussions incorporating Hinduism, Buddhism, and Jainism: Hibbets 2000, 1999a, and 1999b; Brekke 1998; and Babb 1996:174–195.

5. Though this is an aspect of the gift that falls outside the scope of this study, it is also obvious that the gift in Buddhism has had profoundly material and economic consequences. Indeed, the category of the gift has a concrete material presence that many other valued categories within Buddhist discourse utterly lack, for most of the physical objects that embody Buddhism in time and space—such as *stūpas,* images, paintings, texts, monasteries, monks and nuns—can be identified and conceptualized as *gifts.* This material and economic aspect of the gift cannot be overemphasized: the very existence of "Buddhism" as such has been dependent upon the gift (a point made most forcefully, perhaps, in Strenski 1983).

6. Eng. trans. Mauss 1990.

7. Mauss 1990:54–60.

8. Including, for example, Trautmann 1981 and 1986, Parry 1986, Raheja 1988, and Michaels 1997.

9. Mauss 1990:146–147, n. 61.

10. Trautmann 1981:278–282.

11. Trautmann 1981:287.

12. Trautmann 1981:279.

13. Parry 1986:462.

14. Michaels 1997:259.

15. Parry 1986:468.

16. *adāsi meti dānaṃ deti; dassati meti dānaṃ deti* (ed. Morris 1955–1961:4, 236).

17. *pratīkārānapekṣaṃ; na parataḥ pratyupakāraṃ pratyāśaṃsate* (ed. Dutt 1978a:94).

18. See, for example, Hibbets 1999a, Strenski 1983, and Ames 1966. However, Egge (2002:140, n. 149) does cite a passage from the *Itivuttaka* that "praises the reciprocity of the lay-monastic relationship," in which "laypeople supply monastics with their material needs, and monks teach the Dharma to laypeople; thus homeless and householders live the religious life in mutual dependence." He also speculates that "similar notions of reciprocity have no doubt played a much larger role in the attitudes of Buddhists than they do in textual ideologies."

19. See Spiro 1982:410 and Bunnag 1973:60. The same is true of Hindu *dāna;* as Trautmann (1981:287–288) notes, "Because the donee is the benefactor, it is a feature of this etiquette that he makes no expression of thanks, a characteristic of Indian life much puzzling to Westerners."

20. See, for example, Spiro 1982:200, Gombrich 1971:117–118, and King 1964:153.

21. See Schopen 1997:114–147, 148–164, 258–289.

22. *kathaṃ tatrāpratigṛhṇati kasmiṃścit puṇyam* (v. 4.121, ed. Pradhan 1975:272).

23. *yadi hi puṇyaṃ parānugrahād eva syāt maitryādyapramāṇasamyagdṛṣṭibhāv anāyāṃ na syāt* (v. 4.121, ed. Pradhan 1975:272).

24. *abhyatīte 'pi; svacittaprabhavaṃ* (v. 4.121, ed. Pradhan 1975:272).

25. *caitye tyāgānvayaṃ puṇyaṃ paribhogānvayaṃ puṇyaṃ nāsti* (v. 4.121, ed. Pradhan 1975:272).

26. See, for example, Gombrich 1971:150–152 and Ames 1966.

27. Compare the similar distinction drawn in the *Bhagavad Gītā,* where gifts "given in due time and place to a fit recipient who can give no advantage" are classified as *sāttvika,* and gifts "given reluctantly, to secure some service in return or to gain a future reward" are classified as *rājasa* (vv. 17.20–21, trans. Miller 1986:140).

28. Trautmann 1981:281.

29. Such passages are too numerous to cite individually, but see, for example, *Dīgha Nikāya* (ed. Rhys Davids and Carpenter 1975–1982: 3, 258–260) and *Aṅguttara Nikāya* (ed. Morris 1955–1961: 2, 62–64; 2, 202–205; 3, 32–34; 3, 172–173).

30. *piyassa dātā piyaṃ labhatīti* (from the Pāli *Jātaka* collection, ed. Fausboll 1875–1997: 4, 401); *sahassena samaṃ mitā* (from *Saṃyutta Nikāya,* ed. Feer 1960:1, 18).

31. See the Pāli *Jātaka* collection (ed. Fausboll 1875–1897:3, 471).

32. See *Saṃyutta Nikāya* (ed. Feer 1960:1, 18).

33. Spiro 1982:111–112.

34. *sugatiṃ saggaṃ lokaṃ uppajjissāmīti dānaṃ deti* (ed. Morris 1955–1961:4, 236).

35. *ekacco sāpekho dānaṃ deti paṭibaddhacitto dānaṃ deti sannidhipekho dānaṃ deti imaṃ pecca paribhuñjissāmiti dānaṃ deti* (ed. Morris 1955–1961:4, 60).

36. *cittaṃ hīne 'dhimuttaṃ* (ed. Rhys Davids and Carpenter 1975–1982:3, 258–260, *passim*).

37. Malinowski 1932: chapter 6.

38. *yo vītarāgo vītarāgesu dadāti dānaṃ . . . taṃ ve dānaṃ āmisadānānam agganti* (ed. Trenckner 1888–1925:3, 257).

39. *sarveṣāṃ tu dānānām agraṃ muktasya muktāya* (v. 4.117, ed. Pradhan 1975:270).

40. *tadvipākabhūmer atyantasamatikrāntatvāt* (v. 4.114, ed. Pradhan 1975:269).

41. Derrida 1992.

42. See the many references in Lamotte 1944–1980:1, 297, n. 2.

43. Michaels 1997:259.

44. Starobinski 1997:64.

45. Silber 1995.

46. *cittaparikkhāratthaṃ* (from *Aṅguttara Nikāya,* ed. Morris 1955–1961:4, 235–236 and 236–237); *uttamārthasya prāptaye* (from *Abhidharmakośabhāṣya,* v. 4.117, ed. Pradhan 1975:270).

47. *vipākānapekṣaṃ; paramabodhāv anuśaṃsadarśī* (ed. Dutt 1978a:94).

48. *na . . . vinā parasukhenāsti sukham; tasyāyutasaukhyatvād* (ed. Lévi 1907–1911: chapter 17, v. 53).

49. This is nicely summed up, in fact, by a single half-verse from the *Kośa*'s discussion of giving (v. 4.117, ed. Pradhan 1975:270). This half-verse first observes that among all gifts, "the best is the gift given by one liberated person to another liberated person" (*agraṃ muktasya muktāya*)—in other words, the gift of an arhat.

It then adds, "or a gift from the bodhisattva" (*bodhisattvasya ca*), and finally concludes, "or the eighth" (*aṣṭamam*)—that is, the gift given for the sake of attaining arhatship (the "eighth" in the Buddha's list of eight gifts). The "best gift" is thus restricted to arhats, those aspiring to arhatship, and all bodhisattvas.

50. Ed. Trenckner 1888–1925:3, 255.

51. Ed. Morris 1955–1961:4, 394–395.

52. *āhuneyyo pāhuneyyo dakkhiṇeyyo añjalikaraṇīyo anuttaraṃ puññakkhettaṃ lokassāti* (found throughout the Pāli Canon; see, for example, the partial list of citations and brief discussion found at Egge 2002:140, n. 1).

53. *viceyyadānaṃ* (a concept found, for example, in the *Saṃyutta Nikāya* [ed. Feer 1960:1, 21] and the Pāli *Jātaka* collection [ed. Fausboll 1875–1897:3, 472]).

54. *sīlavato dinnaṃ mahapphalaṃ vadāmi, no tathā dussīle* (ed. Feer 1960:1, 161).

55. *kṣetradoṣāt tu tad bījam alpaphalaṃ vā bhavaty aphalaṃ vā* (v. 4.121, ed. Pradhan 1975:272–273).

56. Egge 2002:34–39, Hibbets 2000:36–37.

57. *pūjānugrahakāmyayā* (v. 4.113, ed. Pradhan 1975:268).

58. Gombrich 1971:248. The same distinction is common among Burmese monks, according to Melford Spiro (1982:109): "To contribute to the support of a monk, to erect a pagoda, to offer flowers to a Buddha image—these are *dāna.* To contribute to the support of a widow, to build a school, to bring flowers to the sick—these are not, or at best are inferior *dāna;* little if any merit is to be gained from them."

59. *ebhyaḥ pañcabhyaḥ pṛthagjanabhūtebhyo 'py aprameyā phalato dakṣiṇā bhavati* (v. 4.118, ed. Pradhan 1975:271).

60. *Kathāvatthu* 17.11 (trans. Aung and Rhys Davids 1915:321–322).

61. Ed. Morris 1955–1961:1, 161.

62. *kukṣetre 'pīṣṭaphalatā phalabījāviparyayāt* (v. 4.121, ed. Pradhan 1975:272).

63. Egge 2002. Some of the same ground is also covered in Brekke 1998, but Egge's treatment is much more comprehensive.

64. Egge 2002:62. Much the same explanation is offered by Brekke (1998:311), who states: "[The worthy-recipient doctrine] is an ideology serving the interests of the religious specialists. The aspirations to domination of this class rests on this ideology. If people do not believe in the special merit of giving to the renouncers, the renouncer will not receive alms. This has, of course, been clear to monks and Brahmins and they have worked to keep the ideology alive and gloss over its clash with the ethics of intention."

65. Hibbets 2000.

66. Hibbets 2000:34, 38.

67. Hibbets 2000:37. Brekke (1998:293) similarly notes that Jain discussions of *dāna* suggest that the donor should be characterized by *aparibhāvitvā,* or an "absence of condescension towards the recipient," and that the "condescension which naturally arises in the charitable donor towards the beggar" would therefore tend to undermine the donor's proper frame of mind.

68. *natvevāhaṃ ānanda kenacī pariyāyena saṅghagatāya dakkhiṇāya pāṭipuggalikaṃ dānaṃ mahapphalataraṃ vadāmi; dussīlā pāpadhammā* (ed. Trenckner 1888–1925:3, 256).

69. *saṅghaṃ uddissa* (ed. Trenckner 1888–1925:3, 256).

70. As Brekke (1998:290) has pointed out, however, this is not merely a case of muddled thinking, but rather a useful and productive inconsistency that has been "used creatively to invest all gifts with merit. When the gift is seen as a sacrifice the excellent qualities of the recipients are in the foreground. When the gift is seen as charity it is the good intentions of the giver which are highlighted. The good qualities of the recipient ensure the merit in an act of sacrifice whereas the bad qualities of the recipient do not affect the merit in an act of charity. Gifts are never in vain if the giver can switch between the two alternative merit-making mechanisms as he pleases." This flexibility of interpretation is particularly useful when it comes to justifying the practice of almsgiving to religious renunciants, since the renunciant could be viewed as *either* a worthy and godlike recipient who deserves one's worship and offerings *or* a poor and helpless beggar who is dependent upon one's charity.

71. Trautmann 1981:278–288.

72. On the duties and privileges of each of the four *varṇas,* as outlined in the Dharma Śāstras, see Kane 1941:2, pt. 1, 105–164. On brahmins as the exclusive human recipients of religious gifts, the *Manusmṛti,* for example, says: "Whatever wealth exists on this earth—all that belongs to the *brāhmaṇa;* the *brāhmaṇa* deserves everything on account of his superiority due to his descent [from the mouth of the Creator]" (*Manusmṛti* 1.100, as quoted in Kane 1941:2, pt. 1, 135).

73. See Kane 1941:2, pt. 2, 837–888.

74. So says the commentator Medātithi, commenting on *Manusmṛti* 4.5, as quoted in Kane 1941:2, pt. 2, 842.

75. Kane 1941:2, pt. 2, 842.

76. Kane 1941:2, pt. 2, 843.

77. Kane 1941:2, pt. 1, 114; see also 2, pt. 2, 846.

78. Kane 1941:2, pt. 1, 116. He adds (in note 249): "The idea is that *pratigraha* is a privilege, while charity to the poor and the diseased is due to *dayā* (compassion)."

79. On this *kṣatra-dharma,* see Hara 1974.

80. This *kṣatriya*-ethic of conquest and liberality can perhaps be related to the general tendency within Indian thought to assimilate kings to gods—for Gonda (1975) has observed a very similar ethic in relation to the gods as far back as the *Ṛg Veda*. According to him, the hymns of the *Ṛg Veda* consistently suggest that generosity is "an essential part of the god's function" and "characteristic of his very nature as a powerful divine being" (129), that the god gives such gifts by "fall[ing] back upon [his own] abundance of possessions" (130), and that these possessions have generally been "won, gained or acquired . . . by force" (131).

81. Thus, in the *Mahābhārata*, a *kṣatriya* says: "I am a Kṣatriya and never know the expression 'give me.' We are those who say [only] 'give me a battle.'" Similarly, Yudhiṣṭhira says to Duryodhana, "it is not a right thing (*dharma*) for a warrior to accept [what is given]," and King Ikṣvāku says to Kauśika, "Kṣatriyas are said to be the givers [so] how can I take [this] from you?" (*Mahābhārata* 12.192.41, 9.30.53b, and 12.192.73b, as quoted in Hara 1974:302–303).

82. One might compare, for example, the following passages. In the *Mahābhārata, kṣatriyas* are constantly being urged to fight: "Fight with no self-interest, having simply recourse to strength and valour. For there is nothing more auspicious for Kṣatriyas than fighting" (*Mahābhārata* 6.117.32, as quoted in Hara 1974:299). In a similar fashion, Śāntideva encourages the bodhisattva to fight against his enemies, the afflictions: "In the vanguard of the battle, powerful men violently attack those dark enemies of theirs who are destined by nature to die. Ignoring the painful blows of arrows and spears, they do not turn back until they have succeeded. So even if I should experience a hundred misfortunes today, what reason could I possibly have to feel the misery of despair when I have set out to conquer my natural enemies—[the afflictions]—who are the constant cause of every sort of pain? . . . Let my entrails ooze out if they wish to! Let my head fall off—who cares? But never in any way will I bow down before my enemies, the afflictions!" (vv. 4.37–38 and 4.44, ed. Vaidya 1960:46).

83. Hara 1974:297–299. The *Mahābhārata*, for example, says of the *kṣatriya:* "A man of strength [*vīrya*] can overcome enemies, even when he lacks all other virtues. But what will he accomplish, a man without strength, even when he possesses all other virtues?" (*Mahābhārata* 2.15.10, as quoted in Hara 1974:299).

84. Of course, if the bodhisattva is also a monk, then he is obligated to accept the gift of alms—but in some contexts, this receiving-rather-than-giving seems to have caused him some degree of consternation. Thus, in the *Ugraparipṛcchā Sūtra*, it is said that the bodhisattva should beg for alms "for as long as he lives"—yet even as he accepts these alms, he thinks to himself, "I should live by my own power, not in dependence upon another" and "I will not rely on any man, woman, boy, or girl" (trans. Nattier 2003:287–288).

85. *dakṣa utthānasampannaḥ svayaṃkārī sadā bhavet / nāvakāśaḥ pradātavyaḥ kasyacit sarvakarmasu //* (v. 5.82, ed. Vaidya 1960:69).

86. *kleśasvatantro loko 'yaṃ na kṣamaḥ svārthasādhane / tasmānmayaiṣāṃ kartavyaṃ nāśakto 'haṃ yathā janaḥ //* (v. 7.50, ed. Vaidya 1960:128).

87. *mayaivaikena kartavyam* (v. 7.49, ed. Vaidya 1960:128).

88. *yat kiṃcid anavadyaṃ karma āpatitaṃ bhavati sattvānām tat sarvaṃ mayaivaikena kartavyam / nānyasyāvakāśo dātavya ity arthaḥ //* (commentary on *Bodhicaryāvatāra* 7.49, ed. Vaidya 1960:128).

89. Nattier 2003:147.

90. See Strong 1990.

91. For an English translation of this episode, see Strong 1983a:264–268; see also Strong 1990.

5. "A Flexible Gift"

1. Consider, for example, the ordinary laywomen discussed in Durt 1998 who make gifts of their own flesh.

2. This statement is made, for example, in the commentary to the *Cariyāpiṭaka* (see Horner 1975:2, 14, n. 1).

3. Fr. trans. Lamotte 1944–1980:1, 255.

4. See verses 1.6–13 (ed. Meadows 1986:158–161). The Ārya Śūra who authored the *Pāramitāsamāsa* is most likely distinct from, and several centuries later than, the Ārya Śūra who authored the *Jātakamālā* (for this argument, see Meadows 1986:1–21).

5. *dāna-parikkhārā; dānassa pāramī; pārami pūrayiṃ* (ed. Jayawickrama 1974: pt. 2, 13, v. 146). A similar threefold distinction (but applied to all ten Theravādin perfections, not just *dāna*) is discussed in the Conclusions.

6. Fr. trans. Lamotte 1944–1980:2, 750–751.

7. Fr. trans. Lamotte 1944–1980:2, 701.

8. As related, for example, in *Kalpanāmaṇḍitikā* 71, *Avadānasārasamuccaya* 3, and *Mahajjātakamālā* 45.

9. Ed. Yamada 1968: vol. 2, 376, 378, 379.

10. Ed. Cowell and Neil 1970:320.

11. Ed. Vaidya 1959b:2, 334–337. This story is called the *Sarvaṃdadāvadāna* and refers to its main character as Sarvaṃdada throughout, yet tells the traditional story of King Śibi's gift of flesh to ransom a dove.

12. *sarvaṃdado nāma kathaṃ kadā vā yasya svadehe 'pi manaḥprasaṅgaḥ / yathārthanāmā tv adhunā bhaviṣyāmy* (ed. Handurukande 1984:74, v. 47).

13. *yadi dāsyati Sarvaṃdado bhaviṣyati, atha na dāsyati na Sarvaṃdado bhaviṣyati* (ed. Yamada 1968:2, 378–379).

14. *yadi tāvat sarvaṃdado bhaviṣyati mama śiro dāsyaty* (ed. Cowell and Neil 1970:320).

15. "To make a gift of something to someone is to make a present of some part of oneself . . . to accept something from somebody is to accept some part of his spiritual essence, of his soul" (Mauss 1990:12). This identity between *giver* and *gift* is so strong within Indic discourse that Trautmann (1986) and Parry (1986), for example, both speculate that Mauss perhaps derived this idea from the Indic material itself. For even as far back as the *Ṛg Veda,* in fact, Gonda has remarked upon the "close connection between a god's character and the benefits he bestows on his worshippers" (1975:127), and concluded therefrom that the gods are really being "implored to give part of their own nature . . . essence or substance" (126). Thus, "giver and gift are not only connected by a tight bond, the latter is also part of the very being and essence of the former" (128).

16. See, for example, Van Gennep 1960 and Turner 1995, 1987, 1977, and 1974.

17. *mayā bāhiravatthuṃ adinnaṃ nāma natthi, na maṃ bāhiradānaṃ toseti, aham ajjhattikadānaṃ dātukāmo* (ed. Fausboll 1875–1897:4, 402).

18. Ed. Dutt 1978a:80. In other cases, the distinction between "internal" and "external" gifts is clearly assumed, even though this terminology is not made explicit. The *Pāramitāsamāsa,* for example, advises the bodhisattva to think: "May those who desire my flesh take my flesh; may he who desires even my bone marrow take my bone marrow by drawing it out. For I bear this wretched body for the sake of the world—how much more an external object!" (*māṃsārthino māṃsam idaṃ harantu majjānam apy uddharaṇāt tadarthī / ahaṃ hi lokārtham idaṃ bibharmi śarīrakaṃ kiṃ bata vastu bāhyam //;* v. 1.7, ed. Meadows 1986:158).

19. Fr. trans. Lamotte 1944–1980:2, 688.

20. *dāsakammaṃ karissāmi* (ed. Fausboll 1875–1897:4, 402).

21. *suduccajaṃ . . . purisena duccajan* (spoken by King Śibi to describe the gift of his eyes in Pāli *Jātaka* 499, ed. Fausboll 1875–1897:4, 403). The idea that the gift of the body is an exceedingly difficult gift to give is a common conceit within gift-of-the-body stories.

22. Trans. Khoroche 1989:22–25.

23. *evam atyayam apy avigaṇayya ditsanti satpuruṣāḥ / kena nāma svasthena na dātavyaṃ syāt /* (ed. Vaidya 1959a:23).

24. *mahārāja dānaṃ nāma na kevalaṃ samparāyatthaṃ eva dīyati, diṭṭhadhammatthāya pi paccayo hoti* (ed. Fausboll 1875–1897:4, 409). Rouse interprets this sentence as three separate phrases (the first phrase ending after

kevalaṃ), and translates: "The gift is not everything in itself, Your Majesty, it is given with an eye to the future. Yet there is a motive relating to this visible world" (see Cowell 1895–1913:4, 255). I interpret the sentence as two phrases only, with *na kevalaṃ* and *eva* basically performing the same function. I believe this makes better sense.

25. *atha sa rājā pradānasamucitatvād anabhyastayācñākārpaṇyamārgo* (ed. Vaidya 1959a:12).

26. Ed. Vaidya 1959a:12–13.

27. *ko 'yam asmān vikatthayitum atrabhavato nirbandhaḥ* (ed. Vaidya 1959a:13).

28. Ed. Vaidya 1959a:14–15.

29. Ed. Fausboll 1875–1897:3, 51.

30. Ed. Fausboll 1875–1897:4, 401.

31. Sahlins 1996.

32. Lévi-Strauss 1969.

33. Strenski 1983.

34. Mauss 1990:10–13.

35. Lévi-Strauss 1997:55.

36. Lévi-Strauss 1997:53.

37. Bourdieu 1996:135.

38. Bourdieu 1996:142.

39. Gonda 1975:132.

40. Gonda 1975:133.

41. Gonda 1975:133.

42. For example: "Today I will give a gift that has never been given by me before" (*ajjāhaṃ mayā nadinnapubbaṃ dānaṃ dassāmi;* from Pāli *Jātaka* 316, ed. Fausboll 1875–1897:3, 54); "Today I will give you an excellent gift that has never been given before" (*adinnapubbaṃ dānavaraṃ ajja dassāmi te ahaṃ;* from *Cariyāpiṭaka* 1.10, ed. Jayawickrama 1974: pt. 2, 12, v. 12); "I will give a gift that has never been given before" (*adinnapubbadānaṃ dassāmīti;* from Pāli *Jātaka* 499, ed. Fausboll 1875–1897:4, 403); "Today I will give to a supplicant an excellent gift never given before" (*adinnapubbaṃ dānavaraṃ ajja dassāmi yācake;* from *Cariyāpiṭaka* 1.8, ed. Jayawickrama 1974: pt. 2, 6, v. 12).

43. *aho sudinnaṃ mayā akkhidānan ti* (from Pāli *Jātaka* 499, ed. Fausboll 1875–1897:4, 407).

44. *dehaṃ parair dustyajam* (from *Suvarṇabhāsottama Sūtra,* chapter 18, ed. Nobel 1937:212).

45. From *Kalpanāmaṇḍitikā* 69 (Fr. trans. Huber 1908:410).

46. "Good Son, I will tell you in brief of the perfection of generosity. [I will tell you] how, as I was practicing the bodhisattva conduct, I sacrificed the sacrifice of a gift, [and how] no other bodhisattva previously sacrificed the sacrifice of such a gift, [and how] there will be no bodhisattva [in the future] who, as he practices the conduct leading to enlightenment, will sacrifice the sacrifice of such a gift, as I sacrificed [such a gift], when I was practicing the bodhisattva conduct—except for [the following] eight good men . . ." (from *Karuṇāpuṇḍarīka Sūtra,* chapter 5, ed. Yamada 1968:2, 355).

47. From *Kalpanāmaṇḍitikā* 64 (Fr. trans. Huber 1908:336).

48. *utsahe 'haṃ sarvasatvānām arthe eka eva sarvaduḥkhāny udvoḍhuṃ* (from *Maṇicūḍāvadāna,* ed. Handurukande 1967:84).

49. "I have given this gift, along with its fruit, to living beings because their happiness is my happiness. Be as fruitful for them as you can be, if you feel any obligation toward me!" (*saphalaṃ dānaṃ dattaṃ tan me satveṣu tatsukhasukhena / phala teṣv eva nikāmaṃ yadi me kartavyatā te 'sti //;* ed. Lévi 1907–1911: chapter 17, v. 54).

50. *akṛtaṃ na phalasi yasmāt pratikārāpekṣayā na me tulyaṃ / pratikāranirvyapekṣaḥ paratra phalado 'sya kāmaṃ te //* (ed. Lévi 1907–1911: chapter 17, v. 58).

51. *viśuddha-dāna; asaṃbhṛta; na utsahate* (ed. Dutt 1978a:93).

52. *kṣaṇam api dānena vinā dānābhirato bhavati naiva //* (ed. Lévi 1907–1911: chapter 17, v. 57).

53. *bhogā bahuśubhatar[ā]; na hi tatsukhaṃ mataṃ me dāne pāraṃparo 'smi yataḥ* (ed. Lévi 1907–1911: chapter 17, v. 55).

54. Hibbets 2000:37.

55. Shulman 1993:121.

56. *anunnata-dāna; nīcacitto bodhisattvo dānaṃ dadāti / na ca paraspardhayā dadāti / na ca . . . tena dānena manyate aham asmi dātā dānapatir anye ca na tatheti* / (ed. Dutt 1978a:94).

57. Verses 6.112–116 (ed. Vaidya 1960:110–111).

58. As Jan Nattier (2003:135) has noted: "The potential for arrogance on the part of the practitioner who is striving for such a glorious goal [as Buddhahood] is a theme that pervades the earliest bodhisattva literature, and various coping tactics are recommended in order to aid the bodhisattva in dealing with this threat." One especially interesting "coping tactic" cited by Nattier is the "rhetoric of negation" characteristic of many Mahāyāna *sūtras,* or "the use of negative language to undermine reification, and thus the very conceptual basis for pride, in what the bodhisattva is undertaking." She notes that many such negations are applied not to dharmas in general but to the bodhisattva himself and the practices

he engages in, and then adds (135–136, n. 62): "It is my strong suspicion that this 'rhetoric of negation' first emerged as a tactical attempt to undercut the potential for bodhisattvas' arrogance, and was only later generalized to what came to be considered a new (anti-abhidharma) ontology."

59. Trans. Tin 1975:340–375.

60. *sīmāsambhedo kātabbo* (ed. Rhys Davids 1975:307).

61. Fr. trans. Lamotte 1944–1980:1, 255.

62. Fr. trans. Lamotte 1944–1980:2, 750–751.

63. Fr. trans. Lamotte 1944–1980:1, 297–298.

64. Wilson 2002.

65. Cited in Wilson 2002:62.

66. Cited in Wilson 2002:61.

67. That is, *dāna* as a means of purifying the donor through the physical transfer of his "sin" or "inauspiciousness" to the recipient via the medium of the gift. This interpretation of *dāna* has been explored, for example, in Heesterman 1985 and 1993, Parry 1994, and Raheja 1988. Although there seems to be ample ethnographic evidence for this view of *dāna,* its relevance to the textual sources is far less certain. Hibbets (1999a:137–146), for example, denies that there is any evidence for this view in Hindu, Buddhist, and Jain medieval digests on *dāna.* Similarly, I do not see any solid evidence for this view in regard to the bodhisattva's gift of his body; however, I have treated this issue speculatively, at least, in Ohnuma 1997:284–292.

68. See esp. Mauss 1990:33–43.

69. Carrithers 1985 (in reference to Mauss 1985).

70. As Olivelle (1997:445, n. 6) points out: "Carrithers appears to restrict *personne* to those societies that have legally defined citizenship carrying rights and responsibilities" and "denies that such a category is applicable to the Indian *varṇa* system." Olivelle, on the other hand, thinks that "selfhood within the *varṇa* system is very much a *personne,* because it is defined by one's belonging to a particular social group, a belonging that carries rights and responsibilities, even though that group is not the nation-state" (see also his discussion on 429–431).

71. See also Olivelle 1992: chapter 2.

72. Dumont 1980:274–275.

73. Lee 1967.

74. Dumont (1980:274–275) says of the world-renouncer: "In leaving the world he finds himself invested with an individuality which he apparently finds uncomfortable since all his efforts tend to its extinction or its transcendence."

75. *attā hi attano nātho attā hi attano gati / tasmā saññāmay' attānaṃ . . .* (v. 380, ed. Von Hinüber and Norman 1994:107).

76. Parry 1986, esp. 458–459 and 466–469.
77. Parry 1986:469.
78. On this point, see especially Chakravarti 1987 and Findly 2003.

6. *"Bodies Ordinary and Ideal"*

1. Bateson 1908:758. This quote appears to be a summary of the views expressed in Sir Monier Monier-Williams' *Buddhism,* published in 1889.

2. Gregory Schopen (1997:1–22), for example, has discussed the "Protestant" bias by which the disembodied ideas found in Pāli and Sanskrit textual sources have been regarded as the location of "real" religion and overwhelmingly preferred over archaeological, epigraphical, and art historical sources, which are perceived as the abode of "popular" religion precisely because they relate more closely to material things. (His argument is well taken; however, he does tend to construct his own reverse-hierarchy between texts and inscriptions, arguing that inscriptions are a direct reflection of "what Indian Buddhists actually did" [1997:8–9] and what they "actually practiced and believed" [1997:1] instead of perceiving them as another kind of text.) Philip Almond (1988:13) dates this "textual reification of Buddhism" to the first half of the nineteenth century. He states: "Originally existing 'out there' in the Oriental *present,* Buddhism came to be determined as an object the primary location of which was the West, through the progressive collection, translation, and publication of its textual *past.* Buddhism, by 1860, had come to exist, not in the Orient, but in the Oriental libraries and institutes of the West, in its texts and manuscripts, at the desks of the Western savants who interpreted it. It had become a textual object, defined, classified, and interpreted through its own textuality. By the middle of the century, the Buddhism that existed 'out there' was beginning to be judged by a West that *alone* knew what Buddhism was, is, and ought to be. The essence of Buddhism came to be seen as expressed not 'out there' in the Orient, but in the West through the West's control of Buddhism's own textual past." Many of the same issues are discussed in relation to Theravādin Buddhist studies in Hallisey 1995, and in relation to Tibetan Buddhist studies in Lopez 1995a and 1998:156–180.

3. This is not merely a problem of Western assumptions confronting Eastern materials; the same problem is encountered in the interpretation of the West's own past. In regard to Christianity, for example, much of Caroline Walker Bynum's work on medieval religion has aimed to get beyond the dualistic view assumed in modern thought and to show that medieval Christian thinkers perceived of the

person as a psychosomatic unity and highly valued the body as a means of access to the divine (see, for example, Bynum 1987, 1989, 1991, and 1995).

4. The "rematerialization" of religious studies as a discipline can be easily traced, for example, in the recent volume *Critical Terms for Religious Studies* (Taylor 1998) and its highlighting of terms such as "body," "gender," "image," "relic," "performance," "territory," and "writing"—as well as its deconstruction of terms such as "belief" and "rationality." See the review by David Chidester (2000), which notes that "the best essays in this collection suggest an emergent horizon for the study of religion that might be called a new materialism. Attentive to the body, the senses, gender, sexuality, location, exchange, power relations, and other material conditions, most of the authors implicitly recast religion as a category for analyzing materiality" (374). See also the discussion in Terry Godlove's "Saving Belief: On the New Materialism in Religious Studies," which is an argument for "saving belief" (Godlove 2002). The "rematerialization" of religious studies might itself be seen within the context of the "rematerialization" of the humanities and social sciences as a whole, which has resulted in an explosion of "body-focused" scholarship over the last several decades. This body-focused literature is far too vast to cite. However, for some good, representative examples, see the three-volume *Fragments for a History of the Human Body* (Feher et al. 1989); and see the references and discussions found in various bibliographical, "state-of-the-field" articles on body studies from a variety of disciplinary perspectives, such as the following: McGuire 1990, Sullivan 1990, Culianu 1991, Turner 1991, Frank 1991, Porter 1992, Dissanayake 1993, Turner 1997, Asad 1997, LaFleur 1998, and Porter 2001.

5. See the articles collected in Schopen 1997 and 2004.

6. The complete titles of these anthologies are as follows: *Buddhism in Practice* (Lopez 1995b), *The Life of Buddhism* (Reynolds and Carbine 2000), *The Experience of Buddhism* (Strong 1995), *Buddhist Texts Through the Ages* (Conze 1954), *Buddhism in Translations* (Warren 1896), *Buddhist Scriptures* (Conze 1959), and *The Teachings of the Compassionate Buddha* (Burtt 1955).

7. See, for example, Mrozik 2002, which argues for a study of Buddhist ethics that is driven by the concept of "embodied virtue" rather than just virtue.

8. It is instructive, in fact, to compare Bateson's article with a more recent encyclopedia entry: Yuichi Kajiyama's article on "The Body" in the *Encyclopaedia of Buddhism* (Kajiyama 1972), which does include a section on "The Ideal Body" (restricted, however, to a discussion of the Buddha's body).

9. See, for example, Bateson 1908, Kajiyama 1972, Hamilton 1995, Wilson 1996:41–76, Collins 1997, and Williams 1997 (I cannot, however, agree with Hamilton's argument that distinctly negative statements about the body within

the Pāli Canon should be solely attributed to "Brahmanical," "non-Buddhist," or "nondoctrinal" influence). On the tendency within Buddhist literature to gender the "worthless" body as a specifically *female* body, see Lang 1986, Wilson 1995 and 1996, and Blackstone 1998:59–81. Their argument has been refuted—though not convincingly, in my opinion—by other scholars, such as Gross (1993:47), Collins (1997:191, n. 10), Trainor (1993), and Walters (1994:362, n. 11). For a fuller discussion of this dispute, see Ohnuma 1997:203–213.

10. Verses 147–148, 150 (ed. Von Hinüber and Norman 1994:42–43).

11. For a succinct description of body-focused meditations (and citations to the Pāli canonical and commentarial texts in which they are described), see Collins 1997:192–194.

12. Faure 1995:212.

13. By "suicide," I mean self-interested suicide, not voluntary deeds of self-sacrifice for the benefit of others, such as we see in gift-of-the-body *jātakas*. Self-interested suicide was largely condemned, though there were situations (such as degenerative illness) in which it seems to have been condoned or exonerated, as long as the person committing it were truly detached from his body. The problems of textual interpretation surrounding the issue of suicide are complex, however; on this question see, for example, Lamotte 1987, Wiltshire 1983, Keown 1996, and Harvey 2000:286–292.

14. Ed. Rhys Davids 1975:195.

15. See, for example, Keown 1983, Gombrich 1984, and Collins 1997.

16. *kelāyatha mamāyatha; piyo* (ed. Trenckner 1880:73).

17. *ālepena ca ālimpīyati telena ca makkhīyati sukhumena ca colapaṭṭena palivethīyati* (ed. Trenckner 1880:74).

18. *brahmacariyānuggahāya* (ed. Trenckner 1880:74).

19. It is interesting to note, however, that a wound received in battle, though not "dear" to the one who receives it, is described as being cared for "so that the flesh will heal" (*maṃsassa rūhaṇatthāya*) (ed. Trenckner 1880:74). If Nāgasena's analogy between the body and a wound is supposed to be a strict one, this perhaps suggests (albeit subtly) that monastic care for the body somehow "heals" it so that it is no longer a "wound"—perhaps becoming an "ideal body" that overcomes the deficiencies of the ordinary human form.

20. Collins 1997:202.

21. *nirātmake bhedini sārahīne duḥkhe kṛtaghne satatāśucau ca / dehe parasmāy upayujyamāne na prītimān yo na vicakṣaṇaḥ saḥ //* (from *Jātakamālā* 1, ed. Vaidya 1959a:4).

22. *dehe vināśiny asukhāspade ca / vimarśamārgo 'py anudāttatā syān . . .* (from *Jātakamālā* 8, ed. Vaidya 1959a:50).

23. From *Liu du ji jing* (T. 152) (Fr. trans. Chavannes 1910–1934:1, 41 [story no. 10]).

24. From *Liudu ji jing* (T. 152) (Fr. trans. Chavannes 1910–1934:1, 77 [story no. 21]).

25. From *Avadānakalpalatā* 51 (ed. Vaidya 1959b:2, 317, vv. 24–26).

26. From *Divyāvadāna* 32 (ed. Cowell and Neil 1970:472).

27. *suciram api dhṛto 'yaṃ pūtikāyo mahārhaiḥ śayanavasanapānair bhojanair vāhanaiś ca / śatanapatanadharmo bhedanānto duranto na vijahati apūrvaṃ svaṃ svabhāvaṃ kṛtaghnaḥ //* (from *Suvarṇabhāsottama Sūtra,* chapter 18, ed. Nobel 1937:210).

28. From *Sūtra of the Wise and the Fool* 22 (ed. Schmidt 1845:143–144).

29. Ed. Vaidya 1959a:32.

30. *api cāhaṃ āvuso imasmiññ eva byāmamatte kalebare sasaññimhi samanake lokañ ca paññāpemi / lokasamudayañ ca lokanirodhañ ca lokanirodhagāminiñ ca paṭipadan ti /* (ed. Feer 1960:1, 62).

31. *nāsti tasyopajīvyaṃ sarvato mīḍhabhūtatvāt / tam aham idānīṃ satkarmaṇi saṃniyokṣye / tan me janmamaraṇasamudrottaraṇapotabhūto bhaviṣyati //* (ed. Nobel 1937:211).

32. *evaṃvidhe yadi na kāyam imaṃ prayokṣye puṇyāgame nirupamānasukhānubandhe / ko 'rtho 'munā parihṛtena kaḍevareṇa vātāhatāmbunidhibudbudadurbalena //* (ed. Handurukande 1984:42, v. 27).

33. The whole verse reads: *duṣṭavraṇasyeva sadāturasya kaḍe(le)varasyāsya rujākarasya / karomi kāryātiśayopayogād atyartharamyaṃ pratikārakhedam //* (ed. Vaidya 1959a:47).

34. *pūtikāyo; anuttarāyāḥ samyaksaṃbodheḥ saṃbhārabhāvaṃ* (ed. Handurukande 1967:32).

35. *bahurogaśatālayam; eṣāṃ duḥkhaparītānām āpaduttaraṇaplavam* (ed. Vaidya 1959a:211).

36. Ed. Handurukande 1984:74, vv. 49–51.

37. *pūtikāyaṃ . . . abalaṃ; saṃtyājayiṣyaty . . . balātmā jagadvināśāvahitaḥ kṛtāntaḥ* (ed. Handurukande 1984:42, v. 28).

38. *kāyam āsannanāśaṃ; duṣkaraṃ kiṃ nu tatra* (ed. Handurukande 1984:42, v. 31).

39. *mahotsavaḥ puṇyaviśeṣaramyaḥ* (ed. Handurukande 1984:42, v. 30).

40. *akāle kaumudī; pratīkāro . . . vipadām . . . śāśvataḥ* (ed. Handurukande 1984:44, v. 39).

41. *pramodāyatanī kariṣyate mayā śarīraṃ suhṛdāṃ hitāgame* (ed. Handurukande 1984:46, v. 46).

42. The whole verse reads: "If I do not turn this strife called the body from an enemy into a friend, my mind will burn for a long time with the fire of regret, whose flames are sighs" (*amitrabhūtaṃ yadi mitrasād imaṃ kaliṃ kariṣyāmi na kāyasaṃjñakam / vidhakṣyate vipratisāravahninā mano viniśvāsaśikhena me ciram //;* ed. Handurukande 1984:48, v. 48).

43. *sāraṃ śarīrād aham uddhariṣye* (from *Jātakamālā* 8, ed. Vaidya 1959a:49).

44. *kāyād asārād aham adya sāraṃ bhavantam āsādya samujjihīrṣuḥ* (from *Avadānasārasamuccaya* 3, ed. Handurukande 1984:76, v. 53).

45. *adyāhaṃ pūtikād asmād vināśāntāt kaḍevarāt bhavantaṃ mitram āsādya sāram uddhartum udyataḥ* (from *Maṇicūḍāvadāna,* ed. Handurukande 1967:32).

46. *asārāt sāram ādeyaṃ śarīrāt pātukād itaḥ / srotobhinnavalanmūlāt phalaṃ taṭataror iva //* (from *Jātakamālā* [of Haribhaṭṭa] 6, ed. Hahn 1992:54, v. 19).

47. Ed. Bendall 1957:23, 25, 26 (all quotations from the *Vajradhvaja Sūtra*).

48. *lābhā me sulabdhā yasya me 'sārāt kāyāt sāram ādattaṃ bhaviṣyati* (quoted from the *Ratnarāśi Sūtra,* ed. Bendall 1957:200).

49. See Monier-Williams 1979: s.v. *sāra.*

50. This might in part explain why the cliché is associated so closely with the bodhisattva's gift of his body (rather than other meritorious deeds), for the physical image of the "core," "pith," or "sap" of something being "extracted" runs parallel to the image of the bodhisattva's body being mutilated and a body part removed. In fact, it is interesting to note that King Śibi—in both the Pāli *Jātaka* collection and the *Cariyāpiṭaka*—bypasses the cliché itself and compares the removal of his eyes directly to the removal of the pith from a palm tree (*tālamiñja*). In Pāli *Jātaka* 499 he states: "If anyone names my eyes, I will tear out my eyes, as if I were removing the pith of a palm tree, and give them to him" (*sace me koci akkhīnaṃ nāmaṃ gaṇheyya tālamiñjaṃ nīharanto viya akkhīni uppāṭetvā dassāmīti;* ed. Fausboll 1875–1897:4, 402). In *Cariyāpiṭaka* 1.8 the Buddha relates: "Then [the physician] Sīvaka . . . tore out [my eyes] like the pith from a palm tree, and gave [them] to the supplicant" (*tato so . . . sīvako . . . uddharitvāna pādāsi tālamiñjaṃ va yācake;* ed. Jayawickrama 1974: pt. 2, 6, v. 14). The gouging out of the king's eye, the removal of the pith from a palm tree, and the abstract idea of extracting worth from a worthless body all run parallel to each other.

51. Strong 1983a:148–161.

52. Strong 1983a:154, quoting Warder's (1970:405) and Conze's (1962:229) definitions of *dharmadhātu.*

53. Strong 1983a:155.

54. Perez-Remon (1979) goes even further. After analyzing the use of the term *sāra* in many passages throughout the Pāli Nikāyas, he concludes that the designa-

tion of the *skandhas* and so many other things as "essenceless" (*asāra*) implicitly suggests that what the Buddhist follower *should* be looking for is an "essence" that does truly exist—in other words, the self (*ātman*). He believes that the Buddha himself and the earliest generation of Buddhist masters taught a doctrine of the self (*ātman*), but this was corrupted in later times into a doctrine of no-self (*anātman*). I do not find his argument very convincing.

55. Trans. Strong 1983a:149–150.

56. Silk 1994:1, 353, n. 1.

57. I have taken this translation from Nattier (2003:227–228) but (for the sake of consistency) replaced her "substance" and "insubstantial" with "essence" and "essenceless." In addition to extracting the essence from one's essenceless *body*, the full passage also deals with extracting this essence from one's *life* and from one's *wealth*. The latter two are also defined in purely functional (nonsubstantialist) terms—the first as "not damaging the roots-of-goodness that one has previously planted, but causing them to increase," and the second as "restraining the spirit of stinginess, causing the spirit of great liberality to increase, and distributing gifts." Nattier (2003:227, n. 120) notes that "the idea of 'extracting the [essence]' from these three items—viz., body (*kāya*), life (*jīva*), and wealth (*bhoga*)—while at the same time maintaining a view of them as [essenceless] is a well-established trope in Mahāyāna sūtras," appearing both alone and together (see her references). The bodhisattva's gift of his body, of course, might qualify as either of two of these items: "extracting the essence from one's essenceless body" or "extracting the essence from one's essenceless life."

58. Mrozik 1998:78–79.

59. *jarārujāmṛtyukhalūrikām* (ed. Handurukande 1984:74, v. 50); *naikopasargavihite* (ibid., 74, v. 52); *mattavāraṇagatiṃ kanakāvadātaṃ prāṃśuṃ sumerum iva lakṣaṇaratnacitram* (ibid., 78, v. 63).

60. Fr. trans. Huber 1908:334, 332.

61. *kanakagiriśilāviśālavakṣāḥ śaradamalendumanojñavaktraśobhaḥ / kanakaparighapīnalambabāhur vṛṣabhanibhekṣaṇavikramo* . . . (ed. Vaidya 1959a:45).

62. *sa pīyamānakṣatajaḥ kṣitīśaḥ kṣapācarair hemavapuś cakāśe / saṃdhyānuraktair jalabhāranamraiḥ payodharair merur ivopagūḍhaḥ //* (ed. Vaidya 1959a:50).

63. *lohitacandanārcitā . . . hemapratimeva* (from *Jātakamālā* [of Haribhaṭṭa] 6, ed. Hahn 1992:54, v. 22).

64. Ed. Fausboll 1875–1897:5, 37 and 53.

65. Ed. Handurukande 1967:7–9.

66. *na ca manir vā pradīpo vā ulkā vā purastān nīyate api tu svakāt kāyād rājñaś candraprabhasya prabhā niścaranti tad yathā candramaṇḍalād raśmayaḥ /* (ed. Cowell and Neil 1970:316).

67. These corpses are enumerated in various places—for example, the *Mahāsatipaṭṭhāna Sutta* of the *Dīgha Nikāya,* the *Satipaṭṭhāna* and *Kāyagatāsati Suttas* of the *Majjhima Nikāya,* Buddhaghosa's *Visuddhimagga,* Sanskrit Abhidarma texts such as the *Abhidharmakośa,* and various Mahāyāna texts as well. For a succinct summary of these lists, see Lamotte 1944–1980:3, 1311–1313.

68. Verses 34–36 (ed. Vaidya 1959a:214).

69. *kamalapalāśalakṣmīsamṛddhābhyāṃ bhāsurāṅgulībhūṣaṇālaṃkṛtābhyāṃ* (ed. Vaidya 1959a:35).

70. *asthīni vyapagatarudhiramāṃsasnāyūni diśo vidiśaś ca keśān vikīrṇān* (ed. Nobel 1937:221).

71. *samudgataprāṇam api prasannaṃ; lakṣmyā samālabdham iva prakāmaṃ pramṛṣṭacāmīkaracāruvarṇam* (ed. Handurukande 1984:54, v. 58).

72. *magnaṃ . . . janmāvaskarakardame sphuradurukleśakrimivyākule* (ed. Handurukande 1984:54, v. 56).

73. Ed. Fausboll 1875–1897:5, 54.

74. Ed. Cowell and Neil 1970:327.

75. *aho namaskāraviśeṣapātratāṃ prasahya nītāsya guṇātanus tanuḥ //* (ed. Vaidya 1959a:6).

76. Ed. Vaidya 1959a:213.

77. *ebhir Ānandāsthibhir mayaivaṃ kṣipram anuttarā samyaksaṃbodhir abhisaṃbuddheti /* (ed. Nobel 1937:206).

78. *saṃpūrṇe 'dyāpi tad idaṃ śaśabimbaṃ niśākare / chāyāmayam ivādarśe rājate divi rājate //* (ed. Vaidya 1959a:35).

79. This occurs in the *Naḷapāna Jātaka* of the Pāli *Jātaka* collection (ed. Fausboll 1875–1897:1, 172).

80. *pūtikāyo; saṃparipūrṇaśobham* (ed. Handurukande 1967:32 and 45).

81. Ed. Handurukande 1967:94.

82. *datvāna mānusaṃ cakkhuṃ laddham [me] cakkhuṃ amānusaṃ* (ed. Fausboll 1875–1897:4, 412).

83. *mama strīndriyam antardhāya puruṣendriyaṃ prādurbhavet* (from *Divyāvadāna* 32, ed. Cowell and Neil 1970:473).

84. *jagati guṇāśrayas* (from *Jātakamālā* [of Haribhaṭṭa] 6, ed. Hahn 1992:55, v. 34).

85. The whole verse (from *Jātakamālā* [of Haribhaṭṭa] 6) reads: "And when her two breasts, swollen like the frontal globes of an elephant in rut, saw just a few beard-hairs as dark as collyrium powder appearing on that moon-like face, they immediately disappeared into a manly chest, as if out of shame" (*śmaśrūdgamaṃ praviralāñjanacūrṇanīlam āvirbhavantam avalokya tad ānanendau / sadyaḥ payodharayugaṃ gajakumbhapīnam antardadhe pṛthuni vakṣasi lajjayeva //;* ed. Hahn 1992:56, v. 36).

86. Ed. Cowell and Neil 1970:326.

87. Ed. Yamada 1968:2, 381–382.

88. *praṇidhānavaśena cānyonyāḥ prādurbhūtāḥ teṣāṃ ayaṃ Gṛdhrakūṭaparvata-pramāno rāśiḥ syān* (ed. Yamada 1968:2, 382).

89. *sarvatra mānuṣaśirāḥ prādurbhūtāḥ sakeśakarṇanayanānāsauṣṭhadāntāḥ sajihvā anekamukhaśatasahasrāḥ prādurbhūtāḥ /* (ed. Yamada 1968:2, 364).

90. From *Suvarṇabhāsottama Sūtra,* chapter 18 (ed. Nobel 1937:211).

91. . . . *mayāpsyate / abhedyam acchedyam ahāryam avyayaṃ niruttaraṃ dharmaśarīram avraṇam //* (from *Avadānasārasamuccaya* 2, ed. Handurukande 1984:46, v. 47).

92. There is a large body of scholarship devoted to the bodies of the Buddha. See, for example, the following: Akanuma 1922; Anesaki 1908; Demiéville 1929–1967:3, 174–185 (s.v. *Busshin*); Dutt 1978b:136–170; Eckel 1994; Griffiths 1994; Harrison 1992; La Valleé Poussin 1906 and 1913–1914; Makransky 1989; Nagao 1973; Reynolds 1977; Stein 1937; Suzuki 1963: 217–276; and Williams 1989:167–184.

93. *vastiguhyatālakṣaṇa; suvarṇavarṇatālakṣaṇa* (ed. Yamada 1968:2, 380).

94. *sabbaññūtañāṇakkhim* (from Pāli *Jātaka* 499, ed. Fausboll 1875–1897:4, 407).

95. *sabbaññutañāṇadantā* (from Pāli *Jātaka* 514, ed. Fausboll 1875–1897:5, 53).

96. *prākṛtamāṃsacakṣus; anuttaraṃ dharmacakṣuḥ* (from *Karuṇāpuṇḍarīka Sūtra,* ed. Yamada 1968:2, 351).

97. *bodhiratna* (from the *Maṇicūḍāvadāna,* ed. Handurukande 1967:76).

98. *anuttaraśraddhāhasta; anuttarāṃ śīlapādāṃ* (from the *Karuṇāpuṇḍarīka Sūtra,* ed. Yamada 1968:2, 380 and 379).

99. *sarvadharmāgraśiraḥ paramajñānam avataran; śraddhāhastaprayuktenānu-grahacāritreṇa; mahāpratiṣṭhānakramatalavyatihāreṇa; niṣparyavasthānajñānadhar-maśarīrāchinnābhinnāluptakāyasaṃjñaḥ* (ed. Nobel 1937:24).

100. See, for example, Mrozik 1998 and 2002, and Boucher [forthcoming]: chapters 1–2.

101. Mrozik 1998:31.

102. See the translation of the *Lakkhaṇa Sutta* in Walshe 1995:441–460. For a thorough discussion of the thirty-two marks and their relation to specific moral deeds performed in previous lives, see Boucher [forthcoming]: chapters 1–2.

103. This example comes from *Avadānaśataka* 61. On the moral and physical aspects of acts of offering in the *Avadānaśataka,* see Strong 1979.

104. *rogeṇa bādhyante pītapāṇḍukāḥ kṛśośarīrā durbalāṅgā; alpābādho 'lpā taṅko 'rogo balavān* (ed. Speyer 1958:1, 168).

105. *samapākayā ca grahaṇyā samanvāgato yena me aśitapītakhāditāsvāditaṃ samyaksukhena pariṇamati alpābādho rogatātītaś cāsmi* (ed. Speyer 1958:1, 172).

106. *na bhikṣavaḥ karmāṇi kṛtāny upacitāny bāhye . . . vipacyante . . . api tūpātteṣv eva skandhadhātvāyataneṣu karmāṇi kṛtāni vipacyante śubhāny aśubhāni ca* (ed. Speyer 1958:1, 169).

107. *saccapāramitācakkhūnīti* (from Pāli *Jātaka* 499, ed. Fausboll 1875–1897:4, 411).

108. *śīlaguṇaparivāsitāni* (from *Suvarṇabhāsottama Sūtra*, chapter 18, ed. Nobel 1937:206).

109. Mahoney 2002.

110. Adapted from Mahoney 2002:16–17. The corresponding Sanskrit terminology used for each item in quotation marks is as follows: "giving away everything" (*sarva-dāna* or *sarva-utsarjana*); "body" (*ātmabhāva*); "enjoyments" (*bhoga*); "merit" (*puṇya*); "preserve" (√*rakṣ*); "purify" (√*śudh*); "increase" (√*vṛdh*).

111. These statements are interesting for providing a different, much more cautionary perspective on the bodhisattva's gift of his body than we find within gift-of-the-body *jātakas* themselves. At the beginning of chapter 2 Śāntideva explains the relationship between "giving" and "preserving" as follows: "Thus, even though one's body, etc., are given away, they must [also] be preserved. Why is that? Because it is for the enjoyment of living beings that one gives away one's body, etc. If they aren't preserved, then how can they be enjoyed? And if they aren't enjoyed, then where is the gift? Therefore, one should protect one's body, etc., for the sake of living beings' enjoyment" (ed. Bendall 1957:34). In other words, one should focus on preserving one's body (through moral conduct) rather than too hastily giving it away; otherwise it will not be a worthy gift. Similarly, in chapter 3, Śāntideva, again in connection with the topic of "preserving" one's body, tells the bodhisattva to expend "effort" (*vīrya*) in all his activities—but not to such an extent that he produces "exhaustion" (*kheda*). Such "exhaustion" might occur, for example, "if [a bodhisattva] of little strength were to undertake a heavy task, or do so at the wrong time, or if [a bodhisattva] of immature confidence were to undertake a difficult deed such as giving away his flesh. [Of course, the bodhisattva] does give away his body, but he must [also] guard against its premature consumption. For otherwise, the bodhisattva's exhaustion would result in the destruction of his *bodhicitta*, which is the seed [of Buddhahood], and because of this, the great quantity of merit those beings [might have acquired] would be destroyed. This is why the *Gaganagañja Sūtra* tells us that the premature desire [for self-sacrifice] is the work of Māra. . . . Even though one should give away the seed from a beautiful medicinal tree whose many parts are fit for consump-

tion, this seed must also be protected against premature consumption. And the same holds true for the medicinal tree that is the perfectly enlightened Buddha" (ibid., 51).

112. Ed. Bendall 1957:158–159.

113. *abhirucitaṃ bhojanaṃ . . . rājārham api; naivaṃvidhaṃ bhojanaṃ vayam aśnīma iti* (ed. Vaidya 1959a:46).

114. *pratyagroṣmāṇi māṃsāni narānāṃ rudhirāṇi ca / ity annapānaṃ . . . yakṣāṇām* . . . (ed. Vaidya 1959a:46).

115. *sthirapīvarāṇi . . . māṃsāni saśoṇitāni* (ed. Vaidya 1959a:47).

116. *svayaṃmṛtānāṃ hi niruṣmakāṇi bhavanti māṃsāni viśoṇitāni / priyāṇi caiṣāṃ na hi tāni* . . . (ed. Vaidya 1959a:47).

117. *vivardhiteṣv, bṛhatsu, māṃsopacayonnateṣu* (ed. Vaidya 1959a:49).

118. *khādanīyabhojanīyasya mahān rāśir* (ed. Handurukande 1967:30); *sadyohatamāṃsarudhira* (ibid.); *pratyagrāṇi* (ibid., 31).

119. *idaṃ sarudhiramāṃsam idaṃ samedam idaṃ sukumāraṃ* (ed. Handurukande 1967:38).

120. *pūtikād asmād vināśāntāt kaḍevarāt* (ed. Handurukande 1967:32).

121. *sha ni mdangs ldan slar yang ral gri'i lo mas sngon nyid du / rnam bcad rab tu mang po dron mo mdog ni dmar po rnams* (ed. Hahn 1974:132).

122. *bza' ba ji ltar 'dod bzhin lus 'di ni* (ed. Hahn 1974:132).

123. *kye yi bram ze mchod sbyin la / srin po phyugs rnams ci phyir rung / yang na bdud rtsi spangs nas ni / snying po med pas ci zhig bya /* (ed. Hahn 1974:134).

124. *lus 'di yang lha'i yin mod /* (ed. Hahn 1974:134).

125. Ed. Hahn 1974:134.

126. *ring mo nas slong ba'i skye bo mngon shes can re zhig bdag gis mthong ngo /* (ed. Hahn 1974:136).

127. Faure 1991, esp. chapters 7–9; Faure 1995.

128. Faure 1995:212.

129. Faure 1991:135.

130. For a discussion of "ascent" versus "descent" as a persistent theme in Buddhist thought, see Nagao 1984.

131. Nagao 1973:37.

132. Faure 1991:136.

133. E.g., Trainor 1997 and several of the articles in Schopen 1997.

134. Collins 1997:201.

135. Vernant 1989. We could also compare such bodies to Judeo-Christian notions of the resurrected body or the bodies of angels.

136. Vernant 1989:23.

137. Vernant 1989:27, 34.

138. The same strategy of conveying absolute transcendence through physical multiplication or magnification is also employed in the *Bhagavad Gīta,* of course, for when Krishna reveals to Arjuna a physical vision of his supernal form as God, Arjuna is startled by its innumerable body parts: "Seeing the many mouths and eyes of your great form, its many arms, thighs, feet, bellies, and fangs, the worlds tremble and so do I" (v. 11.23; trans. Miller 1986:101).

139. Vernant 1989:39, 43.

140. Dunning 1992:1.

141. Filliozat 1963. The phenomena of autocremation and spontaneous combustion in Indian Buddhism have also been usefully explored in Wilson 2003.

142. Some further idea of the contrast between these two genres can be gained by considering the Act of Truth in the story of Kṣemadatta (from the *Samādhirāja Sūtra*). Like the heroes of so many gift-of-the-body *jātakas,* Kṣemadatta also uses an Act of Truth to restore his injured body to health—but the emphasis of his Act of Truth is completely different from what we have seen in the *jātakas:* "By virtue of the truth by which truth this thing called an arm does not exist, may my arm become as it was previously! . . . This thing that is Kṣemadatta does not exist; because of emptiness, those who investigate the ten directions cannot perceive it . . . [and] the same is true of all things" (trans. Filliozat 1963:25). This explicit emphasis upon the emptiness or nonexistence of the body given away is completely uncharacteristic of the Acts of Truth found within gift-of-the-body *jātakas.*

143. Glucklich 2001.

144. Glucklich 2001:59.

145. Glucklich 2001:96–97.

146. Glucklich 2001:149.

147. Fr. trans. Huber 1908:332.

148. This is the story of the woman Rukmavatī, who sacrifices her breasts to feed another woman who is starving. The entire (introductory) verse reads: "What words can possibly be used to describe the noble conduct of those who think only of protecting the afflicted, who are devoted to compassion? They are joyful as their lives are being extinguished, the wounds made on their bodies by extremely sharp weapons feel like blows from the lotuses that wanton women wear behind their ears, and they are happily amused to be ornamented by hairs that stand on end [from the pain]" (ed. Vaidya 1959b:2, 316, v. 1; reading *prāṇapravāsotsave* rather than *prāṇapravāhotsave* and *vācyocitair* rather than *bālyocitair* [see De Jong 1979:80]).

149. If we remind ourselves, moreover, that "pain" is also an acceptable translation for *duḥkha,* then the double-sided nature of the bodhisattva's pain that I have tried to elucidate here accords nicely with the idea that *duḥkha,* in Buddhist

thought, is both the overwhelming problem and the necessary context for its solution.

7. "Kingship, Sacrifice, Offering, and Death: Some Other Interpretive Contexts"

1. See, for example, Van Gennep 1960 and Turner 1995, 1987, 1974, and 1977.

2. On the theme of the exiled king and the opposition between kingdom and forest in the *Rāmāyaṇa,* see Thapar 1978. On the king's relationship to the wilderness in Indian thought, see Falk 1973.

3. As found, for example, in *Avadānasārasamuccaya* 3, *Mahajjātakamālā* 45, and *Kalpanāmaṇḍitikā* 71.

4. Ed. Handurukande 1984:204, vv. 146–156.

5. As found, for example, in the *Maṇicūḍāvadāna,* the *Lokānandanāṭaka, Avadānakalpalatā* 3, and *Mahajjātakamālā* 49 and 50.

6. As found, for example, in Pāli *Jātaka* 499, *Jātakamālā* 2, and *Mahajjātakamālā* 44.

7. See Falk 1973:3–6 and Auboyer 1949:49–61.

8. Auboyer 1949:177–185.

9. Such as the *Nigrodha, Sonaka,* and *Mahājanaka Jātakas* of the Pāli *Jātaka* collection.

10. Falk 1973.

11. Heesterman 1985:108–127.

12. Heesterman 1985:118.

13. Inden 1978:29.

14. See Falk 1973 and Bloss 1978.

15. Auboyer 1949:177ff.

16. Granoff 1990. Granoff bases her discussion on two versions of the Maṇicūḍa story that are not a part of my corpus (*Avadānakalpalatā* 3 and *Mahajjātakamālā* 49 and 50), but the basic plots of these versions (as well as many of the details) are very close to those of the *Maṇicūḍāvadāna* and the *Lokānandanāṭaka,* which are the two versions of the story in my corpus.

17. When the demons refuse the fine food and drink initially offered to them by King Maitrībala and demand flesh and blood instead, his ministers say to him: "The Gods are pleased with fat and marrow and such things that are offered into the fire at sacrifices. It is no wonder that these demons do not take any pleasure in the fine food you have brought before them" (*Jātakamālā* 8, v. 30 [ed. Vaidya

1959a:48]; I have borrowed Granoff's translation [1990:229]; the same verse also appears in *Mahajjātakamālā* 46, v. 135 [ed. Hahn 1985:562]).

18. Granoff 1990:230–233. The episode of Aśvatthāman is found at *Mahābhārata* 10.15–16 and *Bhāgavata Purāṇa* 1.7.

19. This story is contained in the thirty-fifth chapter. I am not aware of any English translation.

20. *Apastambadharma Sūtra* 1.9.25.12, as paraphrased by Granoff (1990:229). Much the same interpretation has also been offered by Jacques Gernet (1960). In his analysis of numerous cases of self-immolation and mutilation by fire committed by Chinese Buddhist monks between the fifth and tenth centuries C.E. (many of which were directly motivated by the Indian gift-of-the-body theme), Gernet speculates that such immolations functioned as sacrificial rituals, and more particularly as rituals of expiation, in which the martyr takes upon himself the sins of those around him. (However, for a refutation of Gernet's analysis, see Filliozat 1963.)

21. Hubert and Mauss 1964:53–58.

22. Hubert and Mauss 1964:32.

23. Hubert and Mauss 1964:67.

24. Hubert and Mauss 1964:51–52.

25. Parlier 1991.

26. Hubert and Mauss 1964:51.

27. Meadows 1986:72.

28. Granoff 1990:239, n. 40.

29. Hubert and Mauss 1964:114, n. 66.

30. See, for one example, Heesterman 1985, esp. 26–42.

31. For an exploration of how the sacrificial imagery of *heat* and *fire* is adapted in the many Buddhist stories involving the themes of autocremation and spontaneous combustion, see Wilson 2003.

32. Hubert and Mauss 1964:100–101.

33. Orzech 1994. For a succinct introduction to René Girard's theory, see Hamerton-Kelly 1994.

34. Orzech 1994:147.

35. Versions of this story include Pāli *Jātaka* 313 (trans. Cowell 1895–1913:26–29) and *Jātakamālā* 28 (trans. Khoroche 1989:193–204).

36. Orzech 1994:152.

37. Orzech 1994:149. It is interesting to note that the story related in the *Kṣāntivādin Jātaka* is very similar to the story (mentioned above) from the *Samādhirāja Sūtra* that presents itself as an explanation for all gifts of the body performed by the bodhisattva, for both stories deal with a king who kills an ascetic

in anger after his harem has wandered away from him and gone to sit at the feet of the ascetic. Perhaps this suggests, in some way, that it was the killing of the nonviolent "exemplary victim" that gave rise to the violent "sacred victim."

38. Trans. Hurvitz 1976:293–302.

39. See citations in Lamotte 1944–1980:1, 143–145, n. 1, and 2, 975, n. 1.

40. For discussions of self-mutilation and self-sacrifice in the Chinese Buddhist tradition, see Gernet 1960, Jan 1965, Kieschnick 1997:35–50, Benn 1998, and Benn 2001.

41. Kieschnick 1997:35–37.

42. This is the famous *Memorial on the Buddha Relic* (*Lun Fogu biao*), in which Han Yu warns the emperor Xianzong (r. 805–820) that if he honors the Buddha's relics, people "in their tens or hundreds [will] burn the tops of their heads and burn off their fingers in sacrifice . . . [and] cut off their limbs or slice up their bodies in making offerings which will pervert our customs and destroy normal usages, making us a laughing stock to the world" (trans. Benn 2001:193).

43. Including, for example, the *Mingseng zhuan* (compiled around 519 C.E.), *Gaoseng zhuan* (compiled in 531 C.E.), *Xu gaoseng zhuan* (compiled in 667 C.E.), and *Song gaoseng zhuan* (compiled in 988 C.E.). The biographies of "self-immolators" that appear in these and several other collections are exhaustively described and analyzed in Benn 2001.

44. Trans. Hurvitz 1976:295.

45. Trans. Horner 1978:89. (For other references to the same threefold distinction, see note 2 on the same page.)

46. Trans. Hurvitz 1976:298.

47. The development of this practice on the basis of two Chinese apocryphal *sūtras* and its relationship to more dramatic deeds of autocremation are discussed in Benn 1998.

48. Stone 2005. For other general discussions of Buddhism and death, see Reynolds 1992 and Hallisey 2000.

49. Stone 2005:57.

50. MacQueen 1981.

51. Hallisey 2000:17.

52. Huijiao was the compiler of the *Gaoseng zhuan* (531 C.E.), Daoxuan was the compiler of the *Xu gaoseng zhuan* (667 C.E.), and Zanning was the compiler of the *Song gaoseng zhuan* (988 C.E.).

53. Benn (2001) discusses and translates the "critical evaluation" (*lun*) that each of these compilers appends to the "self-immolation" category of his "Biographies of Eminent Monks" collection (see 64–73 for Huijiao, 116–130 for Daoxuan, and 189–205 for Zanning).

54. Benn 2001:70, 125, 200.

55. Harlan 1994:83. For a good introduction to *sati,* see the collected volume Hawley 1994.

56. *Ṛg Veda* 10.34. The hymn's nature as an Act of Truth is discussed in Brown 1963 and 1968:173.

57. Brown 1968:173.

58. Caillois 1959:120–121, cited in Drekmeier 1962:47.

59. Burkert 1996:37.

60. See Burkert 1996:34–55.

BIBLIOGRAPHY OF WORKS CITED

Acharya, Kala. 1993. *Purāṇic Concept of Dāna.* Delhi: Naga Publishers.

Akanuma, Chizen. 1922. "The Triple Body of the Buddha." *Eastern Buddhist* 2:1–29.

Almond, Philip C. 1988. *The British Discovery of Buddhism.* Cambridge: Cambridge University Press.

Ames, Michael. 1966. "Ritual Prestations and the Structure of the Sinhalese Pantheon." In *Anthropological Studies in Theravāda Buddhism,* ed. M. Nash et al., 27–50. Cultural Report Series 13. New Haven: Yale University Southeast Asian Studies.

Anesaki, M. 1908. "Docetism (Buddhist)." In *Encyclopaedia of Religion and Ethics,* ed. James Hastings, vol. 4, 835–840. New York: Scribner's.

Asad, Talal. 1997. "Remarks on the Anthropology of the Body." In *Religion and the Body,* ed. Sarah Coakley, 42–52. Cambridge: Cambridge University Press.

Auboyer, Jeannine. 1949. *Le trône et son symbolisme dans l'Inde ancienne.* Annales du Musée Guimet 55. Paris: Presses Universitaires de France.

Aung, Shwe Zan, and C. A. F. Rhys Davids, trans. 1915. *Points of Controversy; or, Subjects of Discourse, being a translation of the Kathā-vatthu from the*

Abhidhamma-Piṭaka. Pāli Text Society Translation Series 5. London: Pāli Text Society.

Babb, Lawrence A. 1996. *Absent Lord: Ascetics and Kings in a Jain Ritual Culture.* Berkeley: University of California Press.

Bareau, André. 1963. *Recherches sur la biographie du Buddha dans les sūtrapiṭaka et les vinayapiṭaka anciens: De la quête de l'éveil à la conversion de Śāriputra et de Maudgalyāyana.* Paris: Ecole Française d'Extrême-Orient.

Barua, D. L., ed. 1939. *Cariyāpiṭakaṭṭhakathā.* London: Pāli Text Society.

Basak, Radhagovinda, ed. 1963–1968. *Mahāvastu Avadāna.* 3 vols. Calcutta Sanskrit College Research Series 20, 31, 63. Calcutta: Sanskrit College.

Bateson, J. H. 1908. "Body (Buddhist)." In *Encyclopaedia of Religion and Ethics,* ed. James Hastings, vol. 2, 758–760. New York: Scribner's.

Bays, Gwendolyn, trans. 1983. *The Voice of the Buddha: The Beauty of Compassion.* 2 vols. Berkeley: Dharma Publishing.

Beal, Samuel, trans. 1884. *Si-Yu-Ki: Buddhist Records of the Western World. Translated from the Chinese of Hiuen Tsiang (A.D. 629).* 2 vols. in one. London: Kegan Paul, Trench, Trübner & Co. Orig. pub. 1869.

Bendall, Cecil, ed. 1957. *Çikshāsamuccaya: A Compendium of Buddhistic Teaching compiled by Çāntideva chiefly from earlier Mahāyāna-Sūtras.* The Hague: Mouton & Co. Orig. pub. 1902.

Bendall, Cecil, and W. H. D. Rouse, trans. 1990. *Śikṣā Samuccaya: A Compendium of Buddhist Doctrine.* Delhi: Motilal Banarsidass. Orig. pub. 1922.

Benn, James. 1998. "Where Text Meets Flesh: Burning the Body as an Apocryphal Practice in Chinese Buddhism." *History of Religions* 37.4:295–322.

——. 2001. "Burning for the Buddha: A History of Self-Immolation in Chinese Buddhism." Ph. D. diss., University of California at Los Angeles.

Bhat, G. K. 1959. *The Vidūṣaka.* Ahmedabad: New Order Book Co.

Blackstone, Kathryn R. 1998. *Women in the Footsteps of the Buddha: Struggle for Liberation in the Therīgāthā.* Surrey, Great Britain: Curzon Press.

Bloss, Lowell. 1978. "The Taming of Māra: Witnessing to the Buddha's Virtues." *History of Religions* 18.2:156–176.

Boucher, Daniel. [Forthcoming]. *Bodhisattvas of the Forest and the Formation of the Mahāyāna: A Study and Translation of the Rāṣṭrapālaparipṛcchā-sūtra.* Honolulu: University of Hawai'i Press.

Bourdieu, Pierre. 1996. "The Work of Time." In *The Gift: An Interdisciplinary Perspective,* ed. Aafke E. Komter, 135–147. Amsterdam: Amsterdam University Press. Excerpted and reprinted from *The Logic of Practice.* Trans. Richard Nice. Cambridge: Polity Press, 1990. Orig. pub. 1980.

Brekke, Torkel. 1998. "Contradiction and the Merit of Giving in Indian Religions." *Numen* 45:287–320.

Brown, W. Norman. 1940. "The Basis for the Hindu Act of Truth." *Review of Religion* 5.1:36–45.

——. 1963. "Ṛg Veda 10.34 as an Act of Truth." In *Munshi Indological Felicitation Volume,* ed. Jayantkrishna H. Dave et al., 8–10. Bombay: Bharatiya Vidya Bhavan.

——. 1968. "The Metaphysics of the Truth Act (**Satyakriyā*)." In *Mélanges d'Indianisme à la mémoire de Louis Renou,* 171–177. Publications de l'Institut de Civilisation Indienne 28. Paris: Éditions de Boccard.

Bunnag, Jane. 1973. *Buddhist Monk, Buddhist Layman: A Study of Urban Monastic Organization in Central Thailand.* Cambridge: Cambridge University Press.

Burkert, Walter. 1996. *Creation of the Sacred: Tracks of Biology in Early Religions.* Cambridge, Mass.: Harvard University Press.

Burlingame, Eugene Watson. 1917. "The Act of Truth (Saccakiriya): A Hindu Spell and Its Employment as a Psychic Motif in Hindu Fiction." *Journal of the Royal Asiatic Society,* 429–467.

Burnouf, E. 1844. *Introduction à l'histoire du Buddhisme Indien.* Paris: Imprimerie Royale.

Burtt, E. A., ed. 1955. *The Teachings of the Compassionate Buddha: Early Discourses, the Dhammapada, and Later Basic Writings.* New York: Penguin.

Bynum, Caroline Walker. 1987. *Holy Feast and Holy Fast: The Religious Significance of Food to Medieval Women.* Berkeley: University of California Press.

——. 1989. "The Female Body and Religious Practice in the Later Middle Ages." In *Fragments for a History of the Human Body,* ed. Michel Feher et al., vol. 1, 160–219. New York: Urzone.

——. 1991. *Fragmentation and Redemption: Essays on Gender and the Human Body in Medieval Religion.* New York: Zone Books.

——. 1995. *The Resurrection of the Body in Western Christianity, 200–1336.* New York: Columbia University Press.

Caillois, Roger. 1959. *Man and the Sacred.* Glencoe, Illinois: Free Press of Glencoe.

Carrithers, Michael. 1985. "An Alternative Social History of the Self." In *The Category of the Person: Anthropology, Philosophy, History,* ed. Michael Carrithers et al., 234–256. Cambridge: Cambridge University Press.

Chakravarti, Uma. 1987. *The Social Dimensions of Early Buddhism.* Delhi: Oxford University Press.

Chavannes, Édouard, trans. 1910–1934. *Cinq cents contes et apologues extraits du Tripiṭaka chinois.* 4 vols. Paris: Ernest Leroux.

Cheal, David J. 1988. *The Gift Economy.* New York: Routledge.

Chidester, David. 2000. "Material Terms for the Study of Religion." Review of *Critical Terms for Religious Studies,* ed. Mark C. Taylor (University of Chicago Press, 1998). *Journal of the American Academy of Religion* 68.2:367–380.

Coles, Romand. 1997. *Rethinking Generosity: Critical Theory and the Politics of Caritas.* Ithaca: Cornell University Press.

Collins, Steven. 1997. "The Body in Theravāda Buddhist Monasticism." In *Religion and the Body,* ed. Sarah Coakley, 185–204. Cambridge: Cambridge University Press.

——. 1998. *Nirvana and Other Buddhist Felicities: Utopias of the Pali Imaginaire.* Cambridge Studies in Religious Traditions 12. Cambridge: Cambridge University Press.

Cone, Margaret, and Richard F. Gombrich, trans. 1977. *The Perfect Generosity of Prince Vessantara: A Buddhist Epic.* Oxford: Clarendon Press.

Conze, Edward, ed. 1954. *Buddhist Texts Through the Ages.* New York: Philosophical Library.

——, ed. 1959. *Buddhist Scriptures.* Harmondsworth, England: Penguin.

——. 1962. *Buddhist Thought in India.* Ann Arbor: University of Michigan Press.

Cowell, Edward B., gen. ed. 1895–1913. *The Jātaka; or, Stories of the Buddha's Former Births.* 6 vols. and Index. Cambridge: Cambridge University Press.

Cowell, Edward B., and Robert A. Neil, eds. 1970. *The Divyāvadāna: A Collection of Early Buddhist Legends.* Amsterdam: Oriental Press. Orig. pub. 1886.

Croce, Benedetto. 2000. "Criticism of the Theory of Artistic and Literary Kinds." In *Modern Genre Theory,* ed. David Duff, 25–28. Harlow, England: Longman. Excerpted and reprinted from *Aesthetic as Science of Expression and General Linguistic,* 2d ed. Trans. Douglas Ainslie. London: Peter Owen, 1953. Orig. pub. 1902.

Culianu, I. P. 1991. "A Corpus for the Body: A Review Article." *Journal of Modern History* 63:61–80.

Culler, Jonathan. 1975. *Structuralist Poetics: Structuralism, Linguistics, and the Study of Literature.* Ithaca: Cornell University Press.

——. 1981. *The Pursuit of Signs: Semiotics, Literature, Deconstruction.* Ithaca: Cornell University Press.

Cummings, Mary. 1982. *The Lives of the Buddha in the Art and Literature of Asia.* Michigan Papers on South and Southeast Asia 20. Ann Arbor: Center for South and Southeast Asian Studies, University of Michigan.

Das, Nobin Chandra, trans. 1893. "Rukmāvatī." *Journal of the Buddhist Text Society of India* 1.4:1–12.

Dayal, Har. 1970. *The Bodhisattva Doctrine in Buddhist Sanskrit Literature.* Delhi: Motilal Banarsidass. Orig. pub. 1932.

Decaroli, Robert. 2004. *Haunting the Buddha: Indian Popular Religions and the Formation of Buddhism.* Oxford: Oxford University Press.

De Jong, J. W. 1979. *Textcritical Remarks on the Bodhisattvāvadānakalpalatā (Pallavas 42–108).* Studia Philologica Buddhica Monograph Series 2. Tokyo: Reiyukai Library.

Demiéville, Paul, ed. 1929–1967. *Hōbōgirin: Dictionnaire encyclopédique du Bouddhisme d'apres les sources chinoises et japonaises.* 4 vols. Paris: Librairie d'Amérique et d'Orient, Adrien Maissonneuve.

Derrida, Jacques. 1992. *Given Time. 1. Counterfeit Money.* Trans. Peggy Kamuf. Chicago: University of Chicago Press. Orig. pub. 1991.

——. 1995. *The Gift of Death.* Trans. David Wills. Chicago: University of Chicago Press. Orig. pub. 1992.

——. 2000. "The Law of Genre." In *Modern Genre Theory,* ed. David Duff, 219–231. Harlow, England: Longman. Reprinted from *Glyph* 7 (1980): 202–213.

Derris, Karen. 2000. "Virtue and Relationships in a Theravādin Biography of the Bodhisatta: A Study of the *Sotaṭṭhakīmahānidāna.*" Ph. D. diss., Harvard University.

Diprose, Rosalyn. 2002. *Corporeal Generosity: On Giving with Nietzsche, Merleau-Ponty, and Levinas.* Albany: State University of New York Press.

Dissanayake, Wimal. 1993. "Body in Social Theory." In *Self as Body in Asian Theory and Practice,* ed. Thomas P. Kasulis et al., 21–36. Albany: State University of New York Press.

Drekmeier, Charles. 1962. *Kingship and Community in Early India.* Stanford: Stanford University Press.

Dubrow, Heather. 1982. *Genre.* London: Methuen.

Duff, David, ed. 2000. *Modern Genre Theory.* Harlow, England: Longman.

Dumont, Louis. 1980. "World Renunciation in Indian Religions." Trans. D. F. Pocock and R. G. Lienhardt. Appendix B in *Homo Hierarchicus: The Caste System and Its Implications,* rev. ed., 267–286. Chicago: University of Chicago Press. Orig. pub. 1959.

Dunning, A. J. 1992. *Extremes: Reflections on Human Behavior.* Trans. Johan Theron. New York: Harcourt Brace Jovanovich. Orig. pub. 1990.

Durt, Hubert. 1998. "Two Interpretations of Human-Flesh Offering: Misdeed or Supreme Sacrifice." *Journal of the International College for Advanced Buddhist Studies* 1:57–83 or 236–210.

Durt, Hubert. 2000. "Du lambeau de chair au démembrement: Le renoncement au corps dans le bouddhisme ancien." *Bulletin de l'École Française d'Extrême-Orient* 87:7–22.

Dutt, Nalinaksha, ed. 1978a. *Bodhisattvabhūmi.* Patna: K. P. Jayaswal Research Institute.

——. 1978b. *Mahāyāna Buddhism.* Delhi: Motilal Banarsidass.

Eckel, Malcolm David. 1994. *To See the Buddha: A Philosopher's Quest for the Meaning of Emptiness.* Princeton: Princeton University Press.

Edgerton, Franklin. 1985. *Buddhist Hybrid Sanskrit Grammar and Dictionary.* 2 vols. New Delhi: Motilal Banarsidass. Orig. pub. 1953.

Egge, James. 2002. *Religious Giving and the Invention of Karma in Theravāda Buddhism.* Curzon Studies in Asian Religion 5. London: Curzon Press.

Emmerick, R. E., trans. 1970. *The Sūtra of Golden Light: Being a Translation of the Suvarṇabhāsottama Sūtra.* London: Luzac.

Endo, Toshiichi. 1987. *Dāna: The Development of Its Concept and Practice.* Colombo: Gunasena.

Ensink, Jacob, trans. 1952. *The Question of Rāṣṭrapāla.* Zwolle: N. V. Drukkerij en Uitgeverij Van de Erven J. J. Tijl.

Falk, Nancy. 1973. "Wilderness and Kingship in Ancient South Asia." *History of Religions* 13.1: 1–15.

——. 1990. "Exemplary Donors of the Pāli Tradition." In *Ethics, Wealth, and Salvation: A Study of Buddhist Social Ethics,* ed. Russell F. Sizemore and Donald K. Swearer, 124–143. Columbia: University of South Carolina Press.

Faure, Bernard. 1991. *The Rhetoric of Immediacy: A Cultural Critique of Chan/Zen Buddhism.* Princeton: Princeton University Press.

——. 1995. "Substitute Bodies in Chan/Zen Buddhism." In *Religious Reflections on the Human Body,* ed. Jane Marie Law, 211–229. Bloomington: Indiana University Press.

Fausboll, V., ed. 1875–1897. *The Jātaka Together With Its Commentary, Being Tales of the Anterior Births of Gotama Buddha.* 6 vols. and Index. London: Trübner.

Feer, Léon. 1879. "Le livre des cent légendes (Avadāna-çataka)." *Journal Asiatique* 7.14:141–189 and 273–307.

——, trans. 1891. *Avadāna-çataka: Cent légendes (Bouddhiques).* Annales du Musée Guimet 18. Paris: Ernest Leroux.

——. 1895. "Le Chaddanta-Jâtaka." *Journal Asiatique,* ser. 9, vol. 5: 31–85 and 189–223.

——. 1899. "Le Bodhisattva et la famille de Tigres." *Journal Asiatique,* ser. 9, vol. 14: 272–303.

——, ed. 1960. *The Saṃyutta-nikāya of the Sutta-piṭaka.* 5 vols. and Index. London: Pāli Text Society. Orig. pub. 1884–1904.

Feher, Michel, et al., eds. 1989. *Fragments for a History of the Human Body.* 3 vols. Zone 3, 4, and 5. New York: Urzone.

Filliozat, Jean. 1963. "La mort volontaire par le feu et la tradition bouddhique indienne." *Journal Asiatique* 251:21–51.

Findly, Ellison Banks. 2003. *Dāna: Giving and Getting in Pāli Buddhism.* Delhi: Motilal Banarsidass.

Foucher, Alfred. 1917. "The Six-Tusked Elephant: An Attempt at a Chronological Classification of the Various Versions of the *Ṣaddanta-Jātaka.*" In *The Beginnings of Buddhist Art and Other Essays in Indian and Central-Asian Archaeology,* 185–204. Rev. by the author and trans. by L. A. Thomas and F. W. Thomas. Paris: Paul Geuthner. London: Humphrey Milford. Orig. pub. 1911.

——. 1974. *Notes on the Ancient Geography of Gandhara: A Commentary on a Chapter of Hiuan Tsang.* Trans. H. Hargreaves. Varanasi: Bhartiya Publishing House. Orig. pub. 1901.

Fowler, Alastair. 1970. "The Life and Death of Literary Forms." *New Literary History* 2:199–216.

——. 1979. "Genre and the Literary Canon." *New Literary History* 11:97–119.

——. 1982. *Kinds of Literature: An Introduction to the Theory of Genres and Modes.* Cambridge, Mass.: Harvard University Press.

——. 1991. "Genre." In *Encyclopedia of Literature and Criticism,* ed. Martin Coyle, 151–163. London: Routledge. Orig. pub. 1990.

Frank, Arthur W. 1991. "For a Sociology of the Body: An Analytical Review." In *The Body: Social Process and Cultural Theory,* ed. Mike Featherstone et al., 36–102. London and Newbury Park, California: Sage.

Frye, Stanley, trans. 1981. *The Sūtra of the Wise and the Foolish (mdo bdzans blun); or, The Ocean of Narratives (üliger-ün dalai).* Dharamsala: Library of Tibetan Works and Archives.

Gernet, Jacques. 1960. "Les suicides par le feu chez le bouddhistes chinois du Ve au Xe siècle." *Mélanges publiés par l'Institut des Hautes Études chinoises* 2, 527–558. Paris: Institut des Hautes Études.

Giles, H. A., trans. 1956. *The Travels of Fa-hsien (399–414 A.D.); or, Record of the Buddhistic Kingdoms.* London: Routledge and Kegan Paul. Orig. pub. 1923.

Glucklich, Ariel. 2001. *Sacred Pain: Hurting the Body for the Sake of the Soul.* New York: Oxford University Press.

Godage, Charles. 1945. "The Place of Indra in Early Buddhism." *University of Ceylon Review* 3:41–72.

Godbout, Jacques T., and Alain Caillé. 1998. *The World of the Gift.* Trans. Donald Winkler. Montreal: McGill-Queen's University Press. Orig. pub. 1992.

Godelier, Maurice. 1999. *The Enigma of the Gift.* Trans. Nora Scott. Chicago: University of Chicago Press. Orig. pub. 1996.

Godlove, Terry. 2002. "Saving Belief: On the New Materialism in Religious Studies." In *Radical Interpretation in Religion,* ed. Nancy K. Frankenberry, 10–24. Cambridge: Cambridge University Press.

Gombrich, Richard F. 1971. *Precept and Practice: Traditional Buddhism in the Rural Highlands of Ceylon.* Oxford: Clarendon Press.

——. 1972. "Feminine Elements in Sinhalese Buddhism." In *Wiener Zeitschrift für die Kunde Südasiens* 16:67–93.

——. 1984. "Notes on the Brahmanical Background to Buddhist Ethics." In *Buddhist Studies in Honour of Hammalava Saddhātissa,* ed. Gatave Dhammapala et al., 91–102. Nugegoda, Sri Lanka: Buddhist Research Library Trust.

——. 1996. *How Buddhism Began: The Conditioned Genesis of the Early Teachings.* London: Athlone.

Gonda, Jan. 1965. "Gifts." In *Change and Continuity in Indian Religion,* 198–228. The Hague: Mouton.

——. 1975. "'Gifts' and 'Giving' in the *Ṛgveda.*" In *Selected Studies* 4: *History of Ancient Indian Religion,* 122–143. Leiden: Brill.

Granoff, Phyllis. 1990. "The Sacrifice of Maṇicūḍa: The Context of Narrative Action as a Guide to Interpretation." In *Kalyāṇamitra (Festschrift for H. Nakamura),* ed. V. N. Jha, 225–239. Poona: Poona University.

——. 1991–1992. "Seeking the Perfect Words: Teachers and Transmission in Buddhist Story Literature." *Indologica Taurinensia* 17–18, 145–181.

Grey, Leslie. 1994. *A Concordance of Buddhist Birth Stories.* 2d ed. Oxford: Pāli Text Society. 1st ed. pub. 1990.

Griffiths, Paul J. 1994. *On Being Buddha: The Classical Doctrine of Buddhahood.* Albany: State University of New York Press.

Gross, Rita M. 1993. *Buddhism After Patriarchy: A Feminist History, Analysis, and Reconstruction of Buddhism.* Albany: State University of New York Press.

Grousset, Réné. 1932. *In the Footsteps of the Buddha.* Trans. Mariette Leon. London: George Routledge and Sons, Ltd. Orig. pub. 1929.

Guillén, Claudio. 1971. *Literature as System: Essays Toward the Theory of Literary History.* Princeton: Princeton University Press.

Hahn, Michael, ed. and trans. 1974. *Candragomins Lokānandanāṭaka. Nach dem tibetischen Tanjur herausgegeben und übersetzt. Ein Beitrag zur klassischen indischen Schauspieldichtung.* Asiatische Forschungen 39. Wiesbaden: Otto Harrassowitz.

——. 1979. "The Play *Lokānandanāṭaka* by Candragomin." *Kailash* 7:51–67.

——. 1982. "Kumāralāta's *Kalpanāmaṇḍitikā Dṛṣṭāntapaṅkti* Nr. 1. Die Vorzüglichkeit des Buddha." *Zentralasiatische Studien* 16:306–336.

——, ed. 1985. *Der grosse Legendenkranz (Mahajjātakamālā): Eine mittelalteriliche buddhistische Legendensammlung aus Nepal.* Wiesbaden: O. Harrassowitz.

——. 1986–1992. "Variant Readings of Āryaśūra's *Jātakamālā* as Found in *Jātakamālāṭīkā.*" *Journal of Oriental Research* 56–62 [*Dr. S. S. Janaki Felicitation Volume*]: 233–253.

——, trans. 1987. *Joy for the World: A Buddhist Play by Candragomin.* Berkeley: Dharma Publishing.

——. 1992. *Haribhaṭṭa and Gopadatta, Two Authors in the Succession of Āryaśūra: On the Rediscovery of Parts of Their Jātakamālās.* 2d ed. Studia Philologica Buddhica Occasional Paper 1. Tokyo: International Institute for Buddhist Studies. 1st ed. orig. pub. 1977.

——. 1993. "Notes on Buddhist Sanskrit Literature: Chronology and Related Topics." *Genshi Bukkyō to Daijō Bukkyō: Watanabe Fumimaro hakushi tsuitō ronshū (Studies in Original Buddhism and Mahāyāna Buddhism in Commemoration of the Late Prof. Dr. Fumimaro Watanabe),* ed. Egaku Mayeda, 31–58. Kyoto: Nagata Bunshodo.

Hallisey, Charles. 1995. "Roads Taken and Not Taken in the Study of Theravāda Buddhism." In *Curators of the Buddha: The Study of Buddhism Under Colonialism,* ed. Donald S. Lopez Jr., 31–61. Chicago: University of Chicago Press.

——. 2000. "Buddhism." In *Death and the Afterlife,* ed. Jacob Neusner, 1–29. Cleveland: Pilgrim Press.

Hallisey, Charles, and Anne Hansen. 1996. "Narrative, Sub-Ethics, and the Moral Life: Some Evidence from Theravāda Buddhism." *Journal of Religious Ethics* 24.2:305–327.

Hamerton-Kelly, Robert G. 1994. "Religion and the Thought of René Girard: An Introduction." In *Curing Violence: Essays on René Girard,* ed. Mark I. Wallace and Theophus H. Smith, 3–24. Sonoma, California: Polebridge Press.

Hamilton, Sue. 1995. "From the Buddha to Buddhaghosa: Changing Attitudes Toward the Human Body in Theravāda Buddhism." In *Religious Reflections on the Human Body,* ed. Jane Marie Law, 46–63. Bloomington: Indiana University Press.

Handurukande, Ratna, ed. and trans. 1967. *Maṇicūḍāvadāna, Being a Translation and Edition, and Lokānanda, a Transliteration and Synopsis.* Sacred Books of the Buddhists 24. London: Pāli Text Society.

——. 1975. "The Maṇicūḍa Study." In *Bukkyō Kenkyū (Buddhist Studies)* 5:309–168.

Handurukande, Ratna, ed. and trans. 1984. *Five Buddhist Legends in the Campū Style From a Collection Named Avadānasārasamuccaya.* Indica et Tibetica 4. Bonn: Indica et Tibetica Verlag.

Hara, Minoru. 1974. "A Note on the Rākṣasa Form of Marriage." *Journal of the American Oriental Society* 94.3:296–306.

Harlan, Lindsey. 1994. "Perfection and Devotion: Sati Tradition in Rajasthan." In *Sati, the Blessing and the Curse: The Burning of Wives in India,* ed. John Stratton Hawley, 79–91.

Harrison, Paul. 1992. "Is the *Dharma-kāya* the Real 'Phantom Body' of the Buddha?" *Journal of the International Association of Buddhist Studies* 15.1:44–94.

Hartmann, Jens-Uwe. 1977. "Das Candraprabha-jātaka: Nach dem Gilgit-Manuskript ubersetzt und Kommentiert." M.A. thesis, Munich.

Harvey, Peter. 2000. *An Introduction to Buddhist Ethics: Foundations, Values, and Issues.* Cambridge: Cambridge University Press.

Hauerwas, Stanley, and L. Gregory Jones, eds. 1997. *Why Narrative? Readings in Narrative Theology.* Grand Rapids, Michigan: W. B. Eerdmans. Orig. pub. 1989.

Hawley, John Stratton, ed. 1994. *Sati, the Blessing and the Curse: The Burning of Wives in India.* Oxford: Oxford University Press.

Heesterman, J. C. 1985. *The Inner Conflict of Tradition: Essays in Indian Ritual, Kingship, and Society.* Chicago: University of Chicago Press.

———. 1993. *The Broken World of Sacrifice: An Essay in Ancient Indian Ritual.* Chicago: University of Chicago Press.

Hibbets [now Heim], Maria. 1999a. "The Ethics of the Gift: A Study of Medieval South Asian Discourses on *Dāna.*" Ph.D. diss., Harvard University.

———, Maria. 1999b. "Saving Them from Yourself: An Inquiry Into the South Asian Gift of Fearlessness." *Journal of Religious Ethics* 27.3:437–462.

———. 2000. "The Ethics of Esteem." *Journal of Buddhist Ethics* 7:26–42.

Horner, I. B., trans. 1975. *The Minor Anthologies of the Pāli Canon, Part 3: Buddhavaṃsa and Cariyāpiṭaka.* Sacred Books of the Buddhists 31. London: Pāli Text Society.

———, trans. 1978. *The Clarifier of the Sweet Meaning (Madhuratthavilāsinī), Commentary on the Chronicle of Buddhas (Buddhavaṃsa) by Buddhadatta Thera.* London: Pāli Text Society.

Horner, I. B., and Padmanabh S. Jaini, trans. 1985. *Apocryphal Birth-Stories (Paññāsa-Jātaka).* 2 vols. London: Pāli Text Society.

Huber, E. 1904. "Trois contes du Sūtrālaṃkāra d'Açvaghoṣa conservés dans le Divyāvadāna." *Bulletin de l'École Française d'Extrême-Orient* 4:709–726.

——. "Études de littérature Bouddhique: V. Les Sources du Divyāvadāna." *Bulletin de l'École Française d'Extrême-Orient* 6:1–37.

——, trans. 1908. *Aśvaghoṣa Sūtrālaṃkāra.* Paris: Ernest Leroux.

Hubert, Henri, and Marcel Mauss. 1964. *Sacrifice: Its Nature and Function.* Trans. W. D. Halls. Chicago: University of Chicago Press. Orig. pub. 1898.

Hurvitz, Leon, trans. 1976. *Scripture of the Lotus Blossom of the Fine Dharma (The Lotus Sūtra).* New York: Columbia University Press.

Hyde, Lewis. 1979. *The Gift: Imagination and the Erotic Life of Property.* New York: Vintage Books.

Inden, Ronald. 1978. "Ritual, Authority, and Cyclic Time in Hindu Kingship." In *Kingship and Authority in South Asia,* ed. J. F. Richards, 28–73. University of Wisconsin South Asian Studies Publication Series 3. Madison: University of Wisconsin.

Jaini, Padmanabh S. 1988. "Stages in the Bodhisattva Career of the Tathāgata Maitreya." In *Maitreya the Future Buddha,* ed. Alan Sponberg and Helen Hardacre, 54–90. Cambridge: Cambridge University Press.

Jameson, Fredric. 1975. "Magical Narratives: Romance as Genre." *New Literary History* 7:135–163.

Jan, Yün-hua. 1965. "Buddhist Self-Immolation in Medieval China." *History of Religions* 4:243–268.

Jauss, Hans Robert. 1974. "Literary History as a Challenge to Literary Theory." In *New Directions in Literary History,* ed. Ralph Cohen, 11–41. Baltimore: Johns Hopkins University Press.

Jayawickrama, N. A., ed. 1974. *Buddhavaṃsa and Cariyāpiṭaka.* Pāli Text Society Text Series 166. London: Pāli Text Society.

——, trans. 2000. *The Story of Gotama Buddha (Jātaka–nidāna).* Rptd. with corrections. Oxford: Pāli Text Society. Orig. pub. 1990.

Johnston, E. H., ed. and trans. 1984. *The Buddhacarita or Acts of the Buddha, by Aśvaghoṣa.* Delhi: Motilal Banarsidass. Orig. pub. 1936.

Jones, J. J., trans. 1949–1956. *The Mahāvastu.* 3 vols. Sacred Books of the Buddhists 16, 18, and 19. London: Pāli Text Society.

Kajiyama, Yuichi. 1972. "The Body." In *Encyclopaedia of Buddhism,* ed. G. P. Malalasekera, vol. 3, fasc. 2, 255–262. Ceylon: Government Press.

Kalupahana, David J. 1965. "Aṅga." In *Encyclopaedia of Buddhism,* ed. G. P. Malalasekara, vol. 1, fasc. 4, 616–619. Colombo: Government of Sri Lanka Press.

Kane, P. V. 1941. *History of Dharmaśāstra (Ancient and Mediaeval Religious and Civil Law),* vol. 2, pts. 1 and 2. Government Oriental Series, class B, no. 6. Poona: Bhandarkar Oriental Research Institute.

Kent, Thomas. 1986. *Interpretation and Genre: The Role of Generic Perception in the Study of Narrative Texts.* Lewisburg: Bucknell University Press.

Keown, Damien. 1983. "Morality in the *Visuddhimagga.*" *Journal of the International Association of Buddhist Studies* 6.1:61–75.

——. 1996. "Buddhism and Suicide: The Case of Channa." *Journal of Buddhist Ethics* 3:8–31.

Kern, Hendrik, ed. 1891. *The Jātaka-mālā or Bodhisattvāvadāna-mālā by Ārya-çūra.* Harvard Oriental Series 1. Boston: Harvard University.

Khoroche, Peter. 1987. *Towards a New Edition of Ārya-Śūra's Jātakamālā.* Indica et Tibetica 12. Bonn: Indica et Tibetica Verlag.

——, trans. 1989. *Once the Buddha Was a Monkey: Ārya Śūra's Jātakamālā.* Chicago: University of Chicago Press.

Kieckhefer, Richard, and George D. Bond, eds. 1988. *Sainthood: Its Manifestations in World Religions.* Berkeley: University of California Press.

Kieschnick, John. 1997. *The Eminent Monk: Buddhist Ideals in Medieval Chinese Hagiography.* Honolulu: University of Hawai'i Press.

King, Winston L. 1964. *A Thousand Lives Away: Buddhism in Contemporary Burma.* Cambridge, Mass.: Harvard University Press.

Komter, Aafke, ed. 1996. *The Gift: An Interdisciplinary Perspective.* Amsterdam: University of Amsterdam.

LaFleur, William R. 1998. "Body." In *Critical Terms for Religious Studies,* ed. Mark C. Taylor et al., 36–54. Chicago: University of Chicago Press.

Lamotte, Étienne. 1944–1980. *Le traité de la grande vertu de Sagesse de Nāgārjuna.* 5 vols. Bibliothèque du Muséon 18. Louvain: Bureaux du Muséon.

——. 1966. "Vajrapāṇi en Inde." In *Mélanges de sinologie offerts à Monsieur Paul Demiéville,* vol. 1, 113–159. Paris: Presses Universitaires de France.

——. 1987. "Religious Suicide in Early Buddhism." *Buddhist Studies Review* 4.2:105–118.

——. 1988. *History of Indian Buddhism, From the Origins to the Saka Era.* Trans. Sara Webb-Boin. Publications de l'Institut Orientaliste de Louvain 36. Louvain-la-Neuve: Institut Orientaliste de l'Université Catholique de Louvain. Orig. pub. as *Histoire du Bouddhisme indien: Des origines à l'ère Saka* in 1958.

Lang, Karen Christina. 1986. "Lord Death's Snare: Gender-Related Imagery in the Theragāthā and the Therīgāthā." *Journal of Feminist Studies in Religion* 11.2:63–79.

La Vallée Poussin, Louis. 1906. "Studies in Buddhist Dogma: The Three Bodies of a Buddha (*Trikāya*)." *Journal of the Royal Asiatic Society,* 943–977.

——. 1913–1914. "Note sur les Corps du Bouddha." *Le Muséon: Revue d'Études Orientales* 32:258–290.

——. 1928. "Les neuf kalpas qu'a franchis Śākyamuni pour devancer Maitreya." *T'oung pao* 26:17–24.

Lee, Orlan. 1967. "From Acts—To Non-Action—To Acts: The Dialectical Basis for Social Withdrawal or Commitment to This World in the Buddhist Reformation." *History of Religions* 65.4:273–302.

Legge, James, trans. 1965. *A Record of Buddhistic Kingdoms: Being an Account by the Chinese Monk Fâ-Hien of His Travels in India and Ceylon (A.D 399–414) in Search of the Buddhist Books of Discipline.* New York: Dover Publications. Orig. pub. 1886.

Lévi, Sylvain. 1907. "Les éléments de formation du Divyāvadāna." *T'oung pao,* ser. 2, vol. 8, 105–122.

——, ed. and trans. 1907–1911. *Mahāyāna-Sūtrālaṃkāra, exposé de la doctrine du Grand Véhicule selon le système Yogācāra.* 2 vols. Paris: H. Champion.

——. 1925. "Le sūtra du sage et du fou dans la littérature de l'Asie Centrale." *Journal Asiatique,* ser. 12, 6, 207: 305–332.

Lévi-Strauss, Claude. 1969. *The Elementary Structures of Kinship.* Rev. ed. Trans. James Harle Belle and John Richard von Sturmer. Ed. Rodney Needham. Boston: Beacon Press. Orig. pub. as *Structures élémentaires de la parenté* in 1949.

——. 1997. "Selections from *Introduction to the Work of Marcel Mauss.*" In *The Logic of the Gift,* ed. Alan D. Schrift, 45–69. New York: Routledge. Excerpted and reprinted from *Introduction to the Work of Marcel Mauss.* Trans. Felicity Baker. London: Routledge and Kegan Paul, 1987. Orig. pub. as *Introduction à l'oeuvre de Marcel Mauss* in 1950.

Li Rongxi, trans. 1996. *The Great Tang Dynasty Record of the Western Regions, Translated by the Tripitaka-Master Xuanzang Under Imperial Order; composed by Śramaṇa Bianji.* Berkeley: Numata Center for Buddhist Translation and Research.

——, trans. 2002. "The Journey of the Eminent Monk Faxian." In *Lives of Great Monks and Nuns,* trans. Li Rongxi and Albert A. Dalia, 155–214. Berkeley: Numata Center for Buddhist Translation and Research.

Lopez, Donald S., Jr. 1995a. "Foreigner at the Lama's Feet." In *Curators of the Buddha: The Study of Buddhism Under Colonialism,* ed. Donald S. Lopez, Jr., 251–295. Chicago: University of Chicago Press.

——, ed. 1995b. *Buddhism in Practice.* Princeton: Princeton University Press.

——. 1998. *Prisoners of Shangri-La: Tibetan Buddhism and the West.* Chicago: University of Chicago Press.

Lüders, Heinrich, ed. 1926. *Bruchstücke der Kalpanāmaṇḍitikā des Kumāralātā.* Kleinere Sanskrittexte aus den Turfanfunden 2. Leipzig: Deutsche Morgenlandische Gesellschaft.

MacIntyre, Alasdair. 1981. *After Virtue: A Study in Moral Theory.* Notre Dame: University of Notre Dame Press.

MacQueen, Graeme. 1981. "The Conflict Between External and Internal Mastery: An Analysis of the *Khantivādi Jātaka.*" *History of Religions* 20.3:242–252.

Mahoney, Richard. 2002. "Of the Progresse of the Bodhisattva: The Bodhisattvamārga in the Śikṣāsamuccaya." M.A. thesis, University of Canterbury.

Mair, Victor. 1993. *The Linguistic and Textual Antecedents of the Sūtra of the Wise and the Foolish.* Sino-Platonic Papers 38. Philadelphia: University of Pennsylvania, Department of Asian and Middle Eastern Studies.

Makransky, John J. 1989. "Controversy Over *Dharmakāya* in India and Tibet: A Reappraisal of its Basis, *Abhisamayālaṃkāra* Chapter 8." *Journal of the International Association of Buddhist Studies* 12.2:45–78.

Malinowski, Bronislaw. 1932. *Argonauts of the Western Pacific: An Account of Native Enterprise and Adventure in the Archipelagoes of Melanesian New Guinea.* Studies in Economics and Political Science 65. London: G. Routledge and Sons, Ltd. New York: E.P. Dutton and Co. Orig. pub. 1922.

Matsumura, Hisashi, ed. 1980. "Four Avadānas from the Gilgit Manuscripts." Ph.D. diss., Australian National University.

Mauss, Marcel. 1985. "A category of the human mind: the notion of person; the notion of self." Trans. W. D. Halls. In *The Category of the Person: Anthropology, Philosophy, History,* ed. Michael Carrithers et al., 1–45. Cambridge: Cambridge University Press. Orig. pub. as "Une catégorie de l'esprit humain: La notion de personne, celle de 'moi'" in 1938.

——. 1990. *The Gift: The Form and Reason for Exchange in Archaic Societies.* Trans. W. D. Halls. New York: Norton. Orig. pub. as *Essai sur la don* in 1925.

McGuire, Meredith B. 1990. "Religion and the Body: Rematerializing the Human Body in the Social Sciences of Religion." *Journal for the Scientific Study of Religion* 29.3:283–296.

Meadows, Carol, ed. and trans. 1986. *Ārya Śūra's Compendium of the Perfections: Text, Translation, and Analysis of the Pāramitāsamāsa.* Bonn: Indica et Tibetica Verlag.

Michaels, Axel. 1997. "Gift and Return Gift, Greeting and Return Greeting in India: On a Consequential Footnote by Marcel Mauss." *Numen* 44:242–269.

Miller, Barbara Stoler, trans. 1986. *The Bhagavad-Gita: Krishna's Counsel in Time of War.* New York: Bantam.

Monier-Williams, Sir Monier. 1979. *A Sanskrit-English Dictionary.* New ed. Oxford: Oxford University Press. Orig. pub. 1899.

Morris, Richard, ed. 1882. *The Buddhavaṃsa and the Cariyāpiṭaka.* London: Pāli Text Society.

——, ed. 1955–1961. *The Aṅguttara-Nikāya.* 5 vols. and Index. London: Pāli Text Society. Orig. pub. 1885–1910.

Mrozik, Susanne. 1998. "The Relationship Between Morality and the Body in Monastic Training According to the *Śikṣāsamuccaya.*" Ph.D. diss., Harvard University.

——. 2002. "The Value of Human Differences: South Asian Buddhist Contributions Toward an Embodied Virtue Theory." *Journal of Buddhist Ethics* 9:1–33.

Müller, Max, trans. 1881. *Dhammapada.* Sacred Books of the East, vol. 10, part 1. Oxford: Oxford University Press.

Nagao, Gadjin. 1973. "On the Theory of Buddha-Body." *Eastern Buddhist* 6.1:25–53.

——. 1984. "Ascent and Descent: Two-Directional Activity in Buddhist Thought." Presidential Address for the Sixth Conference of the International Association of Buddhist Studies, Tokyo, Japan, September 1983. *Journal of the International Association of Buddhist Studies* 7.1:176–183.

Nath, Vijay. 1987. *Dāna: Gift System in Ancient India (c. 600 B.C.–c. A.D. 300): A Socio-Economic Perspective.* Delhi: Munshiram Manoharlal Publishers.

Nattier, Jan. 2003. *A Few Good Men: The Bodhisattva Path According to The Inquiry of Ugra (Ugraparipṛcchā).* Honolulu: University of Hawai'i Press.

Nobel, Johannes, ed. 1937. *Suvarṇabhāsottamasūtra: Das Goldglanz-sūtra, Ein Sanskrittext des Mahāyāna-Buddhismus.* Leipzig: Otto Harrassowitz.

Norman, K. R., trans. 1971. *The Elders' Verses, Part 2: Therīgāthā.* Pāli Text Society Translation Series 40. London: Pāli Text Society.

——. 1983. *Pāli Literature, Including the Canonical Literature in Prakrit and Sanskrit of All the Hīnayāna Schools of Buddhism.* A History of Indian Literature, ed. Jan Gonda, vol. 7, fasc. 2. Wiesbaden: Otto Harrassowitz.

O'Flaherty, Wendy Doniger. 1981. *Śiva: The Erotic Ascetic.* London: Oxford University Press. Orig. pub. as *Asceticism and Eroticism in the Mythology of Śiva* in 1973.

Ohnuma, Reiko. 1997. "*Dehadāna:* The 'Gift of the Body' in Indian Buddhist Narrative Literature." Ph.D. diss., University of Michigan.

——. 1998. "The Gift of the Body and the Gift of Dharma." *History of Religions* 37.4:323–359.

——. 2000. "The Story of Rūpāvatī: A Female Past Birth of the Buddha." *Journal of the International Association of Buddhist Studies* 23.1:103–145.

——, trans. 2004a. "Why the Buddha Had Good Digestion." In *Buddhist Scriptures,* ed. Donald S. Lopez Jr., 136–141. London: Penguin.

Ohnuma, Reiko, trans. 2004b. "A King Gives Away His Head." In *Buddhist Scriptures,* ed. Donald S. Lopez Jr., 142–158. London: Penguin.

——, trans. 2004c. "Rūpyāvatī Gives Away Her Breasts." In *Buddhist Scriptures,* ed. Donald S. Lopez Jr., 159–171. London: Penguin.

Oldenburg, Serge. 1893. "On the Buddhist Jātakas." *Journal of the Royal Asiatic Society* 25, n.s., 301–350.

Olivelle, Patrick, trans. 1992. *Saṃnyāsa Upaniṣads: Hindu Scriptures on Asceticism and Renunciation.* New York: Oxford University Press.

——. 1997. "Amṛtā: Women and Indian Technologies of Immortality." *Journal of Indian Philosophy* 25.5:427–449.

Orzech, Charles D. 1994. "'Provoked Suicide' and the Victim's Behavior." In *Curing Violence: Essays on René Girard,* ed. Mark I. Wallace and Theophus H. Smith, 137–160. Sonoma, California: Polebridge Press.

Parlier, Edith. 1991. "La légende du roi des Śibi: Du sacrifice brahmanique au don du corps bouddhique." *Bulletin d'Études Indiennes* 9:133–160.

Parry, Jonathan. 1986. "The Gift, the Indian Gift, and the 'Indian Gift.'" *Man* 21.3:453–473.

——. 1994. *Death in Banaras.* Cambridge: Cambridge University Press.

Perez-Remon, Joaquin. 1979. "The Simile of the Pith (Sāra) in the Nikāyas and Its Bearing on the Anattavāda." *Boletín de la Asociación Española de Orientalistas* 15:71–93.

Porter, Roy. 1992. "History of the Body." In *New Perspectives on Historical Writing,* ed. Peter Burke, 206–232. University Park: Pennsylvania State University Press.

——. 2001. "History of the Body Reconsidered." In *New Perspectives on Historical Writing,* ed. Peter Burke, 2d ed., 233–260. University Park: Pennsylvania State University Press.

Pradhan, Prahlad, ed. 1975. *Abhidharmakośa-bhāṣyam of Vasubandhu.* 2d ed. Tibetan Sanskrit Works 8. Patna: K. P. Jayaswal Research Institute. 1st ed. orig. pub. 1967.

Propp, Vladimir. 1958. *Morphology of the Folktale.* Trans. Laurence Scott. Indiana University Research Center in Anthropology, Folklore, and Linguistics 10. Bloomington: Indiana University Press. Orig. pub. as *Morfologiia skazki* in 1928.

——. 1983. *Theory and History of Folklore.* Ed. A. Lieberman. Trans. A. Y. Martin et al. Theory and History of Literature 5. Minneapolis: University of Minnesota Press.

Przyluski, Jean. 1914. "Le Nord-ouest de l'Inde dans le Vinaya des Mūlasarvāstivādin et les textes apparentés." *Journal Asiatique* 4:493–568.

Raheja, Gloria Goodwin. 1988. *The Poison in the Gift: Ritual, Prestation, and the Dominant Caste in a North Indian Village.* Chicago: University of Chicago Press.

Ramanujan, A. K. 1991. "Three Hundred Rāmāyaṇas: Five Examples and Three Thoughts on Translation." In *Many Rāmāyaṇas: The Diversity of a Narrative Tradition in South Asia,* ed. Paula Richman, 22–49. Berkeley: University of California Press.

Reynolds, Frank E. 1977. "The Several Bodies of Buddha: Reflections on a Neglected Aspect of Theravada Tradition." *History of Religions* 16.4:374–389.

——. 1992. "Death as Threat, Death as Achievement: Buddhist Perspectives with Particular Reference to the Theravada Tradition." In *Death and Afterlife: Perspectives of World Religions,* ed. Hiroshi Obayashi, 157–167. Contributions to the Study of Religion 33. New York: Greenwood Press.

Reynolds, Frank E., and Jason A. Carbine, eds. 2000. *The Life of Buddhism.* Berkeley: University of California Press.

Rhys Davids, C. A. F., ed. 1975. *The Visuddhi-magga of Buddhaghosa.* London: Pāli Text Society, 1975. Orig. pub. as 2 vols. in 1920–1921.

Rhys Davids, T. W., trans. 1880. *Buddhist Birth Stories.* London: Trubner's Oriental Series.

Rhys Davids, T. W., and J. E. Carpenter, eds. 1968–1971. *The Sumaṅgala-vilāsinī, Buddhaghosa's Commentary on the Dīgha Nikāya.* 3 vols. London: Pāli Text Society. Orig. pub. 1929–1932.

——, eds. 1975–1982. *The Dīgha Nikāya.* 3 vols. London: Pāli Text Society. Orig. pub. 1890–1911.

Rhys Davids, T. W., and William Stede. 1989. *Pāli Text Society Pāli-English Dictionary.* New Delhi: Munshiram Manoharlal Publishers. Orig. pub. 1921–1923.

Rosmarin, Adena. 1985. *The Power of Genre.* Minneapolis: University of Minnesota Press.

Sahlins, Marshall D. 1996. "On the Sociology of Primitive Exchange." In *The Gift: An Interdisciplinary Perspective,* ed. Aafke E. Komter, 26–38. Amsterdam: Amsterdam University Press. Reprinted and abridged from *Stone Age Economics.* London: Routledge, 1978.

Śāstrī, Swāmī Dwārikādās, ed. 1998. *The Abhidharmakośa & Bhāṣya of Ācārya Vasubandhu with Sphutārthā Commentary of Ācārya Yaśomittrā.* 2 vols. Bauddha Bharati Series 7–8. Varanasi: Bauddha Bharati.

Schlingloff, Dieter. 1988. *Studies in the Ajanta Paintings: Identifications and Interpretations.* Delhi: Ajanta Publications.

Schmidt, I. J., ed. and trans. 1845. *Der weise und der thor: Aus dem tibetischen uebersetzt und mit dem originaltexte herausgegeben.* St. Petersburg: W. Gräff's Erben. Leipzig: Leopold Voss.

Schopen, Gregory. 1997. *Bones, Stones, and Buddhist Monks: Collected Papers on the Archaeology, Epigraphy, and Texts of Monastic Buddhism in India.* Honolulu: University of Hawai'i Press.

———. 2004. *Buddhist Monks and Business Matters: Still More Papers on Monastic Buddhism in India.* Honolulu: University of Hawai'i Press.

Schrift, Alan D., ed. 1997. *The Logic of the Gift: Toward an Ethic of Generosity.* New York: Routledge.

Senart, Émile, ed. 1977. *Mahāvastu avadānaṃ. Le Mahāvastu: texte sanscrit publié pour la première fois et accompagné d'introductions et d'un commentaire.* 3 vols. Tokyo: Meicho-Fukyū-Kai. Orig. pub. 1882–1897.

Shackleton Bailey, D. R., ed. and trans. 1954. "The *Jātakastava* of Jñānayaśas." In *Asiatica: Festschrift Friedrich Weller,* ed. Johannes Schubert, 22–29. Leipzig: Otto Harrassowitz.

Shulman, David. 1993. *The Hungry God: Hindu Tales of Filicide and Devotion.* Chicago: University of Chicago Press.

Silber, Ilana F. 1995. "Gift-Giving in the Great Traditions: The Case of Donations to Monasteries in the Medieval West." *Archives europeennes de sociologie* 36.2:209–243.

Silk, Jonathan Alan. 1994. "The Origins and Early History of the *Mahāratnakūṭa* Tradition of Mahāyāna Buddhism with a Study of the *Ratnarāśisūtra* and Related Materials." 2 vols. Ph.D. diss., University of Michigan.

Snellgrove, David. 1987. *Indo-Tibetan Buddhism: Indian Buddhists and Their Tibetan Successors.* 2 vols. Boston: Shambhala Publications.

Speyer, J. S., trans. 1895. *The Gātakamālā; or, Garland of Birth-Stories by Ārya Sūra.* Sacred Books of the Buddhists 1. London: Oxford University Press.

———, ed. 1958. *Avadānaçataka: A Century of Edifying Tales Belonging to the Hīnayāna.* 2 vols. in one. The Hague: Mouton and Co. Orig. pub. 1902–1909.

Spiro, Melford. 1982. *Buddhism and Society: A Great Tradition and Its Burmese Vicissitudes.* 2d ed. Berkeley: University of California Press. 1st ed. orig. pub. 1970.

Starobinski, Jean. 1997. *Largesse.* Trans. Jane Marie Todd. Chicago: University of Chicago Press. Orig. pub. as *Largesse* (in French) in 1994.

Stein, Otto. 1937. "Notes on the Trikāya-Doctrine." In *Jha Commemoration Volume,* 389–398. Poona Oriental Series 39. Poona: Oriental Book Agency.

Stone, Jacqueline I. 2005. "Death." In *Critical Terms for the Study of Buddhism,* ed. Donald S. Lopez Jr., 56–76. Chicago: University of Chicago Press.

Strathern, Marilyn. 1988. *The Gender of the Gift: Problems with Women and Problems with Society in Melanesia.* Berkeley: University of California Press.

Strenski, Ivan. 1983. "On Generalized Exchange and the Domestication of the Saṃgha." *Man,* n.s., 18:463–477.

Strong, John. 1977. "Making Merit in the *Aśokāvadāna:* A Study of Buddhist Acts of Offering in the Post-*Parinirvāṇa* Age." Ph.D. diss., University of Chicago.

——. 1979. "The Transforming Gift: An Analysis of Devotional Acts of Offering in Buddhist Avadāna Literature." *History of Religions* 18.3:221–237.

——. 1983a. *The Legend of King Aśoka: A Translation and Study of the Aśokāvadāna.* Princeton: Princeton University Press.

——. 1983b. "Buddhist Avadānas and Jātakas: The Question of Genre." Unpublished paper delivered at the Annual Meeting of the American Academy of Religion, Dallas, Texas.

——. 1985. "The Buddhist Avadānists and the Elder Upagupta." In *Tantric and Taoist Studies in Honour of R. A. Stein,* ed. Michel Strickman, vol. 3, 862–881. *Mélanges Chinois et Bouddhiques* 22.

——. 1990. "Rich Man, Poor Man, *Bhikkhu,* King: Aśoka's Great Quinquennial Festival and the Nature of *Dāna.*" In *Ethics, Wealth, and Salvation: A Study in Buddhist Social Ethics,* ed. Russell F. Sizemore and Donald K. Swearer, 107–123. Columbia: University of South Carolina Press.

——. 1992. *The Legend and Cult of Upagupta: Sanskrit Buddhism in North India and Southeast Asia.* Princeton: Princeton University Press.

——, ed. 1995. *The Experience of Buddhism: Sources and Interpretations.* Belmont, California: Wadsworth Publishing Company.

——. 2001. *The Buddha: A Short Biography.* Oxford: Oneworld.

——. 2004. *Relics of the Buddha.* Princeton: Princeton University Press.

Sullivan, Lawrence E. 1990. "Body Works: Knowledge of the Body in the Study of Religion." *History of Religions* 29:86–99.

Suzuki, D. T. 1963. *Outlines of Mahayana Buddhism.* New York: Schocken. Orig. pub. 1907.

Swearer, Donald K., trans. 1995. "Bimbā's Lament." In *Buddhism in Practice,* ed. Donald S. Lopez Jr., 541–552. Princeton: Princeton University Press.

Takahashi, Moritaka, ed. and trans. 1969. *Hdsaṅs Blun; or, the Sūtra of the Wise and the Foolish, Translated from Tibetan Versions and Annotated.* Osaka, Japan: Institute of Oriental and Occidental Studies, Kansai University.

Takahata, Kanga, ed. 1954. *Ratnamālāvadāna, A Garland of Precious Gems or a Collection of Edifying Tales, Belonging to the Mahāyāna.* Oriental Library, series D, vol. 3. Tokyo: Toyo Bunko.

Takakusu, J. 1901. "Tales of the Wise Man and the Fool, in Tibetan and Chinese." *Journal of the Royal Asiatique Society,* 447–460.

Tatelman, Joel. 2000. *The Glorious Deeds of Pūrṇa: A Translation and Study of the Pūrṇāvadāna.* Surrey, England: Curzon.

Taylor, Mark C., ed. 1998. *Critical Terms for Religious Studies.* Chicago: University of Chicago Press.

Thapar, Romila. 1978. *Exile and the Kingdom: Some Thoughts on the Rāmāyaṇa.* Rao Bahadur N. Narasimhachar Endowment Lecture for 1977–1978. Bangalore: Mythic Society.

Thomas, E. J. 1933. "Avadāna and Apadāna." *Indian Historical Quarterly* 9:32–36.

Tin, Pe Maung, trans. 1975. *The Path of Purity, Being a Translation of Buddhaghosa's Visuddhimagga.* Pāli Text Society Translation Series 11, 17, and 21. 3 vols. in one. London: Pāli Text Society. Orig. pub. 1923–1931.

Todorov, Tzvetan. 1976. "The Origin of Genres." *New Literary History* 8:159–170.

Trainor, Kevin. 1993. "In the Eye of the Beholder: Nonattachment and the Body in Subhā's Verse (Therīgāthā 71)." *Journal of the American Academy of Religion* 61.1:57–79.

——. 1997. *Relics, Ritual, and Representation in Buddhism: Rematerializing the Sri Lankan Theravada Tradition.* Cambridge Studies in Religious Traditions 10. Cambridge: Cambridge University Press.

Trautmann, Thomas R. 1981. *Dravidian Kinship.* Cambridge Studies in Social Anthropology 36. Cambridge: Cambridge University Press.

——. 1986. "*The Gift* in India: Marcel Mauss as Indianist." Paper delivered before the Thirty-Eighth Annual Meeting of the Association for Asian Studies, Chicago, Illinois. Unpublished manuscript.

Trenckner, Vilhelm, ed. 1880. *The Milindapañho: Being Dialogues Between King Milinda and the Buddhist Sage Nāgasena.* London: Williams and Norgate.

——, ed. 1888–1925. *The Majjhima Nikāya.* 3 vols. and Index. London: Pāli Text Society.

Turner, Bryan S. 1991. "Recent Developments in the Theory of the Body." In *The Body: Social Process and Cultural Theory,* ed. Mike Featherstone et al., 1–35. London and Newbury Park, California: Sage.

——. 1997. "The Body in Western Society: Social Theory and Its Perspectives." In *Religion and the Body,* ed. Sarah Coakley, 15–41. Cambridge: Cambridge University Press.

Turner, Victor. 1974. *Dramas, Fields, and Metaphors: Symbolic Action in Human Society.* Ithaca: Cornell University Press.

——. 1977. "Variations on a Theme of Liminality." In *Secular Ritual,* ed. Sally F. Moore and Barbara G. Myerhoff, 36–52. Amsterdam: Van Gorcum.

——. 1987. "Betwixt and Between: The Liminal Period in Rites of Passage." In *Betwixt and Between: Patterns of Masculine and Feminine Initiation,* ed. Louise

Carus Mahdi, Steven Foster, and Meredith Little, 3–19. La Salle: Open Court. Reprinted from *The Forest of Symbols: Aspects of Ndembu Ritual.* Ithaca: Cornell University Press, 1967.

——. 1995. *The Ritual Process: Structure and Anti-Structure.* Lewis Henry Morgan Lectures, 1966. New York: Aldine de Gruyter. Orig. pub. 1966.

Vaidya, P. L., ed. 1958. *Avadāna-Śataka.* Buddhist Sanskrit Texts 19. Darbhanga: Mithila Institute.

——, ed. 1959a. *Jātakamālā.* Buddhist Sanskrit Texts 21. Darbhanga: Mithila Institute.

——, ed. 1959b. *Avadāna-kalpalatā of Kṣemendra.* 2 vols. Buddhist Sanskrit Texts 22–23. Darbhanga: Mithila Institute.

——, ed. 1959c. *Divyāvadāna.* Buddhist Sanskrit Texts 20. Darbhanga: Mithila Institute.

——, ed. 1960. *Bodhicaryāvatāra of Śāntideva, with the Commentary Pañjika of Prajñākaramati.* Buddhist Sanskrit Texts 12. Darbhanga: Mithila Institute.

Van Buitenen, J. A. B., trans. 1975. *The Mahābhārata, Book 2: The Book of the Assembly Hall, and Book 3: The Book of the Forest.* Chicago: University of Chicago Press.

Van Gennep, Arnold. 1960. *The Rites of Passage.* Trans. Monika B. Vizedom and Gabrielle L. Caffee. Chicago: University of Chicago Press. Orig. pub. as *Les rites de passage* in 1909.

Vernant, Jean-Pierre. 1989. "Dim Body, Dazzling Body." In *Fragments for a History of the Human Body,* ed. Michel Feher et al., vol. 1, 19–47. New York: Urzone.

Von Hinüber, O., and K. R. Norman, eds. 1994. *Dhammapada.* Oxford: Pāli Text Society.

Walshe, Maurice, trans. 1995. *The Long Discourses of the Buddha: A Translation of the Dīgha Nikāya.* Boston: Wisdom Publications. Orig. pub. 1987 as *Thus Have I Heard: The Long Discourses of the Buddha.*

Walters, Jonathan S. 1994. "A Voice From the Silence: The Buddha's Mother's Story." *History of Religions* 33.4:358–379.

Warder, A. K. 1970. *Indian Buddhism.* Delhi: Motilal Banarsidass.

Warren, Henry Clarke, ed. 1896. *Buddhism in Translations.* Cambridge, Mass.: Harvard University Press.

Watters, Thomas, trans. 1904–1905. *On Yuan Chwang's Travels in India (A.D. 629–45).* 2 vols. London: Royal Asiatic Society.

Weeraratne, W. G. 1967. "Avadāna." In *Encyclopaedia of Buddhism,* ed. G. P. Malalasekera, vol. 2, fasc. 3, 395–398. Colombo: Government of Sri Lanka Press.

——. 1984. "Dāna." In *Encyclopaedia of Buddhism,* ed. Jotiya Dhirasekera, vol. 4, fasc. 2, 307–310. Colombo: Government of Sri Lanka Press.

Weeraratne, W. G. 1989. "Divyāvadāna." In *Encyclopaedia of Buddhism,* ed. G. P. Malalasekera, vol. 4, fasc. 4, 284–290. Colombo: Government of Sri Lanka Press.

Williams, Paul. 1989. *Mahāyāna Buddhism: The Doctrinal Foundations.* London: Routledge.

——. 1997. "Some Mahāyāna Buddhist Perspectives on the Body." In *Religion and the Body,* ed. Sarah Coakley, 205–230. Cambridge: Cambridge University Press.

Wilson, Liz. 1994. "Henpecked Husbands and Renouncers Home on the Range: Celibacy as Social Disengagement in South Asian Buddhism." *Union Seminary Quarterly Review* 48.3–4:7–28.

——. 1995. "The Female Body as a Source of Horror and Insight in Post-Ashokan Indian Buddhism." In *Religious Reflections on the Human Body,* ed. Jane Marie Law, 76–99. Bloomington: Indiana University Press.

——. 1996. *Charming Cadavers: Horrific Figurations of the Feminine in Indian Buddhist Hagiographic Literature.* Chicago: University of Chicago Press.

——. 2002. "Beggars Can Be Choosers: Mahākassapa as a Selective Eater of Offerings." In *Constituting Communities: Theravāda Buddhism and the Religious Cultures of South and Southeast Asia,* ed. John Clifford Holt, Jacob N. Kinnard, and Jonathan S. Walters, 57–70.

——. 2003. "Human Torches of Enlightenment: Autocremation and Spontaneous Combustion as Marks of Sanctity in South Asian Buddhism." In *The Living and the Dead: Social Dimensions of Death in South Asian Religions,* ed. Liz Wilson, 29–50. Albany: State University of New York Press.

Wiltshire, Martin G. 1983. "The 'Suicide' Problem in the Pāli Canon." *Journal of the International Association of Buddhist Studies* 6.2:124–140.

Winternitz, Maurice. 1908. "Jātaka." In *Encyclopaedia of Religion and Ethics,* ed. James Hastings, vol. 7, 491–494. New York: Scribner's.

——. 1933. *A History of Indian Literature, Vol. 2: Buddhist Literature and Jaina Literature.* Trans. S. Ketkar and H. Cohn. Calcutta: University of Calcutta. Orig. pub. as part of *Geschichte der indischen Literatur* in 1908–1920.

Wriggins, Sally Hovey. 1996. *Xuanzang: A Buddhist Pilgrim on the Silk Road.* Boulder: Westview Press.

Yamada, Isshi, ed. 1968. *Karuṇāpuṇḍarīka: The White Lotus of Compassion.* 2 vols. London: School of Oriental and African Studies.

INDEX

Nonspecific citations to gift-of-the-body stories (for example, "tigress, story of") are indexed separately from specific citations to gift-of-the-body stories (for example, "*Jātakamālā* No. 1"), with cross-references from the former to the latter (but not vice-versa). Figures and tables are indexed separately from other page references.